*World Perspectives
on International Politics*

World
Perspectives
on International Politics

Edited by

WALTER C. CLEMENS, JR.
Massachusetts Institute of Technology

LITTLE, BROWN AND COMPANY
Boston   Toronto

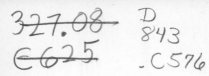
Published simultaneously in Canada
by Little, Brown & Company (Canada) Limited

PRINTED IN THE UNITED STATES OF AMERICA

For
IOLANI LENORE

"Heavenly Bird"

Alle Menschen werden Brüder
Wo dein sanfter Flügel weilt

Preface

This book is a collection of significant and illuminating pronouncements on current key issues by world leaders and publicists from the three distinct camps of world viewpoint — the Western, the Communist, and the nonaligned or developing nations. These views are not presented in a paraphrased and secondary manner. Rather the issues are lucidly expressed in the very words of such policy-makers as Achmed Sukarno, Mikhail A. Suslov, and Charles de Gaulle. The reader, himself, has the opportunity to analyze these juxtaposed views on different crucial problems, determining to his own satisfaction what areas of agreement and disagreement unite and divide international society in the 1960's. Mirroring the driving forces and structure of world politics in this decade, the book presents the material in a unique context of operating powers behind the men and policies of leading nations.

For the convenience of instructor and student, these readings parallel many of the topics covered in standard treatises on world politics, adding a new dimension to their appreciation. Introductory essays to each part of this book are designed to correlate the primary material within the framework of a field theory of international relations.

The structural division of this book into the three world perspectives does not imply that the world corresponds to the troika principle. On the contrary, the sharp disagreements and centrifugal forces within the Western, Communist, and "third" worlds compel a constant awareness of their differences. The readings reflect, however, the unifying as well as the divisive factors at work within each of these worlds. Despite obvious diversities, each world lends itself to categorization according to certain political and other characteristics. Thus, the principle of political identification makes the troika structure a convenient instrument for political analysis of such rich and complex reality.

The introduction to the book expounds a field theory of international relations as one way of comprehending the many viewpoints and problems presented in the readings. Part Two, "Perspectives on National Strategies," projects the basic political and military policies that the leading states from the three worlds have formulated in order to deal with one another. Part Three, "Strategies in Conflict," presents case studies of three recent confrontations between major powers of each world. Part Four, "The Ordering of Conflict," illustrates the diverse approaches of states to arms control and to development of the U.N.

The criterion for the choice of materials finally selected was the degree to which each important statement demonstrated points of difference or similarities in the perspectives of Western, Communist, and developing nations.

This book has profited from the comments of many political scientists. In particular, the author is grateful for the cooperation and advice of many friends, students, and colleagues at the Massachusetts Institute of Technology, especially Norman J. Padelford and Myron Weiner. The perceptive comments of the European fellows at the Salzburg Seminar in American Studies, 95th Session, have strengthened the field theory suggested here. It is a pleasure to acknowledge also the helpful criticisms of Stanley V. Anderson, University of California at Santa Barbara; Bernard Cohen and Constantine Menges, University of Wisconsin; Kenneth N. Waltz, Swarthmore College; Andrew Gyorgy, Boston University; and Daniel Snowman, Sussex University. The author owes a heavy intellectual debt to Stanley H. Hoffmann, Harvard University, whose writings have provided much of the basic framework on the introduction to the readings. Mrs. Beverly B. Major has assisted the author throughout this project and has played a key role not only in locating obscure materials but in offering constructive proposals concerning the entire format. Donald R. Hammonds and Freda Alexander of Little, Brown and Company have offered encouragement and imaginative suggestions. But the final product remains the responsibility of the author alone.

To my family I owe much of the inspiration of this book. My wife, Diane, a scholar in her own right, has been an intellectually stimulating companion, helping to think through many problems connected with the book, as well as providing moral support. It is our hope that, as the dedication page suggests, our daughter Iolani Lenore will grow up to contribute to a world of greater understanding and friendship between East and West . . . a world in which gaps in world perspectives narrow.

WALTER C. CLEMENS, JR.

Center for International Studies,
Massachusetts Institute of Technology

Contents

Communist Strategy

Uniting an Alliance

The Challenge of "Capitalist Imperialism"

Developing the Third World

The Strategy of the Third World

Toward a Third Force

Let Imperialism Be Cast Off

For Political Freedom and Economic Growth

The Rise of the Third World

Military Strategy: The Threat and Uses of Force

Western Strategy

Communist Strategy

PART THREE: STRATEGIES IN CONFLICT

A Confrontation in Europe: Berlin and Divided Germany

"Pacta Sunt Servanda"

New Realities Require New Solutions

The Nonaligned Nations and the Great Powers

A Confrontation in Latin America: The 1962 Cuban Crisis

In Defense of Peace

Peking versus "Adventurism" and "Capitulationism"

A Confrontation in Asia: The Indian-Chinese Frontier

India's View

China's View

International Strategy:
The United Nations and the Rule of Law

The Spirit and Letter of 1945

The Rise of the Third World in the United Nations

The Troika in World Affairs

China Supports Broader Afro-Asian Representation
in the United Nations

Retrospect and Prospect

PART ONE

Introduction

Introduction

Frameworks for Analysis

The statements presented here deal with topical problems, but they represent traditional, almost classical problems of history, philosophy, and political science. The diverse perspectives recorded indicate in microcosm the complexity of reality itself. How can sense be made from such diversity? How can the profound and lasting be distinguished from the superficial or temporary?

The discipline of international relations offers many useful approaches for creating order and meaning from flux. Most of these approaches tend to analyze world politics either from the standpoint of the individual state or, at the other pole, from an overview of the international system as a whole.

From the first of these two viewpoints, political realism will point to the vital interests which affect foreign policy decisions and underlie ideological pronouncements and debating positions. Analysis of the geopolitical and economic foundations of international conflict and cooperation will also deepen appreciation of the material problems at stake. Further, the process of decision-making within each state will be illumined by the insights of the behavioral sciences.

From the second of these two major approaches, an understanding of the international system as a whole will be enhanced by an historical perspective of continuity and change between the present and past eras; by sociological analyses of community building; by the legal and organizational studies of the formal structures uniting the nation-states; and by the models of power and function devised by systems analysts.

Preoccupation either with the process of foreign policy-making within the state or with the international system as a whole, however, may lead to distortions. Political realists attempting to look over the statesman's shoulder may minimize the forces which unite or restrain states even while each pursues its self-interest. The realist theory, moreover, by identifying interest with power tends to neglect the factors that influence or define purposes. Sociologists and students of world law, at the other extreme, may exaggerate the extent to which community and world law are already facts. And systems builders are prone to abstractions based on limited empirical foundations.

A broader approach which can profit from the insights of other approaches while avoiding their narrowness or abstraction has been suggested by Professor Stanley H. Hoffmann of Harvard University.[1] Developing earlier work by Raymond Aron and Quincy Wright, Hoffmann has outlined a field theory of international relations which provides a most useful prism for viewing the materials in this book. The field theory advocated by Hoffmann is eclectic, relativistic, and pluralistic. It assumes that each of the major approaches to international politics mentioned here has value in illuminating some part of the whole.

Hoffmann begins by stressing the need for two kinds of systematic research: first, an historical sociology to examine the past; second, a political philosophy of the purposes, prerequisites, possibilities, and procedures of an improved world order. Both types of research should be stimulated by the world perspectives presented here.

The "historical sociology" would focus on "diplomatic constellations" of given historical situations. Each situation constitutes a field which may be analyzed in terms of four sets of data: (1) the structure of the world in the period under review incorporating the main units or actors, the distribution of power among them, and the "relationships of major

---

[1] "International Relations: The Long Road to Theory," *World Politics*, XI (1959) 346–377. Hoffmann's article and statements of other approaches are included in *International Politics and Foreign Policy: A Reader in Research and Theory* (ed.) James N. Rosenau (New York: Free Press of Glencoe, 1961).

tension"; (2) the transnational forces which form the material and moral context in which the main actors operate; (3) the relations between the domestic and foreign policies of the basic units including their material base, internal constitution, and political culture; and (4) the outcome of these interdependent series, that is, "international relations," as seen from the perspective of the basic units and from an overview of the whole.

Within each historical situation the analyst would study the interaction of two kinds of activities: (a) the striving of the basic units for certain goals, and (b) the basic tasks performed by the formal and informal organization of the international system (e.g., conflict, political accommodation, and economic transformation). The range of the goals essayed by the basic units, the means employed to achieve them, and the mutual relations which result provide the criteria for distinguishing one diplomatic constellation from another.

Analysis of each historical situation should weigh not only the material environment which limits and helps to determine human thought and action, but also the writings of statesmen and theorists. This latter source tends to be neglected as modern sociology of knowledge emphasizes the dependence of ideas upon social environment. But our approach in these readings will be to view the material and moral forces of the world through the eyes of statesmen and theorists, and introductions to each chapter will reiterate the forces with which the various spokesmen are struggling.

The comparative analysis of diverse diplomatic constellations in terms of field theory could produce a typology of historical systems. This book, however, limits its explicit coverage to the situation which has developed since World War II and, more specifically, in the 1960's. True, many of the problems touched upon (such as the relationship of power and ideology) are classical, but they are lifted to another dimension by the unique features of the present era. In two respects the technological revolution has made the present era incomparable with the past: in the potential destructiveness of war and in the political and economic interdependency which makes the "domestic" problem of another age an "international" one today. The reader should therefore ponder the similarities and differences between this and past historical situations, and consider how future eras will respond to the challenges that will grow out of the present international, technological, and intellectual environment.

The comparison of the nuclear age in the 1960's with other periods, past and future, will be facilitated if one attempts to weight the determinants of the present situation according to their relative importance, rather than seeing them merely as "interrelated." A suggestion of the relative weight of different variables should emerge from the saliency of certain problems discussed by Western, Communist, and "third world" statesmen in the present book, but it should be remembered that these leaders may very well be silent on some factors uppermost in their minds.

To move from "historical sociology" to a "political philosophy" for a better world is not easy, partly because of persistent flux in the material and moral context of the international system. This book, together with other, more analytical essays on international relations, may at least point to some approaches. The first problem is to clarify the values which one would like to see promoted in the world at large. From the readings in this book one may get a feel for the value consensus (or lack thereof) in the Communist, Western, and developing countries today.

The reader may also come to appreciate better which of these values are compatible with a "better world." This raises a second task for systematic research: to relate these values to the world as it is, with all its conflict and turmoil. "We must try," in Stanley Hoffmann's phrase, "to build relevant utopias." While this book will provide few answers or even way-markers, it may stimulate the quest.

Field Theory and "World Perspectives"

Each part of this book provides data for the four basic concerns of field theory. Introductions to each part will discuss the relevance of materials in that chapter, but a general overview is sketched here to provide a framework for the parts which follow. This analysis attempts to "fill in" the basic outline of field theory, relying heavily on the collected readings but using supplementary data to round out the interpretation. The same materials, needless to say, may lead others to additional, or quite different conclusions.[2]

[2] Articles by Raymond Aron and others illustrating aspects of Hoffmann's theory are included in the collection edited by Hoffmann, *Contemporary Theory in International Relations* (Englewood Cliffs, N. J.: Prentice-Hall, 1960).

The Basic Actors. The basic unit in international politics today remains the nation-state, although larger (and smaller) entities — formal or informal — are also at work, some of them playing an ever greater role. These broader unities are political, military, economic, technical and/or cultural in nature. One is almost universal in membership and objectives — the United Nations. Others are defined regionally, such as NATO. Some are distinguished by their specific interest, such as the World Health Organization.

Within these larger clusters, the sovereign nation-state remains the primary unit, basically free to withdraw or give its support to international action. Even where sovereignty is formally restricted, little enforcement machinery exists to uphold this limitation.

The basic political entities in international society should not be confused with the individuals who compose and lead them. The "basic actors," in a sense, are the human decision-makers, but this is true whether politics takes place between families or clans at one extreme, or between empires at another. Analysis must be lifted to a more abstract plane if comparisons are to be made concerning different historical situations and diplomatic constellations. To argue that the basic unit in contemporary international relations is the nation-state does not minimize in any way the vital role played by men — by charismatic or phlegmatic leaders, by dynamic or apathetic elites, by aroused or resigned citizenries. The manner in which the human element operates in the objective structure of international relations is especially conditioned by the domestic factors in foreign policy discussed below as one of the series of data in field theory.

The Three Worlds. Most states identify themselves as Western, as Communist, or as nonaligned and therefore, if only by implication, as part of a "third world." These terms reflect the Cold War era before Stalin's death, during which political lines were tightly drawn. Since 1953, the lines have blurred and overlapped. Despite increasing diversity within each world, the unifying characteristics of each group may still be meaningfully defined.

The West. The Western World is united by a common political and cultural heritage and by proximity to the Atlantic Ocean. It includes all of Western Europe and North America. Parts of Eastern Europe belonged to the West historically, but are officially Communist today. Latin America belongs to it by culture and (except for Cuba) by political alliance, but resembles economically the underdeveloped nations of the third world. To some extent any country which adopts Western values, which industrializes, or which allies militarily with the West is "Western." Hence, traditionally Eastern countries such as Japan and Turkey are in some respects part of today's Western world. Islands of Western civilization such as Australia and New Zealand are, of course, also included.

Members of today's Western alliance fought against one another in World Wars I and II and in countless wars before these. The solidarity of the post-World War II alliance has been primarily a response to a perceived Communist threat. The apparent decline in Communist unity and aggressiveness since Stalin's death together with the rise to power of General de Gaulle in 1958 have produced deep fissures in the alliance which are manifested in many readings in this book. Economic and political self-interest, however, still bind most Western governments and inspire efforts toward more effective integration.[3]

The Communist World. The Communist states are those which claim to follow Marxist-Leninism. They are part of a larger movement which includes Communist parties out of power. The increasing diversity within what used to be called the Communist "bloc" has led George F. Kennan to question whether the term "Communist" is not more misleading than revealing.[4] Certainly the word "satellite" no longer fits most East European members of the Warsaw Pact.

The cultural and historical traditions of the Communist world are more variegated than the Western, even if the parties not in power are excluded. Russian Orthodox, Taoist, Buddhist, even Catholic (e.g., in Poland or Cuba) civilizations have provided the substructure for today's Communist regimes. The Communist states' economic development has been more uneven than that of the Western world.

This diversity of background and of present need was plastered over in Stalin's time by a façade of ideological conformity. The seeds for a

---

[3] Despite the wide variety of viewpoints within the West, only the views of the leading proponent and opponent of NATO unity — Washington and Paris — are presented here, for reasons of space. Official U.S. government statements, however, are supplemented by criticisms from the right and the left on the American political spectrum. For a Canadian's analysis of tensions in The Western Alliance, see Lionel Gelber, "A Marriage of Inconvenience," *Foreign Affairs*, XILL, No. 2 (January 1963) 310–322.

[4] George F. Kennan, *On Dealing With the Communist World* (New York: Harper & Row, 1964) introduction.

breakup of his monolith were planted by diverse developments, such as the defection of Yugoslavia in 1948 and China's entry in 1949 into the Communist camp.[5] A breakdown of enforced unity was probably inevitable, but was accelerated by Khrushchev's program of de-Stalinization. The assault on the "personality cult" was taken in Eastern Europe to mean an opportunity for greater independence of Moscow. To Peking it signified a threat to Mao's system of government. As Peking began to challenge Moscow for ideological leadership, Communist governments and parties everywhere began to exploit the Sino-Soviet rift to derive gains like those accruing to the third world from the East-West struggle. "Polycentrism" was the apt term coined by Italian Communist leader Togliatti in 1956 to portray and legitimize the autonomous movements breaking out in the former Soviet empire.

The Communist world is more profoundly divided than the Western as two giants struggle for hegemony within it.[6] The conflict of Moscow and Peking is more serious than that of Washington and Paris for many reasons — it springs from a greater disparity of cultural and racial background, reflects more divergent political and economic needs, represents an attempt of the weaker power not only to be free of the stronger but to rival it, and brings in ideological elements which add sacrosanct overtones to the dispute.

When an apparent Communist monolith confronted the West, the expression "East-West" struggle had relevance. But as the "East" splits into two factions — Soviet (basically European) and Chinese — this phrase, too, becomes misleading. The East European and Soviet Communists may have more in common with the "bourgeois West" than with the Communist regimes of Asia. Therefore, where the term "East" (or "West") appears in this book, its precise connotation must be in-investigated. Only Soviet, Chinese, and Cuban statements are presented here. An adequate appreciation of the diversity within the Communist world (or worlds) would require analysis of materials not only of the parties in power (as in Rumania, Poland, or North Vietnam), but also of those striving for power in all parts of the world.[7]

The Third World. The formation of the world into two hostile

---

[5] See *ibid*, p. 37 ff.

[6] For an opposing view of Sino-Soviet relations see Robert Strausz-Hupé, "The Sino-Soviet Tangle and U.S. Policy," *Orbis*, VI, No. 1 (Spring 1962) 25–38.

[7] See the collection *Diversity in International Communism*, edited by Alexander Dallin (New York: Columbia University Press, 1963) ; and William E. Griffith, *The Sino-Soviet Rift* (Cambridge, Mass.: The M.I.T. Press, 1964).

camps at the onset of the Cold War stimulated a certain loose unity among the states which sought to stand to one side of this battle and to profit from it. Their role and power have increased owing to rifts within the two major alliances and because of the marked influx of former African and Asian colonies into the United Nations since 1955.

The key rallying points for the nonaligned nations have been their common opposition to (1) colonialism and "neocolonialism" in their economic, political, or military aspects; (2) the great power conflict (expressed also in nuclear testing) which endangers their peace and security; (3) great power hegemony in the world and specifically in the United Nations; and (4) unfavorable terms of trade for their products and imports. Objectively they have been driven by a desire to secure political independence and economic growth. Subjectively they have sought psychological gratification from the playing of an articulate role in world affairs, thus giving vent to nationalistic sentiments and helping to determine a scapegoat (Western imperialism) for past and present problems. Some of the divisive factors impeding greater third world unity will be analyzed below.[8]

The main criterion for classifying the members of the *tiers monde* — the third world — is their noncommitment to the Western or Communist alliances. But the formally uncommitted nations of the third world share one or more important characteristics with other states belonging to the Western alliance system[9] or which consider themselves Communist.[10] These characteristics include: (1) economic backwardness, although some are actively developing while others remain static and traditional; (2) geographical proximity (as in Asia or Africa) and/or location to the south of the equator; (3) racial and cultural patterns quite different from those of Europe, Russia, and North America; and (4) a recent history of subjugation to the West, followed by formal independence. Many of these nations are "new," although many of them derive from ancient civilizations or (as in Latin America) have a continuous history as old as the United States. Especially in Africa, however, some members of the third world are genuinely new nations whose

[8] See pp. 44–45. For additional reading see *Neutralism and Nonalignment*, Lawrence W. Martin (ed.) (New York: Praeger, 1962). A review of this work by D. E. T. Luard assails the assumption that "the motley regiments of the nonaligned" can be seen as a "single entity at all." *Survival*, V, No. 2 (March–April, 1963) 89.
[9] For example, Latin members of the OAS, the Middle Eastern members of CENTO, and the Southeast Asian members of SEATO.
[10] Especially the Asian Communist states and Albania.

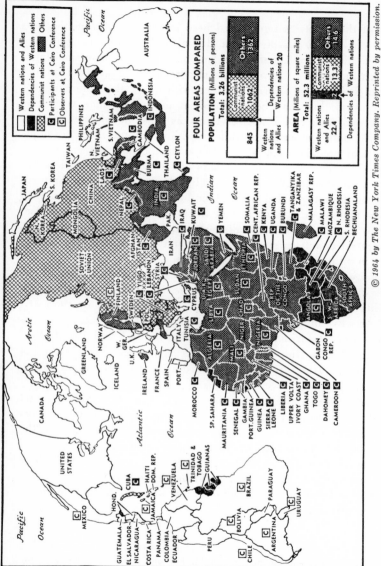

© 1964 by The New York Times Company. Reprinted by permission.

DIVISIONS IN THE WORLD
AND NATIONS ATTENDING THE CONFERENCE IN CAIRO OF NONALIGNED NATIONS
October 11, 1964

boundaries are the artificial constructs of European imperialism and whose sense of identity is presently more fractionated and tribal than national.

Most of the countries represented here in statements from the *tiers monde* — Indonesia, Egypt, Ghana, India, and Yugoslavia — are uncommitted in the bipolar struggle, but have profited from assistance from each major bloc. Two nations also represented in the readings, Cuba and Pakistan, are formally allied with either the Communist or Western world, but may be classified in much the same economic, ethnic, geographic, and historical terms as most nonaligned nations. Yugoslavia, on the other hand, while providing an outstanding example of the art of nonalignment, shares the economic and cultural characteristics of the East European members of the Communist world more than those of most nonaligned nations. Israel, also included in the readings, is not formally allied with either bloc, defies classification with either the underdeveloped nations or the Western, but has been backed mainly by the West and generally opposed by the Communist states. Other neutral countries such as Switzerland and Austria are clearly Western in all but formal alliance structure.

The unity of the third world has been less formal than that of the Western or Communist. It has been manifested in *ad hoc* conferences, such as the Bandung Conference of Afro-Asian Nations in 1955 (attended also by aligned Asian states), and the Conferences of Non-aligned Nations held in Belgrade and Cairo in 1961 and 1964.[11] Portions of the third world, however, such as Africa and — a part thereof — the Arab countries, are groping toward a more formal union among themselves.

The main use of the term "third world" in this book will be to set off those nations which try to remain apart from the East-West political struggle and to profit from it. Little prominence is given here to the political views of the Latin American republics because all are allied with either Washington or Moscow. However, all the discussions here of economic problems in the third world should be understood as applying broadly to the politically aligned, as well as the uncommitted, developing nations.

[11] See readings numbered 13 and 27. For a graphic depiction of the states attending the Cairo Conference, see the map on p. 11. For documents of the Cairo Conference, see *Review of International Affairs* (Belgrade), XV, No. 350 (November 5, 1964).

Hierarchies of Power. Such are the broad parameters which define the three worlds. What is the distribution of power[12] among the basic units, the nation-states? Power means the ability — material or intangible — to influence other states whether by coercion or persuasion. Material power since 1945 has been concentrated in the U.S.A. and the U.S.S.R. to such a degree that they are rightly regarded as superpowers as compared to other states. Secondary and lesser powers have grouped around these two giants to form what has been, at least from 1945 to Stalin's death in 1953, a basically bipolar world.

But the alliances that the superpowers once commanded have been rent by rebellious, centrifugal forces with the net result — as reflected in these readings — that the world is increasingly multipolar politically, even while unquestioned (but sometimes unusable) material power rests with Washington and Moscow. Within each world there are several pretenders to political leadership, with the Communist world likely to be permanently split by the rivalry of two main contenders. Viewed as a whole, international society tends toward increasing political fragmentation as states try to go their own way, deriving what good they can from association with members of any or all of the three (or more) worlds. (At the same time, it will be noted, economic and technological interdependence militates for supranational integration and cooperation on a regional, if not global, basis.)

The world, nevertheless, remains bipolar in the sense that overwhelming physical power still resides in the United States and Soviet Union. Table I shows the estimated gross national product (GNP) and population of the world in 1961. The three great centers of economic power are the U.S.A., the Soviet Union, and — taken as a whole — Western Europe. Europe's production, both in absolute and in per capita terms, exceeds the Soviet Union's, but the latter has sacrificed consumer comfort for military power. The huge obstacles to China's becoming a great industrial or military power are indicated by her low production per capita.

Using GNP figures similar to those given in Table I, although for 1962 instead of 1961, Professor Kenneth N. Waltz has projected the

[12] Professor Ernst Haas has admirably pointed out the confusions which result from using "balance of power" as a prescription, as a concept, and as propaganda. Thus, the term has been used in diverse and even contradictory meanings — to designate an equilibrium, the hegemony of one state, a stable peace or an unstable conflict, power politics generally, a universal law of history, or a guide to policy-making. See *World Politics*, V (1953) 442–477.

Table I

ESTIMATED WORLD GROSS NATIONAL PRODUCT AND POPULATION, 1961

	"Money" GNP		Population		"Real" GNP		GNP per Capita in Dollars	
	Billion Dollars	Per Cent of World Total	Millions	Per Cent of World Total	Billion Dollars	Per Cent of World Total	"Money" GNP	"Real" GNP
	(1)	(2)	(3)	(4)	(5)	(6)	(7)	(8)
DEVELOPED COUNTRIES								
Western Europe	285	20.6	261	8.7	385	22.0	1,091	1,472
Oceania	18	1.3	16	0.5	24	1.4	1,105	1,513
United States	515	37.3	185	6.2	515	29.4	2,790	2,790
Canada	38	2.7	18	0.6	38	2.1	2,048	2,048
Japan	36	2.6	95	3.2	58	3.3	383	613
South Africa	6	0.5	15	0.5	9	0.5	427	598
	898	65.0	590	19.7	1,029	58.7		
COMMUNIST BLOC								
Soviet Union	176	12.7	215	7.2	212	12.1	818	986
Eastern Europe	55	4.0	100	3.3	82	4.7	550	825
China	58	4.2	694	23.2	116	6.6	83	167
North Korea	1	0.1	9	0.3	2	0.1	105	211
North Vietnam	2	0.1	17	0.6	3	0.2	105	199
	292	21.1	1,035	34.6	415	23.7		

UNDERDEVELOPED COUNTRIES								
Africa	21	1.5	206	6.9	34	1.9	100	164
Asia	65	4.7	780	26.1	120	6.8	84	154
Latin America	65	4.7	210	7.0	89	5.1	311	425
Europe	21	1.5	67	2.2	34	1.9	313	501
Middle East	20	1.4	106	3.5	29	1.7	187	257
	192	13.8	1,369	45.7	306	17.5		
TOTAL	1,382	100	2,994	100	1,750	100		

Table I. The first four columns provide information on the estimated population and gross national product (GNP) of all countries of the world in 1961. The gross national product estimates in the first column have been expressed in dollars by converting the estimates in local currencies into dollars at the currently effective rates of exchange. This procedure results in a serious underestimate of the gross national product of the low-income countries, since the domestic purchasing power of their currencies is much higher than would be indicated by their conversion to dollars at foreign exchange rates, which are influenced only by internationally traded goods and services. Accordingly, the fifth column of Table I ("Real GNP") attempts a very rough estimate of what these gross national products might be if each of the products produced in these countries were valued at the price for which it can be bought in the United States. The last two columns of the table, indicating GNP per capita, are arrived at simply by dividing the "money" GNP figures and the "real" GNP figures, respectively, by the population.

Source: Max F. Millikan and Donald L. M. Blackmer, *The Emerging Nations: Their Growth and United States Policy* (Boston: Little, Brown, 1961) pp. 150–151. See also Article No. 5.

GNP that the great powers are likely to attain at the end of this century. The growth rates employed are those most likely to narrow the gap between the greatest and the middle powers to the largest extent presently imaginable. "Even on these bases, it becomes clear that the Soviet Union and the United States to the end of the millennium will remain the preponderant powers in the world unless two or more of the middle powers combine in a way that gives them the ability to concert their political and military actions on a sustained and reliable basis."[13]

[13] The GNP assumed for the U.S.A., the Soviet Union, and China in 1962 is $555 billion, $260 billion, and $50 billion, respectively. The U.S.A. at a growth rate of 3 per cent, will have by the year 2000 a GNP of $2,220 billion; the U.S.S.R., at a rate of 5 per cent, will reach $2,080 billion by the year 2004; while China, at a rate of 7 per cent will have by 2002 A.D. a GNP of $800 billion. See Kenneth N. Waltz, "The Stability of a Bipolar World," *Daedalus* (Summer 1964) pp. 892–893. The 1962 base figures are from *The New York Times*, January 26, 1964, p. E8. Waltz's article is criticized on various grounds by two other essays in the same issue of *Daedalus:* Roger Fisher, "Perceiving the World Through Bipolar Glasses," pp. 910–915; and William E. Griffith, "Eppuor Si Muove," pp. 916–919.

A Soviet forecast made in 1961 predicted a somewhat different picture:*

PERCENTAGE OF WORLD INDUSTRIAL PRODUCTION

	1950	1960	1970	1980
Socialist Camp	18	33	51	60
Imperialist Camp	77	56	37	29
Other Countries*	5	11	12	11

GROWTH RATES AS A PERCENTAGE OF 1960 PRODUCTION

Socialist Camp	28	100	342	832
Imperialist Camp	68	100	146	234
Other Countries	24	100	254	445
Average	50	100	222	452

* S. Strumilin, "Mir Cherez 20 Let [The World in 20 Years]," *Kommunist*, No. 13 (September 1961) 30. No clarification was made as to the countries included in the "other countries" category, although in the population projections below allowance was made for the possibility that some "other" countries would join the socialist camp.

An equally dramatic projection of demographic shifts within the three worlds was attempted. The first variant indicates the trend if no nonaligned countries join the socialist camp. The second forecast, described as "cautious," assumes that in the period from 1960 to 1980 the socialist camp will be joined by 30 per cent of the presently nonaligned states and by 10 per cent of currently imperialistic countries.

A nuclear-missile strategic force represents the distillation of tremendous development of industrial and scientific resources. For decades to come only the United States, the Soviet Union, and — if effectively united — Western Europe will have the economic and technological potential to create and maintain the kinds of forces already possessed by Washington and Moscow. The ability of the Soviet Union itself to rival the United States in strategic forces is in doubt. Although it is within the ability of China and France to develop and procure atomic bombs, they have little prospect of producing delivery systems com-

---

(A higher accession from the West, the article argues, is impeded by the opportunistic belief in the peaceful evolution of capitalism, which is spreading even among the Western proletariat because of improved living standards.)

WORLD POPULATION (MILLIONS) *

Groups of Countries	1960 Total	%	1970 Total	%	1980 Total	%	Percentage Increase In 10 Years	In 20 Years
Variant I:								
Socialist	1050	35	1331	37	1687	40	26.8	60.7
Imperialist	600	20	644	19	733	18	10.6	22.1
Other	1350	45	1551	44	1783	42	14.9	32.1
Total	3000	100	3546	100	4203	100	18.2	40.1
Variant II:								
Socialist	1050	35	1597	45	2295	54	52.1	118.6
Imperialist	600	20	631	18	660	16	5.2	10.0
Other	1350	45	1318	37	1248	30	—2.4	—7.6

* Strumilin, *op. cit.*, p. 30.

Space does not permit a detailed evaluation of Waltz's and Strumilin's predictions except the statement that the former's seem much sounder. Since 1961 none of the expected increase in the population of the socialist camp due to the accession of nonaligned or Western states has taken place. The economic anticipations of 1961 have also been undermined by the sharp downturn of the Soviet economy and upturn of the American since that time. A final caveat — it should be noted that the economic data for 1960 are expressed solely in percentage terms, the base for which may well be disputed. In any case, Strumilin's predictions, published in the official journal of the Soviet Communist Party, give some indication of official thinking at a time when the new Communist Party program was adopted in 1961. As noted on pages 47–48, however, Soviet optimism concerning the political future of the nonaligned countries was jarred by a number of events in 1960–1961. The interested reader will want to compare the Waltz and Strumilin projections with other data and with economic and political developments as they emerge.

parable to the superpowers'. This limitation applies *a fortiori* to other possible nuclear aspirants, such as Egypt, Israel, or Sweden.[14] This qualification in no way minimizes, however, the political and possible catalytic effects of atomic bombs deliverable by airplanes produced or purchased by Paris, Peking, or still lesser powers, for even a minimal *force de frappe* may be a source of tremendous political power.

Military or even economic power, of course, is hardly synonymous with political influence. The nuclear stalemate between the superpowers creates new opportunities for maneuver by lesser powers within the Warsaw Pact and NATO, as well as by uncommitted nations. Intangible political and moral power can result from exploiting the nuclear deadlock, by mediating between contending powers, creating pressures in "world public opinion," and by uniting to form controlling majorities in the United Nations.

The hegemony of Moscow and Washington is challenged materially by Peking and Paris, both of which seek the benefits of at least a symbolic atomic arsenal. The superpowers are challenged politically within their own camps, most notably by the same two states which aspire to the nuclear club. And they are challenged by all the states of their own and particularly of the third world who would exploit the nuclear stalemate to bring new leverage and room for political maneuver by the non-nuclear powers.

Faced with these challenges, the Soviet Union and United States begin to perceive some common interests. Like Alexander I and Napoleon at Tilsit in 1807, the superpowers stand to gain by collaborating to preserve and profit from their material prowess. Militarily their interests call for non-proliferation of nuclear weapons.[15] Politically their interests call for weighting the decision-making process of the United Nations to favor the permanent members of the Security Council.[16] Both these interests are qualified by the desire of each superpower to maintain or increase

[14] See John Beaton and Leonard Maddox, *The Spread of Nuclear Weapons* (New York: Praeger, 1962). The announcement on September 29, 1964 by Secretary of State Rusk that the United States expected China soon to test a nuclear device added that such a detonation "does not mean a stockpile of nuclear weapons and the presence of modern delivery systems." Some U.S. experts put the acquisition of such delivery systems and a meaningful arsenal five to ten years into the future. It was also estimated that the effort required to test atomic bombs required a commitment of about half a billion dollars and a powerful industrial complex, both of which Peking could provide — *The New York Times*, September 30, 1964, pp. 1, 16.
[15] See readings No. 38–41.
[16] See readings No. 45–49.

its power vis-à-vis the other.[17] This desire, however, is increasingly diminished by the growing belief, expressed even by Washington officials, that it may be to U.S. advantage that the Soviet Union achieve the psychological security of military parity and consumer abundance. In any case both Washington and Moscow have an overriding interest in avoiding all-out war and, consequently, in damping local conflicts (as in Southeast Asia) which could escalate. Scientifically and economically the superpowers stand to gain from pooling their resources to reduce the cost of high energy physics, space research, and other endeavors which are costly even for them and almost beyond the capacity of other states. The competition of the superpowers may therefore tend toward an equilibrium moderated by their common interest in preserving and exploiting their privileged positions.

The greatest single variable in this picture is the economic, political, and military potential of Europe — apart from the U.S.S.R. and the U.S.A. If Western Europe's human and material resources were effectively united, they could rival those of the two superpowers. One might add that if the resources of China were effectively developed, they might rival those of one or the other superpower. But vast material problems stand in the way of China's achieving a high production per capita, whereas human, political obstacles are the main deterrent to Europe's development. Will Europe — like America in 1787 — achieve the unity from which to build an economic whole strong enough to compete with Moscow and Washington in military and scientific endeavor? The prospects are cloudy in the mid-1960's due mainly to the influence of General de Gaulle, but after his passing the almost inexorable drives already seen in functional and economic cooperation may be expected to lead toward greater political and economic unity in Western Europe, probably drawing in Eastern Europe as though by gravitational pull. Nevertheless, the arguments in this book's readings that oppose the integration of Europe and, especially, of Europe with North America, may be expected to revive again for years and decades to come, if not in France, then in Germany or elsewhere. The manner in which Europe, if united, will use its pooled resources is, of course, not preordained. Conceivably it would not seek to rival America and Russia militarily or in space, but — counting on a U.S.-Soviet nuclear stalemate — might seek international political power from non-military achievements and/ or concentrate on internal European economic and cultural development.

[17] See readings No. 1–4, 7, 9.

Should Europe become a power like the U.S.A. and the Soviet Union, the existing hegemony of the industrialized North vis-à-vis the slowly developing South would be reinforced. But might not the three northern power centers (Europe, the United States and the Soviet Union) fall out among themselves? This is entirely possible. However, the ties of a relatively common cultural background and joint political and economic interests in the face of the atomic genie and the "have-not" nations will militate for collaboration, as well as competition, among Russia, Europe, and America. In most respects these three superpowers will have more to gain from upholding their "have" status than from seeking to gain a power position which would permit one (or two) of the three to dictate to another. This forecast seems realistic but could, of course, be upset by a revolutionary military-scientific breakthrough by one superpower alone or by the rise to power of a government (say, in Washington or Moscow) hell-bent on attaining unquestioned control over the other superpowers.[18]

Relationships of Major Tension. The view of the structure of international society in the 1960's must consider not only the basic actors and the power distribution among them, but also the relationships of major tension. These relationships may be regarded in various ways, and some might wish to include here the transnational forces discussed shortly — atomic power, the population explosion, nationalism, racism, and others. But most of these forces converge to find expression in three problems which are dramatically defined in the Sino-Soviet polemic, especially since 1963. Our analysis will focus on these three problems

---

[18] Historical analogies are stimulating but precarious. History shows that states with similar interests have often followed disparate policies, as the European powers did before and after 1914. History also suggests that it was Europe's formation into two camps which touched off the war, perhaps by inhibiting the normal flexibility of the "balance of power" system. However, many factors have changed since 1914 and are expressed in the perceived consensus of the great powers today of their common interest in avoiding war. Another variable is that bipolarity currently is based more on the superpower status of two countries rather than on a merely formal alliance of two coalitions, as in 1914. This means that the superpowers have the possibility of restraining their allies (as Washington did in the Suez crisis) to a degree not permitted even to Berlin in 1914. By this same token, however, it may be argued that if a united Europe achieves superpower status, the stability of the present bipolar system will be threatened. (See Waltz, *loc. cit.*, p. 900.) In any event it is sobering to recall Gibbon's dictum: "History is indeed the record of the crimes, follies, and misfortunes of mankind." (Cited in Griffith, *loc. cit.*, p. 917.)

because they help to generalize and simplify a host of tensions which pulse through most parts of the international system.[19]

The first relationship of major tension to be considered is what Moscow terms the "contradiction" between the socialist camp (which it strives to lead) and the capitalist. This, according to Soviet spokesmen, is the major campaign front. True, the national liberation struggle is a crucial element in the coming victory of socialism, but it must be subordinated to and integrated with the growing might and leadership of the socialist (Soviet-led) countries.

A second alternative is stressed by Peking: the conflict between the allegedly oppressed underdeveloped countries (which China hopes to lead) and Western "imperialism."[20] As Robert A. Scalipino has written, "If the 'national-liberation movement' can be made the vital center of the world revolution, and the Chinese model can be advanced, with suitable modifications, as the basic approach to a successful liberation-Socialist revolution, then China will be able to play a crucial role in the world despite her relative lack of military and economic power."[21]

The Western statements in this book, whether from the right or the liberal wing in the U.S.A. or from Gaullist France, tend to agree with the alternative emphasized by Moscow, but with the qualification that international Communist aggression is itself the major source of tension. Rightly or wrongly the West has also tended to see the economic and political demands of the emerging nations merely as an expression of Communist machinations.[22]

[19] International politics, however, is not entirely total and global. Leonard Binder has written of "The Middle East as a Subordinate International System," *World Politics*, X, No. 3 (April 1958) 408–429. Inter-Arab or Arab-Israeli tensions, for example, are in some respects analogous to, but not identical with, the three relationships discussed here.

[20] See item No. 11; also "A Proposal Concerning the General Line of the International Communist Movement," Letter of the Central Committee of the Communist Party of China in Reply to the Letter of the Central Committee of the Communist Party of the Soviet Union of March 30, 1963, dated June 14, 1963. *Peking Review*, VI, No. 25 (June 21, 1963) 6–23.

[21] "The Sino-Soviet Conflict in Perspective," *The Annals of the American Academy of Political and Social Science* (January 1964) p. 10.

[22] Secretary of State Rusk's comment in a news conference on March 1, 1962: "There is no threat to the peace of Southeast Asia from the south or from across the Pacific Ocean; the threat comes only from the north, from those who have declared their intention to force the rest of the world into their pattern — despite the fact that no people has yet chosen that pattern in a genuinely free election."

A third major alternative is implicit in the Sino-Soviet dispute and runs like a red skein throughout this book: the conflict between man and technology. Peking accuses Moscow of "nuclear fetishism," that is, of placing excessive confidence in technology while deprecating morale, ideology, and — by implication — the potential inherent in the sheer numbers of Asia's manpower. The same argument finds expression within the West and within the Soviet Union over the extent to which strategic weapons render conventional forces obsolete or superfluous. A still broader military-political question arises from the Sino-Soviet debate and that between Western advocates of protracted conflict and supporters of *détente:* Can man ensure that his technological ingenuity will not lead to global destruction, whether by accident, escalation, catalysis, or the act of a desperate government?

The question of man versus technology occurs again in debate over modernization of underdeveloped countries. Can any country industrialize? If so, is a bootstrap operation possible? If not, will outside aid prove any more effective?

A deeper understanding of the major fault lines in world politics can be facilitated by an analysis of the driving material and spiritual forces in international society today.

II FORCES IN THE TRANSNATIONAL NET

Statesmen from all three worlds have to deal with forces — material, ideological, and organizational — which cut across or operate within many of the basic units in the international system. From the perspective of historical comparison of different diplomatic constellations, these forces are factors of change, but they are also a "given" at any historical moment. Their number is an index of the intensity of international relations. They are the key to opportunity but also a fundamental restraint upon the action of the basic units. The manner in which the basic actors respond to these forces will be considered in section III immediately following this discussion of the main forces at work in the 1960's.

Objective Factors. One need not be a Marxist to recognize the important role played by material forces throughout history. Indeed, the two greatest dangers confronting modern man stem from changes in the material base of world society. First, the unchaining of the atom and conquest of space have ushered in an age of unparalleled potential for destruction. Second, modern medicine and hygiene have cut death rates so sharply that most countries — especially the poorer ones — are faced with a population explosion which threatens to overfulfill the predictions of Malthus. The first problem pervades the readings in this book. The second — partly because it is as yet less frequently discussed by political leaders — is mentioned here only in the readings dealing with the development of the third world.

The danger of war is exacerbated by the prospect that the Malthusian equation may soon become a reality, for instance, in China, adding to motives for expansion. The very process of attempting to modernize a backward country opens a pandora's box of tensions — personal and societal — which sharpen the dissatisfactions and frustrations which impel nations toward aggressive behavior.[23]

Thus, the relationship of major tension as expressed by "man *vs.* technology" becomes a problem which no country — Communist, Western, or developing — can safely ignore. All are threatened by each other's problems whether military, demographic, or economic. The quantity and quality of the material forces in the transnational net make for an interdependency unique in world history.

Subjective Factors. Linking the "objective" and the "subjective" forces of the present international situation is the communication system produced by modern technology. It provides the vehicle by which nations threaten one another, but also the means by which they trade in goods and ideas, thereby increasing material interdependency and cultural diffusion. The exchange of persons, ideas, and commodities, of course, has great potential for breaking down hostility and differences among peoples, but international tension can result from understanding as well as misunderstanding. This book, in any case, reflects and hopes to increase the cross-cultural flow of ideas.

Principles of Political Unity. Two major subjective forces fill the consciousness of men around the globe. The first is nationalism. Without doubt it is the most powerful force in the transnational network of ideas, values, and sentiments. Each "people," identified by a common language and culture — so runs the prevalent myth — should have political expression in the form of a sovereign nation-state. Some such idea provides the rationale for the organization of families and tribes into "nation-states." Frequently, as in modern Africa, the idea exists only in the consciousness of an elite which

---

[23] See W. Arthur Lewis, "Economic Problems of Development," in *Restless Nations: A Study of World Tensions and Development,* Council on World Tensions (New York: Dodd, Mead & Co., 1962) pp. 68–98; and Pierre Rondot, "Quelques Aspects Sociaux et Moraux des Problèmes de Développement," *Politique Étrangère,* No. 4 (1960) 309–315.

tries to foster symbols of unity among insular tribes. But — as the readings suggest — chauvinist, jingo nationalism persists as a driving force also in the modern societies of the West and the officially "internationalist" Soviet Union. Alternative symbols of unity — whether appealing to race (white, Arab, Negro, etc.), culture (Western or Eastern), class (aristocratic or proletarian), or the ideal of human equality — have paled next to nationalism as effective principles of unity, though racism combined with economic and political grievances threatens to become an increasingly powerful current in world affairs.

Many observers share the view, expressed here by Senator Fulbright, for example, that nationalism is an illusory and dangerous sentiment which should be outgrown and replaced by broader, more realistic and humanistic values.[24] The increasing interdependency of the modern world seems to militate for regional or continental — if not global — principles of identification. Possible patterns for such evolution are suggested in the readings, but the future shape of international society will be the result of human action as well as material forces, of voluntarism interacting with determinism.

Standards of Economic Expectation. The transmission belt by which nationalism has spread today to all parts of the world originated in Napoleon's ostensible liberation of the *patries,* the fatherlands of Europe. About that same time England, the first country to industrialize, ignited a second subjective force which is only now reaching fruition in the third world and the Communist world: the revolution of rising economic and social expectations. The effectiveness of these two subjective forces stemming from France and England is dramatically demonstrated in the Universal Declaration of Human Rights subscribed to by most members of the three worlds since 1948.[25] This declaration and the Draft Covenants of Human Rights which followed it spelled out both political-civil and economic-social-cultural rights. It is significant that virtually all states now pay verbal homage to both kinds of human expectations, even if in practice they abuse them.

Consideration of these objective and subjective forces offers a clue to the relative importance of the three relationships of major tension outlined in section I. All three, of course, interact, and one's estimate

[24] As regards the developing nations, however, see Rupert Emerson, "Nationalism and Political Development," *Journal of Politics,* XXII, No. 1 (February 1960) 3–28.
[25] United Nations General Assembly Resolution, December 10, 1948; in *A Decade of American Foreign Policy: Basic Documents, 1941–1949* (Washington, D.C.: U.S. Government Printing Office, 1950) pp. 1156–1159.

of their respective weights will depend on the time and his place in the three worlds. Clearly, the greatest stakes are involved in the East-West struggle, since nuclear war could result. In another sense there are greater numbers of people involved in the struggle of the emerging nations of Africa, Asia, and Latin America than in the competition between Moscow and the West. But each of these two relationships of major tension derives ultimately from the third alternative: man versus technology — issuing from the forces unleashed by the industrial revolution. It was this revolution which kindled the hope that all men might partake in the blessings of material abundance which new production techniques would provide. It was this revolution which enabled Europe to dominate Russia, Asia, and Africa, only to awaken there the spark of nationalism and the desire to emulate the mass-consumption ways of Europe and America. Thus, both the political and economic strivings of the new nations may justly be regarded as the impact of the West upon the world.[26]

Organizational Factors. The objective and subjective forces common to most countries find expression in various transnational organizations, both informal and formal. Here are included the international forms mentioned above in section I on the Structure of International Politics — the alliances, agencies for functional and cultural cooperation, *ad hoc* conferences, and the United Nations itself. They are the major existing instruments by which the basic actors, the nation-states, can cooperatively deal with the material and spiritual challenges before them.

These intergovernmental agencies are paralleled by other transnational movements which also seek to alter the course of history, but which are not formally governmental. The most powerful group of this nature in history have been the churches — Catholic, Orthodox, Moslem, etc. Their impact has lessened today, but could increase from efforts toward inter-faith harmony. The best financed and most disciplined non-governmental agencies in the twentieth century, however, especially since 1945, have been the Communist Parties and fronts such as the World Peace Council and World Federation of Democratic Youth. Being controlled by the same elites which run the Communist states, these organizations have recently bifurcated along the lines of

[26] For a Soviet discussion of "Technological Progress and the Problem of Maintaining Peace" see G. L. Episkopov, *Tekhnicheskii progress i problema sokhraneniia mira* (Moscow: Institut Mezhdunarodnykh Otnoshenii, 1960). The work is particularly critical of "bourgeois" writing on this subject.

the Sino-Soviet split. By comparison with the churches and international Communism, the efforts of movements in the West and *tiers monde* — such as World Federalism and the World Assembly of Youth — seem feeble. But the final measure of the effectiveness of democratic pluralism versus monolithic centralism has not yet been taken. The outcome must depend somewhat on the validity of the ideas advanced, as well as the structure for their propagation.

Organizational innovation is always possible, but the interplay of basic factors and transnational forces will probably be carried out in the foreseeable future within the framework of existing intergovernmental agencies, prodded and encouraged by the non-governmental movements which rise to prominence.

III   DOMESTIC FACTORS AND FOREIGN POLICY

As the readings make manifest, within each "world" there are unique styles of foreign policy-making which reflect the material base of the government concerned, its political-economic constitution, and its political culture. Such factors condition profoundly the kind of leadership which can emerge in each nation-state and its interaction with the elites and body politic as a whole. The precise weight accorded to "forces" as distinguished from "free will" and "individuals" in history will vary with time and place, but there is no doubt that the domestic environment has a decisive effect upon foreign policy, setting limits and inducements to the kinds of words and deeds to which a Khrushchev, Sukarno, de Gaulle, or Johnson will commit himself.

The peculiar characteristics of each government are relatively easy to define; the qualities common to groups of states more difficult.

Haves and Have-Nots. Objectively, the various nation-states are at different stages of economic development. A leading Western theory sees a trend from traditional society to economic "take-off" culminating in industrial maturity and, finally, consumer abundance.[27] Communist

---

[27] See Walt W. Rostow, *The Stages of Economic Growth* (Cambridge: University Press, 1960). For applications of this theory see items No. 5 and 18, "The Third Choice" and "Guerrilla Warfare in the Underdeveloped Areas." For a Soviet critique of Rostow's theory see Y. Semenov, "Teoriia 'stagii ekonomicheskogo razvitiia,'" ["The Theory of the 'Stages of Economic Growth'"], *Mirovaia Ekonomika i Mezhdunarodnie Otnosheniia*, No. 6 (1963) 32–45. For a Japanese critique see Yoichi Itagaki, "Criticism of Rostow's Stage Approach: The Concepts of Stage, System, and Type," *The Developing Economies*, I, No. 1 (January–June 1963) 1–17.

expectations are similar in some respects but emphasize more the precise form of property relations and foresee an inevitable movement from feudalism to socialism and communism, perhaps bypassing a capitalist stage.

Some states, it is said, are "haves," and others "have-nots." A careful distinction must be made as to what sort of possession is at issue — the quantity or quality of population, raw materials, agriculture, industry, or armaments. The broadest criterion employed in discussions of the rich and the poor nations is per capita production, for this is a reflection of the extent and state of other kinds of material wealth. Using this criterion it may be said that the gap between the rich and the poor nations is generally expanding, as most African, Asian, and Latin American states are barely able to raise production at the same rate as population.

In any event governments and peoples derive varying degrees of satisfaction from their material environment. Each will have a subjective image of "what is" and "what ought to be." The lesser the perceived gap between the two, the more "satisfied" the state will be and the less anxious for change.[28] The government's values, of course, may not be the people's, or the latter's may be manipulated so that relative "have" nations reject the status quo while "have-nots" appear content with it.

The Western governments, on the whole, are relatively satisfied and those of the third world dissatisfied, while the Communist states represent admixtures of these extremes. Of the two superpowers, the Soviet regime is less satisfied with the status quo than the U.S.A., but much more content than Peking or Havana. Of the intermediate powers, Britain is relatively content while France and Communist China are highly revisionist. Of lesser powers, regimes so diverse as Switzerland and Saudi Arabia are basically satisfied for the present, but most (especially those represented in these readings) are not. Precise sources of dissatisfaction must also be distinguished. Thus, frustration over living standards is probably a more compelling force than displeasure with the voting apparatus of the United Nations. On another level, a potential great power, such as China, would be more frustrated with its failure to obtain an atomic arsenal than a government whose pretensions were less grandiose.

---

[28] See Robert C. North, "Soviet and Chinese Goal Values: A Study in Communism as a Behavior System," in *Unity and Contradiction: Major Aspects of Sino-Soviet Relations,* Kurt London (ed.) (New York: Praeger, 1962) pp. 62–63.

The implications for international politics of economic imbalance are manifold. All states try to influence the rate and direction of change to preserve or enhance their own interests. The poorer states perceive a greater discrepancy between "what is" and "what ought to be" than the richer. The have-nots therefore tend to be more desperate for change of some kind than the haves, who lean toward caution. The have-nots are more prone to foreign adventures, whether in bold speeches at the U.N. or in deeds against other states, which promise to divert attention from domestic misfortunes, if not to remedy them. Satisfied powers, whether large like the U.S.A. or small like Switzerland, may understand that their interest requires a channeling of change in the poorer nations, but they will prefer a groping evolution to revolution. While the Soviet Government's ideology pledges aid to wars of national liberation, Moscow, too, is coming to prefer stability over chaos in the emerging nations. The caution of the haves is explained only partly by their own material satisfaction; the extent of their wealth which might be destroyed if chaos led to general war is unprecedented.

There are, of course, different degrees and kinds of satisfaction among the more satisfied powers. The Soviet Union, unlike China, believes itself able to compete economically with the United States. "In this sense the Soviet Union has become a 'have' nation psychologically, not in terms of being satisfied with the status quo, but in terms of being relatively satisfied with the rate and direction of change."[29] Soviet satisfaction, for instance, has derived from a belief that Russia was "overtaking" the "capitalist" world, while the Western countries have measured their contentment more by progress toward fulfillment of internal needs. A major variable in the decades to come is whether the Soviet regime can rest content or endure without visible expansion of its influence abroad.

Even among the Western "haves" there are powers dissatisfied with certain features of the international situation. France, as the readings show, has sought to challenge American influence in Europe and in the world generally, to join the nuclear club, and to regain the privileged position within the United Nations originally accorded to permanent members of the Security Council.[30]

[29] Scalipino, loc. cit., p. 8.
[30] See reading No. 45; see also A. Grosser, "General de Gaulle and the Foreign Policy of the Fifth Republic," International Affairs (London), XXXIX, No. 2 (April 1963) 198–213.

It does not follow that the wealthier the state, the greater opposition to change. The U.S. margin of material power, for instance, allows Washington to be more tolerant of change than another basically have nation with a more precarious position. Thus, the State Department can observe an upgrading of the General Assembly relative to the Security Council with less trepidation than the French Foreign Ministry, because Washington has a greater material influence to wield behind the scenes and, in any case, can *afford* more magnanimity.[31]

Internal Constitutional Factors. A central question to be asked concerning the effect of domestic politics upon foreign policy is how much stability does the government enjoy. Second, to what extent is it free to act or not to act unobstructed by domestic pressure and popular opinion?

A paradoxical situation is emerging in the Western, Communist, and third worlds. There is a general tendency toward more centralized government with ever greater economic and political powers. At the same time governments seem to be increasingly responsive to the peoples who elect them, even on one-party ballots. Even the Communist states refer to themselves as "republics" or "popular democracies." Since 1961 the Soviet regime has claimed to be an "all people's state" rather than a "dictatorship of the proletariat."

The trend toward greater centralization is a response to the increasing complexity of modern life. It also means that the government gains ever greater control over the levers of power and communication. In a showdown, therefore, governments retain the means to resist or remake popular feeling, although they prefer to avoid such conflict.

Some reflection of the centralized nature of modern government emerges in the readings. There is a spectrum of responsiveness to popular sentiments. Thus, Washington is more responsive than Paris; Paris, more than Moscow; Moscow, more than Peking. A certain feeling of pluralism and pragmatism comes through most of the statements by U.S. advocates and critics of government policy. In contrast, the affectionate French references to de Gaulle's wisdom and patriotism produce an image of enlightened despotism. By further contrast it is clear that only dictatorships with totalitarian controls could put forward such absolutistic arguments as those in the Sino-Soviet polemics, revealing discord long kept from the public, but now expecting a new

[31] See readings No. 45 and 49.

line to be accepted overnight.[32] It would also seem, however, that the Kremlin, having approved a pervasive program of de-Stalinization, is riding a tiger that Peking has so far kept chained.

The foreign policy consequences of dictatorship have been noted, for example, by George F. Kennan, who suggested that Stalin's regime required an image of a hostile external foe to justify domestic repression. Other observers have stressed the ability of dictatorships, relative to more democratic systems, to formulate and carry out long-range foreign strategies and execute quick maneuvers when opportunity strikes. They do not confront the problem of the U.S. executive, for example, in persuading Congress to make long-term commitments of foreign aid or to approve some *démarche* to take advantage of change within the Soviet bloc. The American system has had the further disadvantage of promoting a "pacifism-bellicosity" cycle, as executives have proclaimed holy wars to stir the people to protect what was essentially national interest. The growing infeasibility of isolationism, as noted later, is curtailing these traditional patterns of U.S. foreign policy.

Economic power, like political control, seems increasingly to be centralized as government steps in to research, plan, and regulate — if not actually own — vast enterprises. This tendency is probably inevitable in the third world, if rapid modernization is to be possible, and in the Western world, if sustained economic growth and welfare for all citizens is to be assured. In Eastern Europe and the Soviet Union, on the other hand, excessively centralized command economies are being modified to take account of market demands. These trends promise two possible gains for world peace: (1) the convergence (and integration) of national economic systems may reduce grounds for ideological hostilities, although states may still fight over other differences that remain; and (2) increasing effectiveness of national economies may reduce the perceived gap between "what is" and "what ought to be," although for underdeveloped states this may take decades or even generations.[33]

---

[32] In one sense, however, the Kennedy address at American University was also an admission that the American people have long been subjected to a one-sided interpretation of world affairs. See reading No. 3.

[33] For two Soviet attacks upon the view expressed by various Western writers that Soviet and Western societies are converging and are no longer aptly described by the terms "socialist" and "capitalist," see G. Frantsov, "Chto skryvaetsia za lozungom 'ideologicheskogo razoruzheniia'" ["What Lies Behind the Slogan 'Ideological Disarmament'"], *Kommunist*, No. 13 (September 1962) 110–119; Ven.

Economic power, however, tends to generate political power, and there is a profund threat to civic freedom where economic pluralism is replaced by centralism. Thus, it is no accident that the four states placed on a spectrum of political centralization — the U.S.A., France, the Soviet Union, and China — would occupy the same order in terms of economic centralization. Of course, there are other states with highly nationalized economies which are among the most democratic states in the world — Britain, Australia, the Scandinavian countries, and, in another sense, India. The factors conducive to democracy in these countries suggest the kinds of forces needed to counterbalance economic centralization the world over: the affluence and literacy of the citizens, the preservation of private institutions where they are more effective than public, and — most difficult to replicate — a political culture which respects individual differences.

Political Culture. What is the milieu in which the internal constitution functions to formulate and direct foreign policy? What are the public sentiments which, if expressed, might alter the course of foreign policy-making?

The two catchwords of American political campaigns probably express the profoundest hopes of most men everywhere — peace and prosperity. These two goals are intimately connected: without one the other cannot usually be long upheld, although extremely poor societies may lack the will or energy to fight. But, while governments assure their people that they are doing everything possible to promote these objectives, the fact remains that governments will risk violence and impose economic hardship to enhance their over-all power and prestige, and perhaps "to keep the peace." Such is the pragmatic lesson of political realism. Moreover, because of centralized communications, governments can mold opinion to fit their needs. Finally, while the "people" want peace, their nationalist sentiments and yearning for

Motylev, "Predotvrashchenie mirovoi voiny i sovremennyi reformizm" ["The Prevention of War and Contemporary Reformism"], *Mirovaia Ekonomika i Mezhdunarodnye Otnosheniia* [World Economics and International Relations], No. 12 (1963) 127–139. The second article is a review of John Strachey's *On the Prevention of War* (London, 1962), which is criticized, *inter alia*, for offering as an ideological justification for disarmament the convergence of capitalism and socialism. It may be, as Shakespeare suggested, "the lady doth protest too much." The leading Western argument that parallel evolution rather than convergence may be expected of United States and Soviet societies is Zbigniew Brzezinski and Samuel P. Huntington, *Political Power: USA/USSR* (New York: Viking Press, 1964).

vicarious excitement lead them to revel in strong words and actions which manifest their national glory.

The bellicose strains of xenophobia and chauvinism exert a two-fold influence on foreign policy making. First, they reward strong actions, such as pulling Uncle Sam's beard, talking back to Khrushchev, or carrying out reprisals against Israeli (or Arab) raiders. Second, they tend to punish and inhibit government moves to collaborate with an adversary, even where common interests can be promoted, as in the nuclear test ban and U.S.-Soviet wheat deal in 1963.

Isolationist sentiments are no longer a powerful restraint upon foreign policy-making because they are precluded by the transnational net of material and other forces enveloping most states. While a state can hardly be self-sufficient, it can nevertheless seek to avoid alignment with or domination by the superpowers. Thus, while avoiding isolationism, France has attempted a kind of unilateralism. A similar rationale has infused foreign policy in most of the *tiers monde*. A skeptic may ask how such states can survive without great power support. The fact is that many states have received economic aid from both the Communist and Western alliances and that Egypt and India, when attacked in 1956 and 1962 by intermediate powers of one major alliance, were aided militarily by *both* superpowers, to the chagrin of their lesser partners.

The success of the third world at playing off the Communist and Western worlds has encouraged similar policies by members of the Warsaw Pact and NATO, with Rumania and France displaying the most autonomy within these groupings.

The tendency within the Warsaw Pact and NATO alliance to cross ideological frontiers to deal with the adversary is symptomatic of a new development endemic to political cultures of industrialized societies the world over — the decline of ideology. Senator Fulbright and President Kennedy assailed the myths behind much U.S. cold war strategy.[34] French spokesmen have done likewise.[35] The entire Sino-Soviet polemic is rooted in Khrushchev's efforts to modify Communist doctrine to fit the realities of the nuclear era.

Within every society there are divisions between conservatives and modernizers. The former are aided by the desire to adhere to what is

[34] See readings No. 1 and 3; for elucidation see particularly Fulbright's *Old Myths and New Realities* (New York: Random House, 1964).
[35] See items No. 2 and 19.

familiar, but the latter are strengthened by life itself. Support of the status quo is undermined by technological and social change, and dogmatism challenged by empirical scientism. The more traditional or dogmatic the society, the more the conservative-modernist rift is accentuated by the conflict of generations, by the challenge to the old from the young.[36]

The effect of this rift upon foreign policy is illustrated in many of the readings in this book. The rift affects the basic orientation and assumptions of foreign policy as summarized under the headings *Realpolitik* and *Moralpolitik*. The first term denotes a syndrome which tends toward nationalism and caution about the possible, and which looks primarily to the past for guidance. The second term indicates an outlook which is internationalist, optimistic about the desirable, and which looks to reason and human engineering to reform the world.[37] These dichotomies are reflected in the positions which governments take on working with allies, compromise with the adversary, international cooperation and economic assistance, the peaceful settlement of conflicts, the desirability and possibility of arms control, and world law. In another sense, these splits emerge in the strategic debate over the relative utility of wonder weapons and conventional forces.

As will be argued later in more detail, neither *Moralpolitik* nor *Realpolitik* alone provides a sound guide to policy because effective policy will have to balance optimally both ends and means, change and conservation, international and national interests. The rift common to most political cultures between advocates and opponents of change provides still another example of the complications and stresses in public life introduced or accentuated by technological change.

IV THE PRODUCT: INTERNATIONAL RELATIONS

The three series of data — the structure of world politics, the determining forces, and the interaction between domestic and foreign

---

[36] The differences in outlook between "fathers and sons" is an important factor in the alignment between conservatives and modernists in Russia, but in the more modern, less dogmatic United States the conservative-reformist division appears little affected by the conflict of generations. For an analysis of the impact on the new generation in the Soviet Union of Khrushchev's coming to power, see Zbigniew Rapacki, "L'URSS, la Chine, et la Democracies Populaires," *Politique Étrangère*, No. 4 (1962) 338–358.

[37] See also Edward H. Carr, *The Twenty Years Crisis, 1919–1939* (London: Macmillan, 1941) pp. 16–30, 81–122.

policy — do not add to form a sum; they rather multiply and accelerate from interaction to form a dynamic product — "international relations."

This product, it has been argued, may be viewed from the standpoint of decision-making by a basic unit or from an overview of the basic units. Distinctive characteristics of a given historical situation will be (1) the range of goals sought by the basic units and the means used to pursue them; and (2) the manner in which the international system functions to accommodate these pursuits. The present readings suggest a number of features unique in the history of international relations, many of them a function of the transnational net of communications, economic interdependence, and military threat.

The Ends and Means of the Basic Units. The nation-states of the present era, despite their many diversities, probably share the greatest value consensus in recorded history. The United Nations Charter, the Universal Declaration of Human Rights, and other declarations which have been subscribed to by most states of the world record a remarkable agreement on political, economic, and cultural goals. National independence, industrialization and prosperity, cultural development — such are the broad objectives common to virtually all governments today.

Assuming satisfactory progress toward these objectives, most governments will also put a premium on the maintenance of peace. But most states refuse to act as though physical survival were the *sine qua non* for achievement of their other goals. Most members of the third world have used violence or the threat of violence to achieve independence and begin the road to modernization. Further back in time, most regimes of the Communist and Western world also had violent beginnings and have since fought frequently to preserve their way of life. Today, in fact, the U.S.A., the Soviet Union, and Communist China lead multinational alliances which each of the other two powers sees as a physical and moral threat to its existence. "Peace" is presently ensured, if at all, by deterrence based on the threat of retaliation.

Thus, the international system today is unique in two other respects: in the global aspirations of its empire builders, and the general destruction by which they threaten one another. However, the very technology which makes possible these far-reaching objectives and instruments of policy has also created the means to countervail them. While imperial strivings persist, combat can be carried out with nonviolent means — economic and propaganda influence. Such competition leads to a realization that the economic and cultural aims of the superpowers — as well as other states — might profit from cooperation more than conflict. Designs for hegemony may therefore atrophy as independence is tempered by interdependence, Hobbesian diffidence superseded by trust, and fearful poverty replaced by an assured stake in the existing order.

In the meantime, while this greater consensus is only inchoate, the superpowers are learning how to collaborate to preserve the delicate fabric of peace. But the lessons must be quickly applied. The superpowers must avoid situations which leave one another no exit for graceful retreat, prevent conflicts between themselves or third parties which could result in local wars subject to escalation, establish controls to prevent accidental or catalytic war, end nuclear proliferation, agree to an international machinery to settle disputes peacefully, and re-establish peace where violence breaks out among smaller powers. In their own interest, Moscow and Washington must increase technical and cultural collaboration between themselves. More difficult, the rich haves of the industrialized North must find ways of assisting the poor majority in Asia, Africa, and Latin America to develop rapidly but peacefully.

The Functioning of the International System. If the goals of most men are to be achieved, the workings of the state system must avoid a general war while facilitating improvement of economic and cultural standards everywhere, or the present system must be transformed into one which can perform these tasks. The present state system places ultimate responsibility for peace and economic development upon the basic units, especially the two superpowers. The nation-states, however, are surrendering ever greater bits and pieces of their nominal sovereignty to supranational political, economic, and technical agencies which facilitate the achievement of common objectives.

Will functional and even political cooperation lead to federation or some other form of supranational government? The growing needs to regulate population, to develop the poor nations, and to maintain peace seem to militate for such a government. However, cultural lag behind technological change is a reality. There is no assurance that the superstructure, in Marx's terminology, will adjust to the base . . . no guarantee that needs will be satisfied . . . no certainty that opportunities will be maximized. (Even if some supranational structure were established, of course, there is no assurance it would cope with international problems more effectively than unilateral or multilateral efforts of individual states.)

Arnold Toynbee has warned that few people are as yet aware that "in the Atomic Age the human race is in danger of liquidating itself, and therefore the survival of one's own sectional tribe or sectional ideology can only be ensured by ensuring that the human race survives. In this new situation, there is no genuine conflict between sectional loyalty and ecumenical loyalty. Sectional tribes and ideologies can survive now only on condition that mankind is preserved, and therefore we have to give an overriding loyalty to mankind as a whole in order to preserve our precious tribes and ideologies."[38]

The readings in this book — representative and authoritative statements about crucial issues of war and peace from the three worlds of political identification — show how far people are from recognizing an "overriding loyalty to mankind as a whole." As Toynbee states: "There is going to be a race between mass self-reeducation and mass self-destruction. We have to hope that, in this crucial race, the growth and spread of a sense of world citizenship will win, and we have to promote this realization by our personal action."[39]

Thus, we return to the second basic task posed at the outset: the need to develop a political philosophy of an improved international order. The readings of this book illustrate the nature of the present diplomatic constellation with its opportunities and dangers. They reveal the areas of major tension between the industrial North and impoverished South, the collectivist East and more individualist West, and — a deeper problem — between man and his technology.

A clue to effective national and international policy may be found in the rift existing in most political cultures between proponents of change and preservers of the status quo. Since change is inevitable, absolute conservatism cannot succeed. A choice remains between radical, perhaps violent, revolution and directed evolution which builds from existing foundations. This third or intermediate path is recommended by the standard for political wisdom: that politics is the art of the possible. An evolutionist path will steer between the Scylla of futile conservatism and the Charybdis of destructive revolution. It will avoid the shortsighted narrowness of pure *Realpolitik* and the utopias of unbounded *Moralpolitik*. The counsel of moderation will profit from realism and idealism in constructing a policy which balances the feasible with the desirable.

This counsel will, therefore, view with suspicion policy recom-

---

[38] "Conditions of Survival," *Saturday Review*, August 29, 1964, p. 193.
[39] *Ibid.*

mendations which try to freeze the world as it is or which count on radically changing it in the near or intermediate future. To entertain grandiose hopes as the only solution from present problems is to risk practical impotence. The evolutionist path would not count on the global achievement of an overriding loyalty to mankind as a whole, or world federation subsuming nation-states. It would not count on solving all territorial disputes by peaceful means. It would not count on quick and tranquil modernization of the third world or the early elimination of East-West and North-South disputes. It would not assume that all arms must, and therefore can, be abolished.

The evolutionist path would, however, make long-range plans at the same time that it dealt with gradual and partial improvements of the existing situation. It would endeavor to lay the groundwork for future political and economic developments which minimized the bases for aggression and which maximized the prospects of social justice and order. But this path would begin by working from the existing distribution of power and political allegiance. It would seek safeguards to keep military power sheathed while promoting the extension of economic power to help the developing nations. It might look at the views expressed in this book as suggestive of present limitations and future opportunities. It would therefore seek to cultivate consensus and law, while mitigating the consequences of their present lack. It would work to erode the sectionalism of present-day political allegiances (manifest in these readings) in order to undermine collective egoism and spread a respect for the dignity of all men.

PART TWO

Perspectives on

National Strategies

Introduction to Part Two

Political and Economic Strategies: Competition and Cooperation

The term "strategy" derives from the Greek *stratos* for "army." It denotes not only military planning, but also the large scale, long-range formulation of policy by which states endeavor to promote their power and influence. This first group of readings on national strategies sets the stage for the chapters to follow. It provides the broad picture of the way leading states view themselves, their allies, and their adversaries. In particular, these readings indicate the image certain states have of themselves in relation to each of the three "worlds." For the Communist and Western states these problems come under these headings: (1) uniting an alliance; (2) adversary relations; and (3) relations with the third world. For the *tiers monde* the issues are not quite parallel, but may still be regarded under the rubric of relations with other uncommitted (or developing) nations and with the Communist and Western worlds.

I   UNITING AN ALLIANCE

These readings, as noted earlier, point to a structuring of international society into three main camps with polycentrism within each bloc —

the cleavages within each group assuming an importance almost in proportion to its pretension to ideological and formal unity. While material power remains polarized in Washington and Moscow, international politics is increasingly multipolar as political autonomy of the superpowers becomes a goal and reality for the lesser powers.

The partial dissolution of the Western and Communist alliances is reflected here in the rancorous debates between Washington and Paris and between Moscow and Peking. These rifts suggest severe limits on the ability of the United States and Soviet Union — despite their preponderance of power — to dictate to their partners. They also point to the enduring force of national pride in spite of pressures for union in wider confederations. The rifts reveal the fragile foundations of multinational alliances. Ideology had helped to unite the Communist world — and a common culture, the West. But when Peking and Paris no longer perceived compelling military or economic reasons to accept the hegemony of Moscow and Washington, the ties of Communist internationalism or the Western heritage became impotent in the face of a quest for national independence. The demise of a compelling material motive to sustain the alliance was signaled to de Gaulle in 1958 by Washington's refusal to allow Paris to share with London the political control of U.S. nuclear weapons. Similarly the Chinese campaign against Soviet "pacifism" was triggered in 1959 by Moscow's abrogation of its 1957 defense technology pact with Peking and capped by the halting in 1960 of Soviet technical and economic aid to China. These rebuffs were taken the more seriously because of French and Chinese sentiments of cultural superiority over their respective superpower allies, and because of personal pique suffered decades earlier by de Gaulle and Mao Tse-tung in dealing with these allies. Such resentments fanned the flames of nationalism as France and China decided to proceed independently, without regard to the wishes of Washington and Moscow.

The major features which distinguish the intra-Communist rift from the divisions within the West result from the greater role played by ideology in the Communist world. A potential source of strength, ideology also contains seeds of profound dissension. It is natural that allies will differ over tactics and strategy, especially when their interests are so diverse as Moscow's and Peking's. These differences assume a quasi-religious character when couched in the language of ideological disputation. The adversary is painted not only as politically wrong but as morally corrupt when he tries to serve his self-interest rather than *the* truth and *the* cause. Ideological disagreements may be expected to reflect and mask divergent political and economic needs. Ideology is also the cheapest weapon by which the weaker power materially may challenge the stronger. It provides a ready instrument by which Peking may denounce Moscow as the fallen leader of world revolution.[1]

Divergent prescriptions for alliance policy issue from Washington, Paris, Moscow, and Peking. The United States and Soviet Union continue to portray the world in bipolar terms, while Paris explicitly proclaims the obsolescence of this view, and Peking sees a new front emerging which pits the underdeveloped nations against Western (and, by implication, Soviet) imperialism.

Each superpower endeavors to maintain its alliance intact while Paris and Peking, once committed to an independent path, care little for the former unity. A series of countercharges follows in which Washington and Moscow accuse Paris and Peking of chauvinism and fractionalism within the respective alliances. The superpowers, in turn, are accused by France and China of trying to dictate to their alliance partners. As a new twist, the Soviet Union and United States are accused, explicitly by Peking and at least implicitly by Paris, of consorting to dominate the world.

The interest of one superpower in preserving its alliance is shown in Senator Fulbright's vision of an Atlantic partnership of North America and Western Europe.[2] Fulbright argues that Europe's chances of an independent course have been effectively ended by the consequences of two world wars. National nuclear arsenals for European states are infeasible and superfluous. The rational policy, therefore, is to make the most of the bipolar situation. It would be unrealistic to try jumping to a federal union of the Atlantic states, for the nation-state remains a fact of life. It is possible, however, to improve existing machinery to coordinate military strategy[3] and policy toward the underdeveloped

[1] See Walter C. Clemens, Jr., "Ideology in Soviet Disarmament Policy," *Journal of Conflict Resolution*, VIII, No. 1 (March 1964) 7–22.

[2] See item No. 1.

[3] Fulbright's neat assumption is that *possession* of nuclear weapons will not be an overriding issue if consensus can be reached on the conditions when they will be used.

countries. Functional cooperation will cultivate the ground for evolution toward tighter unity.[4]

French spokesmen, in contrast, stress that bipolarity no longer exists and that states must adjust to new opportunities. European interests cannot be upheld by the United States. The Gaullist vision of unity focuses on a Europe of the Inner Six led by Paris and Bonn . . . a "union of fatherlands" joining France, Germany, Italy, Belgium, Luxembourg, and The Netherlands would be the immediate goal. This confederation might develop the political-economic-moral basis for subsequent federation. A national nuclear striking force is seen as feasible (at least for France) and as the only way to achieve freedom from U.S. dictation.[5]

The informal nature of third world unity was outlined above. It may be appropriate to mention here some of the factors which impede greater unity among the nonaligned nations. First, they are chary of formal alliances and prefer to retain a free hand to take advantage of possible gain from the Communist and/or Western worlds. Second, many nations of the third world are troubled by unstable governments which may not be in a position to make long-term commitments. Third, huge geographical distances separate groups of them, e.g., the African from the Asian states. Fourth, and more important, these states are characterized by a tremendous diversity of cultural, political, economic, and technological needs and attainments, a diversity greater even than that of the Communist world. Fifth, power politics within the third world tends to alienate one group of nations from another. Thus, Egypt

---

[4] For other Western comments on the Atlantic alliance see Lionel Gelber, *loc. cit.*; Robert Strausz-Hupé, James E. Dougherty, and William R. Kintner, "The Atlantic Vision: A Question of Choice," *The Atlantic Community Quarterly*, I, No. 3 (Fall 1963) 324–337. For a Western critique of the idea of partnership see Peter Coulmas, "Partnership and Interdependence," *Survival*, V, No. 4 (July–August 1963) 166–172. For a Soviet critique see A. Sovetov, " 'Peace Strategy' and the 'Atlantic Community,' " *International Affairs* (Moscow), No. 9 (September 1963) 24–31. For two Chinese views — the first theoretical, the second rather topical — see Fan Cheng-Hsiang, "The Development of Imperialist Contradictions," *Peking Review*, VI, No. 13 (March 29, 1963), and No. 14 (April 5, 1963) ; Yuan Hsien-Lu, "Division and Realignment," *Peking Review*, VII, No. 13 (March 27, 1964) 13–14.
[5] For elucidation see item No. 2 and also the reading on military strategy, No. 19; A. Grosser, "General de Gaulle and the Foreign Policy of the Fifth Republic," *International Affairs* (London), XXXIX, No. 2 (April 1963) 198–213; and Stanley H. Hoffmann, "De Gaulle, Europe and the Atlantic Alliance," *International Organization*, XVIII, No. 1 (Winter 1964) 1–28.

and Ghana are respectively accused of trying to dominate the Arab League and the Organization of African Unity. An alliance with Indonesia or India could rapidly become unfavorably "entangling" for a nonaligned power, due to the former's conflicts with Malaysia and the latter's difficulties with Pakistan and China.

Even the informal unity of the third world may be jeopardized by the emergence of haves and have-nots among the presently nonaligned nations.[6] As the economic and technological attainments of these states diverge more sharply, so will their political interests. Those which stagnate economically may become more bellicose. Those which advance may come to ally with other supporters of the status quo or they, too, may grow more aggressive, expressing their newly achieved strength.

Finally, the changing nature of the struggle between the Communist and Western worlds will have a profound effect upon the nonaligned states. The emergence of Communist China in particular will present nonaligned Asia with problems quite different from those of the Cold War between Stalinist Russia and the West.

II ADVERSARY RELATIONS

A decision as to which relationship of major tension in the world is most important will reflect one's own preoccupations and commitments. Moscow, because of its historic role in leading the "socialist camp," posits that the revolutionary front is between that camp and Western capitalism.[7] Peking and most emerging nations of the third world regard the key battle line as that between the revolutionary countries of Asia and Africa and their European and American oppressors.[8] The West — represented here in statements from France and from liberal and conservative elements in the United States — sees as the most pressing problem its relations with the Communist world, but acknowledges the long-range importance of the *tiers monde*.[9] While

[6] See Lucian W. Pye, "The Underdeveloped Areas as a Source of International Tension through 1975," *International Stability*, Dale J. Hekhuis, Charles G. McClintock, and Arthur L. Burns (eds.) (New York: John Wiley & Sons, 1964) pp. 53–55.

[7] See item No. 7.

[8] See item No. 12.

[9] For a Western view that the most important relationship of major tension is, or is becoming that between the developed countries — including both the United States and the Soviet Union — and the underdeveloped countries see Werner Plum, "Tensions dans le tiers monde," *Confluent*, No. 38 (February 1964) 124–148.

the nonaligned nations are most concerned with their own independence and development, they too are anxious that tensions between Communism and the West do not erupt in a global holocaust.

Regardless of which tensions are judged to be most important, each state must ask itself how relations with the adversary are to be conducted. Is international politics seen as a zero-sum game — what one side wins the other loses? Or may it be a non-zero-sum game in which both sides may gain from reasonable compromise and cooperation? Peking and the American advocates of a "forward strategy"[10] tend to hold to the first alternative: *either* "we" *or* "they" will win. The other Western statements, including the French, and the Soviet expositions of a peaceful coexistence strategy argue that collaboration among adversaries is both possible and desirable.[11]

Another way to pose the question is to ask how much diversity is tolerable and for how long. The third world is the most ardent supporter of diversity in the Communist and Western worlds, for this creates the optimum conditions for promoting nonaligned interests. The French and liberal U.S. statements (by Fulbright and Kennedy) seem willing to accept diversity indefinitely, perhaps with the assumption that time will modulate present differences. Moscow is also ready to live with diversity, but on the assumption that peaceful competition will eventually communize the globe. Peking and the Strausz-Hupé school in the West hold that diversity is unsafe and that concerted efforts must be made to shape the world into their respectively preferred image — collectivist or "free."

These broad attitudes are refined in practice into methods which seem to have more to do with political expediency than with theoretical purity. Thus, Peking is willing to deal with European capitalism while reserving for the United States the role of arch enemy. Liberal Washington will exploit opportunities for negotiation and *détente* with European and Russian Communism, but not with China or Cuba. Paris admits new realities in Asia but is slower to affirm the possibility of a political settlement with the more proximate Communist power in Moscow. The Gaullist regime is suspicious of a U.S.-Soviet entente impeding the resurgence of Europe and, more specifically, of France. Similarly, while the third world wants peace between the superpowers, some nonaligned nations may fear an end to the Cold War because

[10] See items No. 4 and 10.
[11] See items No. 1, 2, 3 and 9.

of the consequent decrease in opportunities for leverage on Moscow and Washington.

III RELATIONS WITH THE THIRD WORLD

From France and England the fires of nationalism and the quest for the benefits of industrialization have spread to all corners of the globe. These ideals have been spurred by the Bolshevik model of elite manipulation of a permanent revolution to accomplish in a brief span what took decades or centuries in Europe and America. The result has been a major source of international tension: the relationship between the haves and the have-nots, the industrialized North and the under-developed South.

The importance of this relationship is acknowledged from various points along the political spectrum. Peking sees it as the main focus of a revolutionary struggle against imperialist reaction. A similar though not so extreme view prevailed in Moscow from about 1955 to 1961, when the Kremlin leadership seemed confident the emerging nations would move quickly to embrace a kind of national socialism which would soon be supplanted by a Soviet style regime. In this way the road from Moscow to London might move via Cairo and New Delhi. However, third world nations such as Egypt accepted Soviet aid but persisted in an independent path, even persecuting the local Communist Party. The refusal of most new nations to endorse the Soviet *troika* principle in U.N. operations[12] and the thwarting of Moscow's plans in the Congo produced a sharp decline in the Soviet optimistic view that the third world will shortly join the Communist.[13] Moscow maintains, *contra* Peking, that the socialist (Soviet) camp is the main force in the struggle against capitalism, but the Kremlin continues to attach great importance to the nature and direction of political and economic change in the nonaligned nations. This is evident in Khrushchev's greetings in the second Conference of the Heads of Arab States in Alexandria in 1964:

If now there are reasons to acknowledge certain successes in the national liberation movement and a certain relaxation of international tension, the credit goes to the community of all anti-imperialist and anti-colonialist forces. It is pleasant to realize that the Arab peoples who were the first to

[12] See readings No. 46 and 47.
[13] For the 1961 Soviet projections of "the world in 20 years" see pp. 16–17.

raise the banners of independence in Africa and in the Middle East constitute one of the vanguard detachments of this great community.

By proclaiming the policy of nonalignment, the Arab States offer a firm rebuff to the schemes of the imperialists and their agents in the Arab East. They are waging a courageous struggle for peace and improvement of the international situation, for the liquidation of foreign military bases, for elimination of dangerous seats of tension, the western aggressive circles are creating on Cyprus, in the Congo, in South Arabia and other parts of the world. . . . On this path the Arab countries and peoples can, as they could in the past, rely on the support of the Soviet Union, their loyal friend.[14]

The United States and most other Western countries have been preoccupied with containing Soviet and Chinese Communism and have tended to evaluate the third world only as it became a chess piece in this larger conflict. At the same time, most Western leaders grant that, in the long run, the economic development and political allegiance of the developing and nonaligned nations will constitute crucial factors in the distribution of international power. Already the sentiments of these countries carry great weight in the voting arrangements of the United Nations and other international organizations. Gaullist France perhaps more than any other Western nation has sought to enhance her cultural and economic influence in Asia, Africa, and even Latin America, as a way of restoring a lost grandeur.

If the West is generally preoccupied with Communism, most nonaligned states are preoccupied with their own political and economic goals. For them the Communist-Western conflict is basically irrevelant, although an occasion both of dangers and opportunities, and the main task is to proceed with national independence and development.

The readings presented reveal two major areas of debate concerning the *tiers monde:* first, the nature of the desirable and second, the limits to the possible with respect to national independence, internal development, and external alignments.

Formal independence is or soon will be a reality for most parts of the world. It is opposed only from within nations by traditionalists who fear its modernizing effects and dissidents who prefer a different map for their political organization, and from without by governments which seek to perpetuate colonial relationships. Westerners who accept national independence as inevitable do not necessarily imply that it is always a boon, particularly where economic and political conditions are not ripe. And Communists by no means endorse national independence as the

[14] *TASS*, September 5, 1964.

ultimate stage of social development. Only where independence has long been denied to a self-conscious people or elite does it appear an unqualified blessing.

As noted earlier, leading Western analysts as well as Communist theoreticians posit that economic and political growth proceeds in stages and that parallels may be expected as traditional societies grope toward modernity and industrialization.[15] At the same time there is wide disagreement, even within the three worlds, as to the determinants, speed, and direction of this process, and the role to be played by external assistance.

The CENIS study edited by Millikan and Blackmer, which grew out of a report made for the U.S. Senate Committee on Foreign Relations, stresses that modernization is a multifaceted process with psychological, economic, and political dimensions.[16] The study assumes that modernization is inevitable and that it is desirable to conduct and channel it so as to minimize chaos and maximize economic growth and political responsibility and stability. To attempt to preserve the status quo would be futile. To change it by enforced radical surgery, however, is unnecessary, undesirable, and perhaps infeasible. Hence the need for a third, evolutionist choice — one which Western policy can do much to facilitate and encourage. Millikan and Blackmer argue that it is in the interest of the United States and, indeed, all nations to promote such development of the emerging nations. The role of foreign aid should be to assist those nations ready to assist themselves to move to a stage of self-sustaining economic growth. A moderate increase in Western aid could be instrumental in helping many countries ready for economic take-off to raise their rate of growth of income to 2 per cent per year per capita.[17]

[15] See p. 26.

[16] CENIS-Center for International Studies, Massachusetts Institute of Technology. The report to the Senate was entitled "Economic, Social, and Political Change in the Underdeveloped Countries and Its Implications for United States Policy," submitted in January 1960. It was extensively revised and published as *The Emerging Nations: Their Growth and United States Policy*, edited by Max F. Millikan and Donald L. M. Blackmer (Boston: Little, Brown, 1961). Reading No. 5 is from Chapter 7, "The Third Choice."

[17] The CENIS study estimated that the underdeveloped countries could *absorb* about $5.7 billion per year during the period 1961–1966, of which $1.4 billion might take the form of private investment, leaving $4.3 billion to be met by governmental aid. "Aid" consists of grants and long-term loans, but not short- and medium-term loans. Of the total aid of $4.3 billion, the International Bank and

The critique by Professor Banfield[18] is addressed specifically to CENIS and other studies which posit the desirability and possibility of a relatively rapid modernization of the developing nations and which assign a key role to external aid. The CENIS report and Banfield agree that the absorptive capacity and the population growth of each country impose severe limitations upon possible growth per capita. But Banfield is perhaps more pessimistic than Millikan and Blackmer concerning the social, economic, and political effects of such growth if it occurs. He is more optimistic regarding the prospects of U.S. security if such growth does not occur or if it becomes Communist-directed. His fundamental disagreement is with the proposition that external aid can be instrumental in bringing to take-off point countries which could not do so alone or even better if left to their own devices. Even so he grants "there is . . . an important group of middle countries — India is a conspicuous example — which can absorb large amounts of aid and which offer some promise of developing. In time, too, some of the most backward countries may be brought by aid to the condition of this middle group."

The governments of most underdeveloped nations will welcome arguments that their rapid economic growth is possible and, from the viewpoint of the industrialized states, desirable to assist. They will tend to ignore the possible disruptive effects that this growth may have on their social structure and possibly on the maintenance of their regime. They will tend also to deemphasize any prospect that foreign aid may result in economic or political dependence. They usually reject, however, aid with political strings attached.

Peking has warned that such strings are part of Soviet as well as

the International Development Association were deemed likely to provide $500 million net per annum. Aid to be provided by governments was therefore calculated at about $3.8 billion. Using a graduated scale based on national income, the suggested United States contribution was 65 per cent of the total aid burden, i.e., $2.5 billion per year. If technical assistance and emergency funds were added, the total would amount to just under $3 billion. This figure would exclude defense and certain special assistance for other than developmental purposes. The U.S. aid program in 1961 comparably defined amounted to about $2 billion. To raise it to $3 billion annually from 1961 through 1966 was expected to bring the total sum to about 0.6 per cent of the U.S. gross national product. (*Ibid.*, pp. 121–122 and appendices on pp. 149–159; for a more detailed exposition see P. N. Rosenstein-Rodan, "International Aid for Underdeveloped Countries," *The Review of Economics and Statistics*, XLIII, No. 2 [May 1961] 107–138.)
[18] See reading No. 6.

Western aid. China calls on the emerging nations to follow her example of a bootstrap operation which, with proper leadership, can allegedly produce rapid industrialization without foreign assistance. Like the champions of free enterprise, Peking sees a certain purifying value in self-reliance — of the nation, if not of the individual.

The Soviet Union agrees with Peking that rapid development is possible, but stresses the disinterested and useful quality of assistance extended by Moscow to developing nations. The aid benefits that would result from decreases in military spending by the great powers are emphasized. Despite some disenchantment with the *tiers monde* since 1961, Moscow continues to affirm that national socialism will eventually be transformed into a more advanced form. Hence, the national *bourgeoisie* is pictured as a transitional ally in Soviet writings, whereas it is distrusted by Peking and revolutionaries such as Che Guevara.[19] In contrast, the CENIS study stresses the importance of strengthening the urban middle class — not as a temporary expedient — but as a long-range hope for stability and democracy.[20]

The external political allegiances of the developing nations are, of course, major concerns of the Western and Communist worlds. A minimum aim is to keep the nonaligned countries nonaligned; a maximum aim is to bring them formally or informally into one's own alliance. The superpowers themselves, Moscow since about 1955 and Washington since about 1959, have increasingly contented themselves with the minimum goal of maintaining the neutrality of the third world. Both

[19] See items No. 11 and 12.

[20] The CENIS report argues that for practical reasons economic take-off in most countries requires governmental programming and administration of a number of important processes and relationships, but that as development proceeds the potential role of private enterprise increases. (Millikan and Blackmer, *op. cit.*, pp. 56–66.) Banfield, however, stresses that an expansion of government activity may retard economic efficiency and democracy. And the influential "Clay Report" to President Kennedy was adamant that "the U.S. should not aid a foreign government in projects establishing government-owned industrial and commercial enterprises which compete with existing private endeavors. While we realize that in aiding foreign countries we cannot insist upon the establishment of our own economic system, despite its remarkable success and progress, we should not extend aid which is inconsistent with our beliefs, democratic tradition, and knowledge of economic organization and consequences." (*The Scope and Distribution of United States Military Economic Assistance Programs*, Report to the President of the United States from The Committee to Strengthen the Security of the Free World [Washington, D.C.: Department of State, March 20, 1963] pp. 5–6.) The Committee Chairman was General Lucius D. Clay, author of item No. 24.

the major donors of foreign aid have come to appreciate the difficulty of "buying" or indirectly winning the favor of the recipient state. For China and France — countries attempting to break away from super-power domination — it appears desirable to win the moral and voting support of nations which might otherwise lean to the Soviet Union or United States. The nonaligned countries, despite the example of India's treatment by China, seem to prefer an independent course. They may even reason that "neutralist" India has received both Soviet and U.S. support against Chinese aggression.

Military Strategy: The Threat and Uses of Force

The effective weight of the various relationships of major tension is obvious in the military planning of the great powers. Their strategies are geared to the conflict between Communism and the West. Little attention is paid to military operations between the developing nations and the industrialized powers except insofar as Communist subversion confronts the Western desire to uphold existing regimes in the non-aligned or developing countries.

The tension between man and technology also vibrates in the included discussions of military strategy. At one level is the question whether the use of modern military technology can be controlled to serve policy objectives. At another level is the dispute over the relative importance of traditional human factors versus contemporary wonder weapons.

The Clausewitz dictum that war is the continuation of policy by other (violent) means has received wide affirmation in the Communist and Western worlds. The two superpowers and most of their allies since about 1955 appear to be sharply aware that a stalemate has developed in which nuclear war — no matter which side initiates it — would inflict unacceptable damage on both sides. This situation, as subsequent readings indicate, has important consequences for arms control and tension control. While the superpowers continue through research and development to look for possible technological breakthroughs, both have come to acknowledge the existence of a balance of terror.

The consequences of this recognition are manifold. The nuclear deadlock means that there are new opportunities for maneuvering in all areas short of strategic or "central" war. The United States has endeavored to meet this challenge by developing "tactical" nuclear weapons and a credible "counterforce" strategic capability which would permit a "flexible response" to Communist aggression.[21] It has sought to strengthen its conventional forces and "special" forces to deal with limited and guerrilla warfare.[22]

Communist strategy, as shown in the selections from Mao Tse-tung and his Cuban adaptor Che Guevara, recognizes the advantages accruing to protracted, guerrilla operations against a foe which is on the defensive along a wide periphery.[23]

General Gallois, although he recognizes that either counterforce or countercity strategies may be suicidal, argues that France must attain at least a symbolic nuclear force because the *pax atomica* ensures political safety only to nuclear powers. He is, presumably, not oblivious of the bargaining advantages a modest nuclear force would give Paris in dealing with lesser powers.[24]

The difficulty with all these approaches, as Moscow has long stressed, is that they all risk escalation into all-out war. Tactical nuclear weapons, counterforce, and even limited war in the third world may quickly lead one side or the other to increase the level of violence employed. The case studies below of strategies in conflict over Berlin and Cuba indicate the willingness of Moscow and Washington to go to the brink in a massive game of "chicken." But both sides have drawn back from that brink, and especially after the Cuban confrontation of 1962, have been sobered by the risks they had taken to advance or defend their positions.

---

[21] See item No. 17. For an exposition and critique of U.S. strategic doctrine see Robert E. Osgood, "Kinds of Counterforce," *New Republic*, September 10, 1962; also in *Survival*, V, No. 1 (January–February 1963) 23–27, 28. For two Soviet comments see V. Larionov, "The Doctrine of 'Flexible' Aggression," *International Affairs* (Moscow), No. 7 (July 1963) 46–52; A. Nevsky, "Modern Armaments and Problems of Strategy," *World Marxist Review*, VI, No. 3 (March 1963) 30–36. For a Chinese critique see Hung Fan-Ti, "Strategy of 'Flexible Response' and Its Contradictions," *Peking Review*, VII, No. 15 (April 10, 1964) 6–10.

[22] See item No. 18. For a conceptual review of guerrilla warfare see Andrew C. Janos, "Unconventional Warfare: Framework and Analysis," *World Politics*, XV, No. 4 (July 1963) 636–647. For an article on the role of ideology in guerrilla warfare see Eugene H. Methvin, "Ideology and Organization in Counterinsurgency," *Orbis*, VIII, No. 1 (Spring 1964) 106–124.

[23] See items No. 22 and 23.

[24] See reading No. 19. For further elucidation see Pierre Messmer, "The French Military Establishment of Tomorrow," *Orbis*, VI, No. 2 (Summer 1962) 205–216; Pierre Messmer, "Our Military Policy," *The Atlantic Community Quarterly*, I, No. 2 (Summer 1963) 185–187; François de Rose, "Atlantic Relationships and Nuclear Problems," *Foreign Affairs*, XIL, No. 3 (April 1963) 479–490.

Soviet military posture has long relied on the political effect of proto-type weapons which gave rise to an alleged bomber gap followed by a much publicized missile gap. The comparative figures on Soviet-Western military capabilities — nuclear and conventional — given by Defense Secretary McNamara (in No. 17) show the extent to which Moscow has in fact had only a posture of minimum deterrence. Moscow's development of multi-megaton warheads in the 1961 test series has facilitated the Soviet policy of nondiscrimination between countercity and counterforce strategies. Even if Moscow had succeeded in emplacing medium-range missiles in Cuba in 1962, the effect may have been more in the minds of men than on the objective balance of power.[25] That Moscow will resign itself to permanent posture of strategic inferiority vis-à-vis the West cannot, however, be predicted.[26]

A problem which confronts all participants in the arms race is its high cost.[27] To develop diversified forces to deal with any contingency exerts an almost impossible economic burden for any country except the United States. Moscow and Peking have an advantage, however, in being relatively free to select and pursue the weapons systems which fit their campaign plans, while the United States feels it must be ready to defend the Western and even the nonaligned worlds wherever they are attacked and at whatever level of force is required. The priority of various alternatives available to Britain were weighed in 1964 by Labour Party leaders who argued that London had to opt either for a strategic nuclear force, a conventional force to defend Europe, or a mobile system able to maintain order in the Commonwealth and contribute to U.N. police actions.

The extent that military technology has made traditional factors such as manpower, morale, and leadership obsolete has been hotly debated within most nations. The result has been to divide military strategists along "radical" and "conservative" lines like those which distinguish political and economic theoreticians. From 1953 to 1955 Soviet doctrine

[25] The Cuban-based missiles would have been highly vulnerable to a U.S. pre-emptive strike and hardly adequate as the basis for a first Soviet strike against North America, but would have constituted powerful reinforcement for a strategic attack launched from Soviet territory.

[26] For indications in the Soviet press that Moscow may doubt its present ability to surpass U.S. military strength see Thomas W. Wolfe, "Shifts in Soviet Strategic Thought," *Foreign Affairs*, VIIL, No. 3 (April 1964) 484–485.

[27] See Leonard Beaton and John Maddox, *The Spread of Nuclear Weapons* (New York: Praeger, 1962).

came around to discarding Stalin's theory of "permanently operating factors" and upgrading the role of surprise attack and nuclear weapons.[28] The debate continues, however, as can be seen from the two Soviet statements included — one by the head of the Rocket Forces who emphasizes their decisive role in the opening moments of war, and the second statement by the commander of the Soviet Ground Forces who argues that ground forces remain decisive in pursuing a war to a successful completion.[29] Peking has also recognized the importance of nuclear weapons and counted heavily from 1957 until 1959 on the Soviet Union to enable China to become a nuclear power. Although China has her foot in the nuclear door, Peking still ridicules "nuclear fetishism" and reiterates the role which morale, leadership, and sheer manpower can play even in modern war.[30] Since neither Peking nor Paris could hope to rival the strategic delivery systems of the superpowers for decades to come, both seem to attach great symbolic value to the limited nuclear arsenals which are within their present capabilities. Moscow and Washington, anxious to retard proliferation, urge their lesser allies to forgo these futile efforts at defensive "autarky" and rely instead on the protection of the superpower umbrella. Most nonaligned or developing countries would agree with Paris and Peking that even token nuclear forces may have great political influence, but few have the resources to consider their acquisition.[31] Therefore, most members of the third world welcome any limitation on the capabilities of the present nuclear club and any restraint on an expanded membership.[32]

[28] See Raymond L. Garthoff, *Soviet Strategy in the Nuclear Age* (rev. ed.; New York: Praeger, 1962) pp. 61 ff.

[29] See items 20 and 21. For further analysis and references to *Military Strategy*, V. I. Sokolovskii (ed.) (Moscow, 1962 and 1963), see Walter C. Clemens, Jr., "The Soviet Militia in the Missile Age," *Orbis*, VIII, No. 1 (Spring 1964) 84–105.

[30] See Alice L. Hsieh, *Communist China's Strategy in the Nuclear Age* (Englewood Cliffs, N.J.: Prentice-Hall, 1962).

[31] China's successful testing of an atomic bomb in 1964 raised the painful question for the Congress Party whether India's security did not require an indigenous nuclear force or a redefinition of the nonalignment policy, problems more delicate politically than difficult economically.

[32] No statements of third world military strategy are included here because most have only local significance. However, some views of nonaligned countries on arms control — great power and small power — are given in Part IV.

Political and Economic Strategies:
Competition and Cooperation

WESTERN STRATEGY

Uniting an Alliance

| J. WILLIAM FULBRIGHT
| A Concert of Free Nations

"The nations seem to be advancing to unity," wrote Alexis de Tocqueville in 1835. "Our means of intellectual intercourse unite the most remote parts of the earth; and it is impossible for men to remain strangers to each other, or to be ignorant of the events which are taking place in any corner of the globe."[1]

Perceiving the possibility of world community, Tocqueville took it for probability, failing to take account of the human capacity for contact without communication, for knowledge without understanding.

J. William Fulbright, U.S. Senator from Arkansas and Chairman of the Senate Committee on Foreign Relations, delivered this lecture at The Fletcher School of Law and Diplomacy, Tufts University, in April 1963. These excerpts, from his speech which was the first of a series of three lectures in The William L. Clayton Series, are reprinted by permission.

[1] Alexis de Tocqueville, *Democracy in America*, translated by Henry Reever (London: Oxford University Press, 1947) p. 285.

Far from leading to a community of mankind, the economic and technological unification of the world has in fact aggravated, and made far more dangerous, the animosities of national communities that continue to value their separate sovereignty over their common humanity and even their security. Only in the lands bordering the North Atlantic has a tendency toward community recently taken hold and even here the trend has been fragmentary, hesitant, and of uncertain duration.

For at least a century and a half Western history has been shaped by two great contradictory forces, one a tendency toward cooperation and community, the other a baleful nationalism that set the nations against each other and culminated in the great conflicts of the twentieth century. In our own time there is reason to hope that the great paradox is at last moving toward resolution in favor of a broad community of the North Atlantic peoples. Great obstacles remain to be overcome, however, and, as we have had occasion to note in recent history, no trend is irreversible. As of 1963 the unity of the West is neither certain nor even probable; it is no more than a reasonably well-founded hope.

In the past half century the "European age" has come to a close. The passing of European pre-eminence in the world and the emergence of a global system controlled by two non-European powers of continental size mean something more than an alteration of power relationships. As one contemporary writer has put it: "What is meant is that a particular form of political organization, based upon the nation-state, is no longer the determining pattern in world affairs. For European history since at least the close of the Middle Ages has been the history of conflicting and competing nation-states, as Mediterranean history was the record of rival city-states. To say that the European age has closed is to imply that the nation-state is no longer the dominant political form."[2]

The end of the "European era" was brought on by the expansion of the nation-state system beyond Europe itself, westward to include America and eastward to include Russia. As "peripheral" powers, America and Russia were beyond the control of the balance of power system which prevented any European nation from becoming significantly larger or more powerful than any other. The non-European nations were permitted to grow to continental dimensions and to develop power commensurate with their size while Europe remained

[2] George Lichtheim, *The New Europe* (New York: Frederick A. Praeger, 1963) p. 8.

divided against itself, seeking a tenuous stability at the cost of fragmentation. In the two world wars of the twentieth century Europe proved unable to resolve its internal conflicts by its own efforts and the outcome of both conflicts was determined by the intervention of the non-European powers. America and Russia became the arbiters of a global political system of which Europe could never again be the single source and center.

The classical "European era" is over and what is to replace it is the central question confronting the Western world. On this question depends our own internal evolution, our future relations with the Communist world, and the character of our future bonds with Asia, Africa, and Latin America. One alternative, that of General de Gaulle, is to revive the old system on a global scale, to bring a confederated Europe under French hegemony into a world system that would be governed by the same rules as those which governed Europe in its era of pre-eminence. The other possibility, that of Atlantic partnership, is to alter the game as well as its players, to move beyond the system of sovereign entities in precarious equilibrium toward a partnership encompassing all the Western people who share the experience of industrialism and political democracy.

The conflict between the Gaullist and Atlantic approaches is not a matter of mere misunderstanding, failure of communication, or personal predilection. The fundamental issue is one between two different conceptions of the future organization of the West and the world. The Gaullist design, it seems to me, is bold and even creative in tactics but profoundly conservative in its objectives. It seeks to reshape Europe as an essentially *national* entity which would be large enough and strong enough to participate as a great power in a worldwide system of nation-states related to each other in the traditional patterns of rivalry and balance. The Gaullist program is designed to restore and conserve the classical balance-of-power system among sovereign nations, with its inherent instability, by adjusting it to the specifications of the age of super-states and nuclear weapons.

The Atlantic conception, on the other hand, is built on the premise that an international system based on unlimited national sovereignty has become an intolerably dangerous anachronism in the nuclear age, not only for small nations but for great nations as well — indeed especially for great nations. Like the League of Nations Covenant and the United Nations Charter, the idea of Atlantic partnership is an attempt to come to grips with the basic facts of world politics in the twentieth century: that modern warfare has become so destructive that it has ceased to be a rational instrument of national policy; that the international system that worked tolerably well to prevent or limit war before 1914 has broken down irreparably in the last half-century; and that if we are to survive under these new conditions the nation-state can no longer serve as the ultimate unit of law and human association.

The collapse of the League of Nations and the failure of the United Nations thus far to achieve the hopes that attended its creation were not the result of their repudiation of an old order which had failed but rather the result of an effort to out-run history, to move in a single leap from world anarchy to world community. Unfortunately there is no necessary correlation between human need and human capacity. However fully it may comport with our needs, the shaping of a genuine world community is demonstrably beyond our capacity in the world as it is and as it is likely to be for the foreseeable future. We must therefore focus our efforts on the more modest goal of building new bonds among those peoples of the free world who have some feeling of shared values and interests, some feeling of the ability to communicate effectively, some feeling of trust and confidence in each other's purposes.

These are the preconditions of community. They exist, I believe, in substantial measure among the industrial democracies of the North Atlantic area. Because they do, Atlantic partnership is a feasible goal, barely feasible perhaps, but nonetheless one which can be pursued with some reasonably well-founded hope of success. If it is far short of the universal aims of the United Nations Charter, it is also far bolder and more creative than the Gaullist vision of a unified but exclusive Europe. The Atlantic idea, in short, represents the point at which our needs and our capacity seem to converge.

The current crisis in the Western alliance is not a petty quarrel over prestige or personalities. It is a debate on the fundamental question of how the Western community is to be organized now that the postwar dependency of Europe on the United States is at an end. The demand of a resurgent Europe for a status in the world commensurate with its new strength is a natural historical development which is based on much more permanent foundations than the personality and ambitions of General de Gaulle. It is General de Gaulle, however, who is currently giving voice and content to Europe's self-assertion and he is doing so in a manner which, in my opinion, is detrimental to the best interests of both Europe and America. Like Bismarck a hundred years ago, he pursues a vision of unification with formidable skill and resourcefulness but a limited and inadequate vision, one which, if realized, would unite a small community at the cost of dividing a larger one and thereby sowing the seeds of unnecessary and unnatural animosities among peoples whose destinies, like their histories, are inextricably bound together.

If we are to cope with the Gaullist challenge, we must begin by recognizing the true sources of its power. The "new reality," as Walter Lippmann has defined it, is that Western Europe has outgrown the dependence upon America which began with the first World War and will no longer accept American pre-eminence in European affairs. The "new reality" is the result of the great changes of the last decade: the brilliant recovery of Western Europe, the decline of the United States from world financial pre-eminence, the failure of the United States to cope with chronic economic sluggishness, and the shifting of the military balance of power in favor of the West to the extent that the Soviet military threat in Europe has greatly abated. The result of these changes is that Western Europe is much less dependent on the United States than it has been for nearly fifty years.[3]

Being "less dependent" is quite a different matter from being independent. Europe has become less dependent on the United States in the sense that the threat of imminent catastrophe — of war and of political and economic collapse — has receded after a generation of turmoil. In terms of continuing interests, on the other hand, of long-term security and stability, of the opportunity to realize our full economic potential and to improve the lives of our people, Europe and America remain profoundly dependent upon each other. In close partnership Western Europe and America have it within their power to attain greater security than they have known in this century, to help the underdeveloped countries to overcome their ancient affliction of poverty, to bring unexampled material well-being to their own people and, in so doing, to liberate them for the creative pursuits of civilized society.

The postwar era is past. If we are to adjust to this fact and to realize the opportunities of Atlantic unity, we must reconsider the major components of our foreign policy. Fortunately the current crisis in the Western alliance does not pose an immediate threat to our security and we have time in which to think about the new circumstances which

---

[3] Walter Lippmann, "On Not Fidgeting," *Washington Post*, February 21, 1963.

confront us and how best to deal with them. General de Gaulle has struck a blow at the foundations of postwar American policy. The General's challenge has been carefully conceived and skillfully executed and it is not going to be overcome by precipitate action or by spiteful acts of retaliation. My own view is that there are certain specific steps which we can take toward restoring Western unity but that there is little we can do for the present that would strike at the heart of the problem.

Because the dangers posed by Western disunity are long-range rather than immediate, we would do well to reflect for a time on where we stand and where we are going before making major new policy decisions. Specifically, we must think about four main areas of relations among the Western countries, those of defense and trade, those of their political and institutional bonds with each other and their common responsibilities toward the less developed nations. In each of these areas there may be limited measures which can be taken in the immediate future. In none of them does the time seem ripe for major new policy departures.

I DEFENSE

There is no ready solution to the problem of joint command decision in the use of nuclear weapons. Responsibility is inseparable from power, and wars, certainly nuclear war, cannot be conducted by committees. As long as the United States controls the vast preponderance of Western nuclear power, it is bound to retain ultimate responsibility for their use or non-use. The creation of a multilateral seaborne nuclear force will go a way toward meeting Europe's demand for nuclear sharing but it is only a palliative, albeit a costly one that does not go to the heart of the problem. The vast land-based and airborne nuclear capacity of the United States will continue under sole American control and, with it, the ultimate authority to decide on war or peace. It seems to me, therefore, that the creation of a multilateral nuclear force, though a desirable exercise in NATO cooperation, will not solve the problem of giving Europe an adequate voice in determining the conditions of its own survival.

The worst possible outcome of the current debate, of course, would be the multiplication of separate national nuclear arsenals. In addition to being prohibitively expensive and of dubious strategic value, the proliferation of national nuclear arsenals would undermine the foundation of Western political and military collaboration and inject a powerful new element of instability into the world balance of power.

A unified Western strategy is thus essential to our future peace and security. We must find a way to bring our allies into meaningful participation in the vital decisions relating to war and peace. The crux of the problem is the development of a solid strategic consensus among the NATO allies. The development of such a consensus can be approached through a system of allied participation in the planning and shaping of strategic policy, in determining the *conditions* under which the American deterrent would be brought to bear. This, if successful, would provide a basis for ultimate allied control of the nuclear deterrent itself. Once full consensus were achieved, it is unlikely that technical and organizational problems would prove to be insurmountable. In the final analysis, the control of missiles and warheads is secondary to the control of basic policy processes that determine war or peace.

A unified Allied system of strategic planning would serve many purposes. It would in the first place give Europe the voice in determining its own destiny that it rightly demands. More important perhaps in the long run, by elevating the debate on strategic policy from the domestic level to the level of the Alliance as a whole, it would generate an attitude toward Western defense as the defense of a single community. One can conceive of a unified strategic planning system helping to solve immediate problems and at the same time contributing to the broader purposes of Atlantic community.

In times of clear and present danger, custom, inertia, vested interests, and traditional viewpoints give way to the demands of the times. The problem that now confronts NATO is whether it can meet the requirements of a long-term rather than an immediate danger with a spirit similar to that which motivated the Western Allies in the two world wars. If we can forge something like the unity of purpose and common action that we so successfully forged in wartime, we will be well on the way toward a solution of the problem of nuclear weapons control as well as toward meeting the broader challenge of building an Atlantic community.

There is little need of new machinery for unified strategic planning and policy coordination in the Western Alliance. Existing NATO machinery can adequately serve these purposes with certain reforms and, above all, with a concerted will to use this machinery effectively. There is no reason, for example, why the NATO Council cannot in time be developed into an Allied strategic planning body on the model of the Combined Chiefs of Staff of World War II. What is needed in the Western Alliance is not elaborate new machinery, which could all too easily be left to atrophy, but the invigoration of existing NATO organs by the application of a strong new spirit of partnership and trust.

The most useful single step toward the strengthening of NATO as a meaningful instrument of Atlantic partnership would be the elevation of the NATO Council to the stature of a genuine organ of policy co-ordination. It could become the allied forum for long-term political and military planning on the most fundamental questions of war and peace. Through the gradual formulation of an overall strategic consensus among the Atlantic allies, a strengthened NATO Council could in time resolve the problems of nuclear sharing that now seem insuperable.

It is quite possible that such a major enhancement of the NATO policy machinery would not at first commend itself to all of our partners. Should this be the case, even after a considerable period of debate and discussion, it would be appropriate, I think, to proceed with those of our allies who are prepared to cooperate, leaving an "empty chair" and a standing invitation for the reluctant or laggard. The affairs of the Alliance are far too important to be governed indefinitely by the veto of its least cooperative member. The strengthening of NATO, and particularly of the NATO Council, is one of the advances toward full Atlantic partnership that can and should be undertaken without excessive delay. Such measures are both strategically necessary and politically feasible. They are in line with both our needs and the feasibilities of history.

II   TRADE

No less important than the question of nuclear weapons and defense for the Alliance is the challenge of shaping new economic relations among the Atlantic countries. The kind of economic community envisaged by the Treaty of Rome and by the American Trade Expansion Act of 1962 has vast political as well as economic implications. As one contemporary writer has commented: "The reduction of tariff barriers and all the other economic changes which the treaties have set in motion are the outward signs of integration, but at its center lies a profound shift in political relationships, political methods, and political objectives."[4]

The [1962] Trade Expansion Act was the American response to the liberal spirit of Article 110 of the Treaty of Rome, which set forth the

[4] Roy Price, *The Political Future of the European Community* (London: John Marshbank, 1962) p. 20.

intention of the European Community "to contribute, in conformity with the common interest, to the harmonious development of world trade, the progressive abolition of restrictions on international exchanges, and the lowering of customs barriers." The new American approach on trade, adopted in the wake of a significant campaign of national persuasion and education, will fulfill its promise only if the European Community keeps faith with the spirit and intent of Article 110 of the Treaty of Rome. The progressive lowering of tariff barriers, despite transitory hardships and adjustments on both sides, would open the way to substantially expanded trade and accelerated economic growth for both Europe and America. Beyond this, the development of a thriving economic community of the North Atlantic would have enormous implications, political as well as economic, for the entire free world. In the words of a recent Senate Foreign Relations Committee staff study: "From the spreading base of this mutually beneficial trade, the two great communities on either side of the Atlantic should be able to perform a number of tasks that have become indivisible, to reach major goals that neither could reach alone."[5]

An Atlantic trading partnership is neither a conception of pure idealism nor, as certain Europeans have suggested, a sublimated form of American economic colonialism. It is a conception based on the realities of mutual advantage, a project rooted in solid foundations of interest for both Europe and America. The United States needs to participate in a large Atlantic trading area in order to expand its trade and thus be able to earn the hard money needed to finance its military and civilian commitments overseas. If the European Economic Community becomes a closed, restrictive trading area, the United States will be unable to earn the costs of financing its contribution to the defense of Europe. With our mounting obligations in Latin America and Asia and a substantial annual deficit in our balance of payments, we would eventually have no choice but to reduce our contribution to Western European defense. An Atlantic trading partnership is thus far more than a noble dream; it is a necessity of the first priority for both Europe and America. . . .

The implications of European protectionism and autarchy are of course far more than commercial. I believe that the thrust and design of economic exclusiveness, as conceived by General de Gaulle, are

[5] *Problems and Trends in Atlantic Partnership I* (Senate Document No. 132, 1962) p. 30.

toward the creation of a closed European political confederation under French control with German support. The inherent instability of such a European order is quite obvious, not least because of the improbability that a dynamic and productive Germany would long consent to the role of lieutenant in a French-dominated political system. But even if a closed Europe could be made politically viable, I believe, for reasons I have stated, that such a system would be inimical to the real interests of Europe, including France, of America and of the entire free world.

The frontiers of freedom are wider than the frontiers of Europe. If a unified Europe is to make a lasting contribution to the security and prosperity of the free world of which it is an integral part, it must be as part of a broader concert of free nations. The heart of Western civilization embraces the entire community of Atlantic democracies and our future depends less on what we do in confrontation with the Communist world than on the kind of relations we develop and the kind of society we build within our own world. Most especially, our future depends on whether we allow the West to succumb once again to divisive and destructive nationalism or whether we make it so strong and unified that no one will dare attack us and so prosperous and progressive that it will serve as a model and a magnet for the entire world — for the struggling nations of Asia and Africa, for the unhappy peoples of Eastern Europe, and ultimately perhaps, for the Russians themselves.

III   POLITICAL AND INSTITUTIONAL BONDS

Since the exclusion of Great Britain from the European Economic Community, there seems little likelihood for the foreseeable future of a broadening of institutional bonds among the Western nations. It is not possible from our present perspective to foresee the kind of relationship which Britain will ultimately have with Europe or the kind of relationship which we will have with both. These are problems which we must live with for a while. Fortunately there is no great urgency about solving them and we would do well to use the present hiatus for some hard and serious thought about the kind of Atlantic political institutions we would like to shape, if any, and the kinds of sacrifices we would be willing to make, if any, to achieve them.

My own view has been that the most promising road toward Atlantic community is the "functional" rather than the "federal" road, by measured advances toward cooperation in specific and limited fields. This approach was represented by the Brussels negotiations and is for the present foreclosed. We would perhaps do well, therefore, to consider certain limited measures of Atlantic cooperation in areas that remain open to us, with a view to keeping the spirit of Atlantic community alive while we think about more significant advances in the future and await the opportunity to make them.

One avenue of progress, albeit limited progress, that remains open to us is that of improving Atlantic parliamentary institutions. In January 1962 the Atlantic Convention of NATO Nations, an unofficial group of distinguished Europeans and Americans, issued the "Declaration of Paris," in which they recommended the establishment of Atlantic executive and judicial organs and the development of the NATO Parliamentarians' Conference into consultative "Atlantic Assembly." In November 1962 the NATO Parliamentarians' Conference commissioned a special subcommittee to study this proposal. I believe that the establishment of a consultative Atlantic Assembly in the near future would be a desirable and feasible measure for the strengthening of the Atlantic community. The establishment of such a body of parliamentarians would have a salutary effect in alleviating the current atmosphere of disunity and recrimination within the Alliance.

An Atlantic Assembly of parliamentarians superseding the NATO Parliamentarians' Conference should be constituted to serve as a consultative organ for the Organization for Economic Cooperation and Development as well as for NATO. It should embrace the full scope of Atlantic relations, military and political, economic and cultural, as well as the relations of the North Atlantic countries with Asia, Africa, and Latin America.

The constitution of an Atlantic Assembly would of course have to be carefully considered, but one can envision a body authorized to submit recommendations to both NATO and the OECD, which would be expected to reply to all proposals either in writing or by the appearance of authorized representatives before the parliamentary body or any of its subsidiary organs. In addition, the delegates to the Assembly might be empowered to express their confidence or lack of confidence in specific actions or decisions of the two executive bodies. To accommodate those countries who are members of OECD but not of NATO, procedures might be devised for separate consideration of OECD and NATO matters so that the neutrals would be able to abstain entirely from all questions of the military alliance.

It is possible, indeed probable, that the contributions of an Atlantic Assembly would for some time be more symbolic than substantive. In no sense could its creation be regarded as the "answer" to the basic problem of Western unity. Its value for the foreseeable future would be as an organ of counsel and consultation, a forum for the practice of community on the Atlantic level, and an institutional symbol of our interdependence.

IV   THE WEST AND THE DEVELOPING NATIONS

In the discharge of their common obligations to the underdeveloped countries of Asia, Africa, and Latin America, the nations of the West have a surpassing opportunity, by bringing to bear in unity and common purpose a small part of their vast resources, both to strengthen their bonds with each other and to lay the foundations for a worldwide concert of free nations.

It has been said, but it bears repeating, that the nations of Asia, Africa, and Latin America are caught up in a great historic revolution. The essence of this revolution is the demand for human dignity, material and moral, and for an approach to equality with the privileged community of the West. The challenge which this poses for the Atlantic nations is expressed in words that Alexis de Tocqueville wrote over a hundred years ago: "The nations of our time cannot prevent the conditions of men from becoming equal; but it depends upon themselves whether the principle of equality is to lead them to servitude or freedom, to knowledge or barbarism, to prosperity or to wretchedness."[6]

I think it is important to be quite clear about the nature of Western interests in relation to the poor countries of the world. Whatever the extent of its humanitarian motivation and effect, our material assistance to the less developed countries, far from being "nonpolitical" or essentially commercial or altruistic in character, has profound political implications. Foreign aid is one of a number of instruments of policy by which the West seeks to bolster its own security, by fostering a world environment in which our kind of society, and the values in which it is rooted, can survive and flourish. Indeed an adequate conception of Western aid is not one which divorces aid from political objectives but rather one which divorces it from crude and shortsighted, trivial and superficial objectives, by linking it firmly to our most vital long-range political goals.

We must make a major new effort, in close cooperation with our Atlantic allies, to determine our objectives in foreign aid and to reshape our aid programs accordingly. A new approach, it seems to me, must

[6] Tocqueville, *op. cit.*, p. 599.

be in the direction of rigorous *selectivity* — selectivity as to whom we will help and how we will help them. We must evaluate such factors as the ability of a recipient to absorb capital, the presence or absence of trained personnel, the capacity for social reforms and, above all, the potential contribution of the recipient to world peace and stability. In Walter Lippmann's succinct phrase: "Let the bridges we have to build be fewer but let all of them cross the river."[7]

It is important that the West keep firm bearings on the overall objective of its assistance to the poor countries of the world, which, as I have suggested, is to help create a world environment in which free societies can survive and flourish. It is equally important that we interpret this objective in terms of historical rather than immediate prospects. We have reason and the right to hope that our assistance will contribute to the spread of free institutions in the world, but this is a long-term prospect, which has little if any chance of fulfillment in the immediate future. "It is idle," writes Robert Heilbroner, "to pretend that the West can be an effective model for the immediate economic and political development of the backward world. What we must hope and work for is to make it a model for their long-term evolution."[8]

The rigors of economic development for backward countries are such that we must expect protracted periods of instability and, in some cases, of authoritarian government. Economic development is a profoundly revolutionary force, involving the overturn of vested interests and traditional ways of doing things and requiring great sacrifices in the present for the promise of greater rewards in the future. "There is no doubt," writes Eric Hoffer, "that individual freedom is an unequaled factor in the release of social energies. . . . But this source of energy can be tapped only under special conditions: a society must be strong enough to support, and affluent enough to afford, individual freedom. It would thus be wholly unreasonable to expect a backward country to modernize itself in a hurry in an atmosphere of freedom. Its poverty, lack of skill, and its need for fervor and unity militate against it."[9]

With its radically different kind of experience, the West is only beginning to perceive that the ascent from poverty of Asia, Africa, and Latin America involves the revolutionary transformation of societies

[7] Walter Lippmann, "The Clay Report," *Washington Post*, March 26, 1963.

[8] Robert L. Heilbroner, *The Great Ascent* (New York: Harper and Row, 1963) p. 181.

[9] Eric Hoffer, *The Ordeal of Change* (New York: Harper and Row, 1963) pp. 98–99.

and that there is little possibility of this transformation being achieved through the methods of Western political democracy. The basic requirement for economic growth is of course capital and in desperately poor countries, except for limited assistance from outside, capital can only be formed by forced savings, that is, by holding down or further lowering levels of consumption that are barely above subsistence. The rigorous discipline and harsh controls that this involves have already led in some countries and is likely to lead in others to the displacement of parliamentary systems by authoritarian regimes.

It is an unanswered question whether the West, especially the United States, is prepared to assist and support for long periods regimes which do not pursue policies of democratic capitalism. My own view is that we must recognize the exigencies of development, however distasteful they may be, and lend our support to those governments which meet two main tests: first, that they have the will and capacity for economic growth, and, secondly, that they pursue policies which infringe on popular liberties only to the extent absolutely necessary for the country's development plans and are committed to the establishment of democratic institutions at the earliest practicable time.

I believe such an approach to be consistent with our objectives of shaping a concert of free nations. It requires us, in Robert Heilbroner's words, "to distinguish between mere oppression and oppressive but purposeful discipline, between static dictatorship and dictatorial development."[10] In short, we must take a calculated risk in supporting governments which, whatever their present character, seem likely in the long run to achieve both economic growth and political democracy and, in so doing, to contribute to our own long-term purposes.

Success in so difficult and delicate an enterprise is far more likely if the Western nations to the greatest possible extent remove their development efforts from domestic political arenas and channel them through international agencies. A unified Western effort in the field of foreign aid would serve the double purpose of creating new bonds between the Western nations themselves and of giving them a far more effective means of influencing the course of the new nations than they now have in their separate programs of aid. Indeed, if the Atlantic nations are prepared to accept the burden of generous, concerted, and long-term assistance to the more promising of the underdeveloped countries, then they can, I believe, make a powerful, and perhaps decisive,

[10] Heilbroner, *op. cit.*, p. 175.

contribution to the creation of a peaceful and stable world environment.

The unification of Western aid programs will have meaning and effect only if every member of the Atlantic community accepts its fair share of the burden. Unfortunately only a very few of the prosperous countries of the free world have thus far accepted foreign aid responsibilities commensurate with their resources. I think it not improper to point out that while the United States is able and willing to bear its just share of the burden of aid to the poor nations and of the heavier burden of free world defense as well, it cannot carry indefinitely a disproportionate share when other nations, with equally much at stake, are reluctant to accept responsibilities commensurate with their strength.

The political stakes of Atlantic aid to the poor nations are nothing less than whether the Atlantic world is to be an isolated bastion of freedom and prosperity or the vital core of a worldwide concert of free nations. If we are to achieve the latter, we must concert our policies as to the amounts and duration, the priorities and methods of our aid. This is likely to require something more than the coordination of separate national aid programs. Because bargaining between states often produces only a smallest common denominator of agreed action, it is possible that we shall eventually have to apply to our aid programs some such political procedures as those which have proven so effective in the European Economic Community. As Lord Franks has put it: "A new way has to be found: a new organization, institution or commission, which will have sufficient standing, independence and initiative to formulate common solutions and put them forward to the governments of the several nations of the group, so that they will have to face in argument not merely each other but also and at the same time the solution proposed for the partnership as a whole as best realizing its common good."[11]

My own belief is that the "new way" called for by Lord Franks can be developed through existing international machinery. One can envision the development of a unified multilateral aid program either through the International Development Association of the World Bank or the Development Assistance Committee of the OECD, or through the use of both of these agencies. . . .

Whatever the forms and the instrumentalities that the rich nations use in their efforts to help the poor nations, and whatever the disap-

[11] Lord Franks, "Cooperation Is Not Enough," *Foreign Affairs* (October 1962) p. 33.

pointments and reverses that are suffered in the process, we must at all times keep our bearing on the hopes and opportunities that depend upon our success. In unity and common purpose, we have it within our power to shape a concert of free nations and, building thereon, to lead the world toward a new era of hope and progress. "Our age will be well remembered," said Arnold Toynbee, "not for its horrifying crimes or its astonishing inventions but because it is the first generation since the dawn of history in which mankind dared to believe it practical to make the benefits of civilization available to the whole human race."

In all of the great problems that I have commented on tonight — those of defense and trade, of political cooperation and foreign aid, and of the divergence between the Gaullist and the Atlantic concepts of how the free world should be organized — one simple but compelling theme prevails, the theme of unity or division among free peoples. Since the age of discovery when the Atlantic community was formed, its members have periodically fallen upon each other, with mounting savagery reflecting the refinements of their technology. As long as the North Atlantic nations dominated the world and as long as weapons of war were limited in the damage they could do, the "civil war" of the West was something which its members could survive if not afford. That time is now past. The Atlantic nations no longer dominate the world, nor could they expect to survive as organized societies a conflict with those who threaten them. History and reason and common sense tell us that unity is the condition for preventing such a conflict, that in unity lies our best hope of preserving the civilization we have built and of fulfilling its considerable promise.

What are the foundations of French foreign policy under the Fifth Republic? What are its ultimate goals and its intermediate objectives?

Let us look first at the foundations. The foreign policy of France under the Fifth Republic seems to me freed of any ideological bias. I do not mean to imply by this, however, the absence of a world-view and of that certainty which follows from a philosophy of history — quite the contrary. But the world-view and the philosophy of history which, as I see it, inspire the foreign policy of the President of the Republic are defined, first of all, by a reaction against the "ideology" which seemed generally accepted in French governmental circles before 1958. This ideology, characteristic of the postwar period, can be defined as follows:

1. The world is divided in two by the struggle, which characterizes the second half of the twentieth century, between the doctrine of political liberalism and that of communist totalitarianism. The West must, therefore, regroup its material and moral forces in order to counteract the attacks of an enemy which moves sometimes by force, sometimes by wile, but always according to a centralized master plan. One practical consequence of this Manichaean conception is that any rupture in the solidarity of the free world in the face of the adversary could not but aid his ventures.

2. This division of the world into antagonistic ideological camps is accompanied by a bipolar distribution of political, economic and military power. The two great industrial nations alone possess the means to bring the rest of the world to its senses. Consequently, the states of Western Europe have no choice other than to accept the leadership of the United States or to try, by means of integration, to create a third great power.

3. As corollaries of the two principles enunciated above — the world is divided, essentially, into two camps and power is distributed between the two poles — it was generally assumed: (a) by the European powers

Jacques Vernant is Secretary General of the Administrative Council of the Centre d'Études de Politique Étrangère (Center for the Study of Foreign Policy) in Paris and Director of Studies at the École Politique des Hautes Études. These excerpts are reprinted from "Fondements et objectifs de la politique éxterieure française," in *Politique Étrangère*, 6, 1963, pp. 459–467.

that the liquidation of their overseas empires would put an end to their influence in their former dependencies; and (b) by the whole Western world that the liquidation of European and American influence in the third world implied, as a necessary corollary, the augmentation of Soviet influence and progress in the growth of communism.

These three points the leaders of the Fifth Republic, under the inspiration of General de Gaulle, have proceeded to revise in accordance with the deep convictions of the Chief of State, but to revise also in the light of certain unexpected changes in the international system since the immediate postwar period, changes which have occurred quite independently of the personal philosophy of statesmen.

1. The leaders of the Fifth Republic do not consider it possible to found French foreign policy on the principle that the world is divided in two — for several reasons:

(a) First, because regimes change. Even when they strive to safeguard the integrity of their doctrines, the leaders must adapt the political structures of industrialized states to facts, so that they somehow respond to the normal needs of humanity. The erosion of regimes permits, then, hopes that an overly simplistic, Manichaean conception does not allow;

(b) Because the erosion of regimes implies that time can do its work. Now, the conditions of nuclear equilibrium are such that we can allow the effect of time to enter into our calculations of probability. In effect, the nuclear arms which the great powers have at their disposal interdict for all practical purposes any direct military confrontation between them — which implies a sort of peace in competition. It is in this climate, one more and more sensitive, which are found the current relations between states and regimes;

(c) Because, in a general manner, policy is not a matter of ideology. In the world of nation-states, it is a function of realities and possibilities, taking into account the national interests of the state — which must be defined and which in turn define foreign policy — not a function of ideology. Moreover, ideology is nowhere powerful enough to extinguish national interests. Under the ideological system the nation reasserts itself, just as man gradually reappears under the Communist. Thus China affirms her right to her own international position; and so do Poland, Hungary, Rumania. Thus it is indispensable, if one wants to have a rational policy, to take into account the realities — that is to say states and not an ideology, which often is only a smokescreen;

(d) Because the world is by nature much more diverse than dualistic, the "third powers" are more and more numerous and their capacity for action grows to the degree that the postwar period fades into the past;

(e) Because there is no certainty that bipolarity — the division of the world in two — is a guarantee of peace, as has often been thought. Bipolarity, to a large degree, is an effect of international tension; and it helps to maintain it. The fluidity of international relations, which results from the depolarization of the world, restores the normal conditions of diplomatic action and facilitates the peaceful evolution of the differences which separate states. To that extent it provides a restraint to the nuclear menace inherent in any conflict which directly involves the great powers.

2. It is not true that only the United States and the Soviet Union are in a position to follow independent policies. A state such as France, on condition that it wishes to, and that it wishes to provide itself with the means to do so, is perfectly able to follow an independent policy and must in fact follow an independent policy when its vital interests are in question. For France, equipping herself with the nuclear armament for which French scientists were among those primarily responsible, is at one and the same time the inescapable consequence of the scientific and technical capacities of the country, of its presence — thanks to General de Gaulle — on the side of the victors in World War II, and the condition, the symbol, of its participation in world politics.

On the other hand, it is absurd to think that one can formulate a policy without taking as a starting point the existence of national states. Policy is the internal and external behavior of states whose reality is the product of a long history. Policy results from an accumulation of experiences, of traditions, of which the nation is the setting. If one tries to jump out of these settings and mix up nations under the authority of a superstate, one destroys the very conditions of politics. Thus a European supranational state would have no policy at all. In fact, it will have the policy of the most powerful of its allies, the United States.

3. It is not true that the former colonial powers inevitably lose their influence in their former colonies once they become independent. Proof to the contrary is furnished by the fact that an intelligent policy has permitted France, for example, to conserve its cultural and economic, even political, influence in countries which were formerly united to it by various institutional ties. Better still, in a world which is diversifying

at the same time it is unifying, the influence of Europe can spread throughout the new countries or be reborn in those where it flourished at the height of its power. Likewise, the end of empire does not necessarily mean the decline of the colonial powers. This decline can just as easily be caused by the defense of anachronistic empires. The concentration of the efforts of the nation on its own territory is quite the opposite — in certain cases even the beginning of a renaissance, provided, of course, that there is an effort. But if effort is there, notably in the domains of science and technology — and their military application — the "withdrawal" can be proven useful; to the extent that, in the conditions of the modern world, a nation's scientific knowledge and technical capacities, encouraged by intelligent political direction, assure its increasing influence, much more than the extent of its territory, the number of its inhabitants, or statistics on its production of steel.

Each of these principles, which together constitute, if one wishes, the Gaullist doctrine of foreign policy, at least at I interpret it, can be easily illustrated by declarations or diplomatic acts of the Chief of State or members of the government. I will mention only a few of the more recent diplomatic acts illustrating this doctrine, in order to underline the coherence of the system.

A policy is productive and durable only when it takes reality into account; this is the reason why General de Gaulle wants to unify gradually European policies by drawing together the economic, political and military ties of the "Six," because they have accepted the common enterprise as defined in the Treaty of Rome, and particularly the ties between France and the Federal Republic of Germany.

It is because policy must take realities into account that the French government announced its decision to recognize Communist China. . . .

If France has a world role to play, she must prove it by acting. In addition, France has an interest in seeing peace established in Southeastern Asia and the political situation there stabilized. And it is rightly estimated in Paris that these results cannot be attained if one persists in ignoring the existence of China. Since France has retained important material and moral interests in that region, it is normal for French initiative to intervene, even if the American government, for reasons of internal politics, cannot imitate it, or approve it. In doing as it did, the French government only conformed to an enduring and justified tradition of independent countries. . . .

How, in a very general manner, can one define the objectives of French foreign policy? The first, we have said, is to give France the capacity to make her own voice heard and to take actions which conform to her own interests. More precisely [it is necessary] to strengthen the unity of Western Europe in all fields, in order that unity may become not only an economic reality, but a military and political one as well. Europe must be something other than an appendage of the United States; it must participate in the settlement of current international problems and particularly in those which directly concern it, in preparing solutions conforming to its interests, those which will provide a maximum of stability in the future and which take into account a maximum of the historical and geographical givens. The unification of Germany is thus one of the essential objectives of French foreign policy and, as the unification of Germany is impossible without the reunification of Europe, this unification of Europe is also the goal of French foreign policy. In brief, Europe must be reunified in the conditions which assure its internal stability and permit it to play its proper role in world affairs.

Outside of Europe, in a world which, as I have said, is diversifying more and more, the Fifth Republic intends to increase French influence. In Africa, notably in the French-speaking states of Black Africa; in Asia, in those states which have been marked by French presence and in the great Asian powers such as India, Japan and China, who play already, or are called upon to play, an important role on the international scene; finally, in Latin America, that continent which still searches the road to economic development, political liberty, and social equality, France knows that she too can be a model for development. Science and technology, as well as French culture, are appreciated there. French technical and cultural assistance is not compromising for the nonaligned, not does it arouse their distrust. The independence which French foreign policy displays awakens echoes and arouses sympathy in numerous states, old and new. The ideas of the French revolution retain their significance for people who feel that they have not yet completed their emancipation.

The Challenge of International Communism

3 JOHN F. KENNEDY
Toward a Strategy of Peace

"There are few earthly things more beautiful than a University,"
wrote John Masefield, in his tribute to the English universities — and
his words are equally true here. He did not refer to spires and towers,
to campus greens and ivied walls. He admired the splendid beauty of
the university, he said, because it was "a place where those who hate
ignorance may strive to know, where those who perceive truth may
strive to make others see."

I have, therefore, chosen this time and this place to discuss a topic
on which ignorance too often abounds and the truth is too rarely perceived — yet it is the most important topic on earth: world peace.

What kind of peace do I mean? What kind of peace do we seek?
Not a *Pax Americana* enforced on the world by American weapons of
war. Not the peace of the grave or the security of the slave. I am
talking about genuine peace, the kind of peace that makes life on earth
worth living, the kind that enables men and nations to grow and to
hope and to build a better life for their children — not merely peace
for Americans but peace for all men and women, not merely peace in
our time but peace for all time.

I speak of peace because of the new face of war. Total war makes
no sense in an age when great powers can maintain large and relatively
invulnerable nuclear forces and refuse to surrender without resort to
those forces. It makes no sense in an age when a single nuclear weapon
contains almost 10 times the explosive force delivered by all of the
Allied air forces in the Second World War. It makes no sense in an
age when the deadly poisons produced by a nuclear exchange would
be carried by the wind and water and soil and seed to the far corners
of the globe and to generations yet unborn.

Today the expenditure of billions of dollars every year on weapons
acquired for the purpose of making sure we never need to use them

These excerpts are from a speech delivered by John F. Kennedy, President of
the United States, January 1961–November 22, 1963, at the commencement exercises at The American University in Washington, D.C., on June 10, 1963. They are
reprinted from *The Department of State Bulletin*, XLIX, No. 1253 (July 1, 1963)
2–6.

is essential to keeping the peace. But surely the acquisition of such idle stockpiles — which can only destroy and never create — is not the only, much less the most efficient, means of assuring peace.

I speak of peace, therefore, as the necessary rational end of rational men. I realize that the pursuit of peace is not as dramatic as the pursuit of war, and frequently the words of the pursuer fall on deaf ears. But we have no more urgent task.

Some say that it is useless to speak of world peace or world law or world disarmament — and that it will be useless until the leaders of the Soviet Union adopt a more enlightened attitude. I hope they do. I believe we can help them do it. But I also believe that we must re-examine our own attitude, as individuals and as a nation, for our attitude is as essential as theirs. And every graduate of this school, every thoughtful citizen who despairs of war and wishes to bring peace, should begin by looking inward — by examining his own attitude toward the possibilities of peace, toward the Soviet Union, toward the course of the cold war, and toward freedom and peace here at home.

THE POSSIBILITIES OF PEACE

First: Let us examine our attitude toward peace itself. Too many of us think it is impossible. Too many think it unreal. But that is a dangerous, defeatist belief. It leads to the conclusion that war is inevitable, that mankind is doomed, that we are gripped by forces we cannot control.

We need not accept that view. Our problems are manmade; therefore they can be solved by man. And man can be as big as he wants. No problem of human destiny is beyond human beings. Man's reason and spirit have often solved the seemingly unsolvable, and we believe they can do it again.

I am not referring to the absolute, infinite concept of universal peace and good will of which some fantasies and fanatics dream. I do not deny the values of hopes and dreams, but we merely invite discouragement and incredulity by making that our only and immediate goal.

Let us focus instead on a more practical, more attainable peace, based not on a sudden revolution in human nature but on a gradual evolution in human institutions — on a series of concrete actions and effective agreements which are in the interest of all concerned. There is no single, simple key to this peace, no grand or magic formula to be adopted by one or two powers. Genuine peace must be the product of many nations, the sum of many acts. It must be dynamic, not static, changing to meet the challenge of each new generation. For peace is a process, a way of solving problems.

With such a peace there will still be quarrels and conflicting interests, as there are within families and nations. World peace, like community peace, does not require that each man love his neighbor; it requires only that they live together in mutual tolerance, submitting their disputes to a just and peaceful settlement. And history teaches us that enmities between nations, as between individuals, do not last forever. However fixed our likes and dislikes may seem, the tide of time and events will often bring surprising changes in the relations between nations and neighbors.

So let us persevere. Peace need not be impracticable, and war need not be inevitable. By defining our goal more clearly, by making it seem more manageable and less remote, we can help all peoples to see it, to draw hope from it, and to move irresistibly toward it.

COMMON INTERESTS OF U.S. AND SOVIET UNION

Second: Let us reexamine our attitude toward the Soviet Union. It is discouraging to think that their leaders may actually believe what their propagandists write. It is discouraging to read a recent authoritative Soviet text on military strategy and find, on page after page, wholly baseless and incredible claims — such as the allegation that "American imperialist circles are preparing to unleash different types of wars . . . that there is a very real threat of a preventive war being unleashed by American imperialists against the Soviet Union . . . [and that] the political aims of the American imperialists are to enslave economically and politically the European and other capitalist countries . . . [and] to achieve world domination . . . by means of aggressive wars."

Truly as it was written long ago: "The wicked flee when no man pursueth." Yet it is sad to read these Soviet statements — to realize the extent of the gulf between us. But it is also a warning — a warning to the American people not to fall into the same trap as the Soviets, not to see only a distorted and desperate view of the other side, not to see conflict as inevitable, accommodation as impossible, and communication as nothing more than an exchange of threats.

No government or social system is so evil that its people must be considered as lacking in virtue. As Americans we find communism profoundly repugnant as a negation of personal freedom and dignity. But we can still hail the Russian people for their many achievements — in science and space, in economic and industrial growth, in culture and in acts of courage.

Among the many traits the peoples of our two countries have in common, none is stronger than our mutual abhorrence of war. Almost unique among the major world powers, we have never been at war with each other. And no nation in the history of battle ever suffered more than the Soviet Union suffered in the course of the Second World War. At least 20 million lost their lives. Countless millions of homes and farms were burned or sacked. A third of the nation's territory, including nearly two-thirds of its industrial base, was turned into a wasteland — a loss equivalent to the devastation of this country east of Chicago.

Today, should total war ever break out again — no matter how — our two countries would become the primary targets. It is an ironical but accurate fact that the two strongest powers are the two in the most danger of devastation. All we have built, all we have worked for, would be destroyed in the first 24 hours. And even in the cold war, which brings burdens and dangers to so many countries — including this nation's closest allies — our two countries bear the heaviest burdens. For we are both devoting massive sums of money to weapons that could be better devoted to combating ignorance, poverty, and disease. We are both caught up in a vicious and dangerous cycle in which suspicion on one side breeds suspicion on the other and new weapons beget counterweapons.

In short, both the United States and its allies, and the Soviet Union and its allies, have a mutually deep interest in a just and genuine peace and in halting the arms race. Agreements to this end are in the interests of the Soviet Union as well as ours, and even the most hostile nations can be relied upon to accept and keep those treaty obligations, and only those treaty obligations, which are in their own interest.

So let us not be blind to our differences, but let us also direct attention to our common interests and to the means by which those differences can be resolved. And if we cannot end now our differences, at least we can help make the world safe for diversity. For in the final analysis our most basic common link is that we all inhabit this planet.

We all breathe the same air. We all cherish our children's future. And we are all mortal.

THE PURSUIT OF PEACE

Third: Let us reexamine our attitude toward the cold war, remembering that we are not engaged in a debate, seeking to pile up debating points. We are not here distributing blame or pointing the finger of judgment. We must deal with the world as it is and not as it might have been had the history of the last 18 years been different.

We must, therefore, persevere in the search for peace in the hope that constructive changes within the Communist bloc might bring within reach solutions which now seem beyond us. We must conduct our affairs in such a way that it becomes in the Communists' interest to agree on a genuine peace. Above all, while defending our own vital interests, nuclear powers must avert those confrontations which bring an adversary to a choice of either a humiliating retreat or a nuclear war. To adopt that kind of course in the nuclear age would be evidence only of the bankruptcy of our policy — or of a collective death wish for the world.

To secure these ends, America's weapons are nonprovocative, carefully controlled, designed to deter, and capable of selective use. Our military forces are committed to peace and disciplined in self-restraint. Our diplomats are instructed to avoid unnecessary irritants and purely rhetorical hostility.

For we can seek a relaxation of tensions without relaxing our guard. And, for our part, we do not need to use threats to prove that we are resolute. We do not need to jam foreign broadcasts out of fear our faith will be eroded. We are unwilling to impose our system on any unwilling people, but we are willing and able to engage in peaceful competition with any people on earth.

Meanwhile we seek to strengthen the United Nations, to help solve its financial problems, to make it a more effective instrument of peace, to develop it into a genuine world security system — a system capable of resolving disputes on the basis of law, of insuring the security of the large and the small, and of creating conditions under which arms can finally be abolished.

At the same time we seek to keep peace inside the non-Communist world, where many nations, all of them our friends, are divided over issues which weaken Western unity, which invite Communist intervention, or which threaten to erupt into war. . . .

Speaking of other nations, I wish to make one point clear. We are bound to many nations by alliances. Those alliances exist because our concern and theirs substantially overlap. Our commitment to defend Western Europe and West Berlin, for example, stands undiminished because of the identity of our vital interests. The United States will make no deal with the Soviet Union at the expense of other nations and other peoples, not merely because they are our partners but also because their interests and ours converge.

Our interests converge, however, not only in defending the frontiers of freedom but in pursuing the paths of peace. It is our hope — and the purpose of Allied policies — to convince the Soviet Union that she, too, should let each nation choose its own future, so long as that choice does not interfere with the choices of others. The Communist drive to impose their political and economic system on others is the primary cause of world tension today. For there can be no doubt that, if all nations could refrain from interfering in the self-determination of others, the peace would be much more assured.

This will require a new effort to achieve world law, a new context for world discussions. It will require increased understanding between the Soviets and ourselves. And increased understanding will require increased contact and communication. One step in this direction is the proposed arrangement for a direct line between Moscow and Washington, to avoid on each side the dangerous delays, misunderstandings, and misreadings of the other's actions which might occur at a time of crisis.

We have also been talking in Geneva about other first-step measures of arms control, designed to limit the intensity of the arms race and to reduce the risks of accidental war. Our primary long-range interest in Geneva, however, is general and complete disarmament, designed to take place by stages, permitting parallel political developments to build the new institutions of peace which would take the place of arms. The pursuit of disarmament has been an effort of this Government since the 1920's. It has been urgently sought by the past three administrations. And however dim the prospects may be today, we intend to continue this effort — to continue it in order that all countries, including our own, can better grasp what the problems and possibilities of disarmament are.

The one major area of these negotiations where the end is in sight, yet where a fresh start is badly needed, is in a treaty to outlaw nuclear tests. The conclusion of such a treaty — so near and yet so far — would check the spiraling arms race in one of its most dangerous areas. It would place the nuclear powers in a position to deal more effectively with one of the greatest hazards which man faces in 1963, the further spread of nuclear arms. It would increase our security; it would decrease the prospects of war. Surely this goal is sufficiently important to require our steady pursuit, yielding neither to the temptation to give up the whole effort nor the temptation to give up our insistence on vital and responsible safeguards.

I am taking this opportunity, therefore, to announce two important decisions in this regard.

First: Chairman Khrushchev, Prime Minister Macmillan, and I have agreed that high-level discussions will shortly begin in Moscow looking toward early agreement on a comprehensive test ban treaty. Our hopes must be tempered with the caution of history, but with our hopes go the hopes of all mankind.

Second: To make clear our good faith and solemn convictions on the matter, I now declare that the United States does not propose to conduct nuclear tests in the atmosphere so long as other states do not do so. We will not be the first to resume. Such a declaration is no substitute for a formal binding treaty, but I hope it will help us achieve one. Nor would such a treaty be a substitute for disarmament, but I hope it will help us achieve it.

PEACE AND HUMAN RIGHTS

Finally, my fellow Americans, let us examine our attitude toward peace and freedom here at home. The quality and spirit of our own society must justify and support our efforts abroad. We must show it in the dedication of our own lives, as many of you who are graduating today will have a unique opportunity to do, by serving without pay in the Peace Corps abroad or in the proposed National Service Corps here at home.

But wherever we are, we must all, in our daily lives, live up to the age-old faith that peace and freedom walk together. In too many of our cities today the peace is not secure because freedom is incomplete. . . .

All this is not unrelated to world peace. "When a man's ways please the Lord," the Scriptures tell us, "he maketh even his enemies to be at peace with him." And is not peace, in the last analysis, basically a matter of human rights — the right to live out our lives without fear of devastation, the right to breathe air as nature provided it, the right of future generations to a healthy existence?

While we proceed to safeguard our national interests, let us also safeguard human interests. And the elimination of war and arms is clearly in the interest of both. No treaty, however much it may be to the advantage of all, however tightly it may be worded, can provide absolute security against the risks of deception and evasion. But it can, if it is sufficiently effective in its enforcement and if it is sufficiently in the interests of its signers, offer far more security and far fewer risks than an unabated, uncontrolled, unpredictable arms race.

The United States, as the world knows, will never start a war. We do not want a war. We do not now expect a war. This generation of Americans has already had enough — more than enough — of war and hate and oppression. We shall be prepared if others wish it. We shall be alert to try to stop it. But we shall also do our part to build a world of peace where the weak are safe and the strong are just. We are not helpless before that task or hopeless of its success. Confident and unafraid, we labor on — not toward a strategy of annihilation but toward a strategy of peace.

4 **ROBERT STRAUSZ-HUPÉ AND WILLIAM R. KINTNER**
A Forward Strategy Beyond Survival

The greatness of a nation lies neither in the abundance of its possessions nor in the strength of its arms. A people finds greatness in its response to the historical challenge — by how it manages to harness it strivings to the aspirations of the age. Thus, to be great is to fulfill a promise that surpasses the national interest. Rome extended the lawful order of the city to the entire ancient world. Britain's victory over Napoleon opened an era of 100 years of peace and progress for all of mankind.

Robert Strausz-Hupé is Editor of *Orbis*, Director of the Foreign Policy Research Institute, and Professor of Political Science, University of Pennsylvania. William R. Kintner, Colonel U.S.A. (Ret.), is Deputy Director of the Foreign Policy Research Institute and Professor of Political Science, University of Pennsylvania. These excerpts are reprinted from *Orbis*, a quarterly journal of world affairs, published by the Foreign Policy Research Institute of the University of Pennsylvania, and are taken from an article with the same title which appeared in Vol. IV, No. 2 (Summer 1960) 141–158.

Rome and Britain attained, within the limits of the techniques of their day, predominant power — military, political and economic. Each wedded power to a noble idea of community. Greatness lies in the creative use of power and not in its denial.

Like Rome and Britain, each in her day, America stands at a turning point in history. The felt necessities of the times strain towards a new order. The decline and fall of old empires and the calamities of two world wars wrenched the state system of the nineteenth century — the century of peace and progress — from its moorings. The great problem of our times is to wrest a new order from disorder.

FORCES BEYOND

The United States is confronted by environmental changes which are perceptible now. Their consequences are, to some extent, predictable: Of the many forces spurring the world's systemic revolution, scientific-technological advance and the population increase are the most powerful. In the foreseeable future many states will be able to develop nuclear weapons and to exploit their possession for policy purposes which, while perhaps more limited than those of the U.S., Great Britain and the Soviet Union, may collectively and cumulatively alter the world political situation. The diffusion of nuclear military power will take place concurrently with a formidable increase in population pressure. More likely than not, the population explosion will prove to have shaped the history of this century more fatefully than any other event — more fatefully even than the release of atomic energy, the two world wars, the Bolshevik revolution and the exploration of space. . . .

The incipient, world-wide population crisis confronts the West with political, economic, social and military problems unprecedented in history — unprecedented in statistical magnitudes and geographical scope. As the increase of population presses upon the political order, governments will rely increasingly on force in order to maintain order. By sheer necessity, the state will assume ever greater powers over men's lives. At the limit, as in China, an entire society might seek to survive by total and permanent militarization. Population growth may so exacerbate social conflict that states will seek to "export" the domestic crisis and launch upon foreign wars. The population explosion could even trigger universal nuclear war.

The grave problems posed by the proliferation of nuclear power centers and the increase of population pressures will be aggravated by the birth of additional new nation states. The newcomers will press home their claims to an independent say in world politics. They will seek to acquire the instruments of power needed to enforce these claims. Thus the world is confronted with a series of problems that will call for ever closer administrative and purposive integration and cooperation. Yet the essentially divisive nature of the nation state system and the thrust of new nationalisms point towards a dramatic increase of political friction and conflict.

In all past ages, tendencies of this kind have led to social and international conflicts, revolutions and wars. Reduced to the simplest formula, American policy should seek to forestall a catastrophe which is now in the making and to promote a new international system which will accommodate technological acceleration (including the spread of nuclear power), increased world population, and the revolutionary aspirations of mankind.

THE COMMUNIST PATTERN OF CONQUEST

No blame attaches to the communists for the intrusion of nuclear weapons and population pressure into world politics. Neither the industrial-scientific revolution nor the political revolution that shakes the nation state system are of the communists' making. But the problems posed by these two permanent and universal revolutions are immensely complicated by the hostility of the communists to any and all forces of order which they do not control. The ideologies and social systems of the Free World and the communist bloc are locked in conflict over the new world order. This protracted conflict is global and of indefinite duration, multi-dimensional and dialectic.

As for guiding strategic concepts, the Western nations have up until now unsuccessfully pitted a narrow, primarily military strategy against a much broader, much more total strategy developed by Lenin and Stalin, Khrushchev and Mao. The spectrum of weapons employed by the communists is not confined to force, but brackets all possible relationships between states and social groups — ideological, political, economic, psychological, cultural, technological and military. Activities which Western peoples look upon as pursuits of peace, such as diplomacy, education, trade, cultural exchange and scientific research, are regarded by the communists as tools of strategy. The ability to beat plowshares into swords — a concept repellent to the Western mind — has characterized the communist movement ever since Lenin placed his indelible imprint upon it.

The communists have grasped more firmly than have we the meaning of time as a strategic fourth dimension. Whereas everything in our cultural tradition and our psychology prompts us to yearn for the decisive encounter ("to take up arms against a sea of troubles, and by opposing end them"), the communist strategists avoid skillfully decisive encounters until the achievement of final victory has become feasible. Convinced that time is on their side, they are quite content to eschew the frontal assault and calibrate their challenges to a calculus of intermediate risks until the supremacy of power has been gained and technological advantage has shifted overwhelmingly to their side. The indirect approach, at which they excel, is not difficult to practice in the nuclear-missile age, when both sides appear to recognize the risk of excessive military involvement, and in an international environment which furnishes abundant opportunities for exploiting troublesome crises. The communists have been able to carry the fight against the West through a variety of auxiliaries and proxies — local communist parties, satellite governments, partitioned states, neutrals, nationalists, anti-colonialist and pacifist movements, guerrilla armies, and sundry front organizations. Thus they have maintained a relentless pressure against the West without presenting that ultimate challenge — the *casus belli* — which historically proved indispensable to provoke Western nations into going to war against the major adversary.

THE BASIC EQUATION

Protracted conflict is a generic term describing a world situation in which two power blocs are fighting each other over a long period of time in order to achieve global supremacy. The strategy of protracted conflict aims at conclusive victory by increments of subsidiary wars and non-violent campaigns. Yet, total war is an element within protracted conflict. It is more than just the most massive among the individual instruments of protracted conflict strategy. It is potentially the one that brings the over-all conflict to a climax. Even if a total war will never be fought, the necessities and risks of total nuclear war influence and, in many instances, determine the various alternative strategies. . . .

Protracted and *contracted* conflict — total war — are dialectically related to one another. This dialectic relationship may be expressed in the following propositions:

1. For the first time in history there exist weapons permitting a technologically well-equipped super-power to conquer the entire world.

The master method of world conquest is a surprise attack utilizing nuclear explosives of high yield designed to destroy the competing super-power's military force. The attacker must, however, succeed in reaching the objective of annihilating or neutralizing the defender's strategic nuclear forces *without sacrificing, in the process, his own nuclear strength and the basis of his military power.* If he solves this task, he has achieved military supremacy and, since his weapon systems have global range, he can impose his political law over the entire globe. This potentiality is inherent in nuclear explosives and global range delivery systems and constitutes a fundamentally new development in world affairs.

2. *As technology progresses, more and more weapon systems, i.e. delivery systems and nuclear applications, are coming into existence,* widening the strategic choices of a would-be world conqueror.

3. Nuclear weapons and global delivery systems were invented after Mao Tse-tung had formulated the doctrine of protracted conflict. Although the new technology is entirely in line with the notions of Marx and Engels, who envisaged the world revolution as taking place in one fell swoop, it does not invalidate Mao's concept. *The techniques of protracted conflict are designed either to prepare for the climax of the decisive battle, or to render this battle altogether superfluous.*

4. It is most unlikely that the United States can be eliminated as a major factor of world politics by means short of total military annihilation. This is not to say that the United States cannot be weakened by psychological, economic and limited military means; that continuous expansion of the communist empire would not undermine American capabilities and will to resist; and that a communist seizure of Europe and Asia would not place the United States in a position so untenable that it must give up or fight a war of desperation — assuming that, were all these things to come to pass, the domestic situation in the United States would not undergo a radical change.

Actually, such an assumption is untenable: in all likelihood a catastrophic deterioration of the American power position either would bring to power the partisans of appeasement and surrender, or, conversely, American policies would veer towards stronger resistance and even preventive war before the point of no return had been reached. *Precisely because of the devastating power of nuclear weapons and because the United States continues to be the major nuclear power besides the Soviet Union, a reversal of strategy remains possible almost to the last minute.* Even at a moment when the United States faces defeat because, for example, Europe and Asia and Africa have fallen, a sudden nuclear attack against the Soviet Union could turn the trend of defeat or at least avenge the disaster and deprive the opponent of the ultimate triumph. . . . This potentiality acts as a deterrent upon a strategy of world conquest through limited war.

5. It is for this very reason that the communists cannot rely exclusively on a strategy of piecemeal expansion. Precisely if and when the strategy of protracted conflict is about to triumph, the communists must seek to crush American retaliatory power. The communists could not stop short, in prudence, of the total destruction of American power even if a fellow travelling faction were to seize the ruins of American government. . . . (A communist strategy of world conquest would be made increasingly difficult by the spreading of nuclear weapons, for the proliferation of nuclear powers not only complicates the problems of piecemeal conquest and increases the danger of American intervention, but also compels the Soviets to take on, in the last phase of the conflict, all those nuclear forces which may exist in addition to those of the United States.)

6. *Under modern conditions, the significance of what could be called technological positions has become overwhelming.* . . . This does not mean that geographical-positional strategy must now yield its historic place to a new Strategy of Means. It is necessary, however, to recognize clearly the characteristics of a conflict based on technology and nuclear weapons, and to analyze the conflict as a *whole*.

7. In foreign policy, the American people have not infrequently displayed a somewhat excessive fondness of Utopian solutions. Yet, most of the time, they have managed to conduct their foreign affairs soberly and realistically. Consequently, *neither Americans nor communists can assume that, as the conflict progresses, all the initiatives will remain in communist hands.* In fact, they never did. The military weakness of the United States is a derivative only — or almost only — of its decision not to strike the first nuclear blow. But, were there no practical alternatives left and were communist aggression to render a pre-emptive retaliatory American strike both morally defensible and militarily unavoidable, American military power would increase — and increase suddenly — by several magnitudes by virtue of this one decision alone. . . .

8. Another hazard besets the dogmatic application of the protracted conflict techniques and, specifically, the strategies of limited war. *Each communist success, and especially each territorial conquest, brings*

ROBERT STRAUSZ-HUPÉ AND WILLIAM R. KINTNER

with it the risk of a strong American reaction, including the quickening of arms preparation in general and the acceleration of weapons programs suitable to balance or partly compensate for the loss suffered in particular. From the communist point of view, this danger must be added to that of retaliation. To put it differently, a minor success by piecemeal conquest would render more difficult a victory in the *decisive* battle.

9. A strategy of limited wars is an opportunistic strategy. It is a strategy designed to take advantage of windfalls. It is not a strategy of world conquests — unless it so weakens the will-to-resist of the opponent that he lays down his arms for total war. Each war between minor nations or, for that matter, each revolution requires policy decisions by the great powers including, possibly, intervention. Thus an aggressive state such as the Soviet Union may, because of accidents and prestige consideration, trigger or intervene in limited wars. Yet, from the point of view of a strategy aiming at ultimate decisive victory, such actions may not always be expeditious.

10. A sequence of limited wars might precede the transition from the strategy of protracted conflict to that of total war under the following conditions: a diversion is intended; or a specific limited operation is launched as a curtain raiser to the main event — either as a test of strength, or as a provocation, or as a stratagem designed to facilitate pre-emption. Precisely because of these interrelationships between limited and total war, lack of U.S. and Free World capabilities for limited war jeopardizes our *total* war posture.

11. Changes in force relationships, as they bear on total nuclear conflict, bear directly and significantly on protracted conflict strategy. For example, the initial penetrations into space did not upset the military balance. Certainly, their significance in terms of limited war was negligible. These penetrations constituted, however, a major change in the over-all balance inasmuch as they altered the psychological climate, disclosed technological capabilities and opened new fronts of conflict. Hence the importance of space, in terms of the protracted conflict, has been immense and will continue to grow. . . .

12. *A thermonuclear exchange would be the climactic phase of the protracted conflict.* This phase is fraught with prohibitive risks so long as the defender is strong, vigilant, resolute and capable of retaliating with devastating force. Consequently, as a preliminary to contracted conflict, it is necessary to use the means, especially the non-violent means, of protracted conflict strategy designed to reduce the defender's

force levels and technological strength, to weaken his warning and recuperation systems, and, above all, to undermine his will to resist so that in the end total nuclear war need not be waged physically, but can be won psychologically through the inducement of surrender.

13. Protracted conflict, possibly including limited war, would serve to carry on the struggle despite mutual deterrence. Its purpose would be to change the "nuclear stalemate" in favor of one or the other competitor. In such a situation, there is a good chance that limited conflict would remain limited, unless one or the other of the two camps is willing to risk enlargement of the contest. By the same token, however, gains would remain limited. . . .

"Stalemate" is a fundamentally erroneous description of the nuclear equation. It does not allow for the importance of delivery and interception systems, and, above all, the dynamic character of the race between military capabilities and vulnerabilities in which the "balance" can be upset *at any moment*. The situation is in constant flux, and basic shifts in technology, force levels and moral climate may terminate abruptly a situation of apparent stalemate or, in turn, may change the quasi-stalemate to such a degree that the would-be aggressor finds it advisable to attack.

Hence, the various techniques of protracted conflict are not quite as much a substitute for a war which cannot take place because of a hypothetical stalemate, but are the chief effort designed to change the strategic balance in such a way that either the aggressor can risk the plunge or, conversely, that the defender succeeds in maintaining the power to deter the would-be aggressor.

14. *Protracted conflict serves to create the conditions in which the aggressor can risk the attack or issue the ultimatum for surrender, without exposing his own power base to devastation and destruction.* Obviously, these efforts must be combined with direct preparations for the central war. But protracted conflict methods will serve to train and utilize insurgent and revolutionary forces in the target country to seize power and install a new government willing to do business with the victor. Precisely because, under modern technological conditions, the physical occupation of the United States by Soviet ground forces, or vice versa, will continue to be extremely difficult if not impossible, the nuclear strike must be followed by political conquest or revolution. In this sense, therefore, protracted conflict is one of the indispensable prerequisites for "contracted" war.

15. Given the unpredictable vagaries of political life, technological

breakthroughs and other contingent events, it is entirely possible that, at one time or another, a unique opportunity may present itself for waging total nuclear war under optimum conditions for the aggressor. . . . Given an extraordinary opportunity, a would-be world conqueror obviously would be stupid if he did not take advantage of it and terminate the struggle once and for all on his terms, rather than continue indefinitely with protracted conflict methods which probably never would present him with a chance as favorable as the one he allowed to pass.

In sum, it is in the very nature of the nuclear era that its most important battles may not be fought in the form of exchanges of fire power, but like the conflicts of the sixteenth and seventeenth centuries consist largely of diverse maneuvers designed to achieve a decisive advantage or to prevent the opponent from gaining such a decisive advantage.

It has been argued, fallaciously, that since in all likelihood the conflict will continue as a protracted conflict, to be fought mostly by limited methods of conflict, most of our efforts and appropriations should be devoted to this type of struggle. The above discussion has shown that this is a fallacy inasmuch as the probability of the continuation of protracted conflict is a *function of the United States efforts designed to preclude a nuclear surprise attack.*

It has been argued, no less fallaciously, that concentration upon efforts designed to preclude a surprise attack upon the United States will provide not only the necessary but also the sufficient basis of our national security and that the strategy of protracted conflict is but the icing of the national security cake. . . .

On the first glance, the problem, or rather paradox, appears to defy a rational solution. Yet it becomes manageable once we conceive of protracted and contracted conflict as the two prongs of *one* strategy — the strategy of conflict as an organic whole.

There is no reason, subjective or objective, why the United States cannot develop and pursue a unified strategy of its own — run the race for technological supremacy and at least maintain the nuclear balance, *and,* at the same time, press for the transformation of the societies under communist rule. Both tasks are intimately linked to the mandate of the systematic revolution: the unification of the globe. The communists are prepared to execute this mandate; their doctrine tells them what the new order should be and how to create it. The American people, by force of circumstance, must seek to make the settlement of the twentieth century systemic revolution *their* mission, for only thus can they create the universal order that ensures the survival of American society — an open society — rather than as a hive of human beings, objects of a sociological experiment designed by the rulers of a closed society. The alternatives are stark — as stark as the strategic confrontation. . . .

THE ISSUES AT STAKE

The real issues at stake between the West and the communist bloc are more complicated than Premier Khrushchev would have us believe. If the struggle were in fact merely a clash between two economic systems, then its solution would be infinitely easier than it is. When we say that Soviet society must undergo a change, we do not refer to a change in its economic organization or method. A free, capitalist system can co-exist with a planned, socialist one. This has been amply demonstrated within the West itself, where diverse economic systems not only co-exist but cooperate intimately.

The real issue is not economic but political — totalitarianism versus the open, liberal, democratic society, and the approaches adopted by each in its relations with other states. Different political systems can exist side by side, but not when one system is aggressive, geared to conflict, and bent upon conquest. The nature of the Soviet system exacerbates the problem of arriving at a settlement, because the communists can appear to renounce aggression for a few years in order to lull the West to sleep. In short, the communist system itself is the most disturbing and dangerous source of world tensions.

The Soviet system, irrespective of its domestic popularity, is not a legitimate, constitutional government in the Western sense of the term. Its concept of treaty obligations is based on entirely different assumptions from those which underlie the Western legalist approach to international relations. So long as the succession of leadership power in the Soviet Union continues to hinge upon the crudest type of conspiratorial politics within the party hierarchy, the United States cannot enter into any agreement with the Soviets which might lead to a weakening of the American military posture. Even conceding for the sake of the argument that one communist leader or dominant faction may earnestly desire peace with the West on mutually beneficial terms, there is no way of knowing what will be the attitude of their successors. A totalitarian system is capable of rapid reversals of policy. Its political leadtime problems are much less formidable than those of democratic societies, where basic policy shifts occur very slowly and only after a great deal of governmental debate and public discussion.

If our analysis has any validity, then it should be profitable for us to examine the emerging world picture from that unified viewpoint and suggest the outlines of a forward United States strategy to counter the communist conflict pattern. Perhaps in this way we can put ourselves on guard against the possibility that some of the policies which we are now tempted to espouse may play into the Soviets' hands and contribute to the further success of their strategy. Such an analysis might also enable us to discern the broad outlines of what our policies — both functional and regional — should be in the years ahead. It could furnish some valuable criteria by which the appropriateness and consistency of actual U.S. policies and programs might be measured in terms of basic Free World goals.

America has the men and the tools wherewith to fashion the instruments of victory. American society — the open society — has brought forth an idea of order and a style of life that appeal to many peoples. America has loyal allies. The question is thus not one of means or ideas or friends. Specifically, the question is as to whether the people of the U.S. can shake off that chronic apathy which seems to afflict all Western democratic peoples when they think themselves at peace while in fact the aggressor moves stealthily to destroy them. . . .

We can design the positive policies that will render impregnable the position of the West and place the communists on the defensive; but these policies and the concomitant means must be devised now. The task of rallying the scattered forces of the West is difficult because we have suffered defeats, and, for a while at least, some of these cannot be reversed. Fortunately, we have all the building blocks we need to devise a strategy that aims at turning lost battles into a victorious campaign.

FREEDOM AND POWER

It would be comforting to believe that all of the social and economic, the human and ethical problems posed by the technological-scientific revolution can be solved rationally and humanely. It would be comforting to believe that we have the time, two or three generations at least, to put the affairs of mankind in order, so that by the year 2000, let us say, the most dangerous cliffs of readjustment have been rounded and orderly, peaceable progress will henceforth be assured.

Unfortunately, what stands between us and this pleasant vista is the power struggle which the communists have imposed on us. The require- ment of foreign policy is to assert authority, to enhance prestige, to stand firm, to face down threats, to take risks, to stand by one's friends, to punish one's enemies, and, whenever pursuing these tasks calls for the use of force, to use force. The singlemindedness and intransigence of the communist bid for world power leaves us no other choice but to think soberly about force and to accept the ever present contingency that force will be used against us and that we will have to counter it in kind. Our essentially "other-directed" foreign policy has not only failed to alter the international equation in our favor, but has also managed to deceive our own people about the grim, the true nature of the struggle.

Compassion and generosity are not alternatives for resolution in taking the risks and bearing the sacrifices with which the use of power is fraught. If men of good will, when they confront the challenge of the aggressor, shirk the use of power, they court not only their own defeat but also the defeat of those humane causes which they seek to further. The issue before us is not the future of mankind in some ideal state of harmony, but how to assure mankind a future under freedom. The communists charge that the cry for freedom is merely a pretense; that democracy itself is a form of special privileges; that the democratic nations, having acquired by force a major portion of the world's wealth, and having set up a controlling power over the world, have used that power to exploit other peoples for their own advantage, and are now fighting to retain these superior benefits.

Communist rule is government by power above any law, human or divine. No man living under communism can enjoy freedom. But gov- ernment is legitimate and genuine only so far as its ruling end is the protection of human freedom. Foremost in the mind of every legitimate ruler must be the desire to protect the freedom of those whom he governs. For the sake of this end he must continually restrain his own will and subordinate it to the rule of law. Hence, if we are to assure the future of mankind morally, we must break communist power.

To do this we might pursue alternative strategies. The question might well be as to whether we should strive to root out communist power where it now holds sway, or contain it in such a way that it can no longer wreak evil upon the Free World. Whichever of the two strategies we adopt, however, neither can be carried farther than the reach of our power. They can each be pursued by many different means, but chief among them is our willingness and capability to use force whenever the nature of the communist challenge leaves us no other choice. It is necessary to speak clearly on the use of power. Our friends must be certain that we will not desert them in the hour of supreme test. If that certainty is not given we will have no friends. Then all talk about American leadership is mere exercise in rhetoric. Then we will not be able to lead in building the community of freedom that will stand as the true monument of our greatness.

As the systemic revolution approaches its climax, both the communists and we are faced with imperatives: to grasp the meaning of conflict in the nuclear age and to master the forces of systemic change. The communists, informed by a theory of history and armed with their doctrine of protracted conflict, have integrated nuclear weapons into a comprehensive strategy of world conquest. The United States cannot let the decision go to Sino-Soviet leadership by intellectual and moral default. The United States, on its part, must design a forward strategy that accords with the logic of the systemic revolution and the dynamics of nuclear power. The leadtime of survival is short.

Developing the Third World

5 MAX F. MILLIKAN AND DONALD L. M. BLACKMER
The Third Choice

[All the societies we refer to as underdeveloped are passing through a process of highly complex social, political, and economic change.] . . . The complexity results partly from the fact that modernization involves interaction among psychological, political, social, economic, and cultural factors and partly from the fact that the histories, traditions, resources, and values of the various countries of the underdeveloped world are very different. The process of continuous interaction among so many variables in so many different circumstances would be impos-

Max F. Millikan is Professor of Economics and Director of the Center for International Studies, Massachusetts Institute of Technology. Donald L. M. Blackmer is Assistant Director of the Center for International Studies and Assistant Professor of Political Science at the Massachusetts Institute of Technology. These excerpts, from Max F. Millikan and Donald L. M. Blackmer, Eds., *The Emerging Nations: Their Growth and United States Policy* (Boston: Little, Brown, 1961) pp. 93–102, are reprinted by permission.

sible to trace and to describe with precision even if all the variables could be described in mathematical terms and each assigned a firm statistical weight. Obviously, in dealing with men and societies, neither the qualitative relations nor the quantities can be firmly and unambiguously established.

Nonetheless, sufficient common elements can be discerned to allow some generalizations about the American and free-world interest in the forms taken by the transition process in the modernizing nations and to permit the identification of some broad guidelines for policy toward those nations. As with any simplification of highly complex phenomena, such generalizations will do violence to some of the characteristics of each case. However, although in designing specific policies it is essential that the unique features of each country be taken fully into account, there is need as well for an overview to guide the philosophy and general direction of policy. To provide such a perspective is the purpose of this chapter.

Perhaps the most pervasive element in the modernization process is the profound and progressive widening of men's perceptions of the realistic alternatives open to them, sometimes referred to as the revolution of rising expectations. Too frequently the term has been used as if it referred exclusively to expectations in the economic sense, to newly perceived possibilities of consumption and standards of living which in traditional societies men would have regarded as wholly unattainable. Such new perceptions do indeed exist, but there are also more profound and far-reaching changes in men's views of the world and of the individual's place in it. Men begin seriously to contemplate new values, new forms of political organization, new kinds of careers, new access to knowledge, new relations with those who have traditionally been their superiors, their inferiors, and their peers. They perceive new patterns of social organization, new possibilities of movement, new kinds of leisure.

The pace varies, but this widening of perceived alternatives is universal and inevitable. Three forces tend to start it and keep it moving: widened contact and communication with more modern societies, the rise of trade and of cities, and the emergence of new generations born into a world where modern activity is increasingly a fact of life rather than a perceived break with the past. The widening of perceptions occurs first among a limited element of the elite of the society, especially those exposed through education, government, or commerce to life outside the traditional society. It gradually spreads to wider segments of the population until it becomes a popular rather than an elite phenomenon; and today there is almost no backward segment of the most traditional society which has not been to some degree touched by this process, though its more massive consequences still lie ahead.

The movement toward modernization sets up many opposing political, economic, and social currents within traditional societies. . . .

On the one hand, the process of modernization is profoundly disturbing to all those deeply committed to the traditional society. They may fear that it will deprive them of the power, respect, affection, income, or security afforded them by the traditional way of life. Moreover, the traditional leadership may see the new aspirations as imposing on them responsibility for new kinds of activity which they have neither the resources nor the skills to carry out successfully. They are likely to pay lip service to modernization in recognition of its attractions to others, but, especially if they feel that they cannot effectively promote it without danger to their own position and interests, they are likely to attempt to divert attention from it by stirring up other issues and to repress its advocates.

On the other hand, those growing groups to whom modernization is attractive will be seeking with mounting insistence for ways to promote it. The forms their pressure for modernization takes will depend on how rapidly and how effectively the sectors of society with which they are most intimately concerned appear to be moving in the right directions. If existing institutions appear to be pliable enough, if change is being fostered with some competence, and especially if those with new aspirations are themselves being given opportunities to participate actively in the modernization process, they may accept gradual evolution as a tolerable path toward their new goals. But if their aspirations are being frustrated, if the leadership is rigidly traditional, or incompetent, or opposed to change, and if the new aspirants are being given no role to play in building a new society, they may well conclude that their aims can be advanced only by violent overthrow of the whole existing structure. In such circumstances extremist philosophies like communism, arguing that violent revolution followed by authoritarian control is the only route to modernization, will have great appeal.

That such a sequence of events is a real possibility is suggested in varying degrees by the recent histories of Cuba, Egypt, and Iraq. Each country was ruled for a substantial period by a repressive government whose power was based on landowners and other conservative elements linked to the traditional society. The regimes of Batista in

58837

Cuba, Farouk in Egypt, and Nuri Said in Iraq thus generated in time revolutionary reactions directed simultaneously against the powerful classes in the society and against the agricultural and commercial interests which, in association with foreign influence, dominated the domestic scene. But these and other revolutionary movements have themselves often been transformed into regimes as authoritarian as those they have struggled to displace. Why should this so often have been the case?

Much of the answer lies in the fact that the old regimes had harshly suppressed moderate reform movements, killing their leaders or driving them into hiding, exile, or passivity. Such repression gradually convinces the mass of the people that they can place no hope in moderate movements for reform. Increasingly they may tend to find emotional satisfaction in nothing less than extreme and violent opposition to their rulers, in following fanatically a leader who promises to deliver them from oppression. A revolutionary movement, moreover, tends to develop an authoritarian dynamic of its own. If it is to succeed in such conspiratorial circumstances, it must often develop a highly disciplined and hierarchical style of organization which may influence the structure of its rule over the country once the revolution has taken place. In addition, a repressive framework of political activity tends to draw into underground revolutionary activity individuals who themselves are characterized by one type of authoritarian personality. One common trait of this type of personality appears to be a tendency to see a mortal threat in any rival power and to feel safe only when possessing undisputed supreme power, or when following a leader with such power. Such personality types seek to make their way to positions in which there is no competing authority, and the governments they set up in the name of liberty tend, in a familiar historical pattern, to be authoritarian ones.

But this is only one of many possible patterns. The essential point is that the course which each underdeveloped society takes will depend heavily on the realistic choices which various influential members of the society see as open to them.

One possibility is likely to be seen as the preservation of many features of traditional society, the maintenance of the existing hierarchy by repression if necessary, the destruction of forces promoting change, and perhaps the diversion of dissatisfaction through external adventure. Another will certainly be perceived by some as the radical destruction by extremist measures, probably involving violence, of the whole political, social, and economic fabric of the traditional society and its replacement by something entirely different.

If both traditionalists and modernizers view these two choices as the only ones open to them, tension and conflict are almost inevitable, and the prospect for modernization under democratic forms of consent is remote. Those in power, having everything to lose by revolution, become increasingly obsessed with devices to retain and solidify their power in the face of the mounting pressures for change. Because the sheer maintenance of authority absorbs their energies, they are unable to devote consistent attention to modernization even when they accept its desirability. In the long run they are doomed because time steadily swells the ranks of the opposition. Those who are discontented, with a decreasing stake in the existing order and nothing to lose from its overthrow, focus increasingly on the revolutionary discipline necessary for an attempt to seize power and decreasingly on how to use it constructively once they have it. If they do acquire power, they take over a society which is demanding modernization but which has few of the required institutions, skills, or resources. In these circumstances the dispersion of decision-making and initiative so essential to democratic modernization is too dangerous to the new leadership, and they either retain power by the same techniques by which they acquired it or are forced to yield to yet another revolutionary group.

But these two choices, fortunately, are not the only ones men perceive. There are almost always some traditionalists and some modernizers who, with varying degrees of clarity and hope, perceive a third choice — the gradual modification of the institutions, practices, and structure of the traditional society in the direction of modernization while retaining some of its traditional cohesive features.

The third choice is also a conditional one. If progress is too slow, if opportunities to participate in promoting it are too limited, if existing institutions cannot adapt in time, there will be widespread frustration and disenchantment with this alternative. On the other hand, if the forms of modernization are adopted more rapidly than they can be made to function effectively, then traditional values, institutions, and gratifications will be destroyed before modern substitutes have been developed, and again the third choice will be unacceptable. The extent to which this evolutionary choice continues to be regarded as attractive and realistic by major segments of the society depends upon the rate at which effective modernization occurs in each segment as compared to the rate at which aspirations there are changing.

MAX F. MILLIKAN AND DONALD L. M. BLACKMER   *101*

This summary review of the major alternatives perceived by men in transitional societies can be related to the interests of the United States and the rest of the free world in the evolution of the underdeveloped nations. From this perspective, our overall objective can be described as an effort to maximize the attractiveness and feasibility of the third choice: to help make the evolution to modernization successful enough that major groups will not struggle either to repress change entirely or to promote it by ruthless and extremist measures.

These general objectives can be viewed from the perspective of each of the interacting psychological, political, economic, and social forces of modernization.

In a psychological context the fundamental interest is that the peoples of the underdeveloped countries perceive constructive alternatives both to regressive clinging to old values and to radical overthrow of those values and an ill-considered and desperate rush to totally new ones. The danger is that the old gratifications will lose their stabilizing appeal before new ones have been developed to take their place. As the old ties weaken, men must be offered opportunities to shape a new identity and a new image of a meaningful life in the performance of new and constructive functions. Throughout the society opportunities must be created for individuals to find political, economic, and social roles in aspects of modernization which give them a psychological stake in its continued success.

Politically the guiding interest is that chaos, tensions, and failure do not lead people to accept a repressive concentration of power in the hands either of a traditional elite or of a revolutionary dictatorship. This means that as increasing numbers of people become politically conscious they must see opportunities to exert some influence on the political process and on the decisions that affect their lives. This condition cannot be assured merely by the imposition of democratic forms. Indeed, in societies with little experience of decentralized authority and little consensus on national goals, too rapid a delegation of power is a sure route back to repressive authoritarianism. Where traditionally the individual has had little opportunity to shape his own destiny, the third choice requires the development of a wide range of activities that bring home to each group a sense of its responsibility for building its own future in the context of a wider loyalty to the society as a whole. For constructive political evolution to occur, these new activities must touch all aspects of life, not only politics. Public and private institutions of all sorts must be established to provide a framework within which these activities can take place.

Our objective can also be considered from the standpoint of social structure. In the early stages of modernization the perception of both the possibilities and the dangers of modernization are likely to be found mainly in small elite groups — the traditional feudal or tribal leaders, the military, the initially small but growing urban commercial and business class, the landowners, and the intelligentsia. As the process takes on momentum and the perception of new alternatives spreads through the society, new groups become important — the peasantry, urban labor, the new student class. If evolution is to proceed in an orderly fashion, each of these groups must come to perceive the practicality and attractiveness of the third choice.

Finally, there is the economic dimension. If the economy does not move forward, the prospects for progress in other areas will not appear bright. Economic progress must be regarded both as a result of a movement toward modernization on other fronts and as a force making for further change. Economic progress needs, for example, a minimum group of modern men in the society before it can begin; and the expansion of modern economic activities itself trains more such essential men. Similarly, a certain degree of effective central direction is required before economic progress can get well under way; and a central government gains in efficiency, authority, and stability by the very act of taking effective lendership in economic development. Economic progress requires a dispersion of initiative and decision-making to a growing number of groups throughout the society; and economic progress itself creates new kinds of professionals, new urban technicians, new initiatives among the peasantry, new attitudes toward saving, and a new mobilization of capital resources for productive purposes. Economic progress itself also generates both the new attitudes and the new resources which permit such progress to continue. Finally, the phase of take-off, if successful, not only consolidates the capacity of the society to grow regularly but also tends to consolidate the political, social, and psychological benefits of modernization.

Thus the problem of making the evolutionary third-choice alternative seem both real and attractive is one with many facets. It is useful to look at it from the varied perspectives of the psychologist, the political scientist, the sociologist, and the economist; but it is one problem, not four. If action from the outside is to influence the choice, those wielding the various instruments of international policy must see the problem in these terms and see it whole, since each instrument affects the whole course of a society's evolution.

By way of summary, we may refer to the [following] four objectives . . . as representing the basic American interests in the transitional process.

First, the emerging nations must be able to maintain their independence, especially of powers hostile or potentially hostile to the United States. We have noted that if the third choice appears unlikely to effect progress toward meeting the goals of important groups, conflict is almost certain to result between regressive forces of tradition and groups that see their only hope in the violent overthrow of these forces. The former may triumph for a time, but cannot do so indefinitely. The latter will not hesitate to seek support where they can find it, notably from powerful countries which themselves have an interest in instability and in the overthrow of "bourgeois" regimes. In this period of history the Communist powers are more than eager to assist revolutionary movements, at the price of subservience to their own broader international goals.

The second interest is in the emergence of states that do not resort to violence in their external relations. Traditionalist leaders, unwilling or unable to contain disaffection by promoting internal change, have historically tended to engage in external adventure as a distraction. New revolutionary dictatorships likewise, unable to cope effectively with the popular demands they have helped to stimulate, have a similar motive for aggression. Although modernization does not by any means eliminate the possibility of an aggressive external policy, it does lower the probability of erratic and irresponsible adventurism in foreign affairs.

Third, it is in the American interest to see the emerging states maintain effective and orderly governments without resort to totalitarian controls. Regimes, whether traditional or revolutionary, which cannot at least partially satisfy the rising demands for modernization on the part of all important groups can maintain order only by increasingly repressive measures. It is a necessary condition for attaining the other objectives, therefore, that the developing societies be capable of progressively meeting the aspirations of their people.

Fourth is the interest in seeing states emerge which accept the principles of an open society and which are willing to cooperate in international economic, political, and social control measures. Neither of these conditions is likely to be met by a dictatorship, regressive or revolutionary, which has confidence neither in the loyalty of its own people nor in its own capacity to deal with either external or internal forces. Evolutionary and balanced progress toward modernization will not assure behavior in the American interest, but it is a necessary condition for such behavior. ...

6 EDWARD C. BANFIELD
Foreign Aid Doctrines

Technical assistance and capital grants and loans to underdeveloped countries for non-military purposes ("foreign aid" or "aid") have in the last decade become a conspicuous feature of our foreign policy. In comparison with the total of defense spending the amount of aid has not been large (roughly 3 per cent for the decade), and in comparison with Gross National Product it has been very small (less than 1 per cent). But aid is nevertheless coming to be regarded as a principal instrument of our foreign policy. The use of it to supplement, and in some degree to substitute for, the traditional means of diplomacy is to be explained in part by the impracticability of using force or threats of force under the conditions that now prevail. Many people, however, believe it is in general a better way of achieving our objectives. In their widely read and influential book, *A Proposal,* Max F. Millikan and W. W. Rostow, for example, say that "we have put relatively too much emphasis in recent years on pacts, treaties, negotiations and international diplomacy and too little on measures to promote the evolution of stable, effective and democratic societies abroad," and they emphasize this by subtitling their book "Key to an Effective Foreign Policy."

Most of those who write about aid justify it mainly or ultimately, but usually not solely, on the ground that it will contribute to national security. This position is based on one or the other of two largely incompatible doctrines. One, which will be called the doctrine of indirect influence, asserts that national security will be promoted by using aid to transform fundamentally the cultures and institutions of the

Dr. Edward C. Banfield is Professor of Government, Harvard University, and a member of the Joint Center for Urban Studies of Massachusetts Institute of Technology. These excerpts, from a chapter with the same title, are taken from *Conservative Papers,* pp. 77–95. Copyright © 1964 by Ralph de Toledano and Karl Hess. Reprinted by permission of Doubleday & Company, Inc.

recipient countries. The other, which will be called the doctrine of direct influence, takes the cultures and institutions of the recipient countries as given and seeks to achieve the purpose (promotion of national security) by bringing influence to bear directly either upon the governments of the countries concerned or upon their public opinions.

A widely accepted doctrine asserts that foreign aid may serve the vital interests of the United States by setting off or bringing about fundamental changes in the outlook and institutions of the recipient societies and that these changes will lead to others — especially the spread of freedom and democracy — that will promote peace and thus indirectly serve our ultimate purpose, which is to increase our national security.

One school of thought emphasizes economic effects. A marked rise in average income will change profoundly the outlook of the masses of the people in underdeveloped countries. People who have enough to eat and something to look forward to will be much less receptive to Communist and other extremist appeals. Prosperity and opportunity will engender a taste for democracy and peace as, presumably, they have in our own society. The one great need, therefore, is to bring about rapid economic development. All the other effects that are desired will follow automatically.

On this theory, aid should be distributed among countries solely on the basis of their ability to use it to increase incomes. In principle, Russia and China might be given the highest priorities.

Another school of thought, represented principally by Millikan and Rostow, says that increases in income will not of themselves produce the desired effects (freedom, stability, democracy, and peace). To be sure, "some" economic improvement is a necessary condition for achieving these effects. But Millikan and Rostow are severely critical of the "crude materialist" thesis that economic development will of itself either reduce revolutionary pressures or lead to orderly political development. They regard it as a serious misconception to think that the spirit of revolt spreads easily among people who are chronically destitute or that the mere creation of wealth can satisfy a people's expectations. In their view, aid is important principally because it will set off social, political, and psychological changes that will energize the society.

Since they insist that the desired effects can only be secured through certain social, political, and psychological changes, Millikan and Rostow might be expected to make suggestions for using aid to bring about these changes. They do not. All of their recommendations would be congenial to a "crude materialist."

They refer to the purpose of aid as "economic development" and make recommendations that are all directed toward purely economic goals and that have little or no relation to (indeed, are probably somewhat in conflict with) the goal of setting off social, political, and psychological changes. For example, the key recommendation is that the distribution of aid "be determined by absorptive capacity rather than by considerations of equity or politics."

Millikan and Rostow, then, not only say nothing about how the changes they regard as crucial are to be brought about, but, by laying out a program which looks entirely to economic objectives, they implicitly contradict the main point of their analysis.

All who hold the doctrine of indirect influence agree that a significant (Millikan and Rostow say "some") improvement in levels of living is necessary to secure the effects that are ultimately desired. "Crude materialists" believe that the greater the improvement the more marked these secondary effects will be. To the extent that there is reason to believe improvements will not take place, confidence in these doctrines must be weakened.

The improvement that is necessary is in the income of the ordinary man, not in aggregate income. A large increase in aggregate income could leave most people in the society worse off than before if, for example, population grew faster than income or if the growth in income was accompanied by an increased concentration of income in the hands of a small elite or was siphoned off for military or other governmental purposes that did not raise standards of life. In order to bring about the necessary improvement in levels of living, therefore, a proper equilibrium must be achieved among three variables: the productivity of the economy, the size of the population, and the evenness with which income is distributed. Conceivably a satisfactory relationship among these variables might be secured by changing only one of them; in the usual case, however, it will be essential to change them all.

In most of the underdeveloped areas aggregate income has been increasing in recent decades. These gains, however, are being nearly offset, and in some cases more than offset, by growth of population. The rate of population growth is in most places enough to absorb the increase in aggregate income that will result from normal saving. Although their incomes are rising, the underdeveloped countries, with some exceptions, are not increasing their per capita food supply.

EDWARD C. BANFIELD   *107*

Estimates by Professor P. N. Rosenstein-Rodan on very optimistic assumptions (e.g., that the underdeveloped countries will get all the aid they can absorb and that they will make reasonably good use of it) indicate that from 1961 to 1976 gross national product in the under-developed parts of the world may rise from an average of $140 to $192 per capita. Whether an increase of this magnitude would suffice to change the political outlook of the underdeveloped countries decidedly is, of course, anyone's guess.

If the aid doctrine requires not merely *some* improvement in levels of living but the "modernization" of the economy, the outlook is even more discouraging. That aggregate and in some cases per capita in-comes in these countries have been growing in recent years does not mean that they will continue to do so. The growth that has occurred so far may be in the nature of "taking up slack"; additional growth may be impossible without basic changes within the societies — changes that will not occur. . . .

Even those underdeveloped countries which are not primitive may lack certain cultural or other prerequisites of development. One such prerequisite is the presence in the society of at least a small class of persons having talents and incentives that lead them to organize, in-novate, and take risks. Other prerequisites are traits which must prob-ably be fairly widespread in order for such a class to arise, or to function effectively if it does arise. These include the desire for material improvement, the belief that economic activity is worthy of respect, willingness to concert activity for common purposes or at least to allow others to concert it without interference, and ability to maintain at least that minimum of political stability that is essential in order for the government to carry out certain critical tasks.

These and other prerequisites are not all present in any of the under-developed areas.

Such factors are in general more important obstacles to development than are lack of technical knowledge or of foreign capital. If cultural and other conditions favor development, it will occur without aid. (Japan and Russia, to cite recent cases, did in fact develop without it.) If cultural conditions do not favor development, no amount of aid will bring it about. (Haiti, for example, has received large amounts of both technical assistance and foreign capital without development taking place.) *Probably no country is so poor that it cannot accumulate capital, Simon Kuznets has written, and the Western world could not if it tried prevent the wholesale borrowing of its technical knowledge by under-developed countries able to make use of it.*

American aid doctrine certainly exaggerates greatly the importance of both technical assistance and foreign capital in the development process. Only in the most backward countries can either kind of aid make a crucial difference, or perhaps even an important one. In the nature of the case, the greater the need of a country for aid, the less evidence there is that it has a capability to develop. The most prosperous and promising of the underdeveloped countries — Mexico, for example — may not require any aid in order to grow at a satisfactory rate. There is, to be sure, an important middle group of countries — India is a conspicuous example — which can absorb large amounts of aid and which offer some promise of developing. In time, too, some of the most backward countries may be brought by aid to the condition of this middle group. Nevertheless, despite these qualifications, there is a built-in perversity in the situation which makes it impossible to use large amounts of aid with effectiveness in most places.

Although aid is seldom, or perhaps never, an indispensable prerequisite to economic development and although even under the most favorable circumstances it is not likely to be the "key" to development, it may, as such dissimilar analysts as Milton Friedman and J. K. Galbraith have emphasized, do much to retard development if improperly used. There is much that should be done by government in under-developed areas (e.g., provision of roads, elementary education, a monetary system, law and order), Friedman says, but there are crucial advantages in letting private business do as much as possible. *One such advantage is that private individuals, since they risk their own funds, have a much stronger incentive to invest wisely. Another is that private individuals are more likely than state bureaucracies to abandon unsuccessful ventures.* The availability of resources at little or no cost to a country inevitably stimulates "monument-building," i.e., investment in projects adding little or nothing to the productivity of the economy. Under these circumstances, he concludes, countries would develop faster without aid than with it.

But even if economic growth does occur it will not necessarily lead to the spread of freedom and democracy. . . .

If by democracy and freedom are meant "respect for the individual" and its corollary "government by discussion" (however these principles are expressed institutionally), there is certainly little basis for optimism. Respect for the individual is unique to the Judaeo-Christian tradition. In those parts of the world which do not participate in this tradition, the idea is unintelligible or nearly so. That this particular conception — of the sacredness of the individual — might enter into and transform alien cultures in those parts of the world where the worthlessness of the individual human life is a conspicuous fact of everyday experience (a circumstance which indeed constitutes the very problem that aid seeks to solve) is so improbable as to be incredible.

The prospects are better if democracy is defined to mean merely government through institutions that are in some sense representative (i.e., which take account of the wants and interests of the major elements of the population and which by a peaceful process like an election can be made to respond to public opinion). But democracy even in this restricted sense will have a slow and fitful growth in most of the underdeveloped world. The political institutions of the West cannot be copied, as its technology can, by people whose ways of thinking and valuing are fundamentally different.

The expansion of state activity which aid engenders tends in some ways to discharge the growth of democracy. In a prosperous and politically experienced society, democracy and extensive governmental participation in economic affairs may coexist. But the situation of the underdeveloped countries precludes this. The best choice open to many of them is between governments that are not incompetent and ones that are not tyrannical. Aid, by encouraging governments to undertake tasks beyond their capabilities, is likely to lead to waste through the incompetence of the recipients, to the extension and hardening of governmental power — or, perhaps most likely, to both at once. . . .

Successful application of the doctrine of indirect influence (supposing this to be possible) will require concentration of aid efforts on the most promising and amenable countries, and this, of course, will almost certainly create disaffection among those that are not favored. It is quite likely that the promising and amenable — and hence favored — countries will be ones of little strategic importance to the United States and that the disfavored — and hence disaffected — ones will be of great strategic importance.

Millikan and Rostow assert that as underdeveloped countries gain confidence they will become easier to deal with.

Once they see that they are wholly capable of standing on their own feet, they can afford to be less quixotic and nervous in their foreign policies. A confident nation, making progress at home is likely to conduct its foreign policy with poise and good sense.

This also overlooks the fact of power. The Soviet Union is a confident nation, but it is nevertheless infinitely dangerous to us. Twenty-five years ago, when its confidence was much less, it was no danger at all. The difference is that its power has increased. What counts is not the confidence of nations but their power.

Along with the probability of achieving the effect that is ultimately desired must be considered another: that of achieving it *in time.* The peril to America exists now and in the immediate future; it makes little difference to us how peaceful the presently underdeveloped countries will be a hundred years from now, or even thirty years from now, if by then we will have been destroyed. One unit of present advantage is worth much more to us than many units of advantage thirty years hence, and more, perhaps, than any possible number a hundred years hence. It is certainly wildly optimistic to believe that the underdeveloped areas may become "mature" and "healthy" democracies within a generation, but even if they did, success might come too late.

Whatever the benefits that may be judged probable on this basis, account must also be taken of the costs. One cost which may not be obvious is the possibility of making matters worse. We may, for example, set off armaments races and wars between the underdeveloped countries. Indeed, there is reason to suppose that we have already done so. Israel's attack on Egypt was probably made possible by American aid, for although the aid was non-military, it freed foreign exchange for the purchase of armaments. In time, perhaps, our non-military aid to Egypt will enable that country to attack Israel. The arms competition between India and Pakistan is largely financed by us. By giving India non-military aid we make it possible for her to buy arms (Indian expenditures for arms have for several years equaled the value of the aid received from us), which causes Pakistan to demand ever larger amounts of military assistance. We are therefore financing both sides of an arms race.

This is not the only danger. We ourselves may eventually be menaced by countries that are now weak and friendly but will by our aid be made strong and hostile.

Another doctrine asserts that aid may serve the vital interests of the United States by directly influencing the recipient governments and peoples to act as the interests of the United States require or, more often, to refrain from acting in ways injurious to the United States. In contrast to the doctrine of indirect influence, this doctrine does not expect aid to work by changing the character of the recipient society economically or otherwise, though it acknowledges that economic and other effects may be by-products.

Several versions of this doctrine may usefully be distinguished:

1. *Quid Pro Quo.* The aid is part of a bargain between two governments in which there are clearly specified advantages to both sides. For example, we might agree to build a system of highways in return for assurances that the Soviet Union would not be allowed to penetrate the country.

2. *Business Friendship.* The aid is given to create or maintain a relationship that is expected to have mutual advantages over time. The aid is, so to speak, a payment on an open account, it being tacitly understood that political advantages will be given in return.

3. *Maintenance of Friendly Governments.* The aid is intended to strengthen and to keep in power a government which is friendly, or at least not unfriendly. This may be done by undertakings, including of course economic development, which will increase the prestige of the recipient government or the confidence its public have in it.

4. *Prestige.* The aid is intended to exhibit dramatically the power of the giver and thereby to increase it. As Hobbes said in *Leviathan,* "Reputation of power is power, because it draweth with it the adherence of those that need protection."

5. *Good Will.* The aid is intended to make the recipient feel well disposed toward the giver and to put him under an implied obligation to return kindness for kindness. Few people expect governments to be moved by such sentiments as gratitude, but it is fairly widely believed that public opinion may be so moved and that it may have some effect on the policy of governments.

6. *Moral Force.* The aid is expected to affect public opinion by exerting moral force. The giver expects that the nobility of his action will inspire the recipient to act nobly too.

In most discussions of the doctrine of direct influence, these differences of approach are not clearly recognized. The term "impact" is sometimes used to describe any approach that is expected to make its effect by influencing opinion. It is evident, however, that different approaches require different means. For example, measures to promote "business friendship" would not generate "moral force."

It is not obvious why Americans so generally condemn the *"quid pro quo"* and "business friendship" versions of the direct influence doctrine. To bribe a foreign government to keep its country free may not be evil at all. But if it is, it is a kind of evil that respectable statesmen have always deemed it their duty to do when the security and welfare of their countries demanded. Where bribery is not involved, the justification of "reason of state" is not necessary. If a government is willing to give political favors in exchange for material resources, it is hard to see why either it or a government which accepts its offer should be criticized. As Aristotle remarked, the expression "friendly governments" means governments that exchange favors, not ones that love each other.

Instead of regretting the occasional necessity of putting aid on a business basis, we should wish that we could do it more often. Unfortunately, our opportunities will be few. The underdeveloped countries are in most cases pathologically sensitive about national "honor," and the suggestion that we should get something for what we give is always bitterly resented.

For the United States to seek to increase its prestige by the use of aid makes little sense. The power of this country is not underrated. (The Soviets are in a different position; their power is new and has to be seen to be believed.) Military prestige, moreover, is of little value so long as it is understood on all sides that Soviet power, world opinion, and our own scruples will prevent us from using force in any event. Our experience with Cuba is a case in point. The case for using aid to increase our reputation for non-military power is even poorer. No underdeveloped country doubts our ability to give or withhold enormous advantages.

"Good will" and "moral force" can make their effect only by working upon public opinion rather than upon governments. The public opinion in an underdeveloped country does not include the opinion of the peasants, who in most places are the vast majority. If our grain prevents the peasant from starving, he may be grateful, but his gratitude has no effect upon the policy of his country because politically he does not exist. Those who *do* make a difference are the people of the cities, especially the primate cities, and, above all, the small group which rules.

To suppose that the masses in the cities will feel grateful toward us because we have improved the peasant's lot or saved him from starvation is probably unrealistic. It is hardly less so, perhaps, to suppose that the ruling groups will be moved to gratitude or respect by our generosity.

They will assume that our actions are really selfishly motivated and that our claims to the contrary are hypocrisy. Although they are largely Western-educated, these elites do not entirely share our moral standards. In some places, the very idea of public-spiritedness is incomprehensible; actions we think noble appear as merely foolish.

These considerations suggest that if aid is to have political effect it must work upon the educated class. Undertakings which stir national pride or afford direct material benefits to that class are likely to succeed best. Building an ostentatious capital city or supporting schools, theaters, and supermarkets in primate cities may do more to create politically significant sentiment in favor of the United States than much more costly projects in the hinterland.

Even at its most effective, "impact" aid is not likely to change matters fundamentally. To make countries that are already friendly somewhat more so will avail us little. To bring friendly countries into a condition of "total dependency" (assuming this to be desirable) would require vast amounts of aid. To change basically the policy of uncommitted countries by this means is probably out of the question. There is a danger too, as President Kennedy pointed out to Congress, that "if we encourage recipient countries to dramatize a series of short-term crises as a basis for our aid . . . we will dissipate our funds, our good will and our leadership."

It is often asserted that if we do not give them aid the underdeveloped countries will eventually fall under the control of the Soviet Union and be used by it to bring about our destruction. There is, however, reason to think that this is not a realistic view of the alternative. For one thing, assistance for non-military purposes (the only kind of aid under discussion here) is not our sole means of preventing countries from falling under Soviet domination. Except where aid is the practical equivalent of military assistance (the recipient using it, as India does, to release for military expenditure funds that would otherwise have to be used for non-military expenditure), it is not decisive in keeping a country out of the hands of the Soviets. *What* is *decisive is military assistance or the threat of it.*

However, even if we gave neither aid nor military assistance, it is not likely that all of the underdeveloped countries would fall completely under Soviet control. Nationalism would be a barrier to Communist imperialism, as it has been to Western, and even if all of the countries in question did become in some sense Communist, the Kremlin probably could not impose a tight discipline upon all of them in all things.

Tensions like those that now exist between the Russians and the Chinese and between both the Russians and the Chinese and the Yugoslavs would certainly arise. But even if they did not — even if all of the underdeveloped countries entered fully into a monolithic bloc hostile to the United States — we would not necessarily be cut off and isolated.

Let us, however, assume the worst: viz., that all of the underdeveloped countries fall completely under the control of the Soviet Union and that it uses its control to try to isolate and destroy us. Even in this event, we could probably survive and we might even prosper.

The economic consequences of such isolation would be endurable. Trade with the underdeveloped countries is relatively unimportant to us. They are comparatively cheap sources of certain raw materials, but at some additional cost we could either produce these raw materials ourselves or find substitutes for them from within our borders. The cost might be no greater than that of extending aid at the levels that would be necessary in order to achieve much by it (say $6 billion a year).

That we could probably survive if all of the underdeveloped countries fell to the Communists is not, of course, a reason for letting them fall to them if we can help it — any more than the fact that one can survive with a broken leg is a reason for letting one's leg be broken. The dangers and disadvantages of such a thing to us, even though not likely to be fatal, obviously justify very strenuous efforts — more strenuous, perhaps, than we are now making — to prevent it from happening. Even if aid is only moderately effective in keeping the underdeveloped countries out of the hands of the Communists, it is a small price to pay for a large benefit.

This, however, is very different from saying that our very existence as a nation depends upon our giving aid.

There are those who believe that a humanitarian desire to improve the welfare of the people of the underdeveloped areas amply justifies extensive aid and would justify it even if no security advantages could be expected from it — even if, indeed, there were some loss of security to be expected from it. . . .

Sometimes moralizing is half hidden behind an affectation of political realism. For example, Eugene R. Black, president of the World Bank, tells us that by sacrificing our present political advantage to promote long-term economic development we will serve our *real* political interests. And Reinhold Niebuhr, who is known as a political realist, explains that the art of statecraft is to find "the point of concurrence" between the national and the international common good; apparently he is confident that there is such a point, for he goes on to say that "this policy means that we must try to persuade the nation that what is good for the alliance of the free nations is good for our own Nation *in the long run.*" Such statements conjure the crucial problems of choice out of existence by making it appear that conflicts of interest only *seem* to exist — that "in the long run" there are no conflicts and "the proper and the practical courses coincide," presumably at the "point of concurrence."

This mentality, evident in most of the writing on aid, ignores the very facts that constitute the problem: that vast areas of the world show little prospect of achieving self-sustaining economic growth or of governing themselves reasonably well within the foreseeable future; that development, when it does take place, is as likely to be inspired by blood and hate as by peace and rational management; that the development of the underdeveloped countries may not on balance be in the interest of the United States or, indeed, of civilization; and that the measures most effective in relieving misery and promoting economic growth are in general least effective in serving the urgent necessities of the West. Instead of facing up to these tragic facts and endeavoring to frame a course of action that is workable and represents the least among evils for us and for mankind, writers on aid generally proffer a few sententious principles of everyday morality and issue stern warnings against using aid for political purposes.

When policy based upon such misconceptions fails, the moralizer knows whom to blame. Not, surely, anyone in the underdeveloped countries — not even if the obvious cause of the trouble is there. Still less those like himself upon whose naïve and sentimental notions the policy was based. The fault, he says, is with the United States; it was not generous enough, or not tactful enough, or not firm enough, or it did not organize and plan effectively. That the failure may have been unavoidable, the natures of givers and receivers being what they are, is a possibility that escapes him altogether.

COMMUNIST STRATEGY

Uniting an Alliance

7 MIKHAIL A. SUSLOV
On the Struggle of the C.P.S.U. for the Unity of the International Communist Movement

Comrades, our Party has every right to say that we have done, and are still doing everything in our power to overcome the differences and to resorte co-operation between the C.P.C. and the C.P.S.U., to strengthen the friendship between the C.R.P. and the Soviet Union and to cement the unity of the world Communist movement. In spite of the inadmissible methods of debate used by the leaders of the C.P.C., in spite of their open struggle against the C.P.S.U. and other fraternal parties, our Party has shown the maximum of restraint, the maximum sense of responsibility, and the maximum concern for the cohesion of the communist ranks.

In the last few years, acting on the initiative of Comrade Khrushchev, the C.C. C.P.S.U. and the Soviet Government undertook many practical measures aimed at uniting our parties and at preserving and expanding cooperation with the C.P.R. in the political, economic, scientific, technical and cultural spheres. If these measures have failed to yield results, the blame rests entirely with the Chinese leaders.

When the Chinese leaders began their unveiled attacks on our Party, the C.C. C.P.S.U. addressed several letters to the C.C. C.P.C., pointing out that the fundamental interests of the Socialist and Communist cause require that our Parties should, as before, in spite of the existing differences, pursue an agreed policy in all matters of principle. We suggested stopping the needless controversy over questions on which opinions differ, and to cease making any public statements, which only tend to deepen the differences. The letters put forward concrete pro-

Mikhail A. Suslov, a Presidium Member and a Secretary of the Central Committee of the Communist Party of the Soviet Union, is noted as an expert on ideology and propaganda. The report, given at the Plenary Meeting of the February 14, 1964, Central Committee, Communist Party of the Soviet Union, was first published in April 1964. Conclusions of the report are reprinted here from the translation of *Information Bulletin*, supplement to *World Marxist Review* (Prague) Nos. 8–9, 1964, pp. 343–348.

posals envisaging coordinated actions in world affairs, greater exchange of foreign policy information and agreed action in the international democratic organisations, etc.

In October 1962, Comrade Khrushchev asked the Chinese Ambassador to the USSR, who was returning home, to tell the Chinese leaders that we proposed to "abandon all arguments and differences, to stop discussing who is right and who is wrong, not to rake up the past, and to begin our relations over again with a clean slate."

Although the Chinese press had by then published a whole series of articles containing gross attacks on the C.P.S.U. and other fraternal parties, Comrade Khrushchev declared in a conversation with the new Chinese Ambassador in January 1963 that "we want to return to our previous fraternal relations and are ready to do everything for this purpose."

But the leaders of the C.P.C. invariably responded to these acts of good will on the part of the Central Committee of our Party by deliberately doing everything possible to aggravate the differences, and mounted fresh attacks on the C.P.S.U., the Soviet Government and the general line of the world Communist movement.

In the struggle against the C.P.S.U. and its Leninist policy, the Chinese leaders are concentrating their fire mainly against Nikita Sergeyevich Khrushchev. To be sure, they cannot fail to see that it is Nikita Sergeyevich Khrushchev who stands in the van of the remarkable developments that have taken place in our Party and country since the Twentieth Congress and which ensure the successful progress of the Soviet people to communism. That is why they would like to isolate Comrade Khrushchev from the Central Committee for their subversive ends and to oppose our Central Committee to the Party and the Soviet people.

But this foul plan is adventuristic and hopeless, and is doomed to complete and ignominious failure.

The Chinese leaders, and not they alone, should know once and for all that our Central Committee, headed by the loyal Leninist, Nikita Sergeyevich Khrushchev, has never been so united and monolithic as now.

Comrade Khrushchev with his inexhaustible energy, his truly Bolshevik zeal and devotion to principle, is the recognised leader of our Party and our people. He expresses the most cherished thoughts and aspirations of the Soviet people. The Leninist line pursued by our Party cannot be separated from the Central Committee, from Nikita Sergeyevich Khrushchev. This line has elevated our country's world prestige to unprecedented heights, it has elevated its prestige in the eyes of the working people of the whole world. This Leninist line is supported wholeheartedly by all the Communists and all the people of our land.

Our Party has never feared ideological struggle. But it believes that ideological differences should be settled on the basis of Leninist principles and that the polemics be subordinated to the interests of the working-class movement.

The C.C. C.P.S.U. clearly foresaw the danger that the Chinese leaders would seek to use the open polemics not as a means of ironing out disputed questions but as an excuse for piling up absurd, slanderous charges, an instrument of ideological and political struggle against the Communist movement.

Together with the other Marxist-Leninist parties, our Party has exerted considerable effort to terminate the open polemics forced upon us by the C.P.C. leaders. The C.C. C.P.S.U. has repeatedly taken the initiative to that end — notably in January 1963, in the speech of Comrade Khrushchev, First Secretary of the C.C. C.P.S.U., at the Sixth Congress of the Socialist Unity Party of Germany. This initiative was backed by the overwhelming majority of Marxist-Leninist parties. But the Chinese leadership refused to discuss this proposal and saw fit to extend the range of questions in dispute, to aggravate and provoke the polemics.

Last spring an agreement was reached on a bilateral meeting of C.P.S.U. and C.P.C. representatives. We hoped that at this meeting the Chinese comrades would be ready to concentrate efforts not on what divides us, but on what unites the C.P.C. with the C.P.S.U. and with other fraternal parties. The C.P.S.U. delegation suggested that all questions in dispute be thoroughly thrashed out, in order to clear the path for a normalisation of relations, to cement the unity of our Parties and of the world Communist movement as a whole. We submitted a concrete programme for the development of relations between the U.S.S.R. and the C.P.R.

But the C.P.C. delegation took advantage of the meeting to exacerbate the differences and to level violent and groundless attacks at the C.P.S.U. and other Marxist-Leninist parties. After reading prepared statements, which completely ignored our arguments and proposals, the Chinese delegates called for an adjournment of the bilateral talks.

All the measures taken by the C.C. C.P.S.U. were prompted by a sincere desire to strengthen the unity of the Marxist-Leninist parties and the cohesion of the socialist countries. Our task was to utilize every available opportunity to remove the differences and prevent a split, and not be carried away by the heat of the struggle.

The Chinese leadership, however, apparently understood these measures of ours differently. It became clear that they took our restraint, our striving towards unity, for a sign of weakness. Lately they have begun saying that they will not agree to any improvement of relations with the C.P.S.U., except on the basis of our "unconditional surrender." What do the Chinese leaders want?

In substance, they want the Communist movement to retreat from its positions on all the basic problems of our times.

The world Communist movement considers it vitally necessary to utilize the present situation to unite all the revolutionary forces of our time ever more closely and to develop the world revolutionary process further.

In contrast to this the Chinese leaders have set their sights on dividing the main revolutionary forces of our time — the socialist world system, the international working class, and the national-liberation movement. This can only act as a break on the development of the world revolutionary process.

Marxists-Leninists believe that it is the cardinal task of the Communist parties to marshal all the peace-loving forces for the defence of peace and the deliverance of mankind from a nuclear disaster. They consider peaceful coexistence to be the general principle of relations between the socialist and the capitalist countries.

The Chinese leaders scorn this task. What they are doing, in effect, is whipping up the nuclear arms race and calling for new powers to join it. They are pursuing a line that is liable to cause an atomic war, and consider the struggle for peace a secondary task, opposing it to the struggle for socialism.

The Marxists-Leninists consider it their duty to strengthen in every possible way the unity and cohesion of the socialist community on the principles of Marxism-Leninism, and to concentrate the special attention of the socialist countries on economic development in order that socialism should win the peaceful economic competition with capitalism.

The actions of the Chinese leaders are subverting and undermining the unity of the socialist camp. They are isolating China more and more from the other socialist countries. The C.C. C.P.C. underrates economic development and ignores the tasks confronting the socialist countries in their economic competition with the capitalist countries. This policy tends to weaken the might of the socialist countries and impedes their struggle against imperialism.

Marxists-Leninists, the working class of the capitalist countries see it as their task to step up the struggle against monopoly capital, in defence of the vital interests of the masses, to make maximum use of the now available opportunities to effect a peaceful socialist revolution not involving a civil war, and at the same time be ready to take the non-peaceful way, to suppress the resistance of the bourgeoisie by armed force.

In contrast, the C.P.C. leaders vilify in every way the struggle of the working class and its Communist vanguard for the vital interests of the working people, for peace and democracy, and reject the tactics of broad anti-monopoly alliances, the possibility of effecting social revolution peacefully. They call for reckless armed actions irrespective of the concrete situation.

Marxists-Leninists and the peoples fighting for national liberation consider it their duty to complete the anti-imperialist, democratic revolution, to create and consolidate the national front, and to work for the establishment of states of national democracy, for the non-capitalist way of development.

The Chinese leaders ignore the essence of the present stage of the national-liberation revolution. They are blind to the differences in the situation prevailing in the various countries and offer the peoples of all countries one and the same prescription — armed struggle and establishment of the dictatorship of the proletariat. Such prescriptions may, if put into practice, undermine the national front and strengthen the positions of the colonialists and neo-colonialists.

Marxists-Leninists are eager to strengthen the unity and cohesion both of each individual Communist Party and the entire army of Communists in the world on the basis of the principles laid down in the [1957] Declaration and the [1960] Statement.

The Chinese leaders are disrupting the unity of the Communist movement and of the democratic organisations. They are founding factions and are striving to split our movement and its national contingents.

In brief, the C.P.C. leaders are opposing the Communist movement in all the basic questions of strategy and tactics. Theirs is a course in which petty-bourgeois revolutionism and nationalistic, great-power aspirations merge.

In a malicious anti-Soviet article, slanderous from beginning to end, which appeared on February 4 in the C.C. C.P.C. publications, the Chinese leaders declare for everybody to hear that they will step up their subversive activities against the world Communist movement. With nationalistic arrogance they boast that they will continue their attacks on the C.P.S.U. in order to disorganise the work of the Party founded by the great Lenin.

To the Soviet Communists, the sons and daughters of the October Revolution, the pioneers of the new, Communist world, who have withstood so many gruelling ordeals, such threats sound ridiculous.

The Soviet Communists will not keep silent while the Chinese leaders prosecute an unbridled offensive against our great cause of communist construction, against the Leninist course of our Party and the positions of the world Communist movement. We shall have to explain the substance of the anti-Marxist, neo-Trotskyite position of the Chinese leaders publicly.

The urgent task at present is to protect Marxism-Leninism from the distortions to which it is being subjected by the Chinese leaders. The interests of preserving the purity of the Marxist-Leninist teaching, the interests of the world Communist movement and, in the final analysis, the interests of the Chinese people itself, require that we come out openly and strongly against the incorrect views and dangerous actions of the C.P.C. leadership.

We stand for strengthening friendship with the Chinese people and are ready to develop co-operation with the C.P.R. in all fields. The Soviet Communists have a sincere regard for the great people of China and a deep respect for the revolutionary traditions of the Communist Party of China. We are sure that nobody will ever succeed in undermining the foundations of the friendship of the great Soviet and Chinese peoples and that the present attitude of the C.P.C. leadership does not reflect the true national interests of the Chinese people. We shall do everything in our power to bring the relations between the Soviet Union and the People's Republic of China back to a path that conforms with the fundamental interests of the working class and all the working people of our countries.

We are fully aware of the danger of the present attitude of the Chinese leaders. The facts show that a grim and, evidently, long struggle lies ahead for the strengthening of the unity of all the socialist forces, for friendship and cooperation between the Soviet and Chinese peoples. It is now perfectly clear that the C.P.C. leaders intend to persist in their incorrect stand, that they intend to carry on with their factional activities in the world Communist movement. Together with the other fraternal parties, our Party will resolutely defend Marxism-Leninism; it will firmly defend the unity and cohesion of the Communist movement on the basis of the principles of the Declaration and Statement of the 1957 and 1960 Moscow Meetings of Communist and Workers' parties. It will firmly defend the unity and cohesion of all the forces working for peace, democracy, national independence and socialism. . . .

The C.C. C.P.S.U. is certain that no matter how great the difficulties experienced by the world Communist movement, that movement will be strong enough to surmount them and to cement its ranks in the struggle for the great Communist cause.

The Communist Party of The Soviet Union will continue to pursue the policy of promoting unity with all the fraternal parties on the basis of the principles of Marxism-Leninism and proletarian internationalism and on the basis of the Programme documents of the world Communist movement — the 1957 Declaration and the 1960 Statement.

The road followed by our Party, by the world Communist movement is the Leninist road and, therefore, the only true road. We have adopted a new Programme, in which we have charted our development twenty years ahead. Our Party and the whole Soviet people regard fulfilment of this Programme, resolute and purposeful progress to the heights of communism, as their supreme internationalist duty to the international working-class and Communist movement. As always, our Party will perform its internationalist duty honourably!

Under the invincible banner of the great Lenin, the Communist Party of the Soviet Union will continue consistently and undeviatingly to pursue a line aimed at carrying out the C.P.S.U. Programme for the building in our country of the most just social system, communism.

THE EDITORS OF "PEOPLE'S DAILY" AND "RED FLAG"
The Leaders of the C.P.S.U. Are the Greatest Splitters
of Our Times

Never before has the unity of the international communist movement been so gravely threatened as it is today when we are witnessing a deluge of modern revisionist ideology. Both internationally and inside individual Parties, fierce struggles are going on between Marxism-Leninism and revisionism. The international communist movement is confronted with an unprecedentedly serious danger of a split.

It is the urgent task of the Communists, the proletariat and the revolutionary people of the world to defend the unity of the socialist camp and of the international communist movement.

The Communist Party of China has made consistent and unremitting efforts to defend and strengthen the unity of the socialist camp and the international communist movement in accordance with Marxism-Leninism and the revolutionary principles of the 1957 Declaration and the 1960 Statement. It has been and remains the unswerving position of the Chinese Communist Party to uphold principle, uphold unity, eliminate differences and strengthen the struggle against our common enemy. . . .

While presenting themselves as champions of unity, the leaders of the C.P.S.U. are trying to pin the label of splittism on the Chinese Communist Party. In its open letter the Central Committee of the C.P.S.U. says:

> The Chinese leaders are undermining the unity not only of the socialist camp but of the entire world communist movement, trampling on the principles of proletarian internationalism and grossly violating accepted standards of relations between fraternal Parties.

. . . But what are the facts? Who is undermining the unity of the socialist camp? Who is undermining the unity of the international communist movement? Who is trampling on the principles of proletarian internationalism? And who is grossly violating the accepted standards of relations between fraternal Parties? In other words, who are the real, out-and-out splitters?

These excerpts, from the seventh Chinese reply to the Open Letter of the Central Committee of the Communist Party of the Soviet Union on July 14, 1963, are reprinted from the *Peking Review*, VII, No. 6 (February 7, 1964) 5–21.

Only when these questions are properly answered can we find the way to defend and strengthen the unity of the socialist camp and the international communist movement and overcome the danger of a split.
. . . The struggle between Marxism-Leninism and opportunism and between the forces defending unity and those creating splits runs through the history of the development of the communist movement. This is the case both in individual countries and on the international plane. In this prolonged struggle, Marx, Engels and Lenin expounded the true essence of proletarian unity on a theoretical level and, by their deeds, set brilliant examples in combating opportunism, revisionism and splittism. . . .

EXPERIENCE AND LESSONS

What does the history of the development of the international communist movement demonstrate?

First, it demonstrates that like everything else, the international working-class movement tends to divide itself in two. The class struggle between the proletariat and the bourgeoisie is inevitably reflected in the communist ranks. It is inevitable that opportunism of one kind or another should arise in the course of the development of the communist movement, that opportunists should engage in anti-Marxist-Leninist splitting activities and that Marxist-Leninists should wage struggles against opportunism and splittism. It is precisely through this struggle of opposites that Marxism-Leninism and the international working-class movement have developed. And it is also through this struggle that the international working-class movement has strengthened and consolidated its unity on the basis of Marxism-Leninism. . . .

Secondly, the history of the international communist movement demonstrates that in every period the struggle between the defenders of unity and the creators of splits is in essence one between Marxism-Leninism and opportunism-revisionism, between the upholders of Marxism and the traitors to Marxism.

Both internationally and in individual countries, genuine proletarian unity is possible only on the basis of Marxism-Leninism.

Both internationally and in individual countries, wherever opportunism and revisionism are rampant, a split becomes inevitable in the proletarian ranks. Every split in the communist movement is invariably caused by the opportunist-revisionist opposition to and betrayal of Marxism-Leninism.

What is splittism?

It means a split with Marxism-Leninism. Anyone who opposes and betrays Marxism-Leninism and undermines the basis of proletarian unity is a splitter.

It means a split with the revolutionary proletarian party. Anyone who persists in a revisionist line and turns a revolutionary proletarian party into a reformist bourgeois party is a splitter.

It means a split with the revolutionary proletariat and the broad masses of the working people. Anyone who follows a programme and line running counter to the revolutionary will and fundamental interests of the proletariat and the working people is a splitter. . . .

By disrupting proletarian unity, splittism serves the bourgeoisie and meets its needs. It is the constant policy of the bourgeoisie to create splits within the ranks of the proletariat. Its most sinister method of doing so is to buy over or cultivate agents within the proletarian ranks. And agents of the bourgeoisie are exactly what the opportunists and revisionists are. So far from seeking to unite the proletariat in the fight against the bourgeoisie, they want the proletariat to cooperate with it. . . .

In brief, opportunism and revisionism are the political and ideological roots of splittism. And splittism is the organizational manifestation of opportunism and revisionism. It can also be said that opportunism and revisionism are splittism as well as sectarianism. The revisionists are the greatest and vilest splitters and sectarians in the communist movement.

Thirdly, the history of the international communist movement demonstrates that proletarian unity has been consolidated and has developed through struggle against opportunism, revisionism and splittism. The struggle for unity is inseparably connected with the struggle for principle.

The unity the proletariat requires is class unity, revolutionary unity, unity against the common enemy and for the great goal of communism. The unity of the international proletariat has its theoretical and political basis in Marxism-Leninism. Only when it has theoretical and political unity can the international proletariat have organizational cohesion and unity of action. . . .

Faced with the challenge of the opportunist-revisionists who are openly splitting the international communist movement, the Marxist-Leninists must make no compromise in matters of principle, but must resolutely combat this splittism. This is an invaluable behest of Marx,

Engels and Lenin, as well as the only correct way to safeguard the unity of the international communist movement.

THE GREATEST SPLITTERS OF OUR TIMES

The events of recent years show that the leaders of the C.P.S.U. headed by Khrushchev have become the chief representatives of modern revisionism as well as the greatest splitters in the international communist movement.

Between the [1956] 20th and [1961] 22nd Congresses of the C.P.S.U., the leaders of the C.P.S.U developed a rounded system of revisionism. They put forward a revisionist line which contravenes the proletarian revolution and the dictatorship of the proletariat, a line which consists of "peaceful coexistence," "peaceful competition," "peaceful transition," "a state of the whole people" and "a party of the entire people." They have tried to impose this revisionist line on all fraternal Parties as a substitute for the common line of the international communist movement which was laid down at the meetings of fraternal Parties in 1957 and 1960. And they have attacked anyone who perseveres in the Marxist-Leninist line and resists their revisionist line.

The leaders of the C.P.S.U. have themselves undermined the basis of the unity of the international communist movement and created the present grave danger of a split by betraying Marxism-Leninism and proletarian internationalism and pushing their revisionist and divisive line.

Far from working to consolidate and expand the socialist camp, the leaders of the C.P.S.U. have endeavoured to split and disintegrate it. They have thus made a mess of the splendid socialist camp.

They have violated the principles guiding relations among fraternal countries as laid down in the Declaration and the Statement, pursued a policy of great-power chauvinism and national egoism towards fraternal socialist countries and thus disrupted the unity of the socialist camp.

They have arbitrarily infringed the sovereignty of fraternal countries, interfered in their internal affairs, carried on subversive activities and striven in every way to control fraternal countries.

In the name of the "international division of labour," the leaders of the C.P.S.U. oppose the adoption by fraternal countries of the policy of building socialism by their own efforts and developing their economies on an independent basis, and attempt to turn them into economic appendages. They have tried to force those fraternal countries which are comparatively backward economically to abandon industrialization and become their sources of raw materials and markets for surplus products.

The leaders of the C.P.S.U. are quite unscrupulous in their pursuit of the policy of great-power chauvinism. They have constantly brought political, economic and even military pressure to bear on fraternal countries.

The leaders of the C.P.S.U. have openly called for the overthrow of the Party and government leaders of Albania, brashly severed all economic and diplomatic relations with her and tyrannically deprived her of her legitimate rights as a member of the Warsaw Treaty Organization and the Council of Economic Mutual Assistance.

The leaders of the C.P.S.U. have violated the Sino-Soviet Treaty of Friendship, Alliance and Mutual Assistance, made a unilateral decision to withdraw 1,390 Soviet experts working in China, to tear up 343 contracts and supplementary contracts on the employment of experts and to cancel 257 projects of scientific and technical cooperation, and pursued a restrictive and discriminatory trade policy against China. They have provoked incidents on the Sino-Soviet border and carried on large-scale subversive activities in Sinkiang. On more than one occasion, Khrushchev went so far as to tell leading comrades of the Central Committee of the C.P.C. that certain anti-Party elements in the Chinese Communist Party were his "good friends." He has praised Chinese anti-Party elements for attacking the Chinese Party's general line for socialist construction, the big leap forward and the people's communes, describing their action as a "manly act."

Such measures which gravely worsen state relations are rare even between capitalist countries. But again and again the leaders of the C.P.S.U. have adopted shocking and extreme measures of this kind against fraternal socialist countries. Yet they go on prating about being "faithful to proletarian internationalism." We would like to ask, is there a shred of internationalism in all these deeds of yours?

The great-power chauvinism and splittism of the leaders of the C.P.S.U. are equally glaring in their conduct vis-à-vis fraternal Parties.

Since the 20th Congress of the C.P.S.U. its leaders have tried, on the pretext of "combating the personality cult," to change the leadership of other fraternal Parties to conform to their will. Right up to the present they have insisted on "combating the personality cult" as a precondition for the restoration of unity and as a "principle" which is "obligatory on every Communist Party."[1]

Contrary to the principles guiding relations among fraternal Parties laid down in the Declaration and the Statement, the leaders of the C.P.S.U. ignore the independent and equal status of fraternal Parties, insist on establishing a kind of feudal patriarchal domination over the international communist movement and turn the relations between brother Parties into those between a patriarchal father and his sons. Khrushchev has more than once described a fraternal Party as a "silly boy" and called himself its "mother."[2] With his feudal psychology of self-exaltation, he has absolutely no sense of shame.

The leaders of the C.P.S.U. have completely ignored the principle of achieving unanimity through consultation among fraternal Parties and habitually make dictatorial decisions and order others about. They have recklessly torn up joint agreements with fraternal Parties, taken arbitrary decisions on important matters of common concern to fraternal Parties and forced *faits accomplis* on them.

The leaders of the C.P.S.U. have violated the principle that differences among fraternal Parties should be settled through inter-Party consultation; they first used their own Party congress and then the congresses of other fraternal Parties as rostrums for large-scale public attacks against those fraternal Parties which firmly uphold Marxism-Leninism.

The leaders of the C.P.S.U. regard fraternal Parties as pawns on their diplomatic chessboard. Khrushchev plays fast and loose, he blows hot and cold, he talks one way one day and another the next, and yet he insists on the fraternal Parties dancing to his every tune without knowing whence or whither.

The leaders of the C.P.S.U. have stirred up trouble and created splits in many Communist Parties by encouraging the followers of their revisionist line in these Parties to attack the leadership, or usurp leading positions, persecute Marxist-Leninists and even expel them from the Party. It is this divisive policy of the leaders of the C.P.S.U. that has given rise to organizational splits in the fraternal Parties of many capitalist countries. . . .

[1] "For the Unity and Solidarity of the International Communist Movement," article by the editorial board, *Pravda*, December 6, 1963.

[2] Cf. Khrushchev's interview with Gardner Cowles, Editor of the U.S. magazine *Look*, April 20, 1962; report by Khrushchev to the Session of the Supreme Soviet of the U.S.S.R., December 12, 1962.

THE EDITORS OF "PEOPLE'S DAILY" AND "RED FLAG"   *129*

In addition, they are imposing the revisionist line on the international democratic organizations, changing the correct line pursued by these organizations and trying to create splits in them.

The leaders of the C.P.S.U. have completely reversed enemies and comrades. They have directed the edge of struggle, which should be against U.S. imperialism and its lackeys, against the Marxist-Leninist fraternal Parties and countries.

The leaders of the C.P.S.U. are bent on seeking Soviet-U.S. co-operation for the domination of the world, they regard U.S. imperialism, the most ferocious enemy of the people of the world, as their most reliable friend, and they treat the fraternal Parties and countries adhering to Marxism-Leninism as their enemy. They collude with U.S. imperialism, the reactionaries of various countries, the renegade Tito clique and the Right-wing social democrats in a partnership against the socialist fraternal countries, the fraternal Parties, the Marxist-Leninists and the revolutionary people of all countries. . . .

These facts show that the leaders of the C.P.S.U. have taken the road of complete betrayal of proletarian internationalism, in contravention of the interests of the Soviet people, the socialist camp and the international communist movement and those of all revolutionary people.

These facts clearly demonstrate that the leaders of the C.P.S.U. counterpose their revisionism to Marxism-Leninism, their great-power chauvinism and national egoism to proletarian internationalism and their sectarianism and splittism to the international unity of the proletariat. Thus, like all the opportunists and revisionists of the past, the leaders of the C.P.S.U. have turned into creators of splits in many fraternal Parties, the socialist camp and the entire international communist movement.

The revisionism and splittism of the leaders of the C.P.S.U. constitute a greater danger than those of any other opportunists and splitters, whether past or present. As everyone knows, this revisionism is occurring in the C.P.S.U., the Party which was created by Lenin and which has enjoyed the highest prestige among all Communist Parties; it is occurring in the great Soviet Union, the first socialist country. For many years, Marxist-Leninists and revolutionary people the world over have held the C.P.S.U. in high esteem and regarded the Soviet Union as the base of world revolution and the model of struggle. And the leaders of the C.P.S.U. have taken advantage of all this — of the prestige of the Party created by Lenin and of the first socialist country

— to cover up the essence of their revisionism and splittism and deceive those who are still unaware of the truth. At the same time, these past masters in double-dealing are shouting "unity, unity," while actually engaged in splitting. To a certain extent, their tricks do temporarily confuse people. Traditional confidence in the C.P.S.U. and ignorance of the facts have prevented quite a few people from recognizing the revisionism and splittism of the leaders of the C.P.S.U. sooner. . . .

The revisionism and splittism of the leaders of the C.P.S.U. are the product both of the lush growth of the bourgeois elements inside the Soviet Union, and of imperialist policy, and particularly of the U.S. imperialist policies of nuclear blackmail and "peaceful evolution." In turn, their revisionist and divisive theories and policies cater not only to the widespread capitalist forces at home but also to imperialism, and serve to paralyse the revolutionary will and to obstruct the revolutionary struggle of the people of the world.

Indeed, the leaders of the C.P.S.U. have already won warm praise and applause from imperialism and its lackeys. . . .

REFUTATION OF THE CHARGE OF BEING ANTI-SOVIET

The leaders of the C.P.S.U. accuse all who resist and criticize their revisionism and splittism of being anti-Soviet. This is a terrifying charge. To oppose the first socialist country in the world and the Party founded by the great Lenin — what insolence!

But we advise the leaders of the C.P.S.U. not to indulge in histrionics. The anti-Soviet charge can never apply to us.

We also advise the leaders of the C.P.S.U. not to become self-intoxicated. The anti-Soviet charge can never silence Marxist-Leninists.

Together with all other Communists and revolutionary people the world over, we Chinese Communists have always cherished sincere respect and love for the great Soviet people, the Soviet state and the Soviet Communist Party. For it was the people of the Soviet Union who, under the leadership of Lenin's Party, lit the triumphant torch of the October Revolution, opened up the new era of world proletarian revolution and marched in the van along the road to communism in the years that followed. It was the Communist Party of the Soviet Union and the Soviet state which, under the leadership of Lenin and Stalin, pursued a Marxist-Leninist domestic and foreign policy, scored unprecedented achievements in socialist construction, made the greatest contribution to victory in the war against fascism and gave internationalist support to the revolutionary struggles of the proletariat and working people of all other countries. . . .

But, beginning with the 20th Congress, the leaders of the C.P.S.U. headed by Khrushchev have been launching violent attacks on Stalin and taking the road of revisionism. Is it possible to say that they have justified the hopes of all Communists? No, it is not.

In its *Proposal Concerning the General Line of the International Communist Movement,* the Central Committee of the Communist Party of China points out that it is the common demand of the people in the countries of the socialist camp and of the international proletariat and working people that all Communist Parties in the socialist camp should:

1. Adhere to the Marxist-Leninist line and pursue correct Marxist-Leninist domestic and foreign policies;

2. Consolidate the dictatorship of the proletariat and the worker-peasant alliance led by the proletariat and carry the socialist revolution forward to the end on the economic, political and ideological fronts;

3. Promote the initiative and creativeness of the broad masses, carry out socialist construction in a planned way, develop production, improve the people's livelihood and strengthen national defence;

4. Strengthen the unity of the socialist camp on the basis of Marxism-Leninism, and support other socialist countries on the basis of proletarian internationalism;

5. Oppose the imperialist policies of aggression and war, and defend world peace;

6. Oppose the anti-communist, anti-popular and counter-revolutionary policies of the reactionaries of all countries; and

7. Help the revolutionary struggles of the oppressed classes and nations of the world. . . .

It is none other than the leaders of the C.P.S.U. headed by Khrushchev who are anti-Soviet.

The leaders of the C.P.S.U. have completely negated Stalin and painted the first dictatorship of the proletariat and socialist system as dark and dreadful. What is this if not anti-Soviet?

The leaders of the C.P.S.U. have proclaimed the abolition of the dictatorship of the proletariat, altered the proletarian character of the C.P.S.U. and opened the floodgates for capitalist forces in the Soviet Union. What is this if not anti-Soviet?

The leaders of the C.P.S.U. seek U.S.-Soviet co-operation and tirelessly fawn upon U.S. imperialism, and have thus disgraced the great Soviet Union. What is this if not anti-Soviet?

The leaders of the C.P.S.U. pursue the policy of great-power chauvinism and treat fraternal socialist countries as dependencies, and have thus damaged the prestige of the Soviet state. What is this if not anti-Soviet?

The leaders of the C.P.S.U. obstruct and oppose the revolutionary struggles of other peoples and act as apologists for imperialism and neo-colonialism, and have thus tarnished the glorious internationalist tradition of Lenin's Party. What is this if not anti-Soviet?

In short, the actions of the leaders of the C.P.S.U. have brought deep shame upon the great Soviet Union and the C.P.S.U. and seriously damaged the fundamental interests of the Soviet people. They are anti-Soviet action through and through.

Naturally, in these circumstances, the Chinese Communist Party and other Marxist-Leninist parties and Marxist-Leninists are bound to subject the revisionist and divisive line of the leaders of the C.P.S.U. to serious criticism for the purpose of defending the purity of Marxism-Leninism and the unity of the international communist movement and unholding the principle of proletarian internationalism. We oppose only the revisionist and divisive errors of the leaders of the C.P.S.U. And we do so for the sake of defending the C.P.S.U. founded by Lenin and safeguarding the fundamental interests of the Soviet Union, the first socialist country, and of the Soviet people. How can this be described as anti-Soviet? . . .

REFUTATION OF THE CHARGE OF SEIZING THE LEADERSHIP

The leaders of the C.P.S.U. ascribe our criticisms and our opposition to their revisionist and divisive line to a desire to "seize the leadership."

First, we would like to ask the leaders of the C.P.S.U.: You say we want to seize the leadership. From whom? Who now holds the leadership? In the international communist movement, is there such a thing as a leadership which lords it over all fraternal Parties? And is this leadership in your hands?

Apparently, the leaders of the C.P.S.U. consider themselves the natural leaders who can lord it over all fraternal Parties. According to their logic, their programme, resolutions and statements are all infallible laws. Every remark and every word of Khrushchev's are imperial edicts, however wrong or absurd they may be. All fraternal

Parties must submissively hear and obey and are absolutely forbidden to criticize or oppose them. This is outright tyranny. It is the ideology of feudal autocrats, pure and simple.

However, we must tell the leaders of the C.P.S.U. that the international communist movement is not some feudal clique. Whether large or small, whether new or old, and whether in or out of power, all fraternal Parties are independent and equal. No meeting of fraternal Parties and no agreement unanimously adopted by them has ever stipulated that there are superior and subordinate Parties, one Party which leads and other Parties which are led, a Party which is a father and Parties which are sons; or that the leaders of the C.P.S.U. are the supreme rulers over other fraternal Parties.

The history of the international proletarian revolutionary movement shows that, owing to the uneven development of revolution, at a particular historical stage the proletariat and its party in one country or another marched in the van of the movement. . . .

Even the vanguard position . . . does not remain unchanged for a long time but shifts according to changing conditions. This shift is decided not by the subjective wishes of any individual or Party, but by the conditions shaped by history. If conditions change, other Parties may come to the van of the movement. When a Party which formerly held the position of vanguard takes the path of revisionism, it is bound to forfeit this position despite the fact that it has been the largest Party and has exerted the greatest influence. . . .

In the present international communist movement, the question of who has the right to lead whom simply does not arise. Fraternal Parties should be independent and completely equal, and at the same time they should be united. On questions of common concern they should reach unanimity of views through consultation, and they should concert their actions in the struggle for the common goal. . . .

Because of their different historical backgrounds, the fraternal Parties naturally find themselves in different situations. Those Parties which have won victory in their revolutions differ from those which have not yet done so, and those which won victory earlier differ from those which did so later. But these differences only mean that the victorious Parties, and in particular the Parties which won victory earlier, have to bear a greater internationalist responsibility in supporting other fraternal Parties, and they have absolutely no right to dominate other fraternal Parties. . . .

The question confronting all Communists and the entire international communist movement today is not who is the leader over whom, but whether one should uphold Marxism-Leninism and proletarian internationalism or submit to the revisionism and splittism of the leaders of the C.P.S.U. In spreading the slander that we want to seize the leadership, the leaders of the C.P.S.U. are in fact insisting that all fraternal Parties, including our own, must bow to their revisionist and divisive leadership.

REFUTATION OF THE CHARGE OF FRUSTRATING THE WILL OF THE MAJORITY AND VIOLATING INTERNATIONAL DISCIPLINE

In their attacks on the Chinese Communist Party since 1960, the leaders of the C.P.S.U. have most frequently resorted to the charge that we "frustrate the will of the majority" and "violate international discipline." . . .

Yet even now the leaders of the C.P.S.U. keep on clamouring that "the minority should submit to the majority." This can only mean that they wish to deny the independent and equal status of all fraternal Parties and to abolish the principle of achieving unanimity through consultation. They are trying to force some fraternal Parties to submit to their will on the pretext of a "majority," and to use the sham preponderance thus obtained to attack fraternal Marxist-Leninist parties. Their very actions are sectarian and divisive and violate the Declaration and the Statement. . . .

The fundamental question is: Who stands with the broad masses of the people? Who represents their basic interests? And who reflects their revolutionary will? . . .

Today, more than 90 percent of the world's population desire revolution, including those who are not yet but will eventually become politically conscious. The real majority are the revolutionary Marxist-Leninist parties and Marxist-Leninists who represent the fundamental interests of the people, and not the handful of revisionists who have betrayed these interests.

REFUTATION OF THE CHARGE OF SUPPORTING THE ANTI-PARTY GROUPS OF FRATERNAL PARTIES

. . . The fact is, the splits that have occurred in certain Communist Parties in recent years have largely been due to the forcible application by the leaders of the C.P.S.U. of their revisionist and divisive line.

The leaders of certain Communist Parties have led the revolutionary movement of their own countries astray and brought serious losses to the revolutionary cause either because they accepted the revisionist line imposed on them by the leaders of the C.P.S.U. or because their own revisionist line was encouraged by the leaders of the C.P.S.U. By following the leaders of the C.P.S.U. and banging the drum for them in the struggle between the two lines in the international communist movement, they adversely affect the unity of the movement. Inevitably this arouses widespread dissatisfaction inside their own Parties and resistance and opposition from the Marxist-Leninists in them.

Aping the leaders of the C.P.S.U., their followers practise a divisive policy inside their own Parties. Violating the principle of democratic centralism, they forbid normal inner-Party discussion of differences concerning the Party line and of major problems confronting the international communist movement. Moreover, they illegitimately ostracize, attack and even expel Communists who adhere to principle. As a result the struggle between the two lines within the Parties inevitably takes on a particularly acute form.

In essence, the struggle within these Communist Parties turns on whether to follow the Marxist-Leninist line or the revisionist line, and whether to make the Communist Party a genuine vanguard of the proletariat and a genuine revolutionary proletarian party or to convert it into a servant of the bourgeoisie and a variant of the Social-Democratic Party. . . .

Communists are makers of revolution. If they refuse to make revolutions, they cease to be Marxist-Leninists and become revisionists and such-like. As Marxist-Leninists, Communists by their very nature should adhere to their revolutionary stand and oppose revisionism. Similarly, a Marxist-Leninist party should as a matter of course give firm support to revolutionaries and to Communists who oppose revisionism.

The Chinese Communist Party has never concealed its position. We support all revolutionary comrades who adhere to Marxism-Leninism. In the international communist movement, we have contacts with revisionists; why then can we not have contacts with Marxist-Leninists? The leaders of the C.P.S.U. describe our support for Marxist-Leninists in other countries as a divisive act. In our opinion, it is simply a proletarian internationalist obligation which it is our duty to discharge. . . .

In short, whatever the country or place, where one finds oppression, there one finds resistance; where one finds revisionists, there one finds Marxist-Leninists fighting them, and where one finds expulsion of Marxist-Leninists from the Party and other divisive measures, there outstanding Marxist-Leninists and strong revolutionary Parties inevitably emerge. Changes contrary to the expectations of the modern revisionists are taking place. The revisionists are producing their own opposites and will eventually be buried by them. This is an inexorable law.

THE PRESENT PUBLIC DEBATE

In the last analysis, the present great debate in the international communist movement centres on whether to adhere to Marxism-Leninism or to revisionism, whether to adhere to proletarian internationalism or to great-power chauvinism and whether to desire unity or a split. This dispute over fundamental principles began long ago, following the 20th Congress of the C.P.S.U. It went on in private talks between fraternal Parties for a considerable time until it came into the open a little more than two years ago.

As everybody knows, the leaders of the C.P.S.U. first provoked and insisted on the open polemics in the international communist movement. . . .

Apparently, things have not developed according to the expectations of the launchers of these polemics. The public debate, which the leaders of the C.P.S.U. at first thought would be to their advantage, is developing in a way contrary to their wishes. Truth is not on the side of the leaders of the C.P.S.U., and therefore in their attacks on others they can only depend on lies, slanders, distortion of the facts and confusion of right and wrong. When argument develops and it becomes necessary to produce facts and reason things out, they find the ground slipping from under their feet and take fright. . . .

The stand of the Chinese Communist Party on public polemics is known to all. From the very beginning, we have held that differences among fraternal Parties should be resolved through private consultations. The public polemics were neither provoked nor desired by us. . . .

The essence of the matter is that the existing differences in the international communist movement are between Marxism-Leninism and revisionism and between proletarian internationalism and great-power chauvinism. These major differences of principle cannot be solved in a fundamental way by a cessation of the public debate. On the contrary, only through public debate, setting forth the facts and reasoning things out will it be possible to clarify matters, distinguish right from wrong and safeguard and strengthen the unity of the international communist movement on the basis of Marxism-Leninism and proletarian internationalism. . . .

THE EDITORS OF "PEOPLE'S DAILY" AND "RED FLAG"   *137*

The revisionism and great-power chauvinism of the leaders of the C.P.S.U. are an unprecedented menace to the unity of the socialist camp and the international communist movement. By taking a revisionist and great-power chauvinist position, the leaders of the C.P.S.U. are standing for a split. So long as they maintain such a position, they are in fact working for sham unity and a real split no matter how volubly they may talk of "unity" and abuse others as "splitters" and "sectarians." . . .

If the leaders of the C.P.S.U. genuinely want unity and are not just pretending, they should loyally abide by the fundamental theories of Marxism-Leninism and by the Marxist-Leninist teachings concerning classes and class struggle, the state and revolution, and especially proletarian revolution and the dictatorship of the proletariat. It is absolutely impermissible for them to substitute class collaboration or class capitulation for class struggle, and social reformism or social pacifism for proletarian revolution, or abolish the dictatorship of the proletariat no matter under what pretext. . . .

If the leaders of the C.P.S.U. genuinely want unity and are not just pretending, they should draw a sharp line of demarcation between enemies and comrades and should unite with all socialist countries, all fraternal Marxist-Leninist parties, the proletariat of the whole world, all oppressed people and nations and all peace-loving countries and people in order to oppose U.S. imperialism, the arch-enemy of the people of the world, and its lackeys. . . .

If the leaders of the C.P.S.U. genuinely want unity and are not just pretending, they should be faithful to proletarian internationalism and strictly abide by the principles guiding relations among fraternal countries and Parties, as laid down in the Declaration and the Statement. It is absolutely impermissible for them to replace these principles with policies of great-power chauvinism and national egoism. In other words, they should:

Observe the principle of solidarity and never line up a number of fraternal Parties to attack other fraternal Parties and engage in sectarian and divisive activities;

Adhere to the principle of mutual support and mutual assistance and never try to control others in the name of assistance or, on the pretext of the "international division of labour," impair the sovereignty and interests of fraternal countries and oppose their building socialism through self-reliance;

Observe the principle of independence and equality and never place themselves above other fraternal Parties or impose their own Party's programme, line and resolutions on others; never interfere in the internal affairs of fraternal Parties and carry out subversive activities under the pretext of "combating the personality cult"; and never treat fraternal Parties as their property and fraternal countries as their dependencies;

Follow the principle of reaching unanimity through consultation and never force through their own Party's wrong line in the name of the so-called majority or use the congresses of their own Party or of other Parties and such forms as resolutions, statements and leaders' speeches for public and explicit attacks on other fraternal Parties, and certainly never extend ideological differences to state relations.

In short, if the leaders of the C.P.S.U. genuinely desire the unity of the socialist camp and the international communist movement, they must make a clean break with their line of revisionism, great-power chauvinism and splittism. The unity of the socialist camp and the international communist movement can be safeguarded and strengthened only by remaining loyal to Marxism-Leninism and proletarian internationalism and by opposing modern revisionism and modern dogmatism, great-power chauvinism and other forms of bourgeois nationalism, and sectarianism and splittism, and by doing so not merely in words but in deeds. This is the sole way to defend and strengthen unity.

Taken as a whole, the present world situation is most favourable. The international communist movement has already gained brilliant victories, bringing about a fundamental change in the international balance of class forces. At present the international communist movement is being assailed by an adverse current of revisionism and splittism; this phenomenon is not inconsistent with the law of historical development. Even though it creates temporary difficulties for the international communist movement and some fraternal Parties, it is a good thing that the revisionists have revealed their true features and that a struggle between Marxism-Leninism and revisionism has ensued.

Without any doubt, Marxism-Leninism will continue to demonstrate its youthful vitality and will sweep the whole world; the international communist movement will grow stronger and more united on the basis of Marxism-Leninism; and the cause of the international proletariat and the world people's revolution will win still more brilliant victories. Modern revisionism will undoubtedly go bankrupt. . . .

Despite our serious differences with the leaders of the C.P.S.U., we have full confidence in the vast membership of the C.P.S.U. and in the Soviet people, who grew up under the guidance of Lenin and Stalin. As always, the Communists and the people of China will unswervingly safeguard the unity between China and the Soviet Union, and consolidate and develop the deep-rooted friendship between our two peoples.

Communists of the world, unite on the basis of Marxism-Leninism!

The Challenge of "Capitalist Imperialism"

9 A. A. ARZUMANYAN
Peaceful Coexistence and the World Revolutionary Process

. . . The question of war and peace, and the peaceful co-existence of states with different social and economic systems, is one that affects the whole of humanity. Today, it is an extremely acute question, one which defies approach with the old yardstick. What is involved is the future of the peoples, an issue that does not allow of any vagueness. . . .

One of the greatest services done to humanity by Lenin and the Communist Party of the Soviet Union, which he founded, is that they have worked out the only correct principle of foreign policy for the transition period from capitalism to Socialism — the peaceful co-existence of states with different social systems. In the new historical conditions our Party has been successfully implementing this Leninist principle. The peace-loving policy of the U.S.S.R. leapt into activity in 1953, especially after the 20th Congress of the C.P.S.U., greatly increasing its influence on the entire course of international relations. . . .

In our age, when the most aggressive circles of imperialism are preparing to plunge the world into thermo-nuclear disaster, the importance of the peaceful co-existence of states with different social systems has grown immensely, and this policy has been further developed and has acquired an even more profound content.

The most important theoretical and political conclusion drawn by

A. A. Arzumanyan is Director, Institute of World Economics and International Relations, in Moscow. These excerpts are from an article which appeared in *International Affairs* (Moscow), VIII (August 1963) 3–6.

our Party at the [1956] 20th Congress — that war is not fatally inevitable and that world war can be averted — has been entirely vindicated by the course of events. Mankind can and must bridle the imperialists before they make use of lethal weapons; it must prevent the outbreak of another armed conflict, and ensure the peaceful coexistence of the two opposed social systems based on a reciprocal repudiation of war as a means of solving international disputes. This task can be fulfilled only if all peace-loving forces take the most active and resolute action.

Our Party regards as the main aim of its foreign policy not only to avert a world war but also to exclude world wars forever from the life of society in our time. With the new balance of forces that has now taken shape in the world, there is a real possibility of excluding world war from the life of society even before the full victory of Socialism on the globe, while capitalism continues to exist in a part of the world. These are not Utopian or pacifist good intentions but the result of a strictly scientific analysis of the balance of class forces in the world and a concrete and militant programme of struggle for lasting peace on earth which is based on a sober evaluation of the material and moral forces ensuring the fulfilment of this vital task of our day. Attainment of this aim is now objectively possible.

Karl Marx used to say that history poses before humanity only such tasks as it is capable of solving. World war could not be avoided if it were inherent in the two existing social systems. The roots of war lie only in imperialism. Because of its predatory nature, imperialism is unable to rid itself of the urge to solve international contradictions by means of war. As for Socialist society, it has no need of war as a means of national or foreign policy. Socialism is peace, and that is why the Socialist system is the centre of attraction for all peace-loving forces on earth. Today, when the Socialist world system has become a powerful material and moral factor of peace, capable of bridling imperialism, an entirely new possibility to avert world war has arisen. With the present steadily growing superiority of the forces of peace and Socialism over the forces of aggression and war, peaceful co-existence has become imperative.

In the early days after the October Revolution, the principle of peaceful co-existence was merely a reflection of the policy of the world's first Socialist state; today it has become the general foreign policy line of the Socialist states. A part of the globe is now an extensive peace zone including alongside the Socialist countries a big group of non-

Socialist states which do not want another war. The struggle for peace in the countries within imperialist military blocs can and must prove equally fatal to the aggressive military plans of the imperialists. The forces of peace are immense, modern international conditions are favourable to their struggle, while their aims are in line with humanity's basic interests.

The C.P.C. leadership takes a different stand on these questions of principle. The Chinese comrades are spreading the theses that so long as imperialism exists war cannot be ruled out, that peaceful co-existence is not the general principle of the foreign policy of the Socialist countries, and that the struggle for peace allegedly hampers revolutionary struggle. What is the meaning of these theses? It is that the Chinese comrades do not believe that the peoples of the Socialist countries, the international working class and all peace-loving and democratic forces are capable of thwarting the aggressive designs of the imperialists and ensuring peace for this and coming generations. In taking this attitude, they underrate the forces of peace and Socialism, and overrate the forces of imperialism. The thesis that war is inevitable reflects a lack of confidence in one's own forces, and fear of imperialism. On the questions of war and peace the Chinese comrades take a stand that is contrary to the general course of the international Communist movement.

"The Central Committee of the C.P.S.U. declares," the Open Letter stressed, "that we have conducted, are conducting and will continue to conduct the Leninist policy of peaceful co-existence of states with different social systems. Our Party regards this as a duty to the Soviet people and also to the peoples of all other countries. To ensure peace is to promote most effectively the consolidation of the Socialist system and, consequently, to enhance its influence on the entire course of the liberation struggle and the world revolutionary process." In the minds of great masses of people Socialism and peace are now indivisible.

The opponents of the principle of peaceful co-existence have been attacking this principle from two sides, but their views eventually coincide. Some suggest the following: to accept revolution also means to accept world war. Such a thesis is false and is of a provocative nature. Others say: peaceful co-existence means rejection of revolution which is likewise a false and provocative approach to the problem.

To see the world revolutionary prospect as leading only through war is to adopt an anti-Leninist stand. Lenin and the Communists have always resolutely opposed any acceleration of revolution by means of military cataclysms; they have always denied that the way to revolution must lie through war between states. The fact that both world wars unleashed by the imperialists did end in Socialist revolutions does not at all mean that the way to social revolution lies through world war, especially in our epoch, when the Socialist world system exists and multiplies its forces.

In modern conditions, when monstrous means of mass annihilation have been created, another, thermo-nuclear, war would inflict incredible destruction on entire countries, it would turn to ruins the major centres of world industry and world culture. Such a war would bring death and suffering to hundreds of millions of people. To avoid such a disaster for humanity would not mean delaying but, on the contrary, advancing and accelerating the development of the victorious Socialist revolution. It would seem that those who underrate modern thermo-nuclear weapons and call them "a paper tiger" are simply not entirely aware of their destructive force and fail to realise the full danger of thermo-nuclear war for mankind. But Communists have no right to ignore this danger. They consider it to be their duty to tell the peoples the truth about the consequences of a world war which in present-day conditions cannot but be a thermo-nuclear catastrophe.

The Chinese comrades allow the possibility of sacrificing in a war the lives of hundreds of millions of people, asserting that "on the ruins of imperialism" (in other words, as a result of a thermo-nuclear war) the victorious peoples would very rapidly create a civilisation a thousand times higher than that attained under capitalism, and would build their truly "beautiful future." But this is a reckless course which has nothing in common with the class approach and which is in basic contradiction with Marxism-Leninism. Any Party which truly cherishes the people's interests, which really wants to preserve the lives of hundreds of millions of men, cannot but feel its responsibility in the struggle to avert a new world war and ensure the peaceful co-existence of states with different social systems.

Social revolution is based on an antagonism between labour and capital, between the oppressed and the oppressor nations. Socialist revolution — and this Marxists-Leninists clearly realise — is the result of an extreme aggravation of internal and international contradictions of imperialism, the setting in of a deep nation-wide crisis, and more acute class struggle. It cannot be imposed by means of a world war, from outside. Revolutions do not take place by order. The victorious proletariat cannot impose any kind of "happiness" on another people without undermining its own victory.

A. A. ARZUMANYAN   143

Revolutions are performed by the people, by exploited classes, when the necessary internal and external objective and subjective conditions are mature. That is why the task is to prevent the export of counter-revolution, and the atmosphere of peaceful co-existence creates the most favourable conditions for this. That is why the alternative — "peaceful co-existence or revolution" — is false and hostile to the revolutionary cause of the working class and all working people.

Revolution is not a violation of the principle of peaceful co-existence. It is an internal affair of the people choosing its own way and taking its own future into its own hands. When peaceful co-existence is opposed to revolution, it is in fact an attempt to justify the export of counter-revolution and imperialist attempts to crush the revolution and the national-liberation struggle of the nations.

Peaceful co-existence creates the most favourable possibilities for the struggle of the working class in the capitalist countries, it facilitates the struggle of the peoples of colonial and dependent countries for liberation from imperialism and promotes the further development and acceleration of the victory of the national-liberation revolution. It was no accident that in the atmosphere of peaceful co-existence the Socialist revolution won out in Cuba, that dozens of countries of Asia and Africa won political independence and that capitalism entered a new stage of its general crisis. Peaceful co-existence does not mean reconciliation with imperialism, it does not mean a damping down of the struggle, but a specific form of class struggle and favourable conditions for the unfurling of the revolutionary process.

The struggle for peace, for the implementation of the principles of peaceful co-existence and for disarmament is one of the most important forms of the peoples' struggle against imperialism, against the new wars it is preparing, against the aggressive acts of the imperialists on the territory of other countries, against the arms drive, etc. This struggle serves the interests of the working class, and of all working people, and is in that sense a class struggle. The struggle for peace and peaceful co-existence weakens the front of imperialism, isolates the most aggressive imperialist circles from the people, and helps the revolutionary struggle of the working class and the national-liberation movement of the peoples.

Revolutionary processes develop and can proceed on an ever deeper and wider scale. Socialism can win all over the world not in the few hours of destructive thermo-nuclear war, but in the years of peaceful co-existence which is the basis of peaceful competition between Socialism and capitalism. *It is the victory of the new social system in peaceful economic competition with the social system which is leaving the historical stage that will be of exceptional importance for the choice by all people of the Socialist path as the only correct one.*

The alternative in actual life is the following: either peaceful co-existence between states with different social systems, or a destructive war. There is no other way. In these circumstances, Communists can take no other attitude but that of peaceful co-existence. The banner of peace enables the Communists to rally broad sections of the people and to create a mass political army of which the bourgeoisie and her parties cannot even dream. It is this that makes for the revolutionary optimism of the Communists. . . .

It was repeatedly stressed in the speeches at the [June] Plenary Meeting that the attempts of the bourgeois politicians, who are defending the old world, to impose on Socialism peaceful co-existence in the sphere of ideas is a piece of outright ideological sabotage whose purpose is to disarm the millions of builders of the Communist future ideologically and to make them "peacefully" capitulate to imperialism.

"To agree to peaceful co-existence between Communist and bourgeois ideology is to give the enemy a chance to denigrate everything that we cherish, to encourage slander, to help corrupt the people's consciousness, to disrupt our organisation and in every way to slow down our advance. We have fought and will continue to fight with implacability not only against corrupt bourgeois ideology, but also against its agents in our midst, as against the agents of our class enemies," N. S. Khrushchev told the June Plenary Meeting of the Central Committee of the C.P.S.U.

In these conditions it becomes especially important to make a detailed analysis of every aspect of the ideological battle which is being fought in conditions of the peaceful co-existence of states with different social systems, a battle which today is one of the most important forms of the class struggle.

SHAO TIEH-CHEN
Revolutionary Dialectics and How to Appraise Imperialism

Marxism-Leninism makes a scientific analysis of the development of the class struggle and, on the basis of this analysis, guides the revolutionary struggles of the proletariat and of all the people striving for emancipation. When the proletariat and other revolutionary people are in an oppressed position, their strength is always far inferior to that of the landlords and the bourgeoisie who have long been in the position of oppressors and rulers. However, as they represent the direction in which history advances, their strength is capable of growing with each passing day. Provided they persist in struggle, using the correct methods, and provided they dare to seize victory at the decisive juncture, they will finally be able to defeat the reactionary and decadent ruling forces. Which, after all, are the really powerful forces: the newly rising forces of the people or the decadent forces of reaction? Marxist-Leninists answer without the slightest hesitation: the newly rising forces of the people, not the decadent forces of reaction. This is a profoundly scientific answer, an answer which is full of revolutionary significance.

MAKING A CORRECT ESTIMATE OF THE BALANCE OF FORCES

Hence, in the struggle against the class enemy, the proletariat and other revolutionary people must, first of all, make a correct estimate of the overall balance of class forces, must show dauntless revolutionary spirit and revolutionary aspirations, and must have a firm faith that the revolutionary forces, which are outwardly weak, are certain to defeat the counter-revolutionary forces, which are outwardly strong. . . .

This was precisely the way the great revolutionary teachers, Marx, Engels and Lenin, treated the class enemy in their own revolutionary activity. More than a hundred years ago, when the bourgeoisie held sway over the entire world, Marx, Engels and a few others were the only Communists. They had neither political power nor armed forces, yet they dared to challenge the old world and to pass the death sentence upon the capitalist system in highly inspiring words. "Its fall [the fall of the bourgeoisie] and the victory of the proletariat are equally inevitable." . . .

This article originally appeared in *Red Flag*, I (January 5, 1963) and is reprinted from a translation in the *Peking Review*, VI, No. 2 (January 11, 1963) 10-15; emphases and subheads were added by *Peking Review* editors.

When Lenin was arrested after he began taking part in revolutionary activity, a police officer asked him, "Why must you make trouble, young fellow? You're up against a brick wall!" Lenin replied unruffled, "A brick wall, but it's rotten; touch it and it will crumble."[1] . . . On the second anniversary of the October Revolution Lenin said in retrospect: "It seemed at that time that world imperialism was such a tremendous and invincible force that it was stupid of the workers of a backward country to attempt an uprising against it. Now, however, as we glance back over the past two years, we see that even our opponents are increasingly admitting that we were right. We see that imperialism, which seemed such an insuperable colossus, has proved before the whole world to be a colossus with feet of clay."[2] Lenin has also said that international capitalism was "a decrepit, dying, hopelessly sick old man."

All this shows the combination of a great scientific insight and a high revolutionary spirit in the persons of Marx, Engels and Lenin. They were able to penetrate all the surface phenomena to the weak essence of the seemingly strong reactionary forces, and they therefore dared to lead the proletariat in struggle against the temporarily much stronger enemy. It was for the same reason that Lenin dared to launch against imperialism the onslaught of the Great October Revolution, at a time when the philistines thought it utterly impossible. . . .

MEANING OF THE PAPER TIGER THESIS

Basing himself on the Marxist-Leninist theory of the class struggle, and especially on Lenin's theory of imperialism, Comrade Mao Tse-tung has summed up a wealth of rich, historical experience, stating that imperialism and all reactionaries are paper tigers, that they are powerful only in appearance, that in reality they are inwardly weak though outwardly strong, weak inside though fierce in countenance, and therefore are not terrifying at all. This is completely in accord with the ideas of Marx, Engels and Lenin in their appraisal of the class enemy.

Comrade Mao Tse-tung's thesis that imperialism and all reactionaries are paper tigers was put forward 16 years ago. At that time, with the end of World War II, the international situation underwent a fundamental change and a realignment of class forces took place on an international scale. The fascist bandits of Germany, Italy and Japan were

---

[1] *Lenin, a Biography* (London: Lawrence and Wishart) p. 9.
[2] "Two Years of Soviet Rule," *Lenin on War and Peace* (Peking: Foreign Languages Press) p. 22.

defeated, the imperialists of Britain, France and some other countries were weakened, the socialist camp began to take shape and the forces of peace and democracy and the national-liberation movement of the peoples of the world were growing. However, U.S. imperialism had taken the place of the German, Italian and Japanese fascists and become the centre and bulwark of world reaction. Relying on its economic power gained through the huge profits it derived from the war, and relying on its monopoly of "the might of the atomic bomb," U.S. imperialism rallied the reactionary forces of all countries, pulled together the remnant forces of fascism and formed an imperialist and anti-democratic camp to oppose the socialist and all other democratic forces, in a vain attempt to dominate and enslave the whole world. At that time, a seemingly powerful adverse current emerged both internationally and in China, which was directed against the Soviet Union, against communism and against the people. In China, the Chiang Kai-shek reactionaries, relying on the immense military and financial support given them by U.S. imperialism, launched a war against the people with the aim of wiping out the Chinese people's revolutionary forces. At the same time, they made every effort to spread among the people the myth of the invincibility of U.S. imperialism.

In those conditions of tense and acute class struggle how was one to appraise the balance of class forces? Could the revolutionary forces defeat the counter-revolutionary forces? These were questions about which not only the people of China but the people of the whole world were closely concerned. Taking a revolutionary proletarian stand and applying the Marxist-Leninist scientific method, Comrade Mao Tse-tung analysed the international and domestic situation following the end of World War II. He pointed out that the contradiction between the proletariat and the bourgeoisie within each imperialist country, the contradiction between the imperialist powers, and the contradiction between imperialism and the people of the colonial and semi-colonial countries not only continued to exist but were becoming more acute and widespread. These contradictions were most strikingly exhibited by U.S. imperialism. Its economic power, which had multiplied during the world war, was faced after the war with an unstable and ever shrinking foreign and domestic market. The shrinking of the market would inevitably lead to a new economic crisis. After the war, U.S. imperialism became more and more reactionary and rotten politically. It began to institute a fascist rule at home and gradually discarded even the shadow of democracy and freedom, arousing more and more opposition from the American people. The fact that U.S. imperialism had rallied the reactionary forces of various countries around itself as its tools for ruling and oppressing the peoples of these countries was provoking firm opposition among the people of the whole world. The irreconcilable contradictions facing U.S. imperialism at home and abroad were like volcanoes which threatened it every minute and could erupt into revolutions at any moment. Comrade Mao Tse-tung said that the imperialist enemy "has a weak and fragile foundation, he is disintegrating internally, he is alienated from the people, he is confronted with inextricable economic crises; therefore, he can be defeated."[3]

In the light of the above analysis Comrade Mao Tse-tung pointed out: "All reactionaries are paper tigers. In appearance, the reactionaries are terrifying, but in reality they are not so powerful. From a long-term point of view, it is not the reactionaries but the people who are really powerful." He went on to elaborate, "Chiang Kai-shek and his supporters, the U.S. reactionaries, are all paper tigers too. Speaking of U.S. imperialism, people seem to feel that it is terrifically strong. Chinese reactionaries are using the 'strength' of the United States to frighten the Chinese people. But it will be proved that the U.S. reactionaries, like all the reactionaries in history, do not have much strength."[4] By comparing imperialism and all reactionaries to paper tigers, Comrade Mao Tse-tung provided a fundamental strategic concept for the revolutionary people, armed them ideologically, and strengthened their confidence in victory over the counter-revolutionary forces. This concept played a very great role in the Chinese People's Liberation War.

INTERNATIONAL EVENTS CONFIRM THE CORRECTNESS OF
THE PAPER TIGER THESIS

In the past ten years and more, Comrade Mao Tse-tung's thesis that imperialism and all reactionaries are paper tigers has stood the test of many events in the world arena and been proved correct. The victory of the Chinese people's revolution was one powerful confirmation. Comrade Mao Tse-tung put forward his thesis just when the reactionary Chiang Kai-shek clique had forced a civil war on the Chinese people.

---

[3] Mao Tse-tung, "Revolutionary Forces of the World Unite, Fight Against Imperialist Aggression!" *Selected Works* (Peking: Foreign Languages Press, 1961) IV, 285.
[4] "Talk With the American Correspondent Anna Louise Strong," *ibid.*, pp. 100, 101.

At that time, the balance of forces was tilted in favour of the reactionary Chiang Kai-shek clique. Its military strength amounted to more than 4 million troops, it controlled an area containing more than two-thirds of China's population, it had taken over all the equipment of the one million invading Japanese troops in China and received tremendous aid from U.S. imperialism. The People's Liberation Army, far inferior to the Chiang Kai-shek troops both in numbers and in equipment, had only 1,200,000 men. The liberated areas were much smaller than the areas under the Kuomintang. Yet, through bitter struggles, the Chinese people finally defeated the powerful enemy and put an end to the 22-year-old reactionary rule of the "Chiang Kai-shek dynasty."

The Vietnamese people waged a protracted and arduous struggle in extremely difficult conditions during the eight years from 1946 to 1954. They finally defeated the U.S.-backed French colonialists, bringing to an end the more than 80 years of colonial rule of French imperialism in the northern part of their country. The Iraqi people, in their national-democratic revolution, overthrew the imperialist-supported Faisal monarchy in 1958, thus knocking an important link out of the Baghdad Treaty Organization. The Algerian people started their fight against the French colonialists with a guerrilla force of only 3,000 men. Yet the French colonialists failed to stem the revolutionary torrent of the Algerian people, even though they threw in 800,000 troops. . . .

Beginning with only 12 men and 7 rifles, the revolutionary struggle under Fidel Castro's leadership overthrew the fascist dictatorship of U.S. imperialism's running-dog Batista in a little more than two years of heroic fighting, thus smashing a link in the U.S. imperialist chain binding Latin America, in the Western hemisphere over which U.S. imperialism has been accustomed to ride roughshod. . . .

The thesis that imperialism and all reactionaries are paper tigers has been readily accepted by the revolutionary masses because it fully accords with objective reality. This has severely shaken imperialism and all the reactionaries. The imperialists are in constant fear that the people of the world will recognize them for the paper tigers that they are and will thus hold them in contempt. They therefore seize on every occasion to argue on their own behalf, declaring themselves to be powerful, genuine tigers, and not paper ones. Yet facts are most stubborn things. The self-aggrandizement of the imperialists only proves that the paper tiger thesis has hit them where it hurts most and has exposed to view their true nature.

Some people use a metaphysical approach to interpret the thesis that imperialism and all reactionaries are paper tigers. These people say, if imperialism and the reactionaries are paper tigers, how is it that they are able to go around committing aggression and unleashing wars? Or they say, if they are paper tigers, wouldn't it require scarcely any effort to wipe them out? These people, it is clear, know nothing whatsoever of Marxist dialectics. Marxism teaches us over and over again not to be misled by superficial phenomena but to look at the essence of a problem and discover the essential relationships amid a host of phenomena. Lenin has said: "Dialectics in the proper sense is the study of contradiction in the very essence of objects."[5] In regarding imperialism and the reactionaries as paper tigers, Comrade Mao Tse-tung refers to their essential nature. On the one hand, imperialism and the reactionaries are "tigers," for they can frighten people, can devour people. On the other hand, they are made of "paper," and their strength is not so great. This is the dual nature of imperialism and all reactionaries. Comrade Mao Tse-tung has pointed out, "Just as there is not a single thing in the world without a dual nature (this is the law of the unity of opposites), so imperialism and all reactionaries have a dual nature — they are real tigers and paper tigers at the same time."[6] . . .

LACK OF FAITH IN PEOPLE — FUNDAMENTAL CHARACTERISTIC OF OPPORTUNISM

It is a fundamental characteristic of the opportunists that they have no faith in the strength of the people and do not believe that those forces of the people which are temporarily in an inferior position will grow strong and be able to defeat imperialism and all the reactionaries; hence, they cannot accept the thesis that imperialism is a paper tiger. Contrary to all the opportunists, Marxist-Leninists hold that the strength of the people is the most powerful force of all and is the decisive force pushing social development forward. Every revolutionary struggle is bound to generate inexhaustible strength, provided it is rooted in the

[5] V. I. Lenin, "Conspectus of Hegel's Book, Lectures on the History of Philosophy," *Collected Works* XXXVIII (Moscow: Foreign Languages Publishing House, 1961) 253–254.
[6] Mao Tse-tung, "Talk With the American Correspondent Anna Louise Strong," *op. cit.*, IV, 98.

masses, fully sets the masses in motion and really becomes the business of the masses themselves. This strength has no match in the world and is capable of smashing any reactionary force, however formidable. It was from this standpoint, belief in the strength of the people, that Lenin viewed imperialism as a "colossus with feet of clay." He said, "He wins in war who has the greater reserves, the greater sources of strength, the greater endurance in the mass of people. . . ."[7]

Imperialism always tries to intimidate the people with the weapons at its disposal, but whatever the weapons may be, they cannot alter imperialism's fatal weakness of being divorced from the people. The factor that decides the destiny of humanity has never been any weapon; it is always the masses of the people. Not the nuclear weapon, but the strength of the people, is the greatest power in the world. Imperialism's use of nuclear weapons to intimidate people, and for nuclear blackmail, is also like a paper tiger in the eyes of the revolutionary people, and can never intimidate the masses. . . .

DESPISING THE ENEMY STRATEGICALLY

Proceeding from the appraisal of the essence of imperialism and all reactionaries and basing himself on the experience gained over many years in China's revolutionary struggles, Comrade Mao Tse-tung formulated the strategy and tactics of the revolution and developed the Marxist-Leninist thinking on strategy and tactics. He has said, "In order to struggle against the enemy, we have formed the concept over a long period that strategically we should despise all enemies, but tactically take them seriously. This also means that we should despise the enemy in general but take him seriously on each and every concrete question."[8]

To despise the enemy strategically means to perceive that the class enemy, viewed in its essence and in the long run, is bound to perish in the end, no matter how powerful he may be for a time; and that the revolutionary forces will eventually win, no matter how weak they may be for a time. In the last analysis, it is the masses of the people who are really powerful, and not imperialism and the reactionaries. That is why we should dare to struggle against the enemy, dare to overthrow the rule of imperialism and the reactionaries and dare to seize victory. . . . When the Third Revolutionary Civil War began, Comrade Mao

[7] V. I. Lenin, *The Results of Party Week in Moscow and Our Tasks.*
[8] *Imperialism and All Reactionaries Are Paper Tigers* (Peking) p. 27.

Tse-tung pointed out that the "millet plus rifles" of the people would prove more powerful than the aeroplanes plus tanks of the Chiang Kai-shek reactionary clique. He later added that "Chiang Kai-shek's superiority in military forces was only transient, a factor which could play only a temporary role, that U.S. imperialist aid was likewise a factor which could play only a temporary role, while the anti-popular character of Chiang Kai-shek's war and the feelings of the people were factors that would play a constant role, and that in this respect the People's Liberation Army was in a superior position. Patriotic, just and revolutionary in character, the war waged by the People's Liberation Army was bound to win the support of the people of the whole country. That was the political foundation for victory over Chiang Kai-shek."[9] . . .

TAKING FULL ACCOUNT OF THE ENEMY TACTICALLY

To take full account of the enemy tactically means that with regard to any given part of the whole, and in each specific struggle, it is necessary to take the enemy seriously, to be prudent, to pay careful attention to the art of struggle and to adopt forms of struggle suited to different times, places and conditions in order to isolate and wipe out the enemy step by step. Comrade Mao Tse-tung has used homely analogies to illustrate the idea of taking full account of the enemy tactically. He has said, "In war, battles can only be fought one by one and the enemy can only be annihilated bit by bit. Factories can only be built one by one. The peasants can only plough the land plot by plot."[10] When we were waging the struggle against the Chiang Kai-shek reactionaries, Comrade Mao Tse-tung on the one hand took them as paper tigers, pointing out that the reactionaries would eventually be defeated and the people would eventually triumph. On the other hand, in each specific struggle against the Chiang Kai-shek reactionaries, he was always most serious and circumspect, went painstakingly into the art of struggle and opposed any inclination to take the enemy lightly and any adventurism. In each specific struggle, he always saw to it that our army was fully prepared, and fought no battle unprepared, fought no battle it was not sure of winning. In every battle, our army concentrated an absolutely superior force (two, three, four and sometimes

[9] Mao Tse-tung, "The Present Situation and Our Tasks," *Selected Works* (Peking) IV, 160.
[10] *Imperialism and All Reactionaries Are Paper Tigers* (Peking) p. 27.

even five or six times the enemy's strength), in order to wipe out the enemy completely and gain victory. Comrade Mao Tse-tung has also pointed out that, when we wage a struggle against the enemy, it is necessary not only to gauge the possibilities in our favour, but also to take into account the different kinds of difficulties we might encounter, and that it is necessary to be fully prepared for the maximum difficulties that might emerge. Only in this way can we stand invincible.

The struggle of the revolutionary people against imperialism and the reactionaries is an arduous and complex one, and victory is impossible without paying a considerable price. The road of revolution is not without its twists and turns and is sometimes beset with difficulties and setbacks when certain detours and temporary retreats are necessary. When an unfavourable situation arises, it is all the more necessary that the revolutionary people firmly adhere to the general strategy for defeating the enemy if they are to carry the struggle forward and transform the situation into a favourable one. Lack of courage to scorn the enemy strategically would not only result in loss of revolutionary determination in unfavourable circumstances; but even given an excellent revolutionary situation, such loss of revolutionary determination would deprive one of the courage to use the opportunity to seize victory and would thus damage the revolutionary cause. At the same time, precisely because the road of revolution is tortuous, it is necessary to take full account of the enemy tactically; heedless and reckless action in any specific struggle will also damage the revolution.

DIALECTICAL INTEGRATION OF STRATEGICAL AND TACTICAL CONCEPTS

The two aspects — despising the enemy strategically and taking full account of him tactically — must be integrated dialectically. This is an important Marxist-Leninist principle. All who genuinely want revolution, and want to win victory, must take this attitude in dealing with the enemy; there is and can be no other attitude to take. Departure from this Marxist-Leninist principle in the revolutionary struggle will lead to opportunist errors of one kind or another. Anyone who takes full account of the enemy tactically, but does not dare to despise him strategically, will inevitably commit Right opportunist errors. Anyone who despises the enemy both tactically and strategically will inevitably commit "Left" adventurist errors. Anyone who dares not despise the enemy strategically and moreover does not take full account of him tactically, will commit both Right opportunist errors in strategy and "Left" adventurist errors in tactics. These conclusions are derived from the abundant experience both of success and failure, accumulated by the Chinese people during their protracted revolutionary struggles. Only by despising the enemy strategically and taking full account of him tactically, and by integrating the two closely, is it possible to hold the initiative and to strike with telling effect at the enemy until his defeat is complete.

To despise the enemy strategically is an essential precondition for taking full account of him tactically. Tactics are guided by strategy. Though tactics must vary with the circumstances in specific struggles, the ultimate aim is always to defeat the enemy. If anyone does not dare to despise the enemy strategically, refusing to look upon imperialism and the reactionaries as paper tigers, either he will give up the revolutionary struggle, make one-sided compromise or accommodation with the enemy, and even surrender shamelessly, or he will take reckless, imprudent and adventurist steps in specific struggles. Naturally, in neither case can he be said to take full account of the enemy tactically. Therefore, it is only by really despising the enemy strategically that one can really take full account of him tactically.

The fundamental contradiction in the present-day world between imperialism and its lackeys on the one hand and the people of all countries on the other has not been resolved. The anti-imperialist struggle of the people in all countries is steadily surging forward. For the present, the main danger in this struggle against imperialism and the reactionaries is over-estimation of the enemy's strength and under-estimation of the people's strength. To lack the courage to see imperialism and reactionaries as paper tigers, that is, not daring to despise the enemy strategically, to expose the essence of imperialism and the reactionaries before the people of the world, or to wage a resolute and thoroughgoing struggle against them, is a manifestation of Right opportunism. The task of all Marxist-Leninists and all revolutionaries is to rid the masses of the people of the influence of this Right opportunism, to help them see the essence of imperialism and the reactionaries clearly and to enhance their revolutionary confidence and determination.

Developing the Third World

G. MIRSKY
Whither the Newly Independent Countries

A large, new group of countries which have begun their national renascence has appeared in the world where the struggle and competition between the two world systems is taking place. Most of these countries, as pointed out in the Programme of the C.P.S.U., "have not yet broken free from world capitalist economy even though they occupy a special place in it. They constitute that part of the world which is still being exploited by the capitalist monopolies."

The newly independent countries are faced with a task of historic importance, namely, to put an end to centuries-old backwardness and escape from monopolist domination. They are looking for the most effective and the quickest ways of eliminating their backwardness and dependence and are trying to get onto the highroad of progress and general prosperity. This is the future that hundreds of millions of people in Asia, Africa and Latin America are dreaming of and fighting for. What should their way forward be like? This question has now assumed exceptionally great importance for the development of the entire world.

Industrial output in all the underdeveloped countries has risen noticeably as compared with the period of foreign rule. Whereas before the Second World War the average annual increase in their gross output did not exceed 1 percent, it has in recent years been 4 percent. Industrialisation has been proclaimed almost everywhere as the chief aim in economic development. . . .

Corresponding changes are taking place in foreign trade as well. . . . we are witnessing a slow but steady change in the old status of the underdeveloped countries as mere agrarian and raw material appendages of the metropolitan countries, suppliers of raw materials and importers of consumer goods.

The state sector embracing key industries is becoming a major factor in the economic development of many countries which have won in-

G. Mirsky is senior researcher, Institute of World Economy and International Relations, U.S.S.R. Academy of Sciences. These excerpts are from an article in *International Affairs* (Moscow), XII (December 1962) 23–27.

dependence. Economic planning is becoming the practice in almost all these countries. . . . Today more than 40 young states have adopted economic development programmes.

These states, however, have to contend with numerous and serious difficulties in their economic development. They still hold an unequal position in the world capitalist economy and their economic prospects have even deteriorated in some respects. The share of the agrarian-raw material countries, in particular, is decreasing in the world capitalist market; trade in manufactured goods is growing at a much faster pace than trade in raw materials and food. The U.N. Economic Commission for Asia and the Far East in its report for 1960 pointed to a "shift in favour of trade between industrial countries, rather than between industrial and the primary exporting countries. . . . World economic growth has not increased the demand for the products of primary exporting countries as it has done for the products of industrial countries."[1]

Various factors, such as synthetics production and greater output of other raw materials in the industrial countries themselves, have reduced the share of raw material exports (and consequently the share of the agrarian-raw material countries) in world capitalist trade, although in absolute terms exports of raw materials have risen. The monopolies are extracting more and more wealth from the underdeveloped countries, but in the general balance of world trade the share of minerals and agricultural commodities exported from the African, Asian and Latin American countries is shrinking. This means that the dependence of the industrial states on raw materials supplied by the underdeveloped countries is becoming relatively weaker and the monopolies are getting greater opportunities for artificially reducing the prices of natural raw materials.

Trade between the underdeveloped countries themselves remains insignificant. In 1958, it amounted to only 6.8 per cent of total trade between countries within the capitalist system. In other words, in their foreign trade the underdeveloped countries are still extremely dependent on the advanced capitalist Powers, although the growth of trade with the Socialist states is steadily lessening this dependence.

The newly independent countries are beset by serious financial hardships, yet the development of the economy, ruined and bled white by colonialist rule, requires more and more funds. The shortage of foreign

[1] *Economic Survey of Asia and the Far East*, 1960, p. 1.

exchange compels the young states to attract foreign capital by accepting quite onerous terms.

Political independence by itself has naturally not been able to deliver the peoples from poverty and backwardness. Per capita national income in the underdeveloped countries is now on the average only one-tenth or one-eleventh of that in the industrial capitalist states. There is also a wide gap in food consumption. These countries are still so far unable to provide employment for a substantial part of the population. This is directly bound up with the fact that land reforms have not been completed. Feudalism has not been entirely rooted out, for even in countries where the ownership of large estates has been abolished the peasants are not yet free from having to pay extortionate rents or from the grip of the usurers. Even in countries where the peasants have received land, the majority of them have not been provided with implements and seed and are dependent on the owners of irrigation networks.

The position in regard to agrarian relations and the related problem of employment hamper the efforts of young states towards industrial development. As long as these countries are without a reasonably well organised agriculture, they cannot have a large home market, and this in turn limits the possibilities of industrial development. Industry is unable to absorb the surplus labour which constantly flows from the countryside. The struggle to transform their economic life proceeds within this "vicious circle."

The absolute gap in the volume of production between the underdeveloped and industrial countries is actually widening despite the fact that the growth rates of the former on the whole are higher than those of the latter. But at this pace the young states would need about 80–100 years to overtake the production level of the advanced capitalist countries. . . .

The foreign monopolies preserve a very strong grip on these countries, especially in Africa. Total British capital investments in Africa amount to $6,500 million, French, to about $7,000 million and American, to $1,100 million. In the last nine years private American investments alone in Africa have nearly trebled and grew at a faster rate than in any other area. The monopolies robbing Africa's wealth get fabulous profits. . . .

Moreover there is a lack of skilled personnel in these countries, which similarly hampers the fight against foreign capital penetration. All this hampers the execution of economic development programmes.

Let us now turn to some political factors characterising the position of the young states. In most of them the national bourgeoisie is the most influential class, although in a number of cases it is compelled to share power with other classes or groups. . . .

In most African countries south of the Sahara no class of local bourgeoisie has been formed. Many African leaders quite obviously consider that in the second half of the 20th century when capitalism is already on the wane in the world it is undesirable to encourage private enterprise. They have legitimate doubts as to whether it is worth while setting up numerous private factories and small shops when the country, taking over from the foreign monopolies, can become the complete master of her economic life.

There are however other "theories" which have gained currency in Africa. Their proponents try to claim that Africans should create their own, completely original social system and that the "naive, mysterious and religious African soul" is against Communism. The idea of some kind of a "third path" for Africans is put forward.

There is not and cannot be any "third path" and experience shows that the African peoples are not looking for one. They are firmly in favour of public ownership of the land and the means of production. . . .

What is the situation in those newly independent countries in which features of capitalist development are already in evidence and power is completely in the hands of the national bourgeoisie?

The special position of the national bourgeoisie is due to the fact that it has assumed leadership in the newly independent countries in an epoch when the dominating tendency in world development is towards Socialism, while imperialism continues stubbornly to cling to its positions and seeks to extend them by all possible means.

In these historically formed conditions the bourgeoisie in the underdeveloped countries finds itself caught between two diametrically opposing tendencies in world development and has to manoeuvre between them.

The interests of the national bourgeoisie as an exploiting class, connected by many threads with international finance capital, drag its Right wing into co-operation with imperialism in the struggle against the Left, progressive forces reflecting the true interests of the nation, against forces whose victory — and the bourgeoisie knows this well — would inevitably signify the triumph of Socialism.

On the other hand, the interests of the national bourgeoisie as a class which seeks to break the stranglehold and diktat of the foreign monopolies and win for itself a respected and equal "place in the sun" in the capitalist world, compel it to fight for economic independence and determine its anti-imperialist tendencies.

"In modern conditions," it is pointed out in the Programme of the C.P.S.U., "the national bourgeoisie in those colonial, one-time colonial and dependent countries where it is not connected with the imperialist circles is objectively interested in accomplishing the basic tasks of an anti-imperialist and anti-feudal revolution. Its progressive role and its ability to participate in the solution of pressing national problems are, therefore, not yet spent."

The economic development of the young states so far shows that the national bourgeoisie, although it has a dual nature and is indecisive in its actions, is nevertheless ousting foreign capital. . . . The prospect undoubtedly is one of worsened relations between the national bourgeoisie and imperialism and, on this basis, broad sections of the bourgeoisie could be drawn into the struggle against imperialism.

The dual nature of the bourgeoisie, however, prevents it from making radical reforms in home policy and from destroying everything of the old order that drags their countries back. The national-liberation, anti-imperialist revolution has not been completed and there is a growing discrepancy between what the people hoped for and what they have got. This could to a great extent be said about a number of newly independent countries under bourgeois leadership.

The unwillingness of the exploiting classes to forego their privileges for the benefit of the nation or carry through a redistribution of the national income seriously retards the social and economic development of young states. In his book *The Future of Underdeveloped Countries*, recently published in the United States and prepared with the help of the Study Group of the Council on Foreign Relations, E. Staley says that "in Nicaragua, according to a mission of the International Bank for Reconstruction and Development, if only 10 per cent of the income of the upper 1 per cent of income receivers were to be invested productively, the current rate of productive investment in the country would increase by 50 per cent. One student of Philippine economic problems estimates that as much as one-fifth of the national income could be extracted annually for use in the development programme if a serious effort were made to do so."[2]

But can the bourgeoisie itself make this "serious effort"? The facts

[2] E. Staley, *The Future of Underdeveloped Countries* (New York, 1962) p. 263.

show that the bourgeoisie does not wish to hand over any of its riches or privileges to the nation. The latest economic reforms in the United Arab Republic directed against the big bourgeoisie were introduced by the Nasser Government after it had become convinced that sabotage by the bourgeoisie and its unwillingness to contribute to industrialisation were seriously impeding and even threatening to wreck the country's economic development programme.

Under the leadership of the national bourgeoisie the developing countries can achieve certain successes in the struggle for economic independence and against monopoly oppression, but they cannot completely solve in this way the pressing problem of overcoming their legacy of backwardness. Capitalism, this system that brings suffering to the people, does not hold out any bright prospects for nations which are intent on ending backwardness, poverty and starvation, particularly since the colonialist policy of exploitation reduces to a minimum the possibility of solving the national problems of young states on a capitalist basis.

A chief purpose of imperialist policy in regard to the underdeveloped countries is to isolate them from the Socialist system and preserve them as a backward exploited sector of the world capitalist economy — to keep them as a "world hinterland." To gain these ends the Western Powers are ready to make certain political concessions and at times even reconcile themselves (at least in words) to the neutralism of the national bourgeoisie in the young states. . . .

Had there been no world Socialist system, the developing countries would never have had any prospect of eliminating their backwardness: the economic, political and, lastly, military might of imperialism would not have allowed them to make the swift and radical reforms needed to extricate themselves from the abyss into which the colonialists plunged entire continents. But today such prospects do exist, since the Socialist system has become the decisive factor of world development. "Gone are the days," N. S. Khrushchev pointed out, "when the imperialists were able without difficulty to drive the peoples into a blind alley and doom them to bondage. It is much easier now for the peoples freed from the colonialist yoke to fight against imperialism. The world Socialist community acts now as a shield reliably protecting the peoples fighting for freedom and progress. The possibilities of the Socialist countries to render support to these peoples are growing steadily."

The young states are rapidly developing their economic relations with the Socialist states, whose unselfish assistance has already become an important factor in the national renascence of the Asian and African peoples and is beginning to exert a favourable influence on the economic development of Latin American countries.

In face of this mighty factor which exerts a growing impact on the course of events, the economic diktat of imperialism is no longer as effective as in the past: trade with the Socialist states is reinforcing the positions of raw material-exporting countries in the world market.

Imperialism has been forced to enter into competition with the Socialist states in giving aid to underdeveloped countries. Western capital has been compelled to make concessions, to ease credit terms, etc. This is a kind of indirect assistance by the Socialist states to countries liberated from the colonial yoke.

Now that the underdeveloped countries are able to choose between what they are offered and what they actually need, the imperialist states are being deprived of the opportunity of imposing on the young states economic relations which benefit only the stronger side. Today when the imperialists have lost their monopoly on loans, export of equipment and technical know-how and are often forced to make concessions, the young states can to a certain extent neutralise the colonialist tendencies of the Western Powers and gain equal and more advantageous relations for themselves.

That the young states can attain high rates in their economic growth and cultural development has been demonstrated by the record of the Socialist countries in Europe and Asia which have proved the Marxist thesis that backward countries need not necessarily pass through all the stages of capitalist development. The former colonial border regions of tsarist Russia — Central Asia and Transcaucasia with their multi-national population — have been transformed into developed countries in less than a quarter of a century. Capitalism could have never ensured such amazing growth rates. "We Communists are confident in the strength of Socialism, in its advantages," N. S. Khrushchev stated at the World Congress for General Disarmament and Peace. "It is a thing history has already proved. Socialism has in a short time demonstrated its viability, its superiority in rates of economic development, scientific and technological progress, public education, and the provision of true freedoms to the masses. The heights which the Soviet Union has now scaled are imposing evidence of the advantages of Socialism."

Life itself compels the newly independent countries to take the road of non-capitalist development. The change-over onto this road can be made in different ways and in different time-limits by particular countries. National democracy can be the political form for this transition.

A national democracy is not a Socialist state. Its purpose is to complete the general democratic, anti-imperialist, anti-feudal revolution. The consistent accomplishment of these tasks will greatly accelerate the progress of the revolution, lead the masses into the political arena, expelling the pro-imperialist, reactionary elements. A regrouping of class forces is likewise inevitable: the working class, peasantry and democratic intellectuals will become the ruling and leading force in the coalition holding power in a national democracy.

V. I. Lenin wrote: "Our European philistines never even dream that the subsequent revolutions in Oriental countries, which possess much vaster populations and a much vaster diversity of social conditions, will undoubtedly display even greater peculiarities than the Russian revolution."[3] National democracy is an example of this. On a broad historic scale it can only be a state destined to create the conditions for the transition of the countries liberated from the colonial chains to the road of non-capitalist development.

The entire course of events, confirming the correctness of the Marxist forecast of the socio-historical process, shows that such a transition will take place everywhere.

[3] V. I. Lenin, *Selected Works* (Moscow, 1952) II, Part 2, 727–728.

12 THE EDITORS OF "PEOPLE'S DAILY" AND "RED FLAG" Apologists of Neo-Colonialism

A great revolutionary storm has spread through Asia, Africa and Latin America since World War II. Independence has been proclaimed in more than fifty Asian and African countries. China, Viet Nam, Korea and Cuba have taken the road of socialism. The face of Asia, Africa and Latin America has undergone a tremendous change.

While revolution in the colonies and semi-colonies suffered serious setbacks after World War I owing to suppression by the imperialists and their lackeys, the situation after World War II is fundamentally different. The imperialists are no longer able to extinguish the prairie fire of national liberation. Their old colonial system is fast disintegrat-

These excerpts, from the fourth Chinese reply to the Open Letter of the Central Committee of the Communist Party of the Soviet Union on July 14, 1963, are reprinted from the *Peking Review*, VI, No. 43 (October 25, 1963) 6–15.

ing. Their rear has become a front of raging anti-imperialist struggles. Imperialist rule has been overthrown in some colonial and dependent countries, and in others it has suffered heavy blows and is tottering. This inevitably weakens and shakes the rule of imperialism in the metropolitan countries.

The victories of the people's revolutions in Asia, Africa and Latin America, together with the rise of the socialist camp, sound a triumphant paean to our day and age.

The storm of the people's revolution in Asia, Africa and Latin America requires every political force in the world to take a stand. This mighty revolutionary storm makes the imperialists and colonialists tremble and the revolutionary people of the world rejoice. The imperialists and colonialists say, "Terrible, terrible!" The revolutionary people say, "Fine, fine!" The imperialists and colonialists say, "It is rebellion, which is forbidden." The revolutionary people say, "It is revolution, which is the people's right and an inexorable current of history."

An important line of demarcation between the Marxist-Leninists and the modern revisionists is the attitude taken towards this extremely sharp issue of contemporary world politics. The Marxist-Leninists firmly side with the oppressed nations and actively support the national-liberation movement. The modern revisionists in fact side with the imperialists and colonialists and repudiate and oppose the national-liberation movement in every possible way.

In their words, the leaders of the C.P.S.U. dare not completely discard the slogans of support for the national-liberation movement, and at times, for the sake of their own interests, they even take certain measures which create the appearance of support. But if we probe to the essence and consider their views and policies over a number of years, we see clearly that their attitude towards the liberation struggles of the oppressed nations of Asia, Africa and Latin America is a passive or scornful or negative one, and that they serve as apologists for neo-colonialism.

In the open letter of the Central Committee of the C.P.S.U. of July 14, 1963, and in a number of articles and statements, the comrades of the C.P.S.U. have worked hard at defending their wrong views and attacking the Chinese Communist Party on the question of the national-liberation movement. But the sole outcome is to confirm the anti-Marxist-Leninist and anti-revolutionary stand of the leaders of the C.P.S.U. on the subject.

Let us now look at the theory and practice of the leaders of the C.P.S.U. on the question of the national-liberation movement.

Victories of great historic significance have already been won by the national-liberation movement in Asia, Africa and Latin America. This no one can deny. But can anyone assert that the task of combating imperialism and colonialism and their agents has been completed by the people of Asia, Africa and Latin America?

Our answer is, no. This fighting task is far from completed.

However, the leaders of the C.P.S.U. frequently spread the view that colonialism has disappeared or is disappearing from the present-day world. They emphasize that "there are 50 million people on earth still groaning under colonial rule," that the remnants of colonialism are to be found only in such places as Portuguese Angola and Mozambique in Africa, and that the abolition of colonial rule has already entered the "final phase."

What are the facts?

Consider, first, the situation in Asia and Africa. There a whole group of countries have declared their independence. But many of these countries have not completely shaken off imperialist and colonial control and enslavement and remain objects of imperialist plunder and aggression as well as arenas of contention between the old and new colonialists. In some, the old colonialists have changed into neo-colonialists and retain their colonial rule through their trained agents. In others, the wolf has left by the front door, but the tiger has entered through the back door, the old colonialism being replaced by the new, more powerful and more dangerous U.S. colonialism. The peoples of Asia and Africa are seriously menaced by the tentacles of neo-colonialism, represented by U.S. imperialism. . . .

The facts are clear. After World War II the imperialists have certainly not given up colonialism, but have merely adopted a new form, neo-colonialism. An important characteristic of such neo-colonialism is that the imperialists have been forced to change their old style of direct colonial rule in some areas and to adopt a new style of colonial rule and exploitation by relying on the agents they have selected and trained. The imperialists headed by the United States enslave or control the colonial countries and countries which have already declared their independence by organizing military blocs, setting up military bases, establishing "federations" or "communities," and fostering puppet regimes. By means of economic "aid" or other forms, they retain these countries as markets for their goods, sources of raw material and outlets for their export of capital, plunder the riches and suck the blood of the people of these countries. Moreover, they use the United Nations as an important tool for interfering in the internal affairs of such countries and for subjecting them to military, economic and cultural aggression. When they are unable to continue their rule over these countries by "peaceful" means, they engineer military coups d'etat, carry out subversion or even resort to direct armed intervention and aggression. . . .

This neo-colonialism is a more pernicious and sinister form of colonialism.

We would like to ask the leaders of the C.P.S.U., under such circumstances how can it be said that the abolition of colonial rule has already entered the "final phase"? . . .

The leaders of the C.P.S.U. have also created the theory that the national-liberation movement has entered upon a "new stage" having economic tasks as its core. Their argument is that, whereas "formerly, the struggle was carried on mainly in the political sphere," today the economic question has become the "central task" and "the basic link in the further development of the revolution."

The national-liberation movement has entered a new stage. But this is by no means the kind of "new stage" described by the leadership of the C.P.S.U. In the new stage, the level of political consciousness of the Asian, African and Latin American peoples has risen higher than ever and the revolutionary movement is surging forward with unprecedented intensity. They urgently demand the thorough elimination of the forces of imperialism and its lackeys in their own countries and strive for complete political and economic independence. The primary and most urgent task facing these countries is still the further development of the struggle against imperialism, old and new colonialism, and their lackeys. This struggle is still being waged fiercely in the political, economic, military, cultural, ideological and other spheres. And the struggles in all these spheres still find their most concentrated expression in political struggle, which often unavoidably develops into armed struggle when the imperialists resort to direct or indirect armed suppression. It is important for the newly independent countries to develop their independent economy. But this task must never be separated from the struggle against imperialism, old and new colonialism, and their lackeys.

Like "the disappearance of colonialism," this theory of a "new stage" advocated by the leaders of the C.P.S.U. is clearly intended to whitewash the aggression against and plunder of Asia, Africa and Latin America by neo-colonialism, as represented by the United States, to cover up the sharp contradiction between imperialism and the oppressed nations and to paralyse the revolutionary struggle of the people of these continents.

According to this theory of theirs, of course, the fight against imperialism, old and new colonialism, and their lackeys is, of course, no longer necessary, for colonialism is disappearing and economic development has become the central task of the national-liberation movement. Does it not follow that the national-liberation movement can be done away with altogether? Therefore, the kind of "new stage" described by the leaders of the C.P.S.U., in which economic tasks are in the centre of the picture, is clearly nothing but one of no opposition to imperialism, old and new colonialism, and their lackeys, a stage in which the national-liberation movement is no longer desired.

PRESCRIPTIONS FOR ABOLISHING THE REVOLUTION OF
THE OPPRESSED NATIONS

In line with their erroneous theories the leaders of the C.P.S.U. have sedulously worked out a number of nostrums for all the ills of the oppressed nations. Let us examine them.

The first prescription is labelled peaceful coexistence and peaceful competition.

The leaders of the C.P.S.U. constantly attribute the great postwar victories of the national-liberation movement won by the Asian, African and Latin American peoples to what they call "peaceful coexistence" and "peaceful competition." The open letter of the Central Committee of the C.P.S.U. says:

In conditions of peaceful coexistence, new important victories have been scored in recent years in the class struggle of the proletariat and in the struggle of the peoples for national freedom. The world revolutionary process is developing successfully.

They also say that the national-liberation movement is developing under conditions of peaceful coexistence between countries with different social systems and of economic competition between the two opposing social systems and that peaceful coexistence and peaceful competition "assist the unfolding of a process of liberation on the part of peoples fighting to free themselves from the economic domination of foreign monopolies," and can deliver "a crushing blow" to "the entire system of capitalist relationship."

All socialist countries should practise the Leninist policy of peaceful coexistence between countries with different social systems. But peaceful coexistence and peaceful competition cannot replace the revolutionary struggles of the people. The victory of the national revolution of all colonies and dependent countries must be won primarily through the revolutionary struggle of their own masses, which can never be replaced by that of any other countries.

The leaders of the C.P.S.U. hold that the victories of the national-liberation revolution are not due primarily to the revolutionary struggles of the masses, and that the people cannot emancipate themselves, but must wait for the natural collapse of imperialism through peaceful co-existence and peaceful competition. In fact, this is equivalent to telling the oppressed nations to put up with imperialist plunder and enslavement for ever, and not to rise up in resistance and revolution.

The second prescription is labelled aid to backward countries.

The leaders of the C.P.S.U. boast of the role played by their economic aid to the newly independent countries. Comrade Khrushchev has said that such aid can enable these countries "to avoid the danger of a new enslavement," and that "it stimulates their progress and contributes to the normal development and even acceleration of those internal processes which may take these countries on to the highway leading to socialism."

It is necessary and important for the socialist countries to give the newly independent countries economic aid on the basis of international-ism. But in no case can it be said that their national independence and social progress are due solely to the economic aid they receive from the socialist countries and not mainly to the revolutionary struggles of their own people.

To speak plainly, the policy and the purpose of the leaders of the C.P.S.U. in their aid to newly independent countries in recent years are open to suspicion. They often take an attitude of great-power chauvinism and national egoism in matters concerning aid to newly independent countries, harm the economic and political interests of the receiving countries, and as a result discredit the socialist countries. As for their aid to India, here their ulterior motives are especially clear. India tops the list of newly independent countries to which the Soviet Union gives economic aid. This aid is obviously intended to encourage the Nehru government in its policies directed against communism, against the people and against socialist countries. Even the U.S. imperialists have stated that such Soviet aid "is very much to our [U.S.] interest."

In addition, the leaders of the C.P.S.U. openly propose co-operation with U.S. imperialism in "giving aid to the backward countries." Khrushchev said in a speech in the United States in September 1959:

Your and our economic successes will be hailed by the whole world, which expects our two great powers to help the peoples who are centuries behind in their economic development to get on their feet more quickly.

Look! The mainstay of modern colonialism [namely, U.S. imperialism] will help the oppressed nations "to get on their feet more quickly"! It is indeed astonishing that the leaders of the C.P.S.U. are not only willing but even proud to be the partners of the neo-colonialists.

The third prescription is labelled disarmament.

Khrushchev has said:

Disarmament means disarming the war forces, abolishing militarism, ruling out armed interference in the internal affairs of any country, and doing away completely and finally with all forms of colonialism.

He has also said:

Disarmament would create proper conditions for a tremendous increase in the scale of assistance to the newly established national states. If a mere 8–10 per cent of the 120,000 million dollars spent for military purposes throughout the world were turned to the purpose, it would be possible to end hunger, disease and illiteracy in the distressed areas of the globe within twenty years.

We have always maintained that the struggle for general disarmament should be carried on in order to expose and oppose imperialist arms expansion and war preparations. But one cannot possibly say that colonialism will be eliminated through disarmament.

Khrushchev here sounds like a preacher. Downtrodden people of the world, you are blessed! If only you are patient, if only you wait until the imperialists lay down their arms, freedom will descend upon you. Wait until the imperialists show mercy, and the poverty-stricken areas of the world will become an earthly paradise flowing with milk and honey! . . .

This is not just the fostering of illusions, it is opium for the people.

The fourth prescription is labelled elimination of colonialism through the United Nations.

Khrushchev maintains that if the United Nations takes measures to uproot the colonial system, "the peoples who are now suffering the humiliation arising out of foreign domination, would acquire a clear and immediate prospect of peaceful liberation from foreign oppression."

In a speech at the United Nations General Assembly in September 1960, Khrushchev asked, "Who, if not the United Nations Organization, should champion the abolition of the colonial system of government?"

This is a strange question to ask. According to Khrushchev, the revolutionary people of Asia, Africa and Latin America should not and cannot themselves eliminate colonialism, but must look to the United Nations for help.

At the United Nations General Assembly, Khrushchev also said:

This is why we appeal to the reason and far-sightedness of the peoples of the Western countries, to their governments and their representatives at this high assembly of the United Nations. Let us agree on measures for the abolition of the colonial system of government and thereby accelerate that natural historical process.

It is apparent that what he really means by looking to the United Nations for help is looking to the imperialists for help. The facts show that the United Nations, which is still under the control of the imperialists, can only defend and strengthen the rule of colonialism but can never abolish it.

In a word, the nostrums of the leaders of the C.P.S.U. for the national-liberation movement has been concocted to make people believe that the imperialists will give up colonialism and bestow freedom and liberation upon the oppressed nations and peoples and that therefore all revolutionary theories, demands and struggles are outmoded and unnecessary and should and must be abandoned.

OPPOSITION TO WARS OF NATIONAL LIBERATION

Although they talk about supporting the movements and wars of national liberation, the leaders of the C.P.S.U. have been trying by every means to make the people of Asia, Africa and Latin America abandon their revolutionary struggle, because they themselves are sorely afraid of the revolutionary storm.

The leaders of the C.P.S.U. have the famous "theory" that "even a tiny spark can cause a world conflagration" and that a world war must necessarily be a thermonuclear war, which means the annihilation of mankind. Therefore, Khrushchev roars that " 'local wars' in our time are very dangerous," and that "we will work hard . . . to put out the sparks that may set off the flames of war." Here Khrushchev makes no distinction between just and unjust wars and betrays the communist stand of supporting just wars.

The history of the eighteen years since World War II has shown that wars of national liberation are unavoidable so long as the imperialists and their lackeys try to maintain their brutal rule by bayonets and use force to suppress the revolution of oppressed nations. These large-scale and small-scale revolutionary wars against the imperialists and their lackeys, which have never ceased, have hit hard at the imperialist forces of war, strengthened the forces defending world peace and effectively prevented the imperialists from realizing their plan of launching a world war. Frankly speaking, Khrushchev's clamour about the need to "put out" the sparks of revolution for the sake of peace is an attempt to oppose revolution in the name of safeguarding peace. . . .

THE AREAS IN WHICH CONTEMPORARY WORLD
CONTRADICTIONS ARE CONCENTRATED

The open letter of the Central Committee of the C.P.S.U. accuses the Chinese Communist Party of putting forward a "new theory." It says:

. . . according to the new theory the main contradiction of our time is, you see, contradiction not between socialism and imperialism, but between the national-liberation movement and imperialism. The decisive force in the struggle against imperialism, the Chinese comrades hold, is not the world system of socialism, not struggle of the international working class, but against the national-liberation movement.

In the first place, this is a fabrication. In our letter of June 14, we pointed out that the fundamental contradictions in the contemporary world are the contradiction between the socialist camp and the imperialist camp, the contradiction between the proletariat and the bourgeoisie in the capitalist countries, the contradiction between the oppressed nations and imperialism, and the contradictions among imperialist countries and among monopoly capitalist groups.

We also pointed out: The contradiction between the socialist camp and the imperialist camp is a contradiction between two fundamentally different social systems, socialism and capitalism. It is undoubtedly very sharp. But Marxist-Leninists must not regard the contradictions in the world as consisting solely and simply of the contradiction between the socialist camp and the imperialist camp.

Our view is crystal clear.

In our letter of June 14, we explained the revolutionary situation in

Asia, Africa and Latin America and the significance and role of the national-liberation movement. This is what we said:

1. "The various types of contradictions in the contemporary world are concentrated in the vast areas of Asia, Africa and Latin America; these are the most vulnerable areas under imperialist rule and the storm centres of world revolution dealing direct blows at imperialism."

2. "The national-democratic revolutionary movement in these areas and the international socialist revolutionary movement are the two great historical currents of our time."

3. "The national-democratic revolution in these areas is an important component of the contemporary proletarian world revolution."

4. "The anti-imperialist revolutionary struggles of the people in Asia, Africa and Latin America are pounding and undermining the foundations of the rule of imperialism and colonialism, old and new, and are now a mighty force in defence of world peace."

5. "In a sense, therefore, the whole cause of the international proletarian revolution hinges on the outcome of the revolutionary struggles of the people of these areas, who constitute the overwhelming majority of the world's population."

6. "Therefore, the anti-imperialist revolutionary struggle of the people in Asia, Africa and Latin America is definitely not merely a matter of regional significance but is one of overall importance for the whole cause of proletarian world revolution."

These are Marxist-Leninist theses, conclusions drawn by scientific analysis from the realities of our time.

No one can deny that an extremely favourable revolutionary situation now exists in Asia, Africa and Latin America. Today the national-liberation revolutions in Asia, Africa and Latin America are the most important forces dealing imperialism direct blows. The contradictions of the world are concentrated in Asia, Africa and Latin America.

The centre of world contradictions, of world political struggles, is not fixed but shifts with changes in the international struggles and the revolutionary situation. We believe that, with the development of the contradiction and struggle between the proletariat and the bourgeoisie in Western Europe and North America, the momentous day of battle will arrive in these homes of capitalism and heart-lands of imperialism. When that day comes, Western Europe and North America will undoubtedly become the centre of world political struggles, of world contradictions. ...

DISTORTION OF THE LENINIST VIEW OF LEADERSHIP IN THE REVOLUTION

In its open letter of July 14, the Central Committee of the C.P.S.U. also attacks the standpoint of the Chinese Communist Party on the question of proletarian leadership in the national-liberation movement. It says:

... the Chinese comrades want to "correct" Lenin and prove that hegemony in the world struggle against imperialism should go not to the working class, but to the petty bourgeoisie or the national bourgeoisie, even to "certain patriotically minded kings, princes and aristocrats."

This is a deliberate distortion of the views of the Chinese Communist Party.

In discussing the need for the proletariat to insist on leading the national-liberation movement, the letter of the Central Committee of the C.P.C. of June 14 says:

History has entrusted to the proletarian parties in these areas [Asia, Africa and Latin America] the glorious mission of holding high the banner of struggle against imperialism, against old and new colonialism and for national independence and people's democracy, of standing in the forefront of the national-democratic revolutionary movement and striving for a socialist future. ...
On the basis of the worker-peasant alliance the proletariat and its party must unite all the strata that can be united and organize a broad united front against imperialism and its lackeys. In order to consolidate and expand this united front it is necessary that the proletarian party should maintain its ideological, political and organizational independence and insist on the leadership of the revolution.

In discussing the need for establishing a broad anti-imperialist united front in the national-liberation movement, the letter of the Central Committee of the C.P.C. says:

The oppressed nations and peoples of Asia, Africa and Latin America are faced with the urgent task of fighting imperialism and its lackeys. ...
In these areas, extremely broad sections of the population refuse to be slaves of imperialism. They include not only the workers, peasants, intellectuals and petty bourgeoisie, but also the patriotic national bourgeoisie and even certain kings, princes and aristocrats, who are patriotic.

THE EDITORS OF "PEOPLE'S DAILY" AND "RED FLAG"   *173*

Our views are perfectly clear. In the national-liberation movement it is necessary both to insist on leadership by the proletariat and to establish a broad anti-imperialist united front. What is wrong with these views? Why should the leadership of the C.P.S.U. distort and attack these correct views?

It is not we, but the leaders of the C.P.S.U., who have abandoned Lenin's views on proletarian leadership in the revolution.

The wrong line of the leaders of the C.P.S.U. completely abandons the task of fighting imperialism and colonialism and opposes wars of national liberation; this means it wants the proletariat and the Communist Parties of the oppressed nations and countries to roll up their patriotic banner of opposing imperialism and struggling for national independence and surrender it to others. In that case, how could one even talk about an anti-imperialist united front or of proletarian leadership?

Another idea often propagated by the leaders of the C.P.S.U. is that a country can build socialism under no matter what leadership, including even that of reactionary nationalist like Nehru. This is still farther removed from the idea of proletarian leadership. . . .

THE PATH OF NATIONALISM AND DEGENERATION

In their open letter of July 14, the leaders of the C.P.S.U. attempt to pin on the Chinese Communist Party the charge of "isolating the national-liberation movement from the international working class and its creation, the socialist world system." They also accuse us of "separating" the national-liberation movement from the socialist system and the working-class movement in the Western capitalist countries and "counterposing" the former to the latter. There are other Communists, like the leaders of the French Communist Party, who loudly echo the leaders of the C.P.S.U.

But what are the facts? Those who counterpose the national-liberation movement to the socialist camp and the working-class movement in the Western capitalist countries are none other than the leaders of the C.P.S.U. and their followers, who do not support, and even oppose, the national-liberation movement.

The Chinese Communist Party has consistently maintained that the revolutionary struggles of all peoples support each other. We always consider the national-liberation movement from the viewpoint of Marxism-Leninism and proletarian internationalism, from the viewpoint of the proletarian world revolution as a whole. We believe the victorious development of the national-liberation revolution is of tremendous significance for the socialist camp, the working-class movement in the capitalist countries and the cause of defending world peace. . . .

According to Marxism-Leninism and proletarian internationalism, every socialist country which has achieved victory in its revolution must actively support and assist the liberation struggles of the oppressed nations. The socialist countries must become base areas for supporting and developing the revolution of the oppressed nations and peoples throughout the world, form the closest alliance with them and carry the proletarian world revolution through to completion.

But the leaders of the C.P.S.U. virtually regard the victory of socialism in one country or several countries as the end of the proletarian world revolution. They want to subordinate the national-liberation revolution to their general line of peaceful coexistence and to the national interests of their own country. . . .

AGAINST THE "THEORY OF RACISM" AND
THE "THEORY OF THE YELLOW PERIL"

Having used up all their wonder-working weapons for opposing the national-liberation movement, the leaders of the C.P.S.U. are now reduced to seeking help from racism, the most reactionary of all imperialist theories. They describe the correct stand of the C.P.C. in resolutely supporting the national-liberation movement as "creating racial and geographical barriers," "replacing the class approach with the racial approach," and "playing upon the national and even racial prejudices of the Asian and African peoples."

If Marxism-Leninism did not exist, perhaps such lies could deceive people. Unfortunately for the manufacturers of these lies, they live in the wrong age, for Marxism-Leninism has already found its way deep into people's hearts. As Stalin rightly pointed out, Leninism "broke down the wall between whites and blacks, between Europeans and Asiatics, between the 'civilised' and 'uncivilised' slaves of imperialism."[1] It is futile for the leaders of the C.P.S.U. to try and rebuild this wall of racism.

In the last analysis, the national question in the contemporary world is one of class struggle and anti-imperialist struggle. Today the workers, peasants, revolutionary intellectuals, anti-imperialist and patriotic bourgeois elements and other patriotic and anti-imperialist enlightened people

[1] Stalin, *Collected Works* (Moscow) VI, 144.

of all races — white, black, yellow or brown — have formed a broad united front against the imperialists, headed by the United States, and their lackeys. This united front is expanding and growing stronger. The question here is not whether to side with the white people or the coloured people, but whether to side with the oppressed peoples and nations or with the handful of imperialists and reactionaries.

According to the Marxist-Leninist class stand, oppressed nations must draw a clear line of demarcation between themselves and the imperialists and colonialists. To blur this line represents a chauvinist view serving imperialism and colonialism. . . .

The leaders of the C.P.S.U. have raised a hue and cry about the "Yellow Peril" and the "imminent menace of Genghis Khan." This is really not worth refuting. We do not intend in this article to comment on the historical role of Genghis Khan or on the development of the Mongolian, Russian and Chinese nations and the process of their formation into states. We would only remind the leaders of the C.P.S.U. of their need to review their history lessons before manufacturing such tales. Genghis Khan was a Khan of Mongolia, and in his day both China and Russia were subjected to Mongolian aggression. He invaded part of northwestern and northern China in 1215 and Russia in 1223. After his death, his successors subjugated Russia in 1240 and thirty-nine years later, in 1279, conquered the whole of China. . . .

RESURRECTING THE OLD REVISIONISM IN A NEW GUISE

The policy of the leadership of the C.P.S.U. on the national-colonial question is identical with the bankrupt policy of the revisionists of the Second International. The only difference is that the latter served the imperialists' old colonialism, while the modern revisionists serve the imperialists' neo-colonialism. . . .

The old revisionists opposed wars of national liberation and held that the national question "can be settled only through international agreements" and "advance in all the arts of peace." On this question, Khrushchev has taken over the line of the revisionists of the Second International; he advocates a "quiet burial of the colonial system."

The old revisionists attacked the revolutionary Marxists, hurling at them the slander that "Bolshevism is in essence a warlike type of socialism" and that "the Communist International harbours the illusion that the liberation of the workers can be achieved by means of the bayonets of the victorious Red Army and that a new world war is necessary for the world revolution." They also spread the story that this position had "created the greatest danger of a new world war." The language Khrushchev uses today to slander the Chinese Communist Party and other fraternal Marxist-Leninist parties is exactly the language used by the old revisionists in slandering the Bolsheviks. It is hard to find any difference.

It must be said that in serving the imperialists' neo-colonialism, Khrushchev is not a whit inferior to the old revisionists in their service of the imperialists' old colonialism.

Lenin showed how the policy of imperialism caused the international workers' movement to split into two sections, the revolutionary and the opportunist. The revolutionary section sided with the oppressed nations and opposed the imperialists and colonialists. On the other hand, the opportunist section fed on crumbs from the spoils which the imperialists and colonialists squeezed out of the people of the colonies and semi-colonies. It sided with the imperialists and colonialists and opposed the revolution of the oppressed nations for liberation.

The same kind of division between revolutionaries and opportunists in the international working-class movement as that described by Lenin is now taking shape not only in the working-class movement in capitalist countries but also in socialist countries where the proletariat wields state power.

The experience of history shows that if the national-liberation movement is to achieve complete victory it must form a solid alliance with the revolutionary working-class movement, draw a clear line of demarcation between itself and the revisionists who serve the imperialists and colonialists, and firmly eradicate their influence.

The experience of history shows that if the working-class movement of the capitalist countries in Western Europe and North America is to achieve complete victory, it must form a close alliance with the national-liberation movement in Asia, Africa and Latin America, draw a clear line of demarcation between itself and the revisionists, and firmly eradicate their influence. . . .

Workers of the world and the oppressed nations unite!

THE EDITORS OF "PEOPLE'S DAILY" AND "RED FLAG"   *177*

THE STRATEGY OF THE THIRD WORLD

Toward a Third Force

13 ACHMED SUKARNO
Let a New Asia and a New Africa Be Born!

It is my great honour and privilege on this historic day to bid you welcome to Indonesia. . . .

As I survey this hall and the distinguished guests gathered here, my heart is filled with emotion. This is the first intercontinental conference of coloured peoples in the history of mankind! I am proud that my country is your host. I am happy that you were able to accept the invitations extended by the five Sponsoring Countries. But also I cannot restrain feelings of sadness when I recall the tribulations through which many of our peoples have so recently passed, tribulations which have exacted a heavy toll in life, in material things, and in the things of the spirit. . . .

It is a new departure in the history of the world that leaders of Asian and African peoples can meet together in their own countries to discuss and deliberate upon matters of common concern. Only a few decades ago it was frequently necessary to travel to other countries and even other continents before the spokesmen of our peoples could confer. . . .

Today the contrast is great. Our nations and countries are colonies no more. Now we are free, sovereign and independent. We are again masters in our own house. We do not need to go to other continents to confer.

Already there have been important meetings of Asian States in Asia itself. . . .

Indeed, I am proud that my country is your host.

But my thoughts are not wholly of the honour which is Indonesia's today. No. My mind is for a part darkened by other considerations.

You have not gathered together in a world of peace and unity and co-operation. Great chasms yawn between nations and groups of nations.

Achmed Sukarno, President of Indonesia since its independence in 1949, gave this speech at the opening of the Asian-African Conference, Bandung, on April 18, 1955. Excerpts are from text furnished by the Ministry of Foreign Affairs, Republic of Indonesia, Jakarta, 1955.

Our unhappy world is torn and tortured, and the peoples of all countries walk in fear lest, through no fault of theirs, the dogs of war are unchained once again.

And if, in spite of all that the peoples may do, this should happen, what then? What of our newly-recovered independence then? What of our culture, what of our spiritual heritage, what of our ancient civilisation? What of our children and our parents?

The burden of the delegates to this Conference is not a light one, for I know that these questions — which are questions of the life or death of humanity itself — must be on your minds, as they are on mine. And the nations of Asia and Africa cannot, even if they wish to, avoid their part in finding solutions to these problems.

For that is part of the duties of independence itself. That is part of the price we gladly pay for our independence. For many generations our peoples have been the voiceless ones in the world. We have been the un-regarded, the peoples for whom decisions were made by others whose interests were paramount, the peoples who lived in poverty and humiliation. Then our nations demanded, nay fought for independence, and achieved independence, and with that independence came responsibility. We have heavy responsibilities to ourselves, and to the world, and to the yet unborn generations. But we do not regret them.

In 1945, the first year of our national revolution, we of Indonesia were confronted with the question of what we were going to do with our independence when it was finally attained and secured — we never questioned that it would be attained and secured. We knew how to oppose and destroy. Then we were suddenly confronted with the necessity of giving content and meaning to our independence. Not material content and meaning only, but also ethical and moral content, for independence without ethics and without morality would be indeed a poor imitation of what we sought. The responsibilities and burdens, the rights and duties and privileges of independence must be seen as part of the ethical and moral content of independence.

Indeed, we *welcome* the change which places new burdens upon us, and we are all resolved to exert all our strength and courage in carrying these burdens.

Sisters and Brothers, how terrificly dynamic is our time! I recall that, several years ago, I had occasion to make a public analysis of colonialism, and that I then drew attention to what I called the "Life-line of imperialism." This line runs from the Straits of Gibraltar, through the Mediterranean, the Suez Canal, the Red Sea, the Indian

Ocean, the South China Sea and the Sea of Japan. For most of that enormous distance, the territories on both sides of this lifeline were colonies, the peoples were unfree, their futures mortgaged to an alien system. Along that life-line, that main artery of imperialism, there was pumped the life-blood of colonialism.

And today in this hall are gathered together the leaders of those same peoples. They are no longer the victims of colonialism. They are no longer the tools of others and the playthings of forces they cannot influence. Today, you are representatives of free peoples, peoples of a different stature and standing in the world.

Yes, there has indeed been a "Sturm über Asien" — and over Africa too. The last few years have seen enormous changes. Nations, States, have awoken from a sleep of centuries. The passive peoples have gone, the outward tranquility has made place for struggle and activity. Irresistible forces have swept the two continents. The mental, spiritual and political face of the whole world has been changed, and the process is still not complete. There are new conditions, new concepts, new problems, new ideals abroad in the world. Hurricanes of national awakening and reawakening have swept over the land, shaking it, changing it, changing it for the better.

This twentieth century has been a period of terrific dynamism. Perhaps the last fifty years have seen more developments and more material progress than the previous five hundred years. Man has learned to control many of the scourges which once threatened him. He has learned to consume distance. He has learned to project his voice and his picture across oceans and continents. He has probed deep into the secrets of nature and learned how to make the desert bloom and the plants of the earth increase their bounty. He has learned how to release the immense forces locked in the smallest particles of matter.

But has man's political skill marched hand-in-hand with his technical and scientific skill? Man can chain lightning to his command — can he control the society in which he lives? The answer is No! The political skill of man has been far outstripped by his technical skill, and what he has made he cannot be sure of controlling.

The result of this is fear. And man gasps for safety and morality.

Perhaps now more than at any other moment in the history of the world, society, government and statesmanship need to be based upon the highest code of morality and ethics. And in political terms, what is the highest code of morality? It is the subordination of everything to the well-being of mankind. But today we are faced with a situation

where the well-being of mankind is not always the primary consideration. Many who are in places of high power think, rather, of controlling
the world.

Yes, we are living in a world of fear. The life of man today is
corroded and made bitter by fear. Fear of the future, fear of the
hydrogen bomb, fear of ideologies. Perhaps this fear is a greater
danger than the danger itself, because it is fear which drives men to
act foolishly, to act thoughtlessly, to act dangerously.

In your deliberations, Sisters and Brothers, I beg of you, do not be
guided by these fears, because fear is an acid which etches man's actions
into curious patterns. Be guided by hopes and determination, be guided
by ideals, and, yes, be guided by dreams!

We are of many different nations, we are of many different social
backgrounds and cultural patterns. Our ways of life are different. Our
national characters, or colours or motifs — call it what you will — are
different. Our racial stock is different, and even the colour of our skin
is different. But what does that matter? Mankind is united or divided
by considerations other than these. Conflict comes not from variety of
skins, nor from variety of religion, but from variety of desires.

All of us, I am certain, are united by more important things than
those which superficially divide us. We are united, for instance, by a
common detestation of colonialism in whatever form it appears. We
are united by a common detestation of racialism. And we are united
by a common determination to preserve and stabilise peace in the
world. Are not these aims mentioned in the letter of invitation to which
you responded?

I freely confess it — in these aims I am not disinterested or driven
by purely impersonal motives.

How is it possible to be disinterested about colonialism? For us,
colonialism is not something far and distant. We have known it in all
its ruthlessness. We have seen the immense human wastage it causes,
the poverty it causes, and the heritage it leaves behind when, eventually
and reluctantly, it is driven out by the inevitable march of history. My
people, and the peoples of many nations of Asia and Africa know these
things, for we have experienced them.

Indeed, we cannot yet say that all parts of our countries are free
already. Some parts still labour under the lash. And some parts of
Asia and Africa which are not represented here still suffer from the
same condition.

Yes, some parts of our nations are not yet free. That is why all of us cannot yet feel that journey's end has been reached. No people can feel themselves free, so long as part of their motherland is unfree. Like peace, freedom is indivisible. There is no such thing as being half free, as there is no such thing as being half alive.

We are often told "Colonialism is dead." Let us not be deceived or even soothed by that. I say to you, colonialism is not yet dead. How can we say it is dead, so long as vast areas of Asia and Africa are unfree.

And, I beg of you, do not think of colonialism only in the classic form which we of Indonesia, and our brothers in different parts of Asia and Africa, knew. Colonialism has also its modern dress, in the form of economic control, intellectual control, actual physical control by a small but alien community within a nation. It is a skilful and determined enemy, and it appears in many guises. It does not give up its loot easily. Wherever, whenever, and however it appears, colonialism is an evil thing, and one which must be eradicated from the earth.

The battle against colonialism has been a long one, and do you know that today is a famous anniversary in that battle? On the eighteenth day of April, one thousand seven hundred and seventy five, just one hundred and eighty years ago, Paul Revere rode at midnight through the New England countryside, warning of the approach of British troops and of the opening of the American War of Independence, the first successful anti-colonial war in history. About this midnight ride the poet Longfellow wrote:

A cry of defiance and not of fear,
A voice in the darkness, a knock at the door,
And a word that shall echo for evermore. . . .

Yes, it shall echo for evermore, just as the other anti-colonial words which gave us comfort and reassurance during the darkest days of our struggle shall echo for evermore. But remember, that battle which began 180 years ago is not yet completely won, and it will not have been completely won until we can survey this our own world, and can say that colonialism is dead.

So, I am not disinterested when I speak of the fight against colonialism.

Nor am I disinterested when I speak of the battle for peace. How can any of us be disinterested about peace?

Not so very long ago we argued that peace was necessary for us because an outbreak of fighting in our part of the world would imperil our precious independence, so recently won at such great cost.

Today, the picture is more black. War would not only mean a threat to our independence, it may mean the end of civilisation and even of human life. There is a force loose in the world whose potentiality for evil no man truly knows. Even in practice and rehearsal for war the effects may well be building up into something of unknown horror.

Not so long ago it was possible to take some little comfort from the idea that the clash, if it came, could perhaps be settled by what were called "conventional weapons" — bombs, tanks, cannon and men. Today that little grain of comfort is denied us, for it has been made clear that the weapons of ultimate horror will certainly be used, and the military planning of nations is on that basis. The unconventional has become the conventional, and who knows what other examples of misguided and diabolical scientific skill have been discovered as a plague on humanity. . . .

No task is more urgent than that of preserving peace. Without peace our independence means little. The rehabilitation and upbuilding of our countries will have little meaning. Our revolutions will not be allowed to run their course.

What can we do? The peoples of Asia and Africa wield little physical power. Even their economic strength is dispersed and slight. We cannot indulge in power politics. Diplomacy for us is not a matter of the big stick. Our statesmen, by and large, are not backed up with serried ranks of jet bombers.

What can we do? We can do much! We can inject the voice of reason into world affairs. We can mobilise all the spiritual, all the moral, all the political strength of Asia and Africa on the side of peace. Yes, we! We, the peoples of Asia and Africa, 1,400,000,000 strong, far more than half the human population of the world, we can mobilise what I have called the *Moral Violence of Nations* in favour of peace. We can demonstrate to the minority of the world which lives on the other continents that we, the majority, are for peace, not for war, and that whatever strength we have will always be thrown on to the side of peace. . . .

Ah, Sisters and Brothers, let this Conference be a great success! In spite of diversity that exists among its participants, — let this Conference be a great success!

Yes, there is diversity among us. Who denies it? Small and great nations are represented here, with people professing almost every religion under the sun, — Buddhism, Islam, Christianity, Confucianism, Hinduism, Jainism, Sikhism, Zoroasthrianism, Shintoism, and others. Almost every political faith we encounter here — Democracy, Monarchism, Theocracy, with innumerable variants. And practically every economic doctrine has its representative in this hall — Marhaenism, Socialism, Capitalism, Communism, in all their manifold variations and combinations.

But what harm is in diversity, when there is unity in desire? This Conference is not to oppose each other, it is a conference of brotherhood. It is not an Islam-Conference, nor a Christian Conference, nor a Buddhist Conference. It is not a meeting of Malayans, nor one of Arabs, nor one of Indo-Aryan stock. It is not an exclusive club either, nor a bloc which seeks to oppose any other bloc. Rather it is a body of enlightened, tolerant opinion which seeks to impress on the world that all men and all countries have their place under the sun — to impress on the world that it is possible to live together, meet together, speak to each other, without losing one's individual identity; and yet to contribute to the general understanding of matters of common concern, and to develop a true consciousness of the interdependence of men and nations for their wellbeing and survival on earth.

I know that in Asia and Africa there is greater diversity of religions, faiths, and beliefs, than in the other continents of the world. But that is only natural! Asia and Africa are the classic birthplaces of faiths and ideas, which have spread all over the world. Therefore, it behooves us to take particular care to ensure that the principle which is usually called the "Live and let live" principle — mark, I do not say the principle of "Laissez faire, laissez passer" of Liberalism which is obsolete — is first of all applied by us most completely within our own Asian and African frontiers. Then only can it be fully extended to our relations with our neighbouring countries, and to others more distant. . . .

So, let this Asian-African Conference be a great success! Make the "Live and let live" principle and the "Unity in Diversity" motto the unifying force which brings us all together — to seek in friendly, uninhibited discussion, ways and means by which each of us can live his own life, and let others live their own lives, in their own way, in harmony, and in peace.

If we succeed in doing so, the effect of it for the freedom, independence and the welfare of man will be great on the world at large. The Light of Understanding has again been lit, the Pillar of Cooperation again erected. The likelihood of success of this Conference is proved already by the very presence of you all here today. It is for us to give it strength, to give it the power of inspiration — to spread its message all over the World.

Failure will mean that the Light of Understanding which seemed to have dawned in the East — the Light towards which looked all the great religions born here in the past — has again been obscured by an unfriendly cloud before man could benefit from its warm radiance.

But let us be full of hope and full of confidence. We have so much in common.

Relatively speaking, all of us gathered here today are neighbours. Almost all of us have ties of common experience, the experience of colonialism. Many of us have a common religion. Many of us have common cultural roots. Many of us, the so-called "underdeveloped" nations, have more or less similar economic problems, so that each can profit from the others' experience and help. And I think I may say that we all hold dear the ideals of national independence and freedom. Yes, we have so much in common. And yet we know so little of each other.

If this Conference succeeds in making the peoples of the East whose representatives are gathered here understand each other a little more, appreciate each other a little more, sympathise with each other's problems a little more — if those things happen, then this Conference, of course, will have been worthwhile, whatever else it may achieve. But I hope that this Conference will give *more* than understanding only and goodwill only — I hope that it will falsify and give the lie to the saying of one diplomat from far abroad: "We will turn this Asian-African Conference into an afternoon-tea meeting." I hope that it will give evidence of the fact that we Asian and African leaders understand that Asia and Africa can prosper only when they are united, and that even the safety of the World at large can not be safeguarded without a united Asia-Africa. I hope that this Conference will give *guidance* to mankind, will point out to mankind the way which it must take to attain safety and peace. I hope that it will give evidence that Asia and Africa have been reborn, nay, that a *New Asia* and a *New Africa* have been born!

Our task is first to seek an understanding of each other, and out of that understanding will come a greater appreciation of each other, and out of that appreciation will come collective action. Bear in mind the words of one of Asia's greatest sons: "To speak is easy. To act is hard. To understand is hardest. Once one understands, action is easy."

I have come to the end. Under God, may your deliberations be fruitful, and may your wisdom strike sparks of light from the hard flints of today's circumstances.

Let us not be bitter about the past, but let us keep our eyes firmly on the future. Let us remember that no blessing of God is so sweet as life and liberty. Let us remember that the stature of all mankind is diminished so long as nations or parts of nations are still unfree. Let us remember that the highest purpose of man is the liberation of man from his bonds of fear, his bonds of human degradation, his bonds of poverty — the liberation of man from the physical, spiritual and intellectual bonds which have for too long stunted the development of humanity's majority.

And let us remember, Sisters and Brothers, that for the sake of all that, we Asians and Africans must be united.

As President of the Republic of Indonesia, and on behalf of the eighty million people of Indonesia, I bid you welcome to this country. I declare the Asian-African Conference opened, and I pray that the Blessing of God will be upon it, and that its discussions will be profitable to the peoples of Asia and Africa, and to the peoples of all nations!

Bismillah!

God speed!

Let Imperialism Be Cast Off

14 GAMAL ABDEL NASSER
Ours Is the Side of Peace and Freedom

. . . You all know that the United Arab Republic believes in the policy of non-alignment and adheres to it as a strict yardstick. I hardly need to repeat the story of the sacrifices made by our Arab nation to hold to the policy of non-alignment, animated by our conviction that it ensures its independence on the one hand, and is conducive to the preservation of lasting peace on the other.

In spite of all pressure, we refused to become tools in the cold war. We also spared no efforts to explain underlying principles of that policy, namely that peace cannot prevail while the world is divided up into antagonistic parts or blocs with no link between them but trenches and barbed wire behind which lie the weapons of aggression and the arms of death and destruction. This policy is based on the belief that peace prevails only when there is more understanding among peoples and when fruitful contacts and creative interrelationship exist on the largest scale possible. The Bandung Conference of African-Asian peoples is one of the greatest landmarks on the road of our national struggle in defence of our principles. . . .

I hereby declare before you, in the name of the United Arab Republic and in expression of its thoughts and conscience, that we believe that the problem of peace and war should be shared by all peoples inasmuch as it determines their future and destiny. The big Powers do not alone have the right to speak about peace and war; it is mankind as a whole that has the final word, having obtained this right through the sacrifices of its different peoples for the sake of civilization and the promotion of its development, and its long yearning for security.

Thus, when peace is at stake, we do take sides; ours is the side of peace. If we have any qualification to attach to this definite position

Gamal Abdel Nasser has been Premier and Chairman of the Council of Revolutionary Command of the United Arab Republic since November 1954. These excerpts, from a speech to the United Nations General Assembly on September 27, 1960, are reprinted from United Nations, *Official Records of the General Assembly (Part I), Plenary Meetings, I: Verbatim Records of Meetings 20 September–17 October, 1960,* 149–151.

against war, it is that the peace we aspire to is that based on justice without discrimination.

With this faith deep in our conscience and with this aim in sight we come to this session confident that within the United Nations effective efforts by all of us should be made for the cause of peace. While we believe that every effort should be made for the sake of peace, wherever it may be, it is our conviction that the possibilities of success are much stronger within the United Nations than without it. . . .

No system can provide a wider participation than this Organization, which represents in its essence the personification of the peoples' desire for peace, as well as the framework which all free peoples have accepted to govern this desire. Yet, the necessity of facing the situation sincerely makes it imperative for us to define clearly that the share of each of us in shouldering the responsibility has to be determined by its power and capacity. Thus, the big Powers carry a greater share of responsibility within their material possibilities than other nations, although we are all equal in moral responsibility. If we all hold an equal share of the hope for peace, the big Powers hold the major keys to this hope.

Hope alone cannot, however, ease world tension; it cannot eliminate doubts and fears; it cannot remove lurking military bases and it cannot drown in the ocean the nuclear weapons of destruction piled up in the stores or the atomic warheads of the intercontinental missiles. If the peace-loving peoples can be the echo of the conscience of our world, the big Powers may be considered as the nerves of this world, and on the soundness of these nerves depends the safety of the entire universe. . . .

On this basis, we consider that there are two practical problems facing our world today, and it is there that we can find the real explanation of the events which are taking place around us. The first problem is that of disarmament. The second is the strong drive towards freedom, whether from the political point of view or from the equally important economic point of view.

Regarding the question of disarmament, we find that there is a preparatory stage which is unavoidable before we come to the details of the problem and the solutions thereof. This necessitates the existence, not only of the desire to solve the problem, but of the actual will to act for its solution. . . .

We are of the opinion that non-aligned countries have a big role to play on this stage. We believe that the extension of the scope of consultation and contacts is in itself a positive contribution to facing the prevailing strain and tension.

We are also of the opinion that holding such consultations and contacts within the framework of the United Nations is an attempt to assure that none of us would trace for himself a path separate from the international group. Yet we reiterate that facing the problem within the framework of the United Nations does not absolve the large nations from their great share of the responsibility; for the problem of disarmament is connected with highly complex, scientific and technical considerations.

The big Powers, whose potentialities enabled them to achieve scientific and technical supremacy, which in its turn enabled them to produce nuclear weapons, are more able than others to find the effective means of removing the danger that threatens the world and, thanks to these potentialities, to shift the nuclear energy from the field of destruction to the peaceful sphere, where it becomes a driving power for progress towards unlimited horizons, where God has revealed to us the secrets of the universe.

Thus, on our part, we — the non-aligned nations — are entitled to make the call for peace. We can bridge the gap separating the distant parts with a view to achieving peaceful coexistence among the nations of different social beliefs, and we can contribute to the creation of the atmosphere that helps ease the tension and brings tranquility to the peoples of the world. Subsequently, we cannot hesitate to participate in laying down general rules which can lead us to fruitful results. We cannot help calling for the removal of military bases. We cannot help demanding that an end be put to the nuclear weapons tests and that the big Powers get rid of the huge piles of nuclear weapons stored in their storage areas. We cannot help urging the establishment of a system of controls conducive to tranquility and security. We cannot help calling for a continuous reduction of the armaments budgets. Then there remains the duty of the big Powers to seek the technical and practical solutions to the problems emanating from the scientific supremacy — a duty that must be performed here at the United Nations. . . .

There remains then the problem of the great drive towards freedom, particularly economic independence. We see, and you can see with us, those free and glorious drives going on in Africa, in Asia and in Latin America.

We have but to observe this encouraging increase in the number of

States Members of the United Nations. . . . We do not doubt, as we see the remnants of imperialism retreating everywhere before the march of the peoples looking forward to liberty, that the scope of the United Nations will increase and strengthen and that the next few years will bring with them new flags representing new victories in the sphere of political freedom. We can, however, observe from now that this great expected development will not completely solve the problem of the drive for freedom; we might even say that, if the matter is not dealt with in a spirit of conscious appreciation, the problem of the drive for freedom will grow in dimension as a result of the struggle behind it and of the pull and clash of forces latent in it.

Those peoples who have obtained their political freedom or who expect to gain it in the near future look forward to economic independence and are preparing to fight for it. These newly independent nations are firmly convinced that, if they do not obtain their economic independence, they will not find the sound basis upon which they can preserve their political freedom. Much of what goes on in Africa, Asia and Latin America today — the acute aspects of which may astonish many of us here — constitutes in fact some features of that drive towards economic liberation. The newly independent peoples are convinced that true freedom lies in reaching a higher standard of living for their sons. The newly independent peoples — and this I must state here frankly — are hastening their steps along the road to economic development, and they feel that they cannot afford to waste any time after a long period of lagging behind.

Some may believe that haste leads to error. Yet, if we admitted this, we should be making a greater error — we should be overlooking the nature of circumstances. The nature of the circumstances in which we live today makes a long wait unbearable. Scientific progress is probably the first aspect of the present circumstances. Any farmer in our country, from the extreme south in Aswan to the extreme north in Kamechlieh, for example, may, by means of radio and the Press, observe the high standard of living of the ordinary United States citizen, or he may observe the magnificent achievements performed by the people of the Soviet Union. If this farmer should compare his condition with that of others, he would feel a surge in his breast urging him to raise his standard of living to the level enjoyed by others. Our peoples may be told that patience is necessary and that other nations had to have it, but allow me to state here that any generation's capacity to endure patience is measured according to the circumstances of that generation, and not according to the circumstances of others. Those who had the patience to endure crossing the sea in small boats directed by the winds differed completely from those who are able to cross it now in a few hours by jet aircraft.

These are not mere words. This is a true picture of our times. Our people felt that they had missed the era of steam and the era of electricity, and they feel that they are almost missing the era of atomic energy with all its unlimited potentialities. Hence the people's determination to achieve their economic independence; hence their resolute drive in the fields of agricultural and industrial development and of social equality. If we find that the United Nations has a big role to play in promoting this development, we must declare in all honesty that nations looking forward to economic independence will not wait. They will accept every assistance given to them through the United Nations, and they will not hesitate to accept any unconditional aid offered to them outside the United Nations. They will set forth on every step which they can take. They will eliminate with determination every barrier that stands between them and their aim, while they will be grateful for every assistance which brings them nearer to their goal. They believe sincerely that in a closer approach to their aim lies their road, as well as other people's road, to peace.

In this resolute, historic drive will be found a true interpretation of the striking movements in Africa, Asia and Latin America; and it is in the light of this alone that the real meaning appears of the revolutions which break out in the various countries on these continents. This is the explanation of the revolution towards large-scale industrialization. This is the true explanation of the revolution against the social injustices inherited by our peoples from the age of feudalism. This is the explanation of the revolution against the policy of spheres of influence. This is the explanation of the revolution against the attempts at imperialist exploitation and monopoly and attempts at arbitrary control over the prices of raw material, which aim at hampering the development of the countries producing those materials and keeping them as mere storage areas in a manner inconsistent with the practice of the farmers, and offering a price amounting to no more than a small percentage of the loans and aid offered to them.

We do hope that the United Nations will be able to fulfil the mission of advancing economic independence side by side with political freedom. We conceive of disarmament as a far-reaching revolution in this field if the budgets which are marked for armaments, or fractions of them, are directed towards the industrial and agricultural development of the countries which are eager to achieve their economic independence.

I hope equally that we may become aware of the fact that here there is no such thing as under-developed peoples and advanced nations. Rather there are peoples who have had the chance to learn and others who have been denied this opportunity by force and oppression; peoples who took the test and reacted to it, and peoples who were denied the chance to test their capacities or discover their potentialities and to withstand the trial of life.

We used to be told that we had no right to demand the restoration of the Suez Canal from all aspects — because, they said, the administration of the Canal was a most complicated problem, and because our men, whatever their standard of education and technical knowledge, would not be able to shoulder the responsibilities of administering the Suez Canal before a period of fifty years had elapsed.

Now you all know that the Suez Canal under Arab administration performs its role in the service of world economy more ably and efficiently than was the case before its restoration to the people who dug it as a waterway for the advancement and prosperity of the world. We faced the test of our development and reacted to it. We have proved that, in spite of all the difficulties we faced and in spite of what we had to face through trial and error, the average yearly revenue of the individual in the Egyptian region of the United Arab Republic has increased by 70 per cent in the course of seven years following the achievement of our freedom.

I have endeavoured not to allow our preoccupation with our own problems to divert our attention from the grave international problems. If I have referred to some of our problems without embarking on the details, it is because I tried to confine my approach to the general aspect that relates those causes to peace and to the United Nations. It is obvious, however, that we believe that serving peace in its world context is in fact serving our own cause.

We believe also that the supremacy of the United Nations means the supremacy of principles and the triumph of law and justice over the dreams of conquest and domination. We believe that the spirit of peace based on justice provides the most favourable atmosphere for our country to promote its development and for paving the way for the fulfilment of its hopes for rebuilding our society on a new basis.

For Political Freedom and Economic Growth

15   E. M. DEBRAH
The Commitment of the Uncommitted Nations

"Americans often find it difficult," noted Professor Berliner, "to understand how certain nations that profess a commitment to international morality can insist on remaining 'uncommitted' in the struggle between Soviet Communism and Western Freedom. How can one be neutral in the conflict between good and evil?" The professor went on to add: "It is difficult enough for any nation to 'see ourselves as others see us.' How much more difficult it is to see a second nation as a third sees it!" And how right!

Africans are bewildered when, on attaining independence after years of being what almost amounts to second-rate citizens, they are confronted with the Cold War problem and asked, willy-nilly, to choose sides. I can picture every African nationalist — and there is nothing wrong in being a nationalist, a person who fights for equality and international recognition for his country — saying: Why can't we be left alone? Why can't we be trusted as adults to work out our own salvation? Why should we not be allowed to forget the past and start a fresh page with initial goodwill for all men? Why should we not allow anyone who wants to be our friend to justify that friendship in our own eyes? Haven't we had enough of playing second fiddle in our own country? Look at the past. Consider Ghana.

HISTORICAL PERSPECTIVE

J. D. Fage, commenting on the first meeting of the tribes of the Gold Coast with Europeans, said:

The Gold Coast States did not want Europeans to build themselves fortified trading stations on their shores. But if the construction of forts was the price which Africans had to pay for European trade then it was a price which they were increasingly prepared to pay — on certain conditions. The

E. M. Debrah, Ambassador of Ghana to Ethiopia, is former Counsellor of the Ghanaian Embassy in Washington. These excerpts, from an article originally titled "Will the Uncommitted Nations Remain Uncommitted?" in *The Annals of the American Academy of Political and Social Science*, CCCXXXVI (July 1961) 83–93, are reprinted by permission.

principal one of these conditions came to be that there should be no infringement of the sovereignty of the States.

Of course, by 1874 and 1901 this sovereignty had not only been infringed but destroyed. Before the sovereignty was finally destroyed, Africans had been transported in large numbers to work for people who were soon to "hold these truths to be self-evident, that all men are created equal." The trans-Atlantic slave trade, which in the sixteenth century had run at a mean level of perhaps 9,000 slaves a year, rapidly grew in volume, so that even conservative estimates put the total number of African slaves supplied to America in the eighteenth century at something like seven million.

While the Christian missionaries in Africa certainly did the best they could to preach Christ and Christ crucified, they, unlike St. Peter and Cornelius, often spurned the vessels into which their work was cast. Drums were supposed to be connected with fetishes; to be a good Christian, one must adopt a Christian name, and, to be civilized, one must have a European name. So you find Ghanaians calling themselves Sydney Napoleon Coleman and Isaac Newton Wood, instead of Boateng Amponsem or Kwaku Dua. What is worse, in 1885 and after the First World War, Africa was carved up like a piece of roast beef and divided among nations who could not care two cents whether the unfortunate peoples came under the same administration or not. Contact with the European meant more highways, certainly. It meant more buildings; that's fine. It meant the learning of English or even Portuguese. But it also saw the suppression of the African self. The stream of African culture which should have continued to roll on was dammed. African ways of self-government were prostituted: the Chief became a stooge; and the unifying force of the people, the tribe, became a term of abuse and, in parts of Africa, was linked with gangsterism against colonial powers. Africans who felt all this wrong were often branded as being in league with the atheistic and materialistic philosophy of communism.

And so we come to the years after the Second World War and to the Independence Movement. Africa is not so much "a continent developing a will of its own" as a continent rediscovering itself — the rebirth of African culture, the assertion of the African personality.

I have given this background to enable you to understand the sentiments of every, if not most, African and Asian nations as they achieve independence. You can understand our irritation when we are pressed to commit ourselves in advance to an Eastern or Western bloc. The references to truth and evil become two-edged weapons. We refuse to be involved. We prefer to remain uncommitted.

POLICY OF NONCOMMITMENT

On August 29, 1957 the Prime Minister of Ghana — now President Nkrumah — made a statement to Parliament in which he emphasized Ghana's determination to keep away from the two blocs and to follow a policy of positive neutralism.

Ghana has been born into a world torn and divided in its political relationships. We of Ghana feel, therefore, that our country should not be committed in any respect of its foreign policy and that Ghana should not be aligned with any particular group of powers or political bloc. It is our intention to preserve our independence and to act as we see best at any particular time.

We in Ghana, furthermore, add that our neutralism is of a positive kind. It does not imply the suspension of judgment on the major world issues of today. It means rather the conscientious exercise of judgment strictly in accordance with the merits of each issue, rather than with any regard to who the contesting parties are. Staying away from the United Nations, refusing to negotiate, a perpetual refusal to vote on issues, or the unwarranted and uncritical condemnation of one side is not our brand of neutralism. And we shall always work to preserve this attitude because we believe it is right.

Our neutralism, moreover, presupposes the pursuit of certain principles which cannot be denied by any group of persons of goodwill. We insist on the equality of all men, irrespective of color, race, or creed. We often quote from the American Declaration of Independence in Congress July 4, 1776, and we may be permitted to quote it again:

We hold these truths to be self-evident, that all men are created equal; that they are endowed by their Creator with certain inalienable rights; that among these are life, liberty, and the pursuit of happiness.

Color has nothing to do with intellect, should not have anything to do with position in society or ability to play a constructive role in national or international politics. We, therefore, condemn racial discrimination or prejudice in all its forms. Whether it is black school children being prevented from joining white children of their age at the same school, or whether it is Bantus being called upon to show passes in their own country, we feel it our duty to express our unequivocal condemnation and to call for strong measures to stop such practices. You

E. M. DEBRAH   *195*

often hear some people, when trying to justify their policy of racial discrimination, using the expression "equal but separate." The fact is, if equal, why separate? And, thus, when the problems of South Africa's apartheid come up for discussion, we are surprised at some Christian countries who daily sing:

> In Christ there is no East or West
> In Him no North or South,
> But one great fellowship of love,
> Throughout the whole wide earth.

We are surprised by Christian countries who say, with St. Paul,

> I am not ashamed of the Gospel for it is the power of Salvation unto every one that believeth,

refusing to face up to the issue. The neutrals do not. They speak their mind; and their mind is unfettered and unqualified condemnation. It is not neutralism which is on trial. It is those who, for bloc allegiance, would not uphold their own principles in public who stand for sentence at the bar of public opinion. . . .

Secondly, neutral countries are against colonialism and imperialism and call upon those who are clinging to colonies in the false understanding that they are part of metropolitan countries to prepare the people now for eventual self-government. May I refer to a WRC-TV commentary on Angola, which is one of the remaining pockets of colonialism in Africa, for you yourselves to judge whether there is not all that merit in fighting colonialism tooth and nail:

> Some 60 kilometers from Loanda is the little village of Katit, where one central faucet serves several hundred families. And young girls and old women share the immense burden of the communal water jug. The old, the halt and the lame fetch and carry many miles to and from their village homes, where life goes on much as it has for centuries past in Africa. This is primitive Angola, as much a part of Africa as its nearest neighbor, the Congo. It is Portugal's boast that all her subjects are Portuguese first, and only incidentally white or black in color. But the Negroes who live in villages like this in Angola, know that their chances of achieving full Portuguese citizenship, even for what that is worth, are slender indeed. An African who can prove to the District Administrator's satisfaction that he is a good Portuguese, a good Catholic, a good family man with only one wife and a fair income, may some day achieve the status of [assimelada] first-class citizen, but the last word is with the local administrator. The Portuguese government is proud of its schools — it has provided many in the colonies. Though in theory these schools are open to all, in practice, economic and

bureaucratic roadblocks stand in the path of all but a privileged few. The higher the grade, the fewer the Africans able to sustain their quest for learning. Ninety-nine per cent of Africans in the Portuguese territories are still illiterate — small wonder, when less than one half of one per cent have been deemed by bureaucracy to be sufficiently civilized to be accorded the privilege of assimilation. . . . Deaf to the protests of Africa's black nationalists, Portugal is plying ahead with her schemes for colonization. Here in Mozambique's [Limpopo] River Valley, whites and blacks are bulldozing space in the jungle — space for new settlers who will be sent out from Portugal to relieve the pressure of population there.

It is naked exploitation of this type which forced us in Ghana to declare that as long as one patch of African territory remains under the yoke of colonialism, Ghana's independence and, we believe, the independence of any other African country is meaningless.

Once again, it is the North Atlantic Treaty Organization (NATO) alliance which is on trial, not neutralism. Let us quote from a *Washington Post* editorial of 29th March 1961, when Portuguese mobs attacked the United States Embassy in Lisbon because the United States, in spite of its NATO alliance, decided to side with what is right:

It is an unhappy thing that some 20,000 Portuguese, a people with whom we have ancient ties of friendship and who are allied with us in the North Atlantic Treaty Organization — have stoned the American Embassy in Lisbon and shouted bitter slogans against our country. This they have done, though possibly not too spontaneously, to dramatize their national resentment over our Government's decision to vote against Portugal on the issue of Angola. Up to a point, since the vote represents a sharp modification of policy, and since it has been cast against a NATO ally, the Portuguese reaction is quite understandable and merits sympathy. With that said, however, there is reason to add that Portugal owes it to itself, as well as to the United States, to put emotions to one side and give careful, dispassionate consideration to our Government's position on the matter. The postion may be summarized as follows:

(1) The American vote on Angola represents a carefully calculated decision — not an improvised or whimsical one — to modify past policy.

(2) The modification, which in sense should weaken NATO, is designed to make clear that our country, far from voting automatically and always on the side of the so-called "colonial" powers, intends henceforth to determine its stand in keeping with what it deems to be the facts or merits of each case as it arises.

This is our brand of neutralism which President Nkrumah announced to the world way back in 1957. Maybe we can pat ourselves on the back and say the United States is becoming neutralist! I am happy to refer to a reported statement of Secretary of State Dean Rusk in the *Washington*

Post of 26th March 1961, saying: "We cannot stand aside from the revolutionary forces which we ourselves help to nourish if we wish our own great experiment in freedom to survive."

Neutral countries are against imperialism and imposition of all forms of foreign rule on other countries, and, in this regard, we do not confine ourselves to one group of powers, but to all powers who would like to impose their will against others.

THE PROBLEMS

In a talk at one university, I was asked: "The so-called neutrals are so poor, are so helpless, that it seems they must join one bloc or the other in order to survive. How can they continue to remain neutral?" The answer I have given to the students is the same answer I will give today: The world needs more uncommitted countries; and the larger the number, the safer the world will be. What are the problems?

Military bases. We are told that neither of the blocs wants war. But, in view of the implacable hostility of one to another, it is essential that both sides must be in a state of preparedness in order to deter any aggressor from plunging the world into a fruitless war. One aspect of this preparedness is to ring the other camp with a number of military bases from which to launch a counterattack in case of war. As far as the West is concerned, since these bases are considered part of the free world's defensive system, considerable surprise is expressed in certain quarters that some neutral countries should refuse to have military bases on their soil or refuse to join military alliances set up, as it is put, for their own good.

Really, such remarks to me are unfair, because the neutrals who reject bases do so in the confidence that bases abroad, of both the East and the West, do not lessen the risks of war. They increase them. In any case, in the present development in missiles, is it not necessary to make a new assessment of the usefulness of military bases abroad? . . .

Economic aid. But far more important than military aid is the determination of the neutrals to accept economic assistance from all countries who have the real desire to assist in their economic development. I do not think that we need dwell on the urgent importance of giving economic assistance to the underdeveloped countries. Considerable assistance has come from the West, and some measure of assistance is now going to neutrals from the East. "Is it some subconscious urge toward self-destruction," it has been asked, "that has led the leaders of the underdeveloped countries to accept millions of dollars of Soviet aid?"

I am no apologist for Soviet aid. The Soviets are better equipped to speak for themselves. But I think we must give the leaders of the underdeveloped countries the credit that, when they accept Soviet aid, or Western aid for that matter, they do so with their eyes wide open. And, after all, why should Soviet aid be refused? In spite of the large sums of money which the West has given to assist underdeveloped countries, there is still a great need for more capital in Africa and Asia. If Soviet assistance is offered, why should an independent country refuse to exercise its sovereignty to consider the offer? Communist assistance often has some worth-while attractions, and, if it were to be given in the true interests of the receiving country, why should it be refused because it comes from the Soviet Union?

Moreover, it must be borne in mind that Soviet loans often carry a low rate of interest and are often given with less difficulty. Repayment is often to be made in local currency or with local commodities. As for strings, it is difficult to believe that any country gives assistance without expecting anything in return. The positive expectation is that the recipient will support the giver's policies, and the negative expectation is that the receiver would refuse to have dealings with the other side. All nations which give aid are saying that they do so without strings. Fine! Let us put their words to the test.

I am not, for a minute, upholding Soviet assistance against Western aid. All I am saying is that it is unrealistic to expect an independent country to refuse assistance from a country because it is in the Eastern bloc. Do not forget a great number of Western countries do trade with the Republic of China. Why should neutrals fight shy of other forms of co-operation with the East?

I am reminded of a passage in President Kennedy's inaugural address:

So, let us begin anew — remembering on both sides that stability is not a sign of weakness, and sincerity is always subject to proof. Let us never negotiate out of fear. But let us never fear to negotiate.

In matters of economic aid, it seems to me that the West has a record of which it can be justly proud. The policy for the West, I believe, is not to be alarmed that the Soviet Union is giving assistance to neutral countries; its policy should be to emphasize not so much that its loan or aid programs are superior to that of the East, but to invite the East to join in one great effort to alleviate the poverty, hunger, and disease that obtain in some underdeveloped countries. Unless both sides are willing to work side by side in peace, how can any one survive? . . .

I would emphasize that American aid must not be given necessarily to positively pro-Western countries or neutral countries, but to countries who need the aid, who ask for it, and who would benefit by it. In the very short term, this may seem a silly policy, but I believe it will pay the United States more dividends than a policy of support only to friends. That will be the real example of help without strings attached. . . .

FUTURE OF NEUTRALISM

. . . Is neutralism a position which the United States can accept? I hope my analysis has revealed that it is more in the interest of the United States, for example, to encourage the setting up of neutral countries all over the world. The security of the world will be ensured that way. How far the uncommitted countries can continue to remain uncommitted, depends upon:

(1) Understanding and acceptance that the neutral is an independent sovereign country, that of his own free will he has taken his stand because he is tired of war and believes in the ability of all men, if they wish, to live peacefully with one another. The neutral nation wishes to avoid war and to encourage peaceful contact between all men irrespective of their systems; and it is prepared to co-operate with those who genuinely wish to follow such a policy.

(2) Peace-loving countries assisting the underdeveloped countries to be economically viable, for it is only when in a sovereign society the hungry are fed, the naked clothed, and the uneducated taught, that civil commotion with its attendant invitation to outsiders can be avoided.

(3) Men of goodwill prepared to accept that color is an accident of geography and environment and that the essential thing is that all men are born equal and are entitled to the same treatment of equality, self-respect, and dignity all over the world.

I saw the inscription on the Liberty Bell this morning. It said, "Though silent now for over a century, the old bell still symbolically proclaims liberty throughout the land unto all the inhabitants thereof." May it toll liberty to all men of goodwill throughout the entire world.

The Rise of the Third World

16 N. PARAMESWARAN NAYAR
The Growth of Nonalignment in World Affairs

The trends of international relations in the post-war years have been broadly shaped by three main forces: the Western, the Communist and the Non-aligned. Undoubtedly the major actors in the world drama during these years have been the first two, but the role of the non-aligned nations has been, by no means, insignificant, particularly in the last few years. In other words, the past years have witnessed an increasing importance of non-alignment as a force, or at least as a trend, to be reckoned with in international politics. This growth in importance of non-alignment has been, therefore, one of the most significant aspects of the politics of the post-war world.

I   FACTORS OF NON-ALIGNMENT

In order to understand the factors for the emergence and increasing popularity of the policy of non-alignment among the new nations of Asia and Africa, it is necessary to look at the international background and the internal conditions of these countries during these years. It was the inter-relationship between the two that made the emergence of the policy a "natural" thing.

It was in the background of a rapidly deteriorating international situation of acute cold war tensions threatening to break out into another world war that a number of nations of Asia, and later Africa, achieved national independence. The predominant force underlying the changes in these countries during these years was the upsurge of nationalism. . . .

In the meanwhile, the nations of the world had already become divided into two blocs under the leadership of USA and USSR. Certain forces inherent in the traditions and experiences of the social and political movements of these countries made it difficult for them to identify themselves with either of the blocs. Their greater contacts with the West in the past had led to a natural inclination in their

N. Parameswaran Nayar is Lecturer in Politics at the University of Kerala in Trivandrum, India. These excerpts, from an article in *India Quarterly* XVIII, No. 1 (January–March 1962) 28–57, are reprinted by permission.

thinking on the lines of Western political and economic systems. . . . Moreover, the leadership of the nationalist movements was usually in the educated middle classes who were trained to think and speak in terms of Western political theory and ideals. Differences in local conditions had given particular orientations to these political ideas, but, on the whole, the general predilections of politics in these countries were in favour of the West.

Along with this, however, there was also a basic distrust of the Western Powers. This was mainly due to the imperialist character of most Western Powers. There was an obvious snag in the argument that the Western nations were trying to preserve democracy against totalitarian communism as long as they themselves sought to maintain colonies. The evils of Western Imperialism were much more real and obvious to these nations than those of some distant danger of Communist totalitarianism. The United States was more or less secure from charges of direct colonialism unlike other Western Powers like Britain or France, but American policy in the Philippines and in Latin America had provoked misgivings and doubts. Moreover, postwar American policy showed often an obsession with fighting communism reflected in a tendency to appease Western imperialism and to condemn blindly even nationalist movements as communist. Similarly, racial discrimination, which had been one expression of colonialism, had always been a sensitive issue with the colonial peoples, most of whom are coloured. The social discrimination practised against the Negroes, Mexicans and Red Indians in the United States was an unhappy reminder that the great liberal ideals of the American Revolution and Civil War were still far from realization. The anti-colonial traditions of the nationalist movements were, therefore, against alignment with Western Powers.

Nor was a total alignment with the Soviet bloc easy in the circumstances. The nationalist movements of these countries were mostly led by middle class intellectuals who were in no sense communists or socialists, except possibly in a romantic way. The socialist or communist elements present in the nationalist ranks were comparatively too weak and small to effect any change in the general social character of these nationalist movements. But the impressive economic achievements of the Soviet Union after the revolution and a vague realization that some similar efforts might be required in their own countries, the consistent anti-imperialist attitude of the Soviet Union, the general egalitarian implications of Soviet social theory, the heroic bravery of the Soviet people in the Second World War, the absence of any obvious racial discrimination within the Communist States, helped to develop certain favourable images about the Soviet Union, even though the extreme rigidity of its social and political system had also created a certain amount of uneasiness. Thus, while the general social character of the nationalist movements was against any identification with the Soviet camp, a number of other influences operated to promote a less antagonistic feeling towards it than was present towards the Western countries.

These factors of non-alignment with either of the two blocs were fortified by a general fear of all big Powers, particularly of the West, among these newly independent and weak nations. It was feared that even in those countries where the transfer of power had taken place, the Western Powers might attempt to make a back door entry into them and imperil their independence. This tended to keep them suspicious of and aloof from the big power politics. Proud and jealous of their freedom, and conscious of their material and military weakness, they tended to suspect every move to bring them into bloc alignments. They did not want to recognize the leadership or guidance of any bloc in their national or international policies. At the same time, the impact of world events mercilessly drew them out of any policy of isolationism into which they could have otherwise taken refuge.

The policy of non-alignment with power blocs was an offshoot of the strong sentiments of nationalism in these countries. The pursuit of an "independent" foreign policy provided a tremendous satisfaction to their national pride and sense of independence. They discovered that non-alignment with either of these blocs not only helped them to preserve their newly-won independence better but also endowed them with a greater importance and recognition in world affairs. This relation between nationalism and foreign policy goes a long way to explain why such a policy makes a tremendous mass appeal in all these countries. It is significant that the countries that have pursued a policy of non-alignment in world affairs are almost invariably those where the nationalist revolutions have been in full swing. . . .

A major factor, determining the outlook of these new nations to a considerable extent in their international relations, is economics. Long years of stagnation under a colonial rule have led to the existence of a very backward economy in all these countries. The urge for modernization and rapid economic and social development had been one of the prime motivations of nationalism in these countries, though it had remained submerged under the immediate question of political independence. With the advent of political independence, this urge has become a watchword of nationalism in these countries. But the success of a policy of social and economic development within these countries is dependent for its success on peaceful conditions, internally and internationally. The fear of a third world war which might destroy their national independence, if not existence, and all their hopes of national development have, therefore, prompted these states to seek peace, often at any cost. The states have consequently argued for total disarmament and peaceful settlement of disputes. The support they give to the United Nations is largely based on the hope that the world body is the only workable mechanism for peaceful settlement of international disputes in the present context, though they also find in the world body an organ in which they are able to realise equality with other nations and a means of maximizing their influence in world affairs.   . . .

The existence of these common factors in the national conditions of these countries does not however, mean that they follow identical policies on all issues of international relations. There are important differences in the national factors relating to foreign policy existing in these countries and bringing about significant differences in foreign policy. Internal conditions like the existence of strong right-wing and left-wing political parties, the type of leadership in power, the nature of social organization, the level of economic development, geographic location, needs of security, etc., are some of these factors. Further, the impact of a particular international event on the nation is naturally different from that on another. Finally, the nature and degree of existence of these common factors of foreign policy are different in different countries. For example, the nature of nationalism in these various countries differs widely from one another in spite of certain common features. Such differences account for differences in policies at different times among these nations.   . . .

It is not, therefore, to be expected that non-alignment means a uniform policy for all its adherents on all occasions. It represents a broad similarity in approach to the contemporary international situation, expressing itself in similar policies on certain questions among these nations.

II EVOLUTION OF THE POLICY

The first official declaration of a policy of non-alignment came with the assumption of power by the nationalist leaders in India in 1946.

Immediately after his assumption of charge of Member for External Affairs and Commonwealth Relations in the Government of India in September 1946, Nehru declared that India would "keep away from power politics of groups aligned against one another, which have led in the past to world wars and which may again lead to disasters on an even vaster scale."[1] All the basic premises of the policy, like anti-colonialism, non-alignment with power blocs, and faith in the United Nations were elaborated by him a few days later.[2]

Internal troubles of a very serious nature prevented Burma from devoting full attention to foreign affairs during the first years of independence, but there were firm pronouncements even during these turbulent years that gave definite indications of an independent foreign policy. . . .

Indonesia was admitted to the United Nations only in 1950. The fight with the Dutch forces had prevented the Republic from devoting full attention to foreign affairs earlier but yet the trends of her policy were not very much in doubt even then. The British and American policies of assisting the Dutch and the Soviet policy of supporting the communist insurrectionists during these years of the Republic's fight for freedom were powerful forces influencing its attitude against alignment with either bloc. At the same time, under the call of non-aligned India, Asian nations met at the Asian Conference on Indonesia in New Delhi in January, 1949, to express their support to the cause of Indonesian independence;[3] within the United Nations also similar moves were initiated by these nations.

Pakistan's foreign policy, during these early years was much more independent of bloc alignments than it became later; but before these early tendencies could crystallize, the internal political conditions within Pakistan and its disputes with India tended to drive her more and more into the Western camp.

A very important addition to the non-aligned group during these

---

[1] *Independence and After: A collection of the more important speeches of Jawaharlal Nehru from September 1946 to May 1949* (Delhi: The Publication Division, 1949) p. 340.

[2] *Indian Annual Register*, ed. N. N. Mitra (Calcutta, 1946), II (July–September 1946) 251–258.

[3] The Conference was held in New Delhi in January 1949. It was attended by official representatives of fifteen Asian States. The Conference made recommendations to the Security Council to take action to stop the second Dutch "Police Action" in violation of the "Renville Agreement" of January 1948 and called for the transference of complete sovereignty to Indonesia by 1st January 1950.

early years was Yugoslavia. The conditioning factors in Yugoslavia persuading it to follow the non-alignment policy were to a large extent different from those of the Asian countries. Yugoslavia had belonged to the Communist bloc till its rift with Soviet Union in June 1948. The early violence of this rift seemed to direct it into the Western bloc at first, but soon after it was able to find its moorings in a more "independent" policy. There is little doubt that a strong sense of nationalism was a powerful factor in determining Yugoslavia's rift with the Soviet Union and its later adherence to the policy of non-alignment.

The years between 1950–54 could be described as the most formative period in the evolution of non-alignment. During the earlier years it had not found favour with either of the blocs, but its growing popularity among a large number of countries in Asia and its increasing influence in world affairs were also evident. The end of the period saw the beginnings of a change in attitude of the two blocs and a clearer evolution and enunciation of the principles of non-alignment.

This period witnessed the intensification of the cold war tendencies into the actual outbreak of a hot war in Korea in June 1950. The outbreak of the Korean War led in turn to a further intensification of the cold war on all fronts. The Western programme of containing communism by organizing military pacts went ahead rapidly. The Rio Pact of 1947, the Brussels Treaty of 1948 and the North Atlantic Treaty of 1949 had only been the beginnings of this policy.[4] The Anzus Pact was signed at San Francisco in 1951.[5] The South East Asia Collective Defence Treaty was signed at Manila in 1954.[6] Similarly, in 1955, the Soviet Union and seven other Communist countries in Eastern Europe

[4] The Rio Pact was signed on 2 January 1947 at Rio de Janeiro between U.S.A. and twenty-one Central and South American States. For text see *Documents on International Affairs*, 1947–48 (London: R.I.I.A., 1952) pp. 773–778. The Brussels Treaty was signed on 17 March 1948 at Brussels between United Kingdom, Belgium, France, Luxembourg and the Netherlands. For text see *ibid.*, pp. 225–229. The North Atlantic Treaty was signed on 4 April 1949 at Washington by U.S.A., Canada and ten other West European powers. Greece and Turkey joined later, on 20 February 1952. For text see *Documents on International Affairs* (London: R.I.I.A., 1953) pp. 257–260.

[5] The signatories of this Treaty were Australia, New Zealand and U.S.A. It was signed at San Francisco in September 1951. For text, see *Documents on International Affairs*, 1951 (London: R.I.I.A., 1954) pp. 677–680.

[6] The following eight countries signed the Treaty in September 1954: U.K., U.S.A., France, Australia, New Zealand, Pakistan, Philippines and Thailand. For text see *Documents on International Affairs*, 1954 (London: R.I.I.A., 1957) pp. 153–157.

signed at Warsaw a 20-year Treaty of Friendship, Co-operation, and Mutual Aid, setting up a communist counterpart of NATO with a unified army command.[7] Both American and Russian policies became extremely rigid during this period. This rigidity was reflected within the countries also. It was the period of McCarthyism in the United States and of the Doctors' Plot and the "purges" within the Soviet Union and the Eastern European countries.

The outbreak of the Korean War in 1950 put the non-alignment policy to a severe test, but also afforded it an occasion for a demonstration of its utility. The policy pursued by the non-aligned countries, in particular India and to some extent Yugoslavia both of which were at the time members of the Security Council, contributed in some measure to a lessening of the tensions and to creating the necessary atmosphere for peaceful negotiations between the two blocs. The events in Korea and the common striving for peace helped to bring about a greater sense of unity among the Arab-Asian countries in the United Nations. Both the blocs came to recognize the value of the peace efforts initiated by the non-aligned nations. The three anxious and unhappy years of the Korean crisis thus marked the beginnings of a more positive and creative orientation of non-alignment.

The emergence of successful nationalist movements in Asia and Africa during these years strengthened the number of adherents to the policy. . . .

The emergence of an Afro-Asian Group in the United Nations in these years was an important development in the growth of non-alignment. This was in no sense a deliberate and well-organized group, but on matters of common interest they came to develop methods of consultation and co-operation. . . . Few of the members of this group were non-aligned at this time, but on a large number of occasions the Asian-African nations found increasing opportunities to develop closer understanding and to work in collaboration with one another. . . .

The years since 1954, saw the consolidation of the policy on all fronts — in its popularity, ideology and recognition by the two blocs. There were increasing adherents to the policy in Asia and Africa. A very close understanding was developed with the Communist bloc.

[7] Popularly known as the Warsaw Pact the Treaty was signed on 14 May 1955 by U.S.S.R., Hungary, Poland, Czechoslovakia, Rumania, Bulgaria, Albania and East Germany. For text see *Documents on International Affairs,* 1955 (London: R.I.I.A., 1958) pp. 193–198.

There were also indications of a change in the attitude of the Western Powers. The full conceptual implications of the non-aligned policy had emerged by the end of the period, such as opposition to military pacts, the idea of an expanding peace area and the *Pancha-sheel* or the five principles of peaceful co-existence.

The crisis in Indo-China in 1954 was the second major occasion for the non-aligned nations to demonstrate the significance of their "independent" policy to the preservation of peace in the world. The issues at stake in the Indo-Chinese crisis were not as complicated as in Korea, though intervention by the Big Powers had led to a tense situation. The trends of events became no less ominous than in Korea when the basic question of the liquidation of colonialism came to be entangled with cold war politics. It was the task of the non-aligned nations to try to dissociate the two aspects of the situation from each other. . . .

The Summit Meeting at Geneva and the settlement in Indo-China, the process of liberalization within the Soviet Union, particularly apparent after the 20th Congress of the Soviet Communist Party, the signing of the Austrian Peace Treaty, the change of administration in the United States and the early pronouncements of President Eisenhower were among the factors that contributed to a relaxation of tensions in the world for the next few years. But on a number of problems like the organization of military pacts, Formosa and the Offshore Islands, disarmament, racialism, admission of China to the United Nations and freedom for the colonies tensions persisted.

The Bandung Conference of the twenty-nine Asian-African nations in 1955 was an important landmark in the growing maturity of the Asian-African world. This was in no sense an exclusive conference of the non-aligned nations as the recent Belgrade Conference was. A number of nations openly aligned with either of the blocs had also been invited to the conference. The final communique, embodying the decisions of the conference, was certainly not an essay in the principles of non-alignment. But the leadership of the Conference and the general tone of its communique were certainly of the non-aligned world.[8] It gave them an occasion to meet and develop some common understanding on world affairs.

[8] For text see *Foreign Policy of India: Text of Documents*, 1947–59 (New Delhi: Lok Sabha Secretariat, 1959) pp. 173–181.

The outbreak of the Suez crisis in 1956 gave the non-aligned nations a further occasion to demonstrate their solidarity. The indignant and united voice of the non-aligned nations was very largely effective in rescuing Egypt from the threat to her freedom.

The Hungarian problem, however, proved to be a much more elusive issue for the non-aligned world. A large amount of spontaneous criticism was generated against Soviet action in all these countries. And yet, many of the leading non-aligned countries found it difficult to condemn with equal vigour the Soviet action in Hungary and the Anglo-French action in Suez. . . .

During the following years, the non-aligned nations were consistently seeking to realize their broad assumptions about international relations into actual policies. In urging the liquidation of colonialism in all parts of the world, notably in Algeria and Angola, in attempting to realize through the United Nations and associated bodies peaceful solutions to international problems and aid to under-developed nations for their development programmes, in opposing the racialist policies pursued by certain nations within their territories, and in urging disarmament and banning of nuclear weapons, the non-aligned nations tried to operate as an international pressure group.

Particularly noteworthy in this context have been the policies of the non-aligned nations towards the tragic events in Congo. . . . These events have shown the dangers which an under-developed or undeveloped nation faces when caught in the tentacles of imperialism and intervention by the Big Powers. The non-aligned nations themselves have not shown a uniform approach towards these events at all times, but there has been a basic similarity of objectives in their policies, namely, that Belgian mercenaries should quit the Republic, that big power politics should be purged from the area, that the integrity of the whole state should be preserved and that democratic forces within the country should be encouraged to develop. . . .

An event of major importance in the evolution of non-alignment was the Summit Conference of Non-aligned Powers at Belgrade in September 1961. This Conference was preceded by a preparatory meeting at Cairo in June 1961 when Foreign Ministers or senior diplomats from twenty countries met to draw up the list of invitees to the Belgrade Conference and to prepare its agenda. The importance of these conferences was that these were the first occasions when non-aligned nations met in conferences of their own. . . .

N. PARAMESWARAN NAYAR   *209*

One of the most notable features about non-alignment in world affairs has been the acceptance of the policy by an increasing number of nations of the world. For a few years after 1946, when the first nationalist government of India declared in September 1946, non-alignment as its basis of approach to contemporary international relations, India was practically the only country in the world to pursue the policy. In great contrast to this is the present strength of the non-aligned world. . . . During the course of these last sixteen years the growth in popularity of non-alignment has been phenomenal.

This tremendous growth has been from one main source — the new States in Asia and Africa. A study of the list of participants at the Belgrade Conference shows that, with the possible exception of Ethiopia and Yugoslavia, all others are new States, that attained independence after the end of the Second World War. . . .

The real strength of the non-aligned world is to be seen not actually in the number of governments that claim to pursue the policy. As was noted earlier, many of these governments pursue the policy in a half-hearted measure and not necessarily with reference to its full social implications. The real basis of strength of non-alignment can be seen in the tremendous popular basis which the policy enjoys, not only in those countries where non-alignment is pursued officially, but also in a number of other countries in the under-developed world and in liberal circles in some of the more advanced countries of Europe like Britain, Norway, Sweden, etc. In the under-developed world, it is not by casual design that governments which actively pursue non-alignment are also governments with large popular base as in India, Indonesia, United Arab Republic or Ghana. The popular character of these governments may or may not be expressed through Western forms of democratic institutions, but their mass base cannot be held in doubt. . . .

IV THE CONCEPTUAL DEVELOPMENT

A further aspect of the growth of non-alignment during these years has been the gradual evolution of its conceptual implications. With the passage of years and through practical experience of international politics the non-aligned nations have been able to give an increasingly coherent character to their foreign policies. . . .

Certain general propositions of the policy were derived at the very beginning itself. These were largely inherent in the political experiences of these nations in the immediate past. Opposition to colonialism and racialism, organizing international assistance for economic development of the undeveloped and under-developed areas, the urge for peace and disarmament, and support to U.N. were such. While, thus, there were a number of issues on which the non-aligned nations felt little difficulty in taking a definite attitude from the very beginning, time and experience were required before they could define their policies on a number of other issues.

The foreign policies of these countries during this early period indicated a general inclination towards the West with which they had closer ties. . . .

A clearer distinction between non-alignment and neutrality is also a result of the growth in maturity in ideas over years, largely as a result of the colonial status of the earlier years when the international personality of the nation had lain suppressed under imperialism in the past. With the advent of independence the natural tendency of these nations was to seek expression to their rediscovered personality. Though, therefore, these countries spoke of non-alignment, it was made clear as early as 1947, that it had "nothing to do with neutrality or passivity or anything else."[9] India was non-aligned but not neutral; Indonesian policy was "independent and active;" Egypt sought to pursue "positive neutrality." There have been repeated expressions of this distinction between non-alignment and neutrality over all these years by the leaders of these nations. In June 1961, the Cairo Conference affirmed again that the policy of non-commitment was "a method of approaching *positively* the problems which confront the world at this hour."[10] . . .

On questions of colonialism, racialism, and peace there has not been any tendency for neutrality among these nations. Even as regards the outbreak of a war, Nehru declared:

If there is a big war, there is no particular reason why we should jump into it. Nevertheless, it is a little difficult now-a-days in world wars to be neutral. . . . We are not going to join a war if we can help it; and we are

---

[9] Speech by Prime Minister Nehru delivered at the Constituent Assembly (Legislative) on 4 December 1947. *Ibid.*, p. 200.
[10] Emphasis added. Official Communique at the end of the Preparatory Meeting of the Heads of State and Government of the Uncommitted Countries (*Review of International Affairs* [Belgrade], Belgrade Conference, No. 1, p. 6).

going to join the side which is to our interest when the time comes to make the choice.[11]

At the same time there were also certainly some negative elements in their basic approach to world affairs. It seemed often that they would prefer to be aloof from a number of problems if they could, such as bloc formations, power politics of the Big Powers, the question of communism vs. capitalism and the like. There was, consequently, a hesitation to take the full plunge in world politics if it could be avoided. . . .

The changing attitude to regional military pacts demonstrates further the conceptual development of non-alignment. The earlier reactions of non-aligned states to the formation of military alliances was generally one of unconcern. . . . Even as late as August, 1954, Yugoslavia is seen entering into the Balkan Pact with Greece and Turkey, both members of NATO, providing for mutual military assistance in case of aggression on any.[12] This, however, changed soon after. For example, India felt in 1952 that though the Atlantic Pact was begun as a defensive arrangement, it had widened its scope and had taken upon itself the defence of the colonial possessions of the member nations of the Pact.[13] All round opposition to the formation of these pacts, particularly in Asia and Africa, has been expressed by non-aligned nations during these years. . . .

From this changed attitude to regional pacts emerged a new enlargement to the concept of non-alignment — the idea of a peace area. It was argued that whatever justification there might have been for the formation of regional military pacts in Europe, their extension into parts of Asia would be to bring cold war politics into an area of comparative peace. The Western Powers were accused of taking sides in the disputes between nations of the area with definite cold war motives. . . .

[11] Speech delivered at the Constituent Assembly (Legislative) on 4 December 1947. *Independence and After, op. cit.,* p. 200.

[12] For text see *Documents on International Affairs,* 1954, *op. cit.,* pp. 197–201.

[13] Speech by Prime Minister Nehru in the Indian Parliament dated 12 June 1952. *Jawaharlal Nehru's Speeches,* 1949–53 (Delhi: The Publications Division, 1954) p. 223. However, at a press conference held a year later on 10 June 1953, in answer to a question regarding India's views on EDC and NATO, the Indian Prime Minister said, "We do not wish to get entangled in European problems or in problems apart from those directly affecting us." *Jawaharlal Nehru's Press Conferences,* 1953 (New Delhi: Information Services of India, 1953) p. 7.

One of the most important contributions to the concept of non-alignment since 1953 has been that of the *Pancha sheel* or the five principles of peaceful coexistence. These principles were in fact a further elucidation of the policy rather than any addition to it. They were first enunciated in the Sino-Indian agreement on Tibet and then in the joint statement by the Prime Ministers of India and China in 1954.[14] These were later incorporated in the ten principles enunciated in the final communique of the Bandung Conference.[15] . . . The Belgrade Conference declared that the principles of peaceful coexistence — "which include the right of peoples to self-determination, to independence and to the free determination of the forms and methods of economic, social and cultural development must be the only basis of all international relations" in the present phase. The participating countries proclaimed that "the principles of peaceful coexistence are the only alternative to the 'cold war' and to a possible nuclear general catastrophe."[16] It makes an interesting commentary on the methods of diplomacy of the two blocs that while the Communist bloc has announced enthusiastic adherence to these principles in joint statements with these countries, the Western bloc has tended to look upon them with a certain amount of distrust.

By 1954–55, one notices that all the major premises of the non-alignment policy as are understood today have emerged clearly. The later years have shown attempts at giving practical application to these principles in response to the challenges of the changing international context.

It was in this context of the gradual emergence of these ideas that the representatives of twenty governments claiming to pursue non-alignment met at Cairo in June 1961 in a Preparatory Meeting for the Belgrade Conference and attempted to define a non-aligned country. After long debates, which brought out not only the areas of agreement but of differences as well among the non-aligned countries, the conference adopted five broad criteria to distinguish a non-aligned country,

[14] For texts of the Sino-Indian Agreement on Tibet dated 29 April 1954 and the Chou-Nehru Joint Statement dated 28 June 1954 see *Foreign Policy of India: Texts of Documents 1947–59, op. cit.*, pp. 103–109, pp. 113–114. Extracts are available in *Documents on International Affairs*, 1954, *op. cit.*, pp. 313–315.

[15] For text see *The Foreign Policy of India, op. cit.*, pp. 173–181.

[16] Declaration of the Heads of State or Government of Non-aligned Countries. *Review of International Affairs*, Belgrade Conference, No. 5, p. 20.

on the basis of which invitations were to be issued for the Belgrade Conference. These criteria were that a non-aligned country should

(1) Follow an independent policy based on non-alignment and peaceful coexistence;
(2) Support liberation movements;
(3) Not be a member of a multilateral military pact in the context of the East-West struggle;
(4) Not be a member of a bilateral military pact with a Big Power in the East-West struggle;
(5) Not grant military bases to foreign powers.[17]

These criteria are, however, too broad and general to be taken as a clear guidance to the understanding of non-alignment. There is need for precision because of the political character of the definition, the diversity of the nations that attended the Preparatory Meeting and the nature of non-alignment itself which indicates more a method of approach than a final definite policy.

The Belgrade Conference held in September 1961 made an effort to state clearly the principle of non-alignment as expressed in the foreign policies of the participating nations. The rather lengthy declaration issued at the end of the conference on 6 September 1961 expressed these efforts, though it is not to be taken as a final declaration of non-alignment. The statement of the conference, as well as the speeches at the conference, make it clear that non-alignment does not mean simply aloofness from power blocs, it also implies adherence to a number of other positive concepts like the stabilization of world peace, elimination of colonialism-imperialism and neo-colonialism in all their manifestations, the principles of peaceful coexistence, cooperation and brotherhood between nations, opposition to military alliances, condemnation of the policies of *apartheid* and racial discrimination, faith in fundamental human rights and respect for the right of minorities, disarmament, removal of the economic imbalance inherited from colonialism and imperialism, revision of the U.N. Charter to expand the membership of the Security Council, ECOSOC, etc.[18]

V CHANGING ATTITUDE OF THE BLOCS

The changing attitudes of the two blocs to the policy of non-alignment

[17] *The Times of India* (Delhi) June 12, 1961. *The Statesman* (Delhi) June 12, 1961.
[18] *Review of International Affairs,* Belgrade Conference, No. 5, pp. 19–23.

during the various years is an excellent commentary on the growing importance of the policy, as well as on the methods of diplomacy of the two power blocs.

The attitude of the two blocs to the policy of non-alignment during the early years was one of suspicion and distrust, probably because during this period of the cold war both the blocs could see others only in a black and white pattern. . . .

To the Western bloc countries this was particularly bitter because these new nations — India, Indonesia and Burma, for example, had, till a few years back, been aligned with the West, though not as independent countries, at least as colonies. Their refusal to be aligned with them amounted in their eyes, therefore, to a positive defection from their own ranks. It is interesting to compare this Western attitude towards their ex-colonies with the Soviet reactions to the defection of Yugoslavia from her own camp.

Nor was the Soviet Union, in general, happy about the policy, though on a number of occasions, particularly in the United Nations, it found itself working in close understanding with these countries against the Western Powers. But there were also a number of other issues on which Soviet Union and the non-aligned Powers disagreed. The debates in the U.N. on Greece, Interim Committee and Korea, for example, brought out these differences. During these early years, the general thesis of the Communist bloc about the newly independent Asian countries was that their governments represented a deal between the national bourgeoisie and the imperialists against the peoples of these countries. . . .

Non-alignment during these early years was thus a heretic doctrine, suspected and condemned by both the blocs and practised by few. India was very nearly waging a lone crusade during these early years, for unsettled conditions prevented Indonesia and Burma from following an active foreign policy. The policy was attacked from either side as being either too idealistic or opportunistic.

During the next few years, relations with the Western blocs showed signs of further deteriorations. The early pro-Western tendencies in many non-aligned nations suffered a severe setback. The general approach of Western policy towards non-alignment and the many problems of these countries alienated considerably the earlier friendly feelings towards them. . . .

A basic change in the Soviet attitude was, however, visible by 1953. The change in Soviet attitude can be accounted partly by the clearer emergence of the policy as a really "independent" and "non-aligned" one and partly also due to the increasing divergence between the Western bloc countries and the non-aligned nations; it was also due in some measure to the tremendous changes set in motion within the Soviet Union after the death of Stalin in 1952.

The most significant expression of this changed attitude was made in Khrushchev's Report to the Twentieth Congress of the Communist Party of the Soviet Union. . . . The period also marked the beginnings of substantial economic aid by Soviet Union to these countries, "to help them to build up an independent national economy and to raise the living standards of their peoples without assuming any political or military commitments."[19] It was obvious that Soviet Union had snatched a diplomatic initiative over the Western Powers in their relations with the non-aligned nations. Goodwill and admiration for the Soviet Union increased in these countries as a consequence of these moves.

This happy trend of friendly relations with the communist world received, however, a rude shock in 1959 when Communist China seemed to strike a new attitude towards non-aligned nations. The policy of the Chinese Communists towards the non-aligned world had so far been supposed to be on the same lines as that of Moscow. To many non-aligned nations the victory of the Chinese Communists had seemed as a completion of the Chinese nationalist revolution. The Chinese performance at Bandung was also viewed with approval. With assiduous care China had built up the foundations of a firm friendship with most of the Asian nations. But, by 1959–60, there was an apparent change in policy. In strange coincidence, Chinese relations with Burma, Indonesia, Egypt, Yugoslavia and India — the most important members of the non-aligned world — showed evidences of sudden strain and deterioration. It is not impossible that there had been a reassessment in Peking that the period of giving tactical support to the non-aligned countries was over and that the time had come for "the real class character" of the governments in these countries to be exposed. . . .

Western policy towards the non-aligned countries, particularly towards the so-called moderate nations among them like India and Burma, has been showing some signs of change and improvement in relations since 1956. . . .

[19] For more details, see D. F. Fleming, *The Cold War and Its Origins* 1917–1960 (London: George Allen and Unwin Ltd., 1960) II, 780–784.

This change in attitude of the two blocs was not, perhaps, as much the result of a re-estimate of the merits of the policy by them as one of accepting certain facts and the consequent adoption of a new tactical line by them. It might have come out of the realization that while the immediate possibilities for a Communist revolution in the Western European countries and of counter-revolutions in the Eastern European countries are remote, the under-developed and undeveloped areas of Asia, Africa and other parts of the world presented a different prospect. The extremely fluid social and political conditions in them make them areas of potential revolutionary changes. Both the blocs are therefore interested in maintaining the closest possible contacts with the dominant social forces in them. These have not yet clearly emerged as communist or anti-communist. For the time being, nationalism represents the most dominant social force in these countries. It is, therefore, natural for both the blocs to try to remain friendly with these nationalist forces and to influence them as far as possible.

VI   GENERAL ESTIMATE

A general estimate of non-alignment as it has operated during the last few years indicates that in spite of occasional set-backs and compromises, its total impact has been towards contributing to the stability and maintenance of peace in the world and of preserving the national independence of, maintaining political stability in and advancing the national interests of these countries.

This was made possible by two developments. Firstly, a balance of power was established between the two blocs. With the expansion in its area — particularly after the establishment of a Communist Government in China — development of nuclear weapons and vehicles for their delivery by the Soviet Union, the Communist world achieved a balance of deterrence with the West. Secondly, there was a change in the United Nations due to the entry of a large number of newly independent African states. As most of the new members are non-aligned, the opinions of the uncommitted nations gained in weight in this world forum. The major Powers, therefore, have had increasingly to take note of the policies of the non-aligned nations.

The activities of the non-aligned nations have thus contributed to strengthening the forces of nationalism in the colonies, discrediting the policies of racial discrimination and *apartheid*, protecting the rights of the smaller nations, emphasizing the importance of the economic and social problems of the undeveloped and under-developed nations, etc.

The general trends of the world situation were favourable to such developments, and the efforts of the non-aligned nations have contributed to expediting them.

On the national front, the pursuit of the policy by governments has helped to maintain some stability of structure within their own countries. It provides a broad national front behind which the extremely divergent sections of the population are able to come together. This is particularly obvious in those countries where the Communist parties are very strong. . . .

It would, of course, be unrealistic to state that the non-aligned nations have maintained the peace of the world. Questions of war and peace do not basically depend on them, but on the Big Powers of the world who are the chief actors in the complex drama of world politics today. The role which the non-aligned nations have played is, therefore, only secondary, but by no means a negligible one. They have tried to be "a basic factor for the preservation of peace and international security."[20] They have been able, occasionally, to make useful contributions to creating the conditions for relaxation of tension and to evolve compromise formula to tide over immediate crises.

But possibly, the most important aspect of non-alignment which requires consideration in this respect is the fact that there is a dynamic relationship between foreign affairs and domestic affairs existing in these countries. It is not by accident that governments that pursue a policy of non-alignment are also those which pursue active and conscious policies of national development in social and economic spheres. . . . At the same time, governments in power in the aligned countries do not seem to possess the same consciousness of these requirements of their countries. There is thus a vital correlation between progressive social policies at home and a policy of non-alignment in world affairs. . . . It is this vital relationship between the necessary social revolution in these countries and their foreign policies that gives non-alignment its tremendous popularity and mass basis. . . .

[20] Nehru address to the Indian Council of World Affairs, New Delhi, on 22 March 1949. *Independence and After, op. cit.*, p. 257.

Military Strategy:

The Threat and Uses of Force

WESTERN STRATEGY

Nuclear Deterrence and Graduated Response

17 ROBERT S. McNAMARA
Spectrum of Defense

. . . Some critics have suggested that we have literally hundreds of times more strength than we need; others have accused us of risking the whole future of the nation by engaging in unilateral disarmament. I would like to believe that criticisms bracketing our policy in that fashion prove it to be rational and sound. But a discrepancy of that order cannot be reassuring. Rather, it indicates that we have failed to convey to some part of our audience even the broadest outlines, as we see them, of the problems that our military strategy and force structure are meant to address. I believe we should be able to move from controversy on that scale toward consensus in military affairs,

Robert S. McNamara, Secretary of Defense of the United States under Presidents Kennedy and Johnson, gave this speech before the Economic Club of New York on November 18, 1963. These excerpts are reprinted from *Survival*, VI, No. 1 (January–February 1964), published by the Institute of Strategic Studies Ltd.

not always on details or components of our policies, but at least on an appreciation of the major national security problems confronting us, on the broad alternative paths to their solution and on the dominant goals, obstacles, costs and risks affecting choice. . . . I should like to identify and discuss some basic matters on which a considerable degree of consensus seems to me both possible and desirable, although by no means assured.

These include those over-all comparative strengths and weaknesses of the opposing military alliances that form the bold relief in the strategic environment. In short, they are the considerations that seem to have relatively long-term significance compared to the annual budget cycle.

Matters of that degree of permanence tend to be stamped on our minds as being unchanging and unchangeable, the unquestioned framework of daily and yearly policy-making. Yet these factors of which I shall speak do change: more swiftly and more profoundly than our picture of them tends to change. Indeed I believe it is just the fact that over the last decade this topography has changed — while many maps have not — that accounts for some apparently irreconcilable controversies.

Let me recall the earlier period briefly, for comparison. The strategic landscape at the outset of the 'Fifties was dominated by two outstanding features. One was the practical U.S. monopoly of deliverable, strategic nuclear weapons. The other was the Soviet Union and Communist China's virtual monopoly of ground force on the continents of Europe and Asia.

Both of these determinants of Western military policy had changed considerably by the end of the Korean War. The Soviets had produced atomic explosions and had created a sizeable nuclear delivery capability against Europe, while NATO ground forces had expanded rapidly, and military operations in Korea had greatly tarnished the significance of Chinese Communist superiority in numbers. But the old notions of monopoly persisted as short-cut aids to thinking on policy matters. And they were not so misleading as they came later to be. Soviet armed forces approaching five million men still heavily outweighed the NATO forces in Europe; and Soviet delivery capability against the U.S. was dwarfed by that of SAC. Moreover, tactical nuclear weapons were being heralded as a new nuclear monopoly for the West.

Even as these earlier notions of monopolies grew obsolete, ideas about the feasibility of alternative policies continued to reflect them.

So did ideas about how wars might be fought. Nuclear operations, both strategic and tactical, by the U.S. in response to Soviet aggression against our allies were considered to be virtually unilateral. Hence it was supposed the problem of credibility of the U.S. response would scarcely arise, even in the case of relatively limited Soviet aggressions. Western reliance upon nuclear weapons, in particular strategic systems, both to deter and to oppose non-nuclear attack of any size seemed not only adequate but also unique in its adequacy.

That sort of situation is convenient for policy-makers. It makes policy easy to choose and easy to explain. Perhaps that is why throughout most of the 'Fifties, while the Soviets under various pressures decreased their ground forces and the NATO allies built theirs up, and while the Soviets acquired a massive nuclear threat against Europe and laid the groundwork for a sizeable threat against the U.S., the picture underlying most policy debate remained that appropriate to 1949. It was a picture of a Communist Goliath in conventional strength facing a Western David, almost naked of conventional arms but alone possessed of a nuclear sling.

Towards the end of that decade, the prospect that the Soviets would acquire intercontinental ballistic missiles at a time when our strategic forces consisted almost entirely of bombers focused our attention and our budget even more sharply than before upon our strategic forces. The urgency of the problem of deterring the most massive of attacks was a new reason for thinking that the West could spare neither resources nor thought to deal more specifically with lesser threats. The most urgent task was to provide for deterrence of massive aggression by assuring the survival under any attack of forces at least adequate, in the calculations of a potential attacker, to destroy his society in retaliation. It was now not the assurance of continued nuclear superiority that pre-empted the attention of policy-makers but, on the contrary, the struggle to maintain it.

But it is time for the maps to change by which policy is charted and justified. The old ones, which assumed a U.S. nuclear monopoly, both strategic and tactical, and a Communist monopoly of ground combat strength, are too far removed from reality to serve as even rough guides. Neither we nor our allies can afford the crudities of maps that tell us that old policies are still forced upon us, when a true picture would show important new avenues of necessity and choice.

What most needs changing is a picture of ourselves and of the Western Alliance as essentially at bay, outmanned and outgunned except for nuclear arms no longer exclusively ours. We should not think of ourselves as forced by limitations of resources to rely upon strategies of desperation and threats of vast mutual destruction, compelled to deal only with the most massive and immediate challenges, letting lesser ones go by default. It would be a striking historical phenomenon if that self-image should be justified. We are the largest member of an Alliance with a population of almost 450 million people, an aggregate annual product which is fast approaching a trillion dollars, and a modern and diverse technological base without parallel, facing the Soviet Union and its European satellites with their hundred million fewer people and an aggregate output no more than half that of the West.

OUTDATED PICTURE

And quite apart from ignoring the underlying strengths of the West, the outdated picture I have described takes no account of the military capabilities in being that our investments over the last decade, and specifically in the last few years, have bought for us. If new problems put strong claims on our attention and our resources today, it is very largely because we have come a large part of the way that is feasible toward solving some old ones.

Let me summarize the current status of the balance of strategic nuclear forces, that part of the military environment that has preoccupied our attention for so long. In strictly relative numerical terms, the situation is the familiar one. The U.S. force now [1963] contains more than 500 operational long-range ballistic missiles — *Atlas, Titan, Minuteman, Polaris* — and is planned to increase to over 1,700 by 1966. There is no doubt in our minds and none in the minds of the Soviets that these missiles can penetrate to their targets. In addition, the U.S. has Strategic Air Command bombers on air alert and over 500 bombers on quick reaction ground alert. By comparison, the consensus is that today the Soviets could place about half as many bombers over North America on a first strike. The Soviets are estimated to have today only a fraction as many intercontinental missiles as we do. Furthermore, their submarine-launched ballistic missiles are short range, and generally are not comparable to our *Polaris* force. The Soviets pose a very large threat against Europe, including hundreds of intermediate and medium-range ballistic missiles. This threat is today and will continue to be covered by the clear superiority of our strategic forces.

The most wishful of Soviet planners would have to calculate as a certainty that the most effective surprise attack they could launch would still leave us with the capability to destroy the attacker's society. What is equally pertinent is that the relative numbers and survivability of U.S. strategic forces would permit us to retaliate against all the urgent Soviet military targets that are subject to attack, thus contributing to the limitation of damage to ourselves and our allies.

Deterrence of deliberate, calculated attack seems as well assured as it can be, and the damage-limiting capability of our numerically superior forces is, I believe, well worth its incremental cost. It is a capability to which the smaller forces of the Soviet Union could not realistically aspire. That is one reason, among others, why I would not trade our strategic posture for that of the Soviets at any point during the coming decade.

BEYOND OFFENSIVE REACH

But given the kind of force that the Soviets are building, including submarine-launched missiles beyond the reach of our offensive forces, the damage which the Soviets could inflict on us and our allies, no matter what we do to limit it, remains extremely high.

That has been true for our allies ever since the middle and late 'Fifties. Soviet acquisition of a sizeable delivery capability against the U.S., and more significantly their acquisition of relatively protected forces, submarine-launched or hardened, has been long and often prematurely heralded. Its arrival at last merely dramatizes the need to recognize that strategic nuclear war would under all foreseeable circumstances be bilateral — and highly destructive to both sides.

Larger budgets for U.S. strategic forces would not change that fact. They could have only a decreasing incremental effect in limiting somewhat the damage that the U.S. and its allies could suffer in a general nuclear war. In short, we cannot buy the capability to make a strategic bombing campaign once again a unilateral prospect.

That must, I suggest, be accepted as one of the determinants affecting policy. Another is that the same situation confronts the Soviet leaders, in a way that is even more intensely confining. In fact, enormous increases in Soviet budgets would be required for them to achieve any significant degree of damage-limiting capability. The present Soviet leaders show no tendency to challenge the basis of the U.S. strategic deterrent posture by such expenditures.

In the last two years alone, we have increased the number of nuclear warheads in the strategic alert forces by 100 percent. During that period we have more than doubled the megatonnage of the strategic alert forces. The fact that further increases in strategic force size will at last encounter rapidly diminishing returns — which is largely an effect of the very large investments the U.S. has made in this area — should be reflected in future budgets. The funding for the initial introduction of missiles into our forces is nearing completion. We can anticipate that the annual expenditure on strategic forces will drop substantially, and level off well below the present rate of spending. This is not to rule out the possibility that research now in progress on possible new technological developments, including the possibility of useful ballistic missile defences, will require major new expenditures. In any event, there will be recurring costs of modernization.

In the field of tactical nuclear weapons, the picture is in important respects similar. The U.S. at present has in stockpile or planned for stockpile tens of thousands of nuclear explosives for tactical use on the battlefield, in anti-submarine warfare and against aircraft. They include warheads for artillery, battlefield missiles, demolition munitions, bombs, depth charges, air-to-air missiles and surface-to-air missiles. The consensus is that the U.S. is presently substantially superior in design, diversity and numbers in this class of weapons.

This is an indispensable superiority, as we can readily understand if we consider how our problems of strategic choice would be altered if the tables were reversed and it were the Soviet Union which held a commanding lead in this field. Nevertheless, what we have is superiority, not monopoly, and even if tactical nuclear warfare can be limited, below some ill-defined threshold of strategic exchange, the key fact is that if the West initiates such warfare in the future it must be expected to be bilateral, in any theatre which engaged the Soviet Union. Again, we cannot buy back a monopoly, or the assurance of unilateral use.

Finally, there is the area of what we call our general purpose forces. Within the last two years, we have increased the number of our combat-ready Army divisions by about 45 percent, from 11 to 16. There has been a 30 percent increase in the number of tactical air squadrons; a 75 percent increase in airlift capabilities; and a 100 percent increase in ship construction and conversion to modernize the fleet.

But it is not only force size that matters. The key to the effective utilization of these forces is combat readiness and mobility.

The most recent demonstration of our ability to reinforce our troops presently stationed in Europe occurred [in October 1963] on Operation *Big Lift*, the first of a series of planned large-scale, world-wide exercises. For the first time in military history, an entire division was airlifted from one continent to another. That movement could never have been accomplished without a massive increase in our airlift capability, which is still being expanded. (It will have risen 400 percent between 1961 and 1967.) It required the development of new techniques to preposition combat equipment, of which we have two extra division sets now in Europe. It called for new techniques in military training and administration to make sure that units are really ready to move out on a moment's notice. This exercise, in which some 16,000 airmen and soldiers and more than 350 planes took part, is directly relevant to the needs of Europe, where it brought a seventh division to join the six that are to remain in place. It is also relevant to the ability of the U.S. to fulfil its policy commitments world-wide, swiftly and in effective strength.

But, it might be asked, what is the significance of all this for the realistic security problems of the United States and its allies? To what contingencies are these forces expected to contribute, and how effective might they be, measured against the strength of opposing forces? How meaningful is it to talk of 16 or 20 or 30 divisions in opposing the ground armies of the Soviet Union and Communist China?

Such questions are often meant to be merely rhetorical, in view of the supposed masses of Communist troops. The fact is that they are serious, difficult questions, to which I shall suggest some tentative answers. But it is difficult to encourage realistic discussions of specific contingencies so long as the shadow of the Communist horde hangs unchallenged over the debate. The actual contingencies that seem to be to me most likely and most significant are not those which would involve all, or even a major part, of the Soviet Bloc or Chinese Communist armed forces, nor do they all involve Europe. Hence, aggregate figures of armed strength of NATO and the Warsaw Pact nations are not immediately relevant to them. But it is useful to make these over-all comparisons precisely because misleading or obsolete notions of these very aggregates often produce an attitude of hopelessness toward any attempt to prepare to meet Communist forces in ground combat, however limited in scope.

SOVIET FORCE CUTS

The announced total of Soviet armed forces for 1955 was indeed a formidable 5.75 million men. Today that figure has been cut to about 3.3 million; the Warsaw Pact total including the Soviets is only about

4.5 million. Against that, it is today the members of NATO whose active armed forces number over 5 million. The ground forces of NATO nations total 3.2 million, of which 2.2 million men are in Europe, as against the Soviet ground combat forces' total of about 2 million men, and a Warsaw Pact total of about 3 million. Both the Soviet Union and the U.S. forces of course include units stationed in the Far East. In Central Europe, NATO has more men, and more combat troops, on the ground than does the Bloc. It has more men on the ground in West Germany than the Bloc does in East Germany. It has more and better tactical aircraft, and these planes on the average can carry twice the payload twice as far as the Soviet counterparts.

These facts are hard to reconcile with the familiar picture of the Russian Army as incomparably massive. The usual index cited to support that picture is numbers of total active divisions, and the specific number familiar from the past is 175 divisions in the Soviet Army.

This total, if true, would indeed present a paradox. The Soviet ground forces are reliably estimated to be very close to two million men, compared to about one million for the U.S. How is it that the Soviets can muster ten times the number of active, combat-ready, fully-manned divisions that the United States has manned, with only twice as many men on active duty? The answer is simply that they do not. Recent intensive investigation has shown that the number of active Soviet divisions that are maintained at manning levels anywhere close to combat readiness is less than half of the 160–175 figure.

What remains is a large number, but even that is misleading. For one thing, U.S. divisions have about twice as many men in the division unit and its immediate combat supporting units as comparable Soviet divisions. A U.S. mechanized division has far more personnel in manoeuvring units, far more in armoured cavalry, far more engineers, far more signals, far more light armoured personnel carriers, and far more aircraft available in support than Soviet divisions. In addition to longer staying power, much of the U.S. manpower and equipment margin is muscle that would make itself felt on D-Day. If, on the other hand, we were to reorganize along Soviet lines, we could display far greater numbers of divisions comparable to those of the Soviets.

The Soviet combat-ready force remains a formidable one. Moreover, the Russians do have a power mobilization capability; in particular, they have a large number of lightly manned or cadre divisions to be filled out on mobilization. Still, this reality remains strikingly different from our accustomed maps of it.

I do not wish to suggest that such aggregate comparisons are by themselves a valid index to military capabilities. But they are enough to suggest the absurdity, as a picture of the prevailing military strengths on which new efforts might build, of David and Goliath notions borrowed from 1949.

None of this is to say that NATO strength on the ground in Europe is adequate to turn back without nuclear weapons an all-out surprise non-nuclear attack.

But that is not in any case the contingency toward which the recent and future improvements in the mobility and capabilities of U.S. general purpose forces are primarily oriented. Aggression on that scale would mean a war about the future of Europe and, as a consequence, the future of the U.S. and the U.S.S.R. In the face of threats of that magnitude, our nuclear superiority remains highly relevant to deterrence. The Soviets know that even non-nuclear aggression at that high end of the spectrum of conflict so threatens our most vital interests that we and our allies are prepared to make whatever response may be required to defeat it, no matter how terrible the consequences for our own society.

The probability that the Soviet leaders would choose to invoke that exchange seems to me very low indeed. They know well what even the Chinese Communist leaders must recognize upon further reflection, that a nuclear war would mean destruction of everything they have built up for themselves during the last 50 years.

SPECTRUM OF AGGRESSION

If we were to consider a spectrum of the possible cases of Communist aggression, then, ranging from harassment, covert aggression and indirect challenge at one end of the scale to the massive invasion of Western Europe or a full scale nuclear strike against the West at the other end, it is clear that our nuclear superiority has been and should continue to be an effective deterrent to aggression at the high end of the spectrum. It is equally clear, on the other hand, that at the very low end of the spectrum a nuclear response may not be fully credible, and that nuclear power alone cannot be an effective deterrent at this level in the future any more than it has been in the past.

The fact is that at every level of force, the Alliance in general, and the U.S. Armed Forces in particular, have greater and more effective strength than we are in the habit of thinking we have — and with reasonable continued effort we can have whatever strength we need.

I have spoken already of strategic weapons, where the great superiority of the United States is the superiority also of the Alliance. In tactical nuclear weapons a parallel superiority exists — and while many of our Allies share with us in manning the systems which would use these tactical warheads in the hour of need, it is not unfair to point out that, even more than in the strategic field, the tactical nuclear strength of the Alliance is a contribution of the United States. That strength has been increased, on the ground in Europe, by more than 60 percent in the last two years. Today the thousands of U.S. warheads deployed on the continent for the immediate defence of Europe have a combined explosive strength more than 10,000 times the force of the nuclear weapons used to end the Second World War. Tactical nuclear strength the Alliance has today, and we have provided it.

But neither we nor our Allies can find the detonation of such weapons — and their inevitable bilateral exchange — an easy first choice. At the lower end of the spectrum, therefore, we also need strong and ready conventional forces. We have done our part here and we continue to believe it just — and practicable — for our partners to do theirs.

The most difficult questions arise over the best means for meeting a variety of dangerous intermediate challenges in many parts of the world: those which threaten the possibility of sizeable conflict while still not raising the immediate issue of the national survival of ourselves or of any member of our alliances. Conflicts might arise out of Soviet subversion and political aggression backed up by military measures in non-NATO areas in Europe, Latin America, the Middle East and Africa. There is a range of challenges that could arise from Communist China and its satellites in the Far East and in South-east Asia. Most dangerously, approaching the upper end of the spectrum, there is the possibility of limited Soviet pressures on NATO territory itself, along the vast front running from Norway to Greece and Turkey. Both the flanks and the centre contain potential targets. And always, of course, there are the contingencies that could arise in relation to Berlin.

It is difficult to say just how probable any of these circumstances might be, although they must be regarded as more likely than still larger aggressions. What one can say is that if any of these more likely contingencies should arise, they would be highly dangerous. Inaction, or weak action, could result in a serious setback, missed opportunity or even disaster. In fact, if either a nuclear exchange or a major Soviet attack should occur, it would most likely arise from a conflict on a lesser scale, which Western capabilities had failed to deter and which an inadequate Western response had failed to curb in time.

Since World War II, the expansionist impulse of the Communist Bloc is clear, but equally clear is its desire to avoid direct confrontation with the military forces of the free world. In Greece, in Berlin, and in Cuba, Communists have probed for military and political weakness but when they have encountered resistance, they have held back. Not only Communist doctrine has counselled this caution, but respect for the danger that any sizeable, overt conflict would lead to nuclear war. It would follow that no deterrent would be more effective against these lesser and intermediate levels of challenge than the assurance that such moves would certainly meet prompt, effective military response by the West. That response could confront the Soviets with frustration of their purposes unless they chose themselves to escalate the conflict to a nuclear exchange, or to levels that made nuclear war highly probable — a choice they are unlikely to make in the face of our destructive power.

The basis for that particular assurance cannot be systems in development, or weapons in storage depots, or reserves that must be mobilized, trained and equipped, or troops without transport. We need the right combination of forward deployment and highly mobile combat-ready ground, sea and air units, capable of prompt and effective commitment to actual combat, in short, the sort of capability we are increasingly building in our forces.

LEAN AND FIT

This capability requires of us — as of our Allies — a military establishment that is, in the President's words, lean and fit. We must stop and ask ourselves before deciding whether to add a new and complex weapon system to our inventory, whether it is really the most effective way to do the job under the rigorous conditions of combat. We must examine constantly the possibilities for combining functions, particularly in weapons that could be used by two or more Services. Given this tough-minded sense of reality about the requirements of combat readiness, it should be possible for the United States not only to maintain but to expand this increased strength without over-all increases in our defence budget. As our national productivity and our gross national product expand, the defence budget therefore need not keep pace. Indeed, it appears likely that measured in relative — and perhaps even absolute — terms, the defence budget will level off and perhaps decline a little. At the same time, we are continuing the essential effort to reduce the impact of defence spending on our balance of payments. We have already brought this figure down from $2.7 billion in FY 1961 to $1.7 billion for FY 1963, and we shall continue to reduce it, without reducing the combat ground forces deployed in Europe, and while strengthening our over-all combat effectiveness.

And it must be our policy to continue to strengthen our combat effectiveness. I do not regard the present Communist leaders as wholly reckless in action. But recent experience, in Cuba and, on a lesser scale, in Berlin, has not persuaded me that I can predict with confidence the sorts of challenges that Communist leaders will come to think prudent and profitable. If they were again to miscalculate as dangerously as they did a year ago, it would be essential to confront them, wherever that might be, with the full consequences of their action: the certainty of meeting immediate, appropriate, and fully effective military action.

All of our strengths, including our strategic and tactical nuclear forces, contributed last year, and they would contribute in similar future situations, to the effectiveness of our response, by providing a basis for assurance that the Soviets would not dangerously escalate or shift the locale of the conflict. But above all, in order to fashion that response, and to promise the Soviets local defeat in case of actual ground conflict, we had to use every element of the improvements in combat readiness and mobility that had been building over the preceding year and a half, including combat divisions, air transport, and tactical air. And the last ingredient was also there: the will to use those forces against Soviet troops and equipment.

Let us not delude ourselves with obsolete images into believing that our nuclear strength, great as it is, solves all of our problems of national security, or that we lack the strengths to meet those problems that it does not solve. In the contingencies that really threaten — the sort that have occurred and will occur again — we and our allies need no longer choose to live with the sense or the reality of inferiority to the Soviet Bloc in relevant, effective force. Let us be fully aware of the wide range of our military resources, and the freedom they can give us to pursue the peaceful objectives of the free world without fear of military aggression.

Unconventional Warfare

18 W. W. ROSTOW
Guerrilla Warfare in the Underdeveloped Areas

. . . It does not require much imagination to understand why President Kennedy has taken the problem of guerrilla warfare seriously. When this administration came to responsibility it faced four major crises: Cuba, the Congo, Laos, and Viet-Nam. Each represented a successful Communist breaching — over the previous two years — of the cold-war truce lines which had emerged from the Second World War and its aftermath. In different ways each had arisen from the efforts of the international Communist movement to exploit the inherent instabilities of the underdeveloped areas of the non-Communist world, and each had a guerrilla-warfare component.

Cuba, of course, differed from the other cases. The Cuban revolution against Batista was a broad-based national insurrection. But that revolution was tragically captured from within by the Communist apparatus; and now Latin America faces the danger of Cuba's being used as the base for training, supply, and direction of guerrilla warfare in the hemisphere.

More than that, Mr. Khrushchev, in his report to the Moscow conference of Communist parties (published January 6, 1961), had explained at great length that the Communists fully support what he called wars of national liberation and would march in the front rank with the peoples waging such struggles. The military arm of Mr. Khrushchev's January 1961 doctrine is, clearly, guerrilla warfare.

Faced with these four crises, pressing in on the President from day to day, and faced with the candidly stated position of Mr. Khrushchev, we have, indeed, begun to take the problem of guerrilla warfare seriously.

Walt W. Rostow, Chairman, Policy Planning Council, U.S. Department of State under Presidents Kennedy and Johnson, made this address at graduation ceremonies at the U.S. Army Special Warfare School, Fort Bragg, N.C., on June 28, 1961. These excerpts are from the text in *The Department of State Bulletin*, XLV, No. 1154 (August 7, 1961) 233–238.

To understand this problem, however, one must begin with the great revolutionary process that is going forward in the southern half of the world; for the guerrilla warfare problem in these regions is a product of that revolutionary process and the Communist effort and intent to exploit it.

What is happening throughout Latin America, Africa, the Middle East, and Asia is this: Old societies are changing their ways in order to create and maintain a national personality on the world scene and to bring to their peoples the benefits modern technology can offer. This process is truly revolutionary. It touches every aspect of the traditional life — economic, social, and political. The introduction of modern technology brings about not merely new methods of production but a new style of family life, new links between the villages and the cities, the beginnings of national politics, and a new leadership to the world outside.

Like all revolutions, the revolution of modernization is disturbing. Individual men are torn between the commitment to the old familiar way of life and the attractions of a modern way of life. The power of old social groups — notably the landlord, who usually dominates the traditional society — is reduced. Power moves toward those who can command the tools of modern technology, including modern weapons. Men and women in the villages and the cities, feeling that the old ways of life are shaken and that new possibilities are open to them, express old resentments and new hopes.

This is the grand arena of revolutionary change which the Communists are exploiting with great energy. They believe that their techniques of organization — based on small disciplined cadres of conspirators — are ideally suited to grasp and to hold power in these turbulent settings. They believe that the weak transitional governments that one is likely to find during this modernization process are highly vulnerable to subversion and to guerrilla warfare. And whatever Communist doctrines of historical inevitability may be, Communists know that their time to seize power in the underdeveloped areas is limited. They know that, as momentum takes hold in an underdeveloped area — and the fundamental social problems inherited from the traditional society are solved — their chances to seize power decline.

It is on the weakest nations, facing their most difficult transitional moments, that the Communists concentrate their attention. They are the scavengers of the modernization process. They believe that the techniques of political centralization under dictatorial control — and the projected image of Soviet and Chinese Communist economic progress — will persuade hesitant men, faced by great transitional problems, that the Communist model should be adopted for modernization, even at the cost of surrendering human liberty. They believe that they can exploit effectively the resentments built up in many of these areas against colonial rule and that they can associate themselves effectively with the desire of the emerging nations for independence, for status on the world scene, and for material progress.

This is a formidable program; for the history of this century teaches us that communism is not the longrun wave of the future toward which societies are naturally drawn. On the contrary. But it is one particular form of modern society to which a nation may fall prey during the transitional process. Communism is best understood as a disease of the transition to modernization.

AMERICA'S PURPOSE AND STRATEGY

What is our reply to this historical conception and strategy? What is the American purpose and the American strategy? We, too, recognize that a revolutionary process is under way. We are dedicated to the proposition that this revolutionary process of modernization shall be permitted to go forward in independence, with increasing degrees of human freedom. We seek two results: first, that truly independent nations shall emerge on the world scene; and, second, that each nation will be permitted to fashion, out of its own culture and its own ambitions, the kind of modern society it wants. The same religious and philosophical beliefs which decree that we respect the uniqueness of each individual make it natural that we respect the uniqueness of each national society. Moreover, we Americans are confident that, if the independence of this process can be maintained over the coming years and decades, these societies will choose their own version of what we would recognize as a democratic, open society.

These are our commitments of policy and of faith. The United States has no interest in political satellites. Where we have military pacts we have them because governments feel directly endangered by outside military action and we are prepared to help protect their independence against such military action. But, to use Mao Tse-tung's famous phrase, we do not seek nations which "lean to one side." We seek nations which shall stand up straight. And we do so for a reason: because we are deeply confident that nations which stand up straight will protect their independence and move in their own ways and in their own time toward human freedom and political democracy.

PROTECTING INDEPENDENCE OF REVOLUTIONARY PROCESS

Thus our central task in the underdeveloped areas, as we see it, is to protect the independence of the revolutionary process now going forward. This is our mission, and it is our ultimate strength. For this is not — and cannot be — the mission of communism. And in time, through the fog of propaganda and the honest confusions of men caught up in the business of making new nations, this fundamental difference will become increasingly clear in the southern half of the world. The American interest will be served if our children live in an environment of strong, assertive, independent nations, capable, because they are strong, of assuming collective responsibility for the peace.

The diffusion of power is the basis for freedom within our own society, and we have no reason to fear it on the world scene. But this outcome would be a defeat for communism — not for Russia as a national state, but for communism. Despite all the Communist talk of aiding movements of national independence, they are driven in the end, by the nature of their system, to violate the independence of nations. Despite all the Communist talk of American imperialism, we are committed, by the nature of our system, to support the cause of national independence. And the truth will out.

The victory we seek will see no ticker tape parades down Broadway, no climactic battles, nor great American celebrations of victory. It is a victory which will take many years and decades of hard work and dedication — by many peoples — to bring about. This will not be a victory of the United States over the Soviet Union. It will not be a victory of capitalism over socialism. It will be a victory of men and nations which aim to stand up straight, over the forces which wish to entrap and to exploit their revolutionary aspirations of modernization. What this victory involves, in the end, is the assertion by nations of their right to independence and by men and women of their right to freedom as they understand it. And we deeply believe this victory will come — on both sides of the Iron Curtain.

If Americans do not seek victory in the usual sense, what do we seek? What is the national interest of the United States? Why do we Americans expend our treasure and assume the risks of modern war in this global struggle? For Americans the reward of victory will be, simply, this: It will permit American society to continue to develop along the old humane lines which go back to our birth as a nation — and which reach deeper into history than that — back to the Mediterranean roots of Western life. We are struggling to maintain an environment on the world scene which will permit our open society to survive and to flourish.

U.S. RESPONSIBILITIES

To make this vision come true places a great burden on the United States at this phase of history. The preservation of independence has many dimensions.

The United States has the primary responsibility for deterring the use of nuclear weapons in the pursuit of Communist ambitions. The United States has a major responsibility to deter the kind of overt aggression with conventional forces which was launched in June 1950 in Korea.

The United States has the primary responsibility for assisting the economies of those hard-pressed states on the periphery of the Communist bloc, which are under acute military or quasi-military pressure which they cannot bear from their own resources; for example, South Korea, Viet-Nam, Taiwan, Pakistan, Iran. The United States has a special responsibility of leadership in bringing not merely its own resources but the resources of all the free world to bear in aiding the longrun development of those nations which are serious about modernizing their economy and their social life. And, as President Kennedy has made clear, he regards no program of his administration as more important than his program for long-term economic development, dramatized, for example, by the Alliance for Progress in Latin America. Independence cannot be maintained by military measures alone. Modern societies must be built, and we are prepared to held build them.

Finally, the United States has a role to play . . . in learning to deter guerrilla warfare, if possible, and to deal with it, if necessary.

LOCAL AND INTERNATIONAL RESPONSIBILITIES

. . . the primary responsibility for dealing with guerrilla warfare in the underdeveloped areas cannot be American. There are many ways in which we can help — and we are searching our minds and our imaginations to learn better how to help; but a guerrilla war must be fought primarily by those on the spot. This is so for a quite particular reason. A guerrilla war is an intimate affair, fought not merely with weapons but fought in the minds of the men who live in the villages and in the hills, fought by the spirit and policy of those who run the local government. An outsider cannot, by himself, win a guerrilla war. He can help create conditions in which it can be won, and he can directly assist those prepared to fight for their independence. We are determined to help destroy this international disease; that is, guerrilla war designed, initiated, supplied, and led from outside an independent nation.

Although as leader of the free world the United States has special responsibilities which it accepts in this common venture of deterrence, it is important that the whole international community begin to accept its responsibility for dealing with this form of aggression. It is important that the world become clear in mind, for example, that the operation run from Hanoi against Viet-Nam is as clear a form of aggression as the violation of the 38th parallel by the North Korean armies in June 1950.

In my conversations with representatives of foreign governments, I am sometimes lectured that this or that government within the free world is not popular; they tell me that guerrilla warfare cannot be won unless the peoples are dissatisfied. These are, at best, half-truths. The truth is that guerrilla warfare, mounted from external bases — with rights of sanctuary — is a terrible burden to carry for any government in a society making its way toward modernization. As you know, it takes somewhere between 10 and 20 soldiers to control one guerrilla in an organized operation. Moreover, the guerrilla force has this advantage: its task is merely to destroy, while the government must build and protect what it is building. A guerrilla war mounted from outside a transitional nation is a crude act of international vandalism. There will be no peace in the world if the international community accepts the outcome of a guerrilla war, mounted from outside a nation, as tantamount to a free election.

The sending of men and arms across international boundaries and the direction of guerrilla war from outside a sovereign nation is aggression; and this is a fact which the whole international community must confront and whose consequent responsibilities it must accept. Without such international action those against whom aggression is mounted will be driven inevitably to seek out and engage the ultimate source of the aggression they confront. . . .

In facing the problem of guerrilla war, I have one observation to make as a historian. It is now fashionable . . . to read the learned works of Mao Tse-tung and Che Guevara on guerrilla warfare. This is, indeed, proper. One should read with care and without passion into the minds of one's enemies. But it is historically inaccurate and psychologically dangerous to think that these men created the strategy and tactics of guerrilla war to which we are now responding. Guerrilla warfare is not a form of military and psychological magic created by the Communists. There is no rule or parable in the Communist texts which was not known at an earlier time in history. The operation of Marion's men in relation to the Battle of Cowpens in the American Revolution was, for example, governed by rules which Mao merely echoes. Che Guevara knows nothing of this business that T. E. Lawrence did not know or was not practiced, for example, in the Peninsular Campaign during the Napoleonic wars, a century earlier. The orchestration of professional troops, militia, and guerrilla fighters is an old game whose rules can be studied and learned.

My point is that we are up against a form of warfare which is powerful and effective only when we do not put our minds clearly to work on how to deal with it. I, for one, believe that with purposeful efforts most nations which might now be susceptible to guerrilla warfare could handle their border areas in ways which would make them very unattractive to the initiation of this ugly game. We can learn to prevent the emergence of the famous sea in which Mao Tse-tung taught his men to swim. This requires, of course, not merely a proper military program of deterrence but programs of village development, communications, and indoctrination. The best way to fight a guerrilla war is to prevent it from happening. And this can be done.

Similarly, I am confident that we can deal with the kind of operation now under way in Viet-Nam. It is an extremely dangerous operation, and it could overwhelm Viet-Nam if the Vietnamese — aided by the free world — do not deal with it. But it is an unsubtle operation, by the book, based more on murder than on political or psychological appeal.

When Communists speak of wars of national liberation and of their support for "progressive forces," I think of the systematic program of assassination now going forward in which the principal victims are the health, agriculture, and education officers in the Viet-Nam villages.

W. W. ROSTOW *237*

The Viet Cong are not trying to persuade the peasants of Viet-Nam that communism is good; they are trying to persuade them that their lives are insecure unless they cooperate with them. With resolution and confidence on all sides and with the assumption of international responsibility for the frontier problem, I believe we are going to bring this threat to the independence of Viet-Nam under control.

My view is, then, that we confront in guerrilla warfare in the underdeveloped areas a systematic attempt by the Communists to impose a serious disease on those societies attempting the transition to modernization. This attempt is a present danger in southeast Asia. It could quickly become a major danger in Africa and Latin America. I salute in particular those among you whose duty it is — along with others — to prevent that disease, if possible, and to eliminate it where it is imposed. . . .

Each of us must carry into his day-to-day work an equal understanding of the military and the creative dimensions of the job. I can tell you that those with whom I have the privilege to work are dedicated to that mission with every resource of mind and spirit at our command.

A National "Force de Dissuasion"

19 PIERRE M. GALLOIS
The Raison d'Etre of French Defense Policy

Opponents of France's defence policy should at least recognise that that policy is based on an awareness of the new facts of the nuclear age. It is difficult to criticise — at least as a whole — the ideas of the French Government, because they are fundamentally the same as those followed by the American and British Governments in their own conduct of affairs. Admittedly, France differs considerably in size, in strength and in resources from the United States and from the Soviet Union.

General Pierre M. Gallois was in charge of technical planning at the French Air Ministry 1952–53 and a member of SHAPE's long-range planning group 1953–57; he is author of *La Stratégie de l'Age Nucléaire*, and other works on military and political problems of Europe. These excerpts, from an article in *International Affairs* (London), XXXIX, No. 4 (October 1963) 497–510, are reprinted by permission.

But the British example provides a pattern for a country like France. . . .

To the specialist attempting to assess the political consequences of the technical changes which we have seen, one of the most striking facts — paradoxically, perhaps, at first sight — is the extent to which the United States and the Soviet Union are becoming able to ensure the invulnerability of their respective retaliatory forces. Admittedly, this invulnerability may be only temporary; in fact, it may be assumed that a continued rapidity of technical development will change it. Nevertheless, as it is in the interest of the two great adversaries to ensure, in all circumstances, what they term the "survival" of their respective retaliatory forces, it seems likely that their efforts to ensure their respective invulnerability will in due course converge, and that both sides will, instead, find it more profitable to protect their retaliatory forces rather than continue to expend their energies in trying to discover how to destroy their opponents. The former is, basically, a policy of "passive defence" which does not imply a deliberate recourse to force. The second implies the committing of an act of aggression, the taking of the initiative in breaking a peaceful, or quasi-peaceful, *status quo*, with all the risks (which could easily become excessive) entailed in such a decision. For these reasons, it is probable that in the next five or 10 years the United States and the Soviet Union will concentrate with still greater emphasis on increasing or completing the invulnerability of their retaliatory forces, and that their example will be followed by Great Britain — whose concern to ensure the survival of at least part of her nuclear weapons was shown by the Nassau agreement. . . .

Recourse to war thus becomes a completely irrational act. All the more so, because there is no question today, as there was in the pre-nuclear age, of taking risks which are on the whole proportional to what is at stake in the dispute, to the value of territory, or to the advantages one seeks; today war means risking the whole existence of a country, whatever its stature or its power, in an adventure which, as one knows before it begins, can only lead to national suicide. There has never been such a situation since armed men first confronted each other. Never has the inevitable nature of the disaster which would arise from using forces against another Power possessing a nuclear arsenal been so clear. Even if the composition and equipment of the opposing armed forces was markedly unequal, and one of the belligerents was more powerful than the other, the risk would remain of the outcome being the same for both. Nor would that risk be reduced by concentration of attack on the enemy's centres of population with the object of annihilating his human potential, for the result of that policy would only be to unleash retaliation of all kinds, however desperate they were, because the country attacked would have lost everything, including the control of its own forces.

Everyone would rejoice that war can no longer be an act of policy and that we are being forced to abandon it, if the organisation of the world were not still based, in part and in the last resort, on the threat of recourse to war. What is a military alliance if not a political act which aims to deny certain advantages to the adversary, or to maintain a certain *status quo* in opposition to him, by making it clear that if the member states of the alliance cannot achieve peacefully the aims they have set themselves, they might ultimately resort to force? If the recourse to force is not plausible, if it is not conceivable that the allies would go to the length of using their weapons to fulfil their commitments, then it is clear that such a military alliance does not make sense.

Does this mean that in international relations governments no longer need to take account of the implicit threat of a possible armed conflict? Between nuclear Powers, and to the extent that these Powers keep more or less abreast in the scientific and technical race, a resort to force is only plausible if one of these Powers irrationally attacks the vitals of the other. The possibility of irrational behaviour cannot, of course, be entirely excluded, but neither is it possible to make it the foundation of a political attitude. On the other hand, the imbalance has never been so great as between a nuclear Power and one bereft of the new weapons. A country deprived of nuclear forces suffers a double disadvantage; of being itself without any defence in the face of the other, and of no longer being able to benefit from the guarantee which, even yesterday, was provided by its membership of a military alliance.

In short, every nuclear Power converts itself into what could be termed an inviolable "sanctuary," and ensures its self-defence by the threat of using, in the last resort, an arsenal invulnerable to the first blows of an assailant. Yet it can only ensure its own protection, since it is hardly credible that it should expose its entire property to destruction merely to ensure the protection of another state, even of a neighbour, friend or ally.

Like sorcerers' apprentices, the Americans and the Russians have both invented and brought into widespread use an armament which ensures their own security, but which at the same time paralyses their role in the world because no government can seriously believe that one or the other can either lead a coalition and share their power with its members, or risk its existence for the sake of its allies.

Admittedly, perhaps, this is only a temporary condition, and either the attrition or destruction of the belligerents' forces might again restore some significance to armed confrontations.[1] But it certainly seems likely that in the next five or 10 years mankind will enter upon a period marked by the general invulnerability of the decisive weapons, during which it will consequently be necessary for the countries possessing these weapons to renounce the use of force among themselves. It is not difficult, therefore, to foresee as a corollary of this enforced *status quo,* a general spread of *faits accomplis,* carried out at the expense of those countries not capable of converting themselves into inviolable "sanctuaries." As for those nations which have done so, they know that without running excessive risks only their marginal interests can be threatened. Their only concern will be to provide against any loss in their global strength which could result from a number of successive *faits accomplis* achieved at the expense of their various spheres of influence.

In a world which seems bound to be ruled by laws, which, though they are new, weigh no less heavily on the weak, is it unnatural that a country aware of the danger of the present situation and with sufficient resources should also attempt to convert itself into a "sanctuary"? In such a context, what is meant by describing France as a bad ally, as she is sometimes accused of being? In what way does international morality forbid her to be concerned over the obvious results of a whole sequence of technical achievements — in which France, at the outset at least, took no part? And why ought she systematically to ignore the new international situation, with the chance that one day she might

---

[1] Analysis shows that it is above all the anti-missile missile, and the development of a defensive system which could be effective against ballistic missiles, that could fundamentally modify the "balance of prudence" which already exists between America and the U.S.S.R., and which should be further strengthened in the years to come. On both the American side (Dr. Jerome Wiesner, President Kennedy's scientific adviser) and on the Russian side (Marshal V. D. Sokolovoskii) it is reckoned that the anti-missile missile will take a long time to develop. Nevertheless, the Russians carried out successful experiments in this field in 1961. In fact, opinions differ widely on this point. It would seem that the cessation of atmospheric tests will prevent the Americans from catching up with the Russians, especially if it is true that the latter had already obtained interesting results over three years ago.

become its victim, precisely because she had created no substitute for a system of security which technical developments have condemned to impotence?

In any case, it must be acknowledged that in spite of the suddenness with which the new technical developments have burst upon the world, signs of the approach of such a strategic revolution were not lacking.

Apart from the fact that, in 1949, the Americans found themselves obliged to share their nuclear monopoly with the Russians, they realised between 1957 and 1959 that they had also lost the invulnerability which geography had hitherto granted them. Naturally invulnerable because they were practically out of reach, the United States now found themselves within an hour's range of a Soviet ICBM. . . .

At the beginning of 1959, Soviet technicians successfully fired an ICBM from the shores of the Caspian to those of the China Sea, and the American Press devoted long commentaries to the event. Two months later, when asked by Senator Morse about the conditions under which the new weapons could be used, Mr. Christian Herter, then the new Secretary of State, gave the famous answer that so surprised the Atlantic world: "I cannot conceive of the President [of the United States] involving us in a nuclear war unless it became certain we were in danger of devastation ourselves."[2] . . . Again, at the same time, General Taylor made the oft-quoted statement: "We should recognise and accept the limitations of our nuclear retaliatory forces. Under the conditions which we must anticipate in the coming years, it is incredible to ourselves, to our allies and to our enemies that we would use such forces for any purpose other than to assure our national survival."[3]

But scarcely had the ICBM taken its place in the arsenals of the two Great Powers, and these anxieties and doubts been expressed, when the spread of small and medium-sized nuclear weapons began both to create new problems and to inspire the theory of escalation. It was indeed hard to imagine that two belligerents equipped with the whole nuclear arsenal would be able to confront each other, their weapons in their hands, without both of them risking either surrender or a rise in the scale of destructive weapons employed until they had annihilated each other, at least in theory.

In escalation, the Europeans saw their protection, the Americans their loss. To the first it seemed clear that if tactical nuclear weapons

[2] *New York Herald Tribune* (European ed.) April 22, 1959.
[3] *The Uncertain Trumpet* by Maxwell D. Taylor (London: Stevens, 1960) p. 145.

were deployed as close to the Iron Curtain as possible, the Russians, facing, as they would, a considerable risk and at a relatively low level of incident, would not dare to show any signs of aggression. But to the "experts" of the New Frontier who advise Mr. Kennedy on these matters, there was implicit danger in the installation of such weapons in continental Europe. A minor incident could degenerate into a major conflict in which nuclear weapons would be used; and since the Russians had written in their strategic treatises that the explosion of a single nuclear warhead would unleash a general nuclear war, the American experts took fright and violently objected to the deployment of nuclear weapons in continental Europe. . . . Now, in the eyes of those who had to devise the new American strategy, tactical nuclear weapons had to be withdrawn from continental Europe, and its defence organised on the basis of conventional arms alone. . . .

Thus, without waiting for the invulnerability of the retaliatory forces of the United States and the Soviet Union to shatter from top to bottom all the principles on which for centuries armed confrontation between peoples had depended, the establishment of stocks of ICBMs and the spread of nuclear weapons of small and medium yield had modified the governing factors of the defence of Western Europe. The unconditional security proclaimed by John Foster Dulles had been replaced by a conditional guarantee. From being a "sanctuary" to be defended at any price and by every means, including the most terrible, the military status of Western Europe was devalued to that of a territory for the defence of which Mr. Kennedy intended to have "an option of means," rather than accept the dilemma of a choice between "capitulation or general nuclear war."

This development is logical, and no one in France would contest its appositeness. As technical and strategic conditions have changed, it is natural that the United States should no longer be able, as was the case 10 years ago, to provide the same guarantees to Europe. As for the European nations, if they found it possible before to plead for their security to be ensured, this was because their benefactor — the guarantor country — risked only the loss of an expeditionary force and not its existence as a great people. Today such pleas are equivalent to requesting the death of the benefactor. Who could make such a request, and above all, who could give it a favourable answer? It is only in full awareness of the facts of the new era, and, in particular, of the limitations of a military alliance in the nuclear age, that the problem of the defence of Western Europe must be studied. For her part, it is within this framework that France seeks to draw up an effective defence policy.

Instead of admitting the political consequences of the new technology of armaments, instead of discussing them with the allied governments and adapting NATO to the radical changes which have taken place since its foundation, the new American Administration decided that an increase in the conventional forces deployed in Central Europe would be enough to meet the strategic transformations which the world had just witnessed. To the advent of the ICBM, to the spread of tactical nuclear weapons, to the development of practically invulnerable launching sites, Washington's reaction was to ask the nations of Europe to create a few large additional ground units with conventional arms. In other words, so far as the defence of Europe was concerned, America attuned herself to the strategic concepts of tomorrow by demanding a return to the weapons of 1941–45.

It seemed to the Europeans that the new American defence policy aimed at reserving any possible use of nuclear weapons for the defence only of the *continental* territory of the United States (according to the views expressed by General Taylor) and that they would defend other areas of the world, including *continental* Europe, with forces without nuclear weapons. Meeting during the summer of 1960 to draw up the main lines of a more prudent foreign policy than that of John Foster Dulles, a number of American experts came to the conclusion that Europe should be defended conventionally in the first place, and that if, in the last resort, it were to be given nuclear support, this should be placed solely under American control, with the weapons deployed at sea, and no longer on land in Europe, where they were "provocative" in peacetime and much too vulnerable in time of war. Moreover, Europe could provide an excellent test area for an agreement with the Russians on the "denuclearisation" of certain parts of the world. In this way the idea of a Rapacki Plan was accepted, although that idea had been rejected with horror two years earlier when it had been regarded as aimed at the destruction of NATO. The American experts were thus fully conscious of the political and military consequences of the new military techniques. But they thought that the Europeans would be naïve enough or ignorant enough to believe in the validity of the first substitute offered in exchange for a denuclearisation of continental Western Europe.

To make its allies accept its new conceptions of defence, Washington launched a vast propaganda campaign, using all the resources of politics, diplomacy and the Press to enlist European support for them. The "Foundations" mobilised their grants to this end, and the revulsion inspired by the atom bomb (and of which the Russians had made use at the time of the Stockholm peace appeal) was once more exploited so that the Europeans would of themselves renounce the bomb. The churches, disarmament movements, in short the whole arsenal of instruments which once were more or less manipulated by the opposite camp to weaken the West's will to resist, were enlisted in the service of American policy and of the denuclearisation of Western Europe.

On the official level the White House tried to explain to the countries of Europe that, as they had no alternative, they should accept the decisions of the United States Government. . . . Mr. Kennedy[4] declared that the integration of forces seemed to him to be a good thing, but that it did not seem so to General de Gaulle. Mr. Kennedy was forgetting that he was advocating the integration of other people's forces but not of his own, and that this idea of integration, of which he was so fond, was for export only, good for other countries but never for his own. If the United States do indeed support the integration of forces, why do they hesitate to integrate their own nuclear forces with those of Europe and let their use be decided by the 15 member governments of NATO?

At Athens [in 1962] Mr. McNamara told the representatives of the NATO governments that the non-American nuclear deterrent forces were limited in number and power, that they could only attack the adversary's centres of population, and that if they were used the result would be suicide. The American forces, on the other hand, could conduct a counterforce strategy. But the American Secretary of Defense also said that America — like Russia — had absolutely invulnerable "weapons systems," so that the NATO representatives who were reproved in this way began to wonder how, if that were so, Mr. McNamara could carry out a counterforce strategy at all.

The propaganda in favour of defending Western Europe by purely conventional forces was scarcely better managed. The American experts first explained that Russia had 208 million inhabitants, the NATO nations of Western Europe 230 million, and that in consequence there was no reason why there should not be the same number of combatants on both sides of the Iron Curtain — naturally without nuclear weapons. This calculation not only omitted the population of the satellite states

[4] Press Conference of August 1, 1963.

on the one side, but included on the other that of Great Britain —
although the British have abandoned conscription — and also the inhabitants of countries which, being highly advanced socially, cannot
increase the length of military service. But the fact that the American
arguments bear no relation to any demographic, or, above all, political
or social reality in Europe is of secondary importance compared with
the facts of the military situation. Who could imagine that the Russians
would accept defeat at the hands of the conventional forces of Western
Europe without having recourse to their nuclear weapons? The "whiz
kids" took no account of the imbalance in armaments which would
result from the denuclearisation of Europe. They based their NATO
policy on the belief that the Russians would play the American game,
and, observing the rules laid down by Washington, would accept defeat
without using their nuclear weapons, of which, in such circumstances,
they would have a complete monopoly in Europe! This hypothesis is
so absurd that it is scarcely credible that it was supported by the
State Department, and that official efforts were made to "sell" it to
the European governments.

The affair of the multilateral fleet, first of submarines, then of surface
ships, is just as ridiculous. After declaring that it was intended to
meet the wishes of the allies, Washington used all available means to
secure adoption of the idea by the allied governments who were supposed to be clamouring for it, although none of them wanted it.
Nobody in Europe has yet understood Mr. McNamara's reasoning in
this matter. If a national counter-city nuclear force leads to suicide,
as Mr. McNamara himself says, why would a collective nuclear force,
armed with counter-city weapons like the Polaris, not lead to collective
suicide? Does the American Secretary of Defense really believe that
it is absurd for a nation to risk everything for its liberty and for the
defence of its vital interests, but that it would not be absurd for a
group of five or six nations to undertake collective suicide, in the
defence of the interests of one of them?

Clearly all the attempts made by the new American Administration
to implement the defence policy defined by the Mid-Summer Study
Group of 1960 have not been happy. In fact, they are based on a total
ignorance of the requirements of Western European defence, and on a
complete misunderstanding of European aspirations.

As far as the defence of their own vital interests is concerned,
however, the United States and Great Britain are setting a much more
valuable example than they are in matters relating to the security of

other countries. The U.S. Government has not, any more than has the British Government, accepted the slightest control over its nuclear forces. The process of integration which is recommended to other countries is immediately rejected where the American or British forces are concerned. . . . The French Government says the same thing, and it is strange that it should be reproached for it.

If, as we may readily believe, we are entering, or have already entered, upon a period characterised by the invulnerability of the retaliatory forces of the nuclear Powers, its important implications ought to be admitted. The most obvious are certainly the following:

(1) Collective defence is now hardly valid, except in the case of minor conflicts, in which the forces of the nuclear Powers are not themselves engaged. What country, possessing nuclear weapons, would not in such circumstances be afraid of escalation, or, in a major conflict increased in scale thereby, would sacrifice the "fabric of its society" for the defence of another country, even an ally?

(2) If a counterforce strategy has become impossible, and only a countercity strategy remains feasible, at least for a time, all nuclear Powers find themselves in the same situation. Once a few dozen nuclear weapons are enough to destroy the few dozen urban areas on which the life of a nation depends, it is hard to see the purpose of the huge stocks of weapons which the two Great Powers have accumulated in the attempt to provide themselves with the instruments of a counterforce strategy. If the cessation of nuclear experiments in the atmosphere delays, or even stops, the development of anti-missile weapons, and if a certain *status quo* is established as a result, with the "balance of prudence" preventing a recourse to force, the equalising power of the atom will be seen more clearly, and every nuclear Power will be able to create a big enough arsenal to make a potential aggressor fear a counter-city "spasm."

Is the condemnation of military alliances implied in this situation complete, even as a temporary result of present techniques? Probably not, if an alliance is intended to give its member states adequate guarantees at the price of acceptable risks. At the time when, 14 years ago, the Treaty of Washington was signed, political and strategic conditions were very different from those of today, and the guarantor Power was able to fulfil its commitments by sending an expeditionary force to Europe, and eventually by mobilising its enormous human and industrial potential. Today, if the stake is the same, the risk is of a different order.

Nevertheless, each member of the alliance is asked — at least by implication — both to take the supreme risk when one of its allies is in danger, and to compete alone in the arms race between East and West. *"La stratégie des opérations"* is collective, and thus a major risk is imposed on each one for a stake not directly of vital importance to itself. At the same time, the *"stratégie des moyens,"* that of deterrence, remains a strict national responsibility. Through the Pact, the allies are asked to die together if the security of one of them is at stake, but each is also asked to take care of the financial, technical and industrial burdens of its defence by itself. . . .

In this sphere, it is clear that even if every state has not the resources to fight alone, national prerogatives still hold good, and each state is isolated. . . .

Such a conception of Western defence is out of date. The system would be healthier, more effective, and thus more feared, if the *"stratégie des moyens"* were a common one, and, in certain extreme cases, the *"stratégie de l'emploi"* were national. If need be, a government can take the supreme risk for its own country when it would refuse a similar commitment for the benefit of another. But in every case, the speed of technical developments in the arms race calls for a collective effort in the field of research, development and production of armaments. And such an effort is all the more desirable and all the more realistic, because it does not involve a major risk.

NATO would be fully effective if it were an organisation which collected the financial resources that each nation allocates to collective defence, drew up armament programmes and had the best studied and manufactured, and then distributed them to the member nations so that, in exceptional circumstances, they would be in a position to make use of them against a fundamental threat. By this means the paralysis which always results from collective control over decisive weapons could be obviated, while much greater resources, better adapted to the technology of modern armaments, would be brought together. As long as the Atlantic alliance is based on sharing an immense risk collectively undertaken, and on a huge technical and financial effort borne by the nations individually, these objectives will not be realised. It is true that the Skybolt affair, and the Nassau agreement in general, have shown how difficult it is to work together on the same armaments programme. Only a real interdependence which is based on genuine exchanges will enable the rest to avoid submitting to the interests of the strongest. This interdependence will become less theoretical as the European nations make greater scientific and technical efforts.

Once the resources of the *"stratégie des moyens"* have been organised and properly exploited, the system of defence and nuclear deterrence will come about of itself. The tight Napoleonic order of battle could not survive the introduction of rapid-fire weapons, and the concept of the continuous front had to adapt itself to the combination of tanks and aircraft. Weapons of mass-destruction have brought about still greater changes in their turn. The consequences of this revolution cannot be indefinitely ignored or conjured away. To the extent that security through strength will still make sense tomorrow, it is clear that it cannot be based only on the permanent mobilisation of immense human resources, which are in any case completely ineffective against these new weapons.

Even Walter Lippmann admitted recently that if it was necessary to adapt the alliance to the radical strategic and technical changes which have now occurred, "we had better understand the new conceptions coming out of France." It should be all the less difficult to do this, in that America and Great Britain have no others on which to base their own defence.

COMMUNIST STRATEGY

Moscow: Modern Technology and the
Material-Moral Base

20 N. I. KRYLOV
Strategic Rockets

The imperialist states, in their drive towards an aggressive war against the Soviet Union and the countries of the socialist camp, are intensifying the arms race. In this respect they give first priority to strategic means of waging war: nuclear weapons, intercontinental ballistic missiles, medium range ballistic missiles, nuclear submarines with *Polaris* missiles and missile carrying naval task forces. These weapons are regarded by American strategists as their main strike force in any future nuclear war on a global scale.

The Pentagon has set up a group of strategic offensive forces essential to the unleashing of nuclear war. Future theatres of operations are being rapidly supplied and equipped with the latest types of weapons and means of carrying out military activities. The United States, using the excuse that "multilateral" or "multinational nuclear forces" should be set up, are trying to equip the armies of NATO with nuclear weapons. The ruling circles of the German Federal Republic, with the direct support and help of America have established in a very short space of time armed forces well over 400,000 men strong and are grasping for nuclear weapons. Britain is stepping up the technical re-equipment of her armed forces and is developing the production of her nuclear weapons and her delivery vehicles.

In these circumstances the Communist Party and the Soviet government, which is struggling for a relaxation of tension [and] the prevention of a world nuclear war, had taken active steps to raise the defence capabilities of our country and to equip the armed forces with the very latest nuclear-missile weapons. The brilliant discoveries of Soviet scientists in the field of atomic physics, mathematics, chemistry, and

N. I. Krylov is Marshal of the Soviet Union and Commander-in-Chief of the Soviet Strategic Rocket Forces. This article which originally appeared in *Izvestiia* on November 17, 1963, was translated in *Survival*, VI, No. 1 (January–February 1964) 45–46, published by the Institute of Strategic Studies Ltd.

electronics have provided the base on which we have built up our own atomic and later nuclear weapons. The tremendous achievements of our heavy industry have allowed us to create in a short space of time a powerful base on which to build our atomic weapons in sufficient numbers to deter any aggressor. The dream of V. I. Lenin that new inventions in science and technology would make the defence of our country so strong that any attack upon us would be impossible is coming true.

The existence of stocks of nuclear weapons by itself does not of course solve the problem of the security of our country. We had to build new intercontinental means of delivery too. The equipment of armed forces with strategic rockets — basically a new bold and revolutionary step in the further development of the means of waging war — builds up the defence capability of the country. Soviet strategic missiles have unlimited ranges. They can carry nuclear warheads of colossal yield with great accuracy and with trajectories which make nuclear missile blows sudden and capable of penetrating any defence. They can be carried out at any time of the year or day, and in any weather conditions.

The nuclear missile weapon has brought about a basic change in the international strategic situation. Until these missiles appeared, the U.S.A. was relatively invulnerable. Protected by the oceans and enormous distances, and possessing bases overseas, American statesmen planned to wage war from the territory of their allies, using their allies' manpower, in the belief that retaliatory blows from our side would fall on the countries of Europe and Asia, while the territory of the United States would remain, as in previous wars, untouched. The appearance of strategic missiles with intercontinental ranges, the factor of distance lost its previous importance. The relative invulnerability of the United States came to an end. The United States territory would, if a war broke out, become a theatre of military operations within minutes. Global rockets have put an end once and for all to the concept of geographical isolation.

The nuclear missile weapons possessed by the Soviet armed forces are limitless in their destructive capabilities. One missile with a nuclear warhead releases more energy than all the explosions carried out all over the world during the Second World War. The new series of nuclear warheads have a yield of 50 or 100 megatons, and new types of super powerful missiles tested during the spring of this year [1963] make it possible to annihilate whole countries with a few nuclear weapons. One nuclear warhead with a yield of 100 megatons is 5,000 times more powerful than the atomic bombs which the Americans dropped on Hiroshima and Nagasaki. American experts have reckoned that in the initial period of a war 263 nuclear strikes with an average yield of five megatons each could be dropped on the most important targets in the U.S.A. They would be capable of destroying 71 large towns, affect fifty percent of the population, of which 53 million people would be killed. It must be admitted that these calculations have been made on a realistic basis.

The results of the latest tests of Soviet strategic missiles provide remarkable evidence of their accuracy. They were fired to distances of 12–13,000 kilometres, and covering distances greater than the diameter of the globe, they landed exactly in the target area with what can only be called "super-sniper accuracy."

Our success in firing strategic missiles with nuclear warheads to their targets has been made possible by the great height which they reach — counted in hundreds of kilometres — and their great speed, which enables them to cover more than 10,000 kilometres in 30 to 35 minutes. A modern strategic bomber requires more than 10 hours to cover this distance. The average speed of a strategic missile in flight is 20 times greater than that of a modern fighter and 10 times greater than the muzzle velocity of a shell fired from a field gun.

INVULNERABLE IN FLIGHT

The invulnerability of strategic missiles in flight is affected by their self-operating guidance systems which are completely independent of any radio-technical apparatus on the ground. This means that it is impossible to take measures either against the rocket in flight or when it enters the enemy's anti-ballistic missile defence zone. However strong this defence may be, our strategic missiles will unerringly reach their intended targets.

Soviet strategic missiles also have other high technical qualities. They are relatively easy to use. The time needed to prepare them for firing is counted literally in minutes. They can be fired even from field launching pads without any special site preparation. This considerably increases the invulnerability of the launching pads from blows by the enemy's strategic strike forces.

With the appearance of missiles a new branch of the Soviet armed forces came into being [in 1960] — the strategic rocket forces. Under the leadership of N. S. Khrushchev a stable organizational command structure of the rocket forces has been established, whose role and task in the country's defence system has been worked out in new regulations. The rocket forces have grown in a very short time in organization, quantity and in particular in quality. Our strategic rocket forces are equipped with the most powerful and advanced nuclear warheads in the world, and are capable of carrying out basic tasks in modern warfare. In past wars the main strategic aim of the armed forces was to destroy the enemy's armies in the theatre of military operation. In modern war there is no dividing line between the front and the interior of the country. Strategic rocket forces are able not only to carry out a lightning destruction of the enemy's main concentration of troops, but to destroy utterly his military economic potential, disorganize the government and military direction of the country and wipe out his means of delivering a nuclear attack.

21 V. I. CHUIKOV
Soviet Land Forces in Nuclear War

With the appearance of nuclear weapons and rockets, those new and exceptionally powerful long-range and quick-functioning means of warfare, many military problems began to be considered in a new way. Among these is, in particular, the question of the role of land forces in a nuclear war. As is known, in the past these forces were the main type of armed forces and played a decisive role in past wars. It may be said that previously when new methods of combat appeared the military theorists of different countries always started to reassess the significance and weight of the former means of combat.

The theories of Douhet, Fuller, Eimannsberger, Guderian and McKenna about the possibility of achieving objectives in war with predominantly one type of armed force or arm — aircraft, tanks, the navy — and also by the replacement of people by machines and the creation of small highly-mechanized armies, are well known. These lopsided theories have had a harmful influence on the build-up of armed forces. Disregard of the objective rules of balanced development and

Vasili Ivanovich Chuikov, Commander-in-Chief of Soviet Ground Forces and Marshal of the Soviet Union, is a member of the Central Committee of the Communist Party of the Ukraine. This article which originally appeared in *Izvestiia* on December 21, 1963, was translated in *Survival*, VI, No. 2 (March–April 1964) 86–89, published by the Institute of Strategic Studies Ltd.

the use in war of all types of weapons and troops, has had catastrophic results, a vivid example of which was the bankruptcy of the Hitlerite army, which relied mainly on tanks and aircraft.

In assessing the role of nuclear weapons, the nature of a future war and the place in it of land forces are interpreted differently by foreign scientists and military experts. Not infrequently these experts tend to go to extremes. Let us take as an example the notorious theory of nuclear air warfare. Thus the American Professor Brod[i]e banks on nuclear weapons and declares that the basis of the aerial theory of Douhet is particularly relevant to the nuclear age, that in any war to be waged by the U.S.A. an unlimited strategic aerial campaign must be of decisive importance. In his view, all other types of military operations are quite unnecessary.

There are worshippers of exclusively chemical or exclusively bacteriological warfare. In the West many similar theories are subjugated to political and economic considerations; behind every type of new armament stand the big monopolies which are hungry for military orders and maximum profits. In the military and technical sense these theories show a lack of understanding or an unwillingness to see that the intensive development of technical means of combat do not reduce the role of man in war, but increase it.

The military leaders of the imperialist countries understand that in a future war, too, they will not be able to dispense with mass armies and considerable land forces. Therefore, having nuclear weapons, they keep over 5,000,000 men in the NATO armies, of which 3,200,000 are in the land forces. In Europe alone the NATO armies total 2,200,000.

Not so long ago, the official conception of the U.S. and NATO political and military leadership was the notorious strategy of massive retaliation, based on the imaginary nuclear superiority of the U.S.A. On this basis, and also under the influence of several of the above-mentioned theories, the Pentagon at one time, approximately until 1961, became less concerned with its land forces, reducing their numbers to 870,000 men. However, the change in the balance of forces in the world, in the first place the growth of the U.S.S.R.'s defence potential, compelled them to review this strategy. General Taylor, at present Chairman of the Joint Chiefs of Staff, opposed it in a book, *Unreliable Strategy* [the Russian translation for *Uncertain Trumpet*]. He advanced the strategy of flexible response and proposed a new military programme which also provided for the strengthening of the land forces.

Now the U.S. military command, concurrently with the increase in the rocket-nuclear potential, has started to pay much more attention to the development of its land forces with nuclear, rocket and conventional weapons, believing that in present conditions these troops will have to carry out important military strategical tasks. As a whole, the military commands of the U.S.A. and NATO believe that for waging any, even a general nuclear war, armed forces will be needed whose composition must certainly include strong and mobile land forces. In this connection measures are being adopted for strengthening and developing them. . . .

Therefore, already in peacetime, in the decisive area of Europe, a strong group of NATO land forces is concentrated. Thus the Western countries, in preparation for a nuclear war, are not only not liquidating land forces but, on the contrary, are steadily developing them.

The leading capitalist countries, especially the U.S.A., France, Britain and the German Federal Republic, are persistently improving their land forces so that they meet modern demands. A big step forward has been taken in the technical equipment of the land forces abroad. In the U.S.A., for example, nuclear weapons of various types have been introduced on a wide scale, with a power ranging from 1,500–3,800 kilotons. In addition, nuclear charges of low and super-low power from one to 36 tons are to be used in conjunction with small-size means of delivery at the lowest tactical level.

Rocket weapons have entered firmly into the arsenal of the U.S. land force. They have several types of guided and unguided rockets for tactical and operational-tactical use. The land forces of Britain, France, the German Federal Republic and other member-countries of NATO are being equipped with rocket weapons.

The strike-force of the land troops of the U.S.A. and other main countries of the North Atlantic bloc is being strengthened with tanks. In the past three or four years alone the number of tanks in the NATO armies has increased about 1.5 times. The strong modern motorized infantry of the foreign armies, equipped with automatic personal and group weapons, can fight in armoured troop carriers and other armoured vehicles. Abroad, especially in the U.S.A., great hopes are pinned on the airborne forces, which continue to be developed very intensively.

The artillery in the main capitalist armies is motorized. A considerable part of it is self-propelled. The U.S. army has atomic artillery; the range of conventional artillery has been considerably increased. Rocket artillery is also being developed. Methods of fighting tanks are being developed intensely, particularly anti-tank guided missiles of great armour-penetrating power. . . .

Soviet military science considers that victory in a future nuclear war, if one should be unleashed by the imperialist aggressors, can be achieved only by the joint efforts of all types of armed forces. There is no doubt that a decisive part in achieving the main aims of war will be played by the strategic rocket troops.[1] Therefore, in modern conditions land forces continue to be an essential and a most important integral part of the armed forces. This means that they must be sufficiently strong, mobile, well armed and organized. Our land forces, too, have become quite different in comparison with the last war. The Party and Government, concerned with strengthening the defensive might of the Soviet State, devote great attention to their further development.

NUCLEAR WEAPONS INTEGRATED

Our land forces possess their own nuclear weapons and include arms such as the Operational and Tactical Rocket Troops, which provide the main fire power for routing the enemy. These troops are capable of hitting any objects at ranges of up to 500 km., and more if necessary, quickly creating a decisive change in the battle situation. Our land forces' operational-tactical and tactical-nuclear weapons and rockets are, as is known, not inferior in quality and quantity to foreign types, but superior to them. . . .

The Soviet land troops possess all the modern arms of the forces, various types of weapons and military technical equipment. In the event of war the land troops, availing themselves of the results of blows struck by strategic means and the combined operations forces, will immediately begin active and decisive military operations on vast land fronts. Military operations by land troops will be characterized by great expansive scale — exceptional dynamism, the rapid development of operational directions, and the broad application of various forms of manoeuvre. There will be no continuous fronts. The struggle will take on a most tense nature. The main task will be to carry out a decisive offensive, as a result of which there will often be supporting skirmishes.

---

[1] In its context, this sentence appears to have been inserted later by a higher authority, to modify Marshal Chuikov's claims for the ground forces in view of the current emphasis on Strategic Rocket Forces. [Comment by editors of *Survival*.]

The vast fire and striking power of the Soviet land troops, their complete mechanization, their capability to take effective and quick advantage of strategic blows, make it possible to carry out deep operations with the most decisive aims and speedily. Our land troops can, figuratively speaking, cut to pieces any defensive or offensive grouping of the enemy, and destroy it piecemeal. Moreover, if in the last war such groupings had to be destroyed not infrequently in consecutive operations, then now they can be destroyed simultaneously and in the shortest possible time.

NO DELAYS

In the last war the German fascist command had great hopes that major water obstacles would be able to delay the offensive of the Soviet troops, but neither the Dnieper, the Vistula, nor the Oder could stop the offensive thrust of our troops. Even more naïve are the hopes of those strategists who have great hopes of water obstacles at the present time. If the imperialists dare to unleash war, no such water obstacle could be found in Europe or Asia which our land troops could not overcome on the move. For this they have the necessary technical means, and our troops, during exercises, have successfully mastered various ways of overcoming the most complicated water obstacles.

Nor can they be delayed either by zones with a high level of chemical or radioactive poisoning. The results of experimental research and various exercises carried out in recent times have shown that units and formations of the Soviet land troops can operate successfully for a long time in zones with high levels of radioactive and chemical poisoning. They have also mastered successfully ways of effectively neutralizing these areas.

First-class military technical equipment and the most advanced weapons are in the reliable hands of Soviet soldiers. The men of the land troops posssess high general and military-technical knowledge and excellent training. They are loyally devoted to their native land and ready at any time to fulfil any military task.

Peking: Protracted Conflict

22 MAO TSE-TUNG
On the Protracted War

Since the Sino-Japanese War is a protracted one and the final victory will be China's, we can reasonably imagine that this protracted war will pass through the following three stages. The first stage is one of the enemy's strategic offensive and our strategic defensive. The second stage is one of the enemy's strategic defensive and our preparation for the counter-offensive. The third stage is one of our strategic counter-offensive and the enemy's strategic retreat. It is impossible to predict the concrete situations in the three stages, but certain main trends of the war may be pointed out in the light of present conditions. . . .

The chief form of fighting for us to adopt in this [first] stage should be mobile warfare, supplemented by guerrilla and positional warfare.

The second stage may be termed the stage of strategic stalemate. At the end of the first stage, owing to the insufficiency in his own troops and our firm resistance, the enemy will be forced to fix a point as the terminus of his strategic offensive; halting his strategic offensive on reaching the terminus, he will then enter the stage of retaining the occupied territories. In this stage, the enemy will attempt to keep the territories he has seized and to perpetuate his occupation through the deceitful measure of establishing puppet governments while plundering, with all his might, the possessions of the Chinese people, but he will be confronted again by a stubborn guerrilla war. Since we take advantage of the enemy's unguarded rear, our guerrilla warfare will undergo an extensive development in the first stage, and since many base areas will have been created and will fundamentally menace his retention of the occupied areas, there will still be large-scale fighting in the second stage. In that stage, our form of fighting will be mainly guerrilla warfare, supplemented by mobile warfare. . . . The fighting in this

Mao Tse-tung is Chairman of the Central Committee of the Chinese Communist Party. The first part of this reading is excerpted from Mao Tse-tung, *On the Protracted War* (Peking: Foreign Languages Press, 1954) pp. 183–206. The second is taken from a report of December 25, 1947, entitled "The Present Situation and Our Tasks," as printed in Mao Tse-tung, *Selected Works*, IV (Peking: Foreign Languages Press, 1961) 161–162.

stage will be ruthless and the country will face serious devastation. But the guerrilla war will achieve victory and, if well conducted, will leave the enemy only about one-third of his occupied areas, with the remaining two-thirds back in our hands; this will be a great defeat for the enemy and a great victory for China. . . . The duration of this stage will be determined by the increase or decrease in the relative strength of the enemy and ourselves and by the changes in the international situation; generally speaking, we should be prepared to hold out for a rather long period and should see to it that we get safely through this difficult stage. This will be a very painful period for China and she will be faced with the two big problems of her economic difficulties and the collaborators' subversive activities. The enemy will violently extend his activities to undermine China's united front, while various collaborators' régimes in all the enemy-occupied areas will merge into a so-called "united government." Within our own ranks, owing to the loss of big cities and the hardships of war, vacillating elements will loudly advocate a theory of compromise, and pessimism will grow seriously. Our tasks will then be: to mobilise the people of the whole country, to unite as one man and carry on the war unswervingly, to broaden and consolidate the united front, to sweep away pessimism and theories of compromise of all shades, to promote hard struggle, and to carry out new wartime policies, in order that we can get through this difficult stage in the journey. In this stage, we must call upon the whole country resolutely to maintain a unified government, to oppose splits, to methodically improve our military technology, to reform our armed forces, mobilise the entire people and prepare for the counter-offensive. . . .

The third stage is the stage of our counter-offensive to recover the lost territories. The recovery of China's lost territories will depend mainly upon her own strength, nurtured in the preceding stage and continuing to grow in the present stage. As it is not enough for China to rely on her own strength alone, and as she cannot win without utilising the aid of international forces and the changes within the enemy country, her international propaganda and diplomacy will become more important. In this stage, our war will be no longer one of strategic defensive, but one of strategic counter-offensive in the form of strategic offensive and we shall no longer operate on strategically interior lines, but shift to strategically exterior lines. . . . The third stage is the last stage of the protracted war, and keeping up the war to the end means going through the entire course of this stage. Our main form of fighting in this stage will still be mobile warfare, but positional warfare will also be raised to an important position. If it is said that positional defence in the first stage could not be regarded as important because of the conditions of that time, then attacks on positions in the third stage will become quite important because of changes in the conditions as well as the requirements of the task. Guerrilla warfare in this stage, unlike the second stage when it was the main form, will again become supplementary to, and strategically co-ordinated with, positional warfare and mobile warfare. . . .

WEAPONS NOT DECISIVE

This is the so-called theory of "weapons mean everything," which is a mechanist theory of war, a view arising from a subjective and one-sided approach to problems. Our view is the opposite; we see not only weapons but also the power of man. Weapons are an important factor in war but not the decisive one; it is man and not material that counts. The contest of forces is not only a contest of military and economic power, but also one of the power and morale of man. Military and economic power must be controlled by man. . . .

LENGTH OF CONFLICT

The protractedness of the war is predetermined, but nobody can predict exactly how many months or years the war will take, for this entirely depends upon the degree of change in the relative strength of the enemy and ourselves. Those who wish to shorten the duration of the war have no alternative but to strive to increase our own strength and reduce the enemy's. Specifically speaking, the only course is to strive to win more battles and wear out the enemy's armies; to develop guerrilla warfare so as to reduce the enemy-occupied territories to a minimum; to consolidate and broaden the united front and unite the forces of the whole nation; to build up new armies and develop new war industries; to expedite political, economic and cultural progress; to mobilise the workers, peasants, businessmen, intellectuals and other sections of the people; to disintegrate the enemy troops and to win them over; to engage actively in international propaganda in order to win foreign support; and to win the support of the Japanese people and other oppressed nations. Only when all these things are done can we shorten the duration of the war; there is no short cut or smooth course.

We can affirm that the protracted Anti-Japanese War will make a splendid page unique in the war history of mankind. The "jig-saw" pattern of the war is one of its quite peculiar features, which follows from such contradictory factors as Japan's barbarity and insufficient armed strength and China's progressiveness and extensive territory. There have been other wars of this pattern in history, like Russia's three-year civil war after the October Revolution. But what distinguishes China's war is its peculiar protractedness and its peculiar extensiveness, both of which beat the record in history. Such a jig-saw pattern manifests itself in the following situations.

(1) *Interior and exterior lines.* The Anti-Japanese War as a whole is fought on the interior line; but as far as the relation between the main forces and the guerrilla detachments is concerned, the former are on the interior line while the latter are on the exterior line, forming the spectacle of a pincers attack on the enemy. The same can be said of the relation between the various guerrilla areas. Each guerrilla area regards itself as on the interior line and the other areas as on the exterior lines, and forms with them numerous pincers-like firing lines round the enemy. In the first stage of the war, the regular army operating strategically on the interior line will beat a retreat; but the guerrilla detachments operating strategically on the exterior line will advance in all directions on the enemy's rear in great strides, and advance even more fiercely in the second stage, thereby forming a unique spectacle of both retreat and advance.

(2) *With and without a rear.* It is the main forces that, relying upon the big rear of the country, extend their front to the very line which marks off the enemy's occupied areas. It is the guerrilla detachments that, separated from our big rear, extend the front into the enemy's rear. But in each guerrilla area, there is still a small rear for the guerrilla force upon which the establishment of fluid operational lines depends. Distinguished from these are guerrilla detachments dispatched from each guerrilla area which is also the enemy's rear, to engage in temporary activities; such guerrilla detachments have neither a rear nor operational lines. "Operations without a rear" are a peculiar feature of the revolutionary war waged in a new era under the conditions of a vast territory, a progressive people, an advanced political party and an

advanced army; in this there is nothing to fear but great benefits to reap, and we should not be sceptical about it but advocate it.

(3) *Encirclement and counter-encirclement.* Taking the war as a whole, we are no doubt in the midst of the strategic encirclement of the enemy, because he has adopted strategic offensive and exterior-line operations and we strategic defensive and interior-line operations. This is the first kind of encirclement the enemy imposes on us. As we have, with numerically preponderant forces, adopted a policy for exterior-line operation in campaigns and battles against the enemy forces advancing on us in separate columns from strategically exterior lines, we can place into our encirclement one or several of the separately advancing enemy columns. This is the first kind of counter-encirclement we impose on the enemy. Furthermore, considering the guerrilla base areas in the enemy's rear, each isolated base area is surrounded by the enemy either on three sides, like the north-western region of Shansi, or on four sides, like the Wutai mountain region. This is the second kind of encirclement the enemy imposes on us. But if we look at the interconnections of the various guerrilla base areas as well as the interconnections of these base areas with the fronts of the regular forces, we shall see that we have in turn surrounded a great number of the enemy units. . . . This is the second kind of counter-encirclement we impose on the enemy. Thus the enemy and ourselves each have imposed two kinds of encirclement on the other, resembling in the main a game of *weich'i:* campaigns and battles between us and the enemy are comparable to the capturing of each other's pieces, and the enemy's strongholds (such as Taiyuan) and our guerrilla base areas (such as the Wutai mountains) are comparable to the blank spaces secured on the board. If a game of *weich'i* on a world-wide scale is taken into account, then there will be yet a third kind of encirclement which we and the enemy impose on each other, namely, the relation between the front of aggression and the front of peace. The enemy encircles countries like China, the Soviet Union, France and Czechoslovakia with the former, while we counter-encircle Germany, Japan and Italy with the latter. But our encirclement is like the hand of Buddha which will be changed into the Mountain of Five Elements lying athwart the entire universe, and the modern monkeys — the fascist aggressors — will finally be entombed beneath it, never to rise again. Therefore, if we can by means of diplomacy bring about the formation of a Pacific anti-Japanese front, with China as one of the strategic units, with the Soviet Union and other countries which may participate in it each also as a strategic unit, and with the Japanese

people's movement as another strategic unit, thus forming a world-wide net from which the fascist monkeys can find no escape, our enemy will be doomed. In fact, the day when this world-wide net is on the whole formed is certainly the day for completely overthrowing Japanese imperialism. This is not a joke, but the inevitable trend of the war.

(4) *The bulk and the bits*. It is possible that the territories occupied by the enemy may constitute the major part of China Proper, while the section we keep intact in China Proper constitutes only the lesser part. That is one aspect of the situation. But within that major part, the enemy can, besides the three North-eastern provinces and certain other sections, hold only the big cities, the highways and certain sections on the plains — all of which may rank highest in importance, but, in area and population, constitute only a lesser part of the occupied territory, while the area of widespread guerrilla warfare constitutes the major part. That is another aspect of the situation. If we go beyond the boundaries of China Proper and count in Mongolia, Sinkiang, Tsinghai and Tibet, then, China's unoccupied section would still constitute the major part in area, while the enemy-occupied areas, including the three North-eastern provinces, still constitute the lesser part. That is yet another aspect of the situation.

The section kept intact is of course important, and we should concentrate great efforts to cultivate it, not only in the political, military and economic aspects, but, what is also important, in the cultural aspect. The enemy has already transformed our cultural centres into cultural backwaters and we must transform the former cultural backwaters into cultural centres. Meanwhile the cultivation of the extensive guerrilla areas in the enemy's rear is also extremely important and we should develop them in various aspects, including the cultural. On the whole, China will turn the bulk of the rural areas into areas of progress and light while the small bits occupied by the enemy, especially the big cities, will temporarily become dark and backward regions.

Thus the protracted and extensive Anti-Japanese War is a war of jig-saw pattern in the military, political, economic and cultural aspects — a spectacle in the history of war, a splendid feat of the Chinese nation, a world-shaking achievement. This war will not only affect China and Japan, strongly impelling both to advance, but also affect the world, impelling all nations, first of all the oppressed nations like India, to march forward. Every Chinese should consciously throw himself into this war of a jig-saw pattern, which is the mode of war adopted by the Chinese nation in the struggle for its own liberation and the peculiar mode of war of liberation waged by a big semi-colonial country in the thirties and forties of the twentieth century. . . .

JUST AND UNJUST WARS

Wars in history can be divided into two kinds, just and unjust. All progressive wars are just and all wars impeding progress are unjust. We Communists are opposed to all unjust wars that impede progress, but we are not opposed to progressive, just wars. As for wars of the latter kind, we Communists not only do not oppose them, but will participate actively in them. The First World War, an instance of the wars of the former kind, was fought by both sides in the interest of imperialism, and therefore was firmly opposed by the Communists of the whole world. The way to oppose a war of this kind is to prevent it by all means before it breaks out and, after it has broken out, to oppose war with war, to oppose unjust war with just war, whenever possible. Japan's war is an unjust war impeding progress, which the peoples of the world, including the Japanese people, should oppose and are opposing. In China all sections of the nation, from the people to the government, from the Communist Party to the Kuomintang, have all hoisted the banner of justice and carried on a national revolutionary war against aggression. Our war is sacred, just and progressive and aims at peace. We aim at peace not only in one country but also throughout the world, and we not only aim at temporary peace but at permanent peace. In order to achieve this objective we must wage a life-and-death war, must be prepared to sacrifice anything, and must fight to the last until our aim is achieved. The sacrifice may be great, and the time long, but there already lies clearly before us a new world of permanent peace and permanent light. Our faith in waging war is based upon this struggle for a new China and a new world of permanent peace and permanent light. Fascism and imperialism want to prolong the war indefinitely, but we want to bring it to a conclusion in the not distant future. To attain this end, the great majority of mankind must exert their utmost. The 450 million people of China constitute one-quarter of the world's population; if they can strive together to overthrow Japanese imperialism and create a new China of freedom and equality, their contribution to the struggle for permanent world peace will no doubt be extremely great. This is not a vain hope, for the whole world is approaching this point in the course of its social and economic development and, with the effort of the majority of mankind thrown in, our objective will surely be attained in a few decades.

CONSCIOUS ACTIVITY IN WAR

. . . Conscious activity is man's characteristic. This characteristic is most strongly manifested in man at war. Victory or defeat in a war is of course decided by the military, political, economic and geographical conditions, by the character of the war and of the international support on both sides, but not by these alone; these alone constitute only the possibility of victory or defeat, and do not in themselves decide the issue. To decide the issue, efforts must be added, efforts in directing and waging the war, *i.e.*, man's conscious activity in war.

WAR AND POLITICS

"War is the continuation of politics"; in this sense war is politics and war itself is a political action, and there has not been a single war since ancient times that does not bear a political character. The Anti-Japanese War is a revolutionary war waged by the whole Chinese nation, whose victory is inseparable from its political aim, namely, the ousting of Japanese imperialism and the building up of a new China of freedom and equality; and it is inseparable from the over-all policy of persistently carrying on the War of Resistance and maintaining the united front; from the mobilisation of the people of the whole nation; from such political principles as the unity between officers and men, the unity between the army and the people and the disintegration of the enemy forces; from an excellent carrying through of united front policy; from cultural mobilisation; and from the efforts to win the support of international forces, including the people of the enemy's country. In a word, war cannot for a single moment be separated from politics. Any tendency among the anti-Japanese soldiers to belittle politics, to isolate war from politics, and to become advocates of "war is everything," is erroneous and must be corrected.

But war has its special characteristics and in this sense it is not identical with politics in general. "War is simply the continuation of politics by other . . . means." When politics has developed to a certain stage beyond which it cannot proceed by the usual means, war breaks out to sweep away the impediments in the way. For instance, the semi-independent status of China has been an impediment to the political development of Japanese imperialism, and so Japan started her war of aggression to sweep away that impediment. What about China? Imperialist oppression has long been an impediment to her bourgeois-democratic revolution, hence numerous liberation wars have been waged in an attempt to sweep it away. As Japan is now imposing a war on China to block completely the advance of China's revolution, China cannot but wage an Anti-Japanese War with the determination to sweep away the impediment. When the impediment is cleared away, the political aim will be attained, and the war concluded. But if the impediment is not cleared away, the war must continue to run its full course. Thus anyone is bound to fail who desires a compromise before the task of the Anti-Japanese War is fulfilled, because even if for certain reasons a compromise were reached, war would recur all the same and the broad masses of the people, who are sure to rise in protest, would continue the war until its political objective was completely achieved. It can therefore be said that politics are bloodless war while war is the politics of bloodshed. . . .

POLITICAL MOBILISATION FOR THE WAR OF RESISTANCE

Such a gigantic national revolutionary war as ours cannot succeed without universal and thoroughgoing political mobilisation. It is indeed regrettable that China has already lost a move to the enemy, *i.e.*, she did not undertake anti-Japanese political mobilisation before the War of Resistance. Even after the resistance to Japan began, political mobilisation was far from universal, let alone thoroughgoing. News about the war reached the great majority of the people through the medium of the enemy's shelling and bombing from the air. That also constituted a kind of mobilisation, but it was done by the enemy and not by ourselves. People in remote regions who cannot hear the guns are leading a tranquil life even now. This situation must be changed, otherwise there can be no victory for our life-and-death struggle. We must not again fail to make the move against our enemy; on the contrary, we must fully exploit this move to vanquish him. Such a move is one of the highest significance, in fact a matter of paramount importance, while our inferiority in things like weapons is only secondary. With the common people of the whole country mobilised, we shall create a vast sea of humanity and drown the enemy in it, remedy our shortage in arms and other things, and secure the prerequisites to overcome every difficulty in the war. In order to achieve victory, we must persistently carry on the War of Resistance, maintain the united front, and keep up the protracted war. But none of these can be separated from the mobilisation of the common people. To aim at attaining victory while neglecting political mobilisation means "trying to drive one's chariot south by heading north," a step that would inevitably forfeit victory.

What is political mobilisation? First, it means telling the army and the people about the political objective of the war. Every soldier and every civilian should be made to understand why the war must be fought and how it concerns him. . . . Next, it is not enough simply to explain the objective; the steps and policies to attain this objective must also be made clear, that is, there must be a political programme. . . . Next, how to mobilise? By word of mouth, by leaflets and bulletins, by newspapers, books and pamphlets, through theatrical performances and the films, through schools, through mass organisations and through cadres. . . . Next, it is not enough to mobilise only once; political mobilisation . . . must be done regularly. Our job is not merely to recite our political programme to the people, for nobody would care to listen to such recitations; but we must link it up with the developments in the war and with the life of the soldiers and the people, thereby transforming the political mobilisation for the war into a regular movement. This is a matter of the first magnitude on which victory primarily depends.

THE WAR OBJECTIVE

. . . The objective of war is nothing but "to preserve oneself and to annihilate the enemy." (To annihilate the enemy means to disarm him or "to deprive him of his power of resistance," and not to annihilate him completely in a physical sense.) The spear and the shield were used in ancient warfare: the spear was used to attack and annihilate the enemy while the shield was used to defend and preserve oneself. The weapons of today are but a continuation of these two. The bomber, the machine gun, the long-range gun and poison gas develop from the spear, while the air-raid shelter, the steel helmet, concrete defence works and the gas mask, form the shield. The tank is a new weapon combining the functions of the spear and the shield. Attack is the chief means to annihilate the enemy but defence cannot be dispensed with. To attack is directly to annihilate the enemy but at the same time also to preserve oneself, for, if the enemy is not annihilated, one will be annihilated by him. To defend is directly to preserve oneself but at the same time it is also a means to supplement attack or to prepare to turn to attack. Retreat belongs to the category of defence and is a continuation of defence, while pursuit is a continuation of attack. It should be pointed out that the annihilation of the enemy is the main objective of war, while the preservation of oneself is the secondary one, because it is only by annihilating the enemy in large numbers that one can effectively preserve oneself. Therefore attack as the chief means to annihilate the enemy is primary, while defence, as an auxiliary means to annihilate the enemy or as a means to preserve oneself, is secondary. Although in actual warfare the chief role is sometimes played by defence and at other times by attack, yet if the war is viewed as a whole, attack remains primary.

* * *

Our principles of operation are:

1. Attack dispersed, isolated enemy forces first; attack concentrated, strong enemy forces later.

2. Take small and medium cities and extensive rural areas first; take big cities later.

3. Make wiping out the enemy's effective strength our main objective; do not make holding or seizing a city or place our main objective. Holding or seizing a city or place is the outcome of wiping out the enemy's effective strength, and often a city or place can be held or seized for good only after it has changed hands a number of times.

4. In every battle, concentrate an absolutely superior force (two, three, four and sometimes even five or six times the enemy's strength), encircle the enemy forces completely, strive to wipe them out thoroughly and do not let any escape from the net. In special circumstances, use the method of dealing crushing blows to the enemy, that is, concentrate all our strength to make a frontal attack and also to attack one or both of his flanks, with the aim of wiping out one part and routing another so that our army can swiftly move its troops to smash other enemy forces. Strive to avoid battles of attrition in which we lose more than we gain or only break even. In this way, although we are inferior as a whole (in terms of numbers), we are absolutely superior in every part and every specific campaign, and this ensures victory in the campaign. As times goes on, we shall become superior as a whole and eventually wipe out all the enemy.

5. Fight no battle unprepared, fight no battle you are not sure of winning; make every effort to be well prepared for each battle, make every effort to ensure victory in the given set of conditions as between the enemy and ourselves.

6. Give full play to our style of fighting — courage in battle, no fear of sacrifice, no fear of fatigue, and continuous fighting (that is, fighting successive battles in a short time without rest).

7. Strive to wipe out the enemy through mobile warfare. At the same time, pay attention to the tactics of positional attack and capture enemy fortified points and cities.

8. With regard to attacking cities, resolutely seize all enemy fortified points and cities which are weakly defended. Seize at opportune moments all enemy fortified points and cities defended with moderate strength, provided circumstances permit. As for strongly defended enemy fortified points and cities, wait till conditions are ripe and then take them.

9. Replenish our strength with all the arms and most of the personnel captured from the enemy. Our army's main sources of manpower and matériel are at the front.

10. Make good use of the intervals between campaigns to rest, train and consolidate our troops. Periods of rest, training and consolidation should in general not be very long, and the enemy should so far as possible be permitted no breathing space.

Havana: Guerrilla Warfare

23 ERNESTO CHE GUEVARA
Guerrilla Warfare: A Means

On innumerable occasions guerrilla warfare has been employed in different historical circumstances to achieve different aims. It was employed in people's liberation wars in recent years — the people's vanguards in their wars of liberation followed the road of using irregular armed struggle to oppose a militarily superior enemy. Asia, Africa and America have always been the stage for guerrilla wars where people strive to seize state power in their struggle against the exploitation by feudalism and old and new colonialism. In Europe, guerrilla warfare is treated as a supplementary means by national regular armies and those of their allies.

In America, guerrilla warfare has been waged in different circumstances. A recent, indirect example was Cesar Augusto Sandino who

Ernesto Che Guevara is Minister of Industries in Cuba. This article which originally appeared in *Cuba Socialista* (September 1963) is excerpted from the translation in *Peking Review*, VII, No. 2 (January 10, 1964) 14–21.

fought the U.S. expeditionary army in Segovia in Nicaragua. The most recent example was Cuba's revolutionary war. Ever since, guerrilla warfare has become a question for theoretical discussion within progressive political parties on this continent. Whether it is possible and advantageous to employ guerrilla warfare has become a subject of heated argument.

In this article I shall try to present our views on guerrilla warfare and to explain how to employ this tactic correctly.

A MEANS FOR SEIZING STATE POWER

It must be made clear in the first place that this form of struggle is a means — a means employed to achieve an objective — seizure of state power. It is a necessary and inevitable objective for all revolutionaries. Therefore, in analysing the concrete circumstances of various countries in America, we ought to limit ourselves to the narrow sense of the term "guerrilla warfare," that is, as a means by which to win state power.

The question would probably be raised immediately: Is guerrilla warfare the only form for seizing state power in America, is it the main form, or is it just one form of struggle? Finally some would ask: Can the example set by Cuba be applied to the realities in other parts of this continent? In the course of argument, some criticism is often levelled at those who stand for guerrilla warfare, charging them with having forgotten the mass struggle, as if mass struggle and guerrilla warfare are two opposing forms. We oppose the insinuations of this assertion. Guerrilla warfare is a kind of people's war, a kind of mass struggle. To attempt to carry out this form of war without the support of the local population means certain defeat. The guerrillas are the people's armed, fighting vanguards operating in a certain area of a certain place. They aim to carry out a series of combat activities for the sole, possible strategic goal — seizure of state power. They have the support of the worker and peasant masses of the area in which they operate, or even of the whole territory. No guerrilla warfare can be conducted without these prerequisites.

THREE CONTRIBUTIONS OF THE CUBAN REVOLUTION

"We hold that in the current situation in America the Cuban revolution has made three basic contributions to the revolutionary movement there. They are: firstly, that it is possible for the people's force to win victory over reactionary troops. Secondly, that we ought not wait for all the revolutionary conditions to become ripe, and that the centre of the uprising can create such revolutionary conditions. Thirdly, that in the underdeveloped parts of America, the battlefield for armed struggle should generally be in the villages." [*Guerrilla Warfare*, by Guevara.]

Such are the Cuban revolution's contributions to the development of the revolutionary struggle in America, attainable by any country on the continent where it is possible to wage guerrilla war.

The Second Declaration of Havana pointed out: "In our countries two circumstances are joined: underdeveloped industry, and an agrarian regime of a feudal character. That is why no matter how hard the living conditions of the urban workers are, the rural population lives under even more horrible conditions of oppression and exploitation. But, with few exceptions, it also constitutes the absolute majority, sometimes more than 70 percent of Latin American populations.

"Not counting the landlords who often live in the cities, the rest of this great mass earns its livelihood by working as peons on the plantations for the most miserable wages, or they work the soil under conditions of exploitation indistinguishable from those of the Middle Ages.

"These are the circumstances which determine that the poor population of the countryside constitutes a tremendous potential revolutionary force.

"The armies are set up and equipped for conventional warfare. They are the force whereby the power of the exploiting classes is maintained. When they are confronted with irregular warfare of peasants based on their own homegrounds, they become absolutely powerless: they lose 10 men for every revolutionary fighter who falls. Demoralization among them mounts rapidly when they are beset by an invisible and invincible army which provides them no chance to display their military academy tactics and their fanfare of war, or which they boast so much to repress the city workers and students.

"The initial struggle of small fighting units is constantly nurtured by new forces; the mass movement begins to grow bold, the old order bit by bit breaks up into a thousand pieces and that is when the working class and the urban masses decide the battle.

"What is it that from the very beginning of the fight makes those units invincible, regardless of the number, strength and resources of their enemies? It is the people's support, and they can count on an ever increasing mass support.

"But the peasantry is a class which, because of the ignorance in which it has been kept and the isolation in which it lives, requires the revolutionary and political leadership of the working class and the revolutionary intellectuals. Without that it cannot alone launch the struggle and achieve victory.

"In the present historical conditions of Latin America the national bourgeoisie cannot lead the anti-feudal and anti-imperialist struggle. Experience demonstrates that in our nations this class — even when its interests clash with those of Yankee imperialism — has been incapable of confronting imperialism, paralysed by fear of social revolution and frightened by the clamour of the exploited masses." (Second Declaration of Havana.)

These theses represent the essence of this revolutionary declaration of America. Supplements are found in some other paragraphs of the declaration: "The subjective conditions in each country, the factors of consciousness, of organization, of leadership, can accelerate or delay revolution, depending on the state of their development. Sooner or later, in each historic epoch, as objective conditions ripen, consciousness is acquired, organization is achieved, leadership arises, and revolution is produced.

"Whether this takes place peacefully or comes to the world after painful labour, does not depend on the revolutionaries; it depends on the reactionary forces of the old society; it depends on their resistance against allowing the new society to be born, a society produced by the contradictions of the old society. Revolution, in history, is as the doctor who assists at the birth of a new life: it does not use forces unless it is necessary, but it will unhesitatingly use them every time labour requires them. A labour that brings the hope of a better life to the enslaved and exploited masses.

"Revolution is inevitable in many countries of Latin America. Nobody's will determines this fact. It is determined by the frightful conditions of exploitation which afflict mankind in America. It is determined by the development of the revolutionary consciousness of the masses, by the world crisis of imperialism and by the universal movement of struggle of the world's subjugated peoples." (Second Declaration of Havana.) . . .

We hold that guerrilla warfare is a form of struggle to achieve a definite aim. The first question involved is to analyse the aim and to find out whether it is possible to seize state power on our American continent through means other than armed struggle.

Peaceful struggles can be waged through mass movements, and in special circumstances when there is a crisis, can force a government to make concessions. They enable the forces of the people to seize state power and establish the dictatorship of the proletariat. All this, theoretically speaking, is correct. But when we come to analyse this question in the light of the situation in America the inevitable conclusion is that there exist everywhere in this continent the objective conditions which compel the masses to oppose the governments of the bourgeoisie and the landlords by violent acts, and that many other countries face a government crisis and there the subjective conditions are present, too. Of course, it is criminal not to take action to seize state power in those countries where all these conditions obtain. Naturally, in those countries where the above-mentioned conditions do not exist, different choices may be made and decisions suited to each country should be reached on the basis of theoretical analysis. The only thing history does not permit is that the analysts and executors of proletarian policies make mistakes of judgment. To qualify for the role of a vanguard political party is not like qualifying for a university diploma. Such a party must lead the working class in the struggle for state power and know how to guide it to seize power, leading the struggle to the quickest victory. This is the mission of all our revolutionary political parties. To avoid mistakes, the analysis should be profound and all-embracing. . . .

VIOLENCE IS NOT A HEREDITARY RIGHT OF THE EXPLOITERS

. . . Violence is not a hereditary right of the exploiters and that the exploited can and ought to use violence at the opportune moment. Marti said: "While provokers of an unavoidable war in a country are criminals, those who refuse to wage an unavoidable war are criminals, too."

At the same time, Lenin made this clear: "Social-democracy has never regarded and does not regard war from a sentimental point of view. Unswervingly denouncing wars as a brutal method of deciding the disputes of mankind, social-democracy knows that wars are inevitable as long as society is divided into classes, as long as the exploitation of man by man exists. And in eliminating this exploitation we will not manage to do without wars which the exploiting, dominating and oppressing classes always and everywhere begin themselves." Lenin said this in 1905. Later, he made a penetrating analysis of the characteristics of class struggle when he wrote in his article *The War Programme of the Proletarian Revolution:* "Whoever recognizes the class struggle cannot fail to recognize civil wars, which in every class society are the natural, and under certain conditions, inevitable continuation, development and intensification of the class struggle. All the great revolutions prove this. To repudiate civil war, or to forget about it would mean sinking into extreme opportunism and renouncing the socialist revolution."

That is to say, we should not be afraid of violence, the midwife of a new society; what must be observed is that it should be used only when the people's leaders decide that the situation is most favourable.

What is the most favourable situation? Subjectively, it depends on two interacting factors which become increasingly ripe in the course of the struggle: consciousness of the necessity of revolutionary change and the real possibility of such a change. When to these two factors are added the objective conditions which are most favourable to the development of the struggle on practically the whole of America, and the firm determination to win the struggle and the new balance of world forces, then the conditions for action obtain.

Although the socialist countries are far away, their favourable influence is constantly being felt among the fighting people of all lands and theirs is an example of educational value that will certainly inspire the people of all lands all the more. On July 26 this year [1963] Fidel Castro said: "It is for all revolutionaries, particularly at the present moment, to recognize and to have a good grip on the change that has already taken place in the world balance of forces, and to realize that such a change is to the advantage of the struggle of the people in various countries. Instead of waiting for the miracle of a social revolution in Latin America to arise from this change in the balance of forces, the task of all revolutionaries, and the revolutionaries in Latin America in particular, is to make full use of all factors favourable to the revolutionary movement in this balance of forces and to make revolution!"

There are people who would say: "We admit that, under certain specific conditions, revolutionary war is a proper way to seize power; but where can we find those great commanders, the Fidel Castros who will lead us to victory?" Like all others, Fidel Castro is a product of history. The military and political leaders who lead the struggle of uprisings in America, if it is possible for them to be merged into one man, will learn the art of war in the exercise of war itself. There is not a single craft or trade that can be mastered by textbooks alone. That being the case, struggle is the great teacher.

Naturally, it is no simple task and some serious menace will have to be faced in the entire course.

A SELF-DEFENCE MOVEMENT OF THE PEOPLE

There may be two extremely critical moments for the revolutionary future in the development of the armed struggle. The first one occurs in the preparatory stage; the manner in which this is solved will show how great is the determination of the people's forces to fight and whether its goal is well defined. When the bourgeois state attacks the people's position, self-defence is bound to take place because the enemy launches the attack at a moment favourable to him. If the minimum subjective and objective conditions are all there, the people's forces must go into armed self-defence but they must not allow themselves to be driven into a position of being hit passively; nor should armed self-defence be regarded simply as a desperate remedy for the persecuted when cornered. Guerrilla warfare is a self-defence movement of the people in a given period; it has the capacity to attack the enemy and great efforts must be made to develop this capacity. This capacity, as time goes on, will determine its special character of mobilizing the people's forces. That is to say, *guerrilla warfare is not passive self-defence, but offensive defence,* and from the moment when things are viewed in this way, *guerrilla warfare will finally end up with the seizure of political power.* [Emphasis added.]

This moment is important. In the course of social progress, the difference between violence and non-violence cannot be measured by the number of shots exchanged; it all depends on the concrete and fluctuating situation. In order to avoid an adverse situation from developing one must be good at seizing the right opportunity and know when to use the people's forces (to know their relative weakness and at the same time their strategic strength) to compel the enemy to take the necessary steps. Thus, one must upset the equilibrium between the oligarchies and the pressure of the people. A dictatorial regime always tries to maintain its rule under conditions where it may not need to use violence on a large scale; one must force it to appear undisguised, that is to say, to force it to appear for what it is: a violent dictatorship of the reactionary class. This will help its unmasking and intensify the struggle to a point of no return. How the people's forces, whose job it is to compel the dictatorial regime to make up its mind, fulfil their task — to retreat or to start the struggle — will determine whether or not the armed operations, which have a far-reaching influence, can have a good start.

CONSTANT INTENSIFICATION OF THE REVOLUTIONARY PROCESS

Whether or not the other critical moment can be avoided depends on the daily growth of the people's forces. Marx consistently maintained that once the revolutionary process begins, the proletariat must ceaselessly attack and attack again. Without being continuously intensified, a revolution may move backward. Once the combatants get tired, they will begin to lose confidence and the plots which the bourgeoisie often works out against us may possibly succeed. These plots are probably the holding of elections to hand over state power to some other hypocritical gentlemen more capable of using honeyed words than the old dictator, or the staging of a coup by reactionaries who are headed, generally speaking, by the military, and which has the support, direct or indirect, of progressive forces. There are other plots as well but an analysis of their tactics is not our subject matter here. . . .

Long ago, Engels, in his preface to the third edition of *The Civil War in France*, observed that the workers emerged with arms from every revolution; "therefore," he said, "the disarming of the workers was the first commandment for the bourgeois, who were at the helm of the state. Hence, after every revolution won by the workers, a new struggle, ending with the defeat of the workers. . . ." (Quoted from Lenin: *The State and Revolution.*)

This kind of ebbing and flowing struggle for decades has repeated itself in the capitalist world and in it some kind of formal reforms are at times obtained; there are also strategic retreats. The proletariat in this aspect is constantly being deceived by the same frauds which have appeared again and again in the past century.

It would be also very dangerous if the leaders of a progressive party are over-zealous in utilizing some aspects of bourgeois legality, in the hope of maintaining the most favourable conditions for revolutionary action in a given period, thus confusing the line of demarcation (as is often seen in the course of action) and forgetting that their final strategic objective is to seize state power.

As long as the leading Marxist-Leninist party knows thoroughly the danger in a given period, and is capable of mobilizing the masses to the greatest extent possible, and leading them to the correct path of solving the fundamental contradictions, these two difficult moments in a revolution, which we have briefly analysed, can be avoided.

WHY GUERRILLA WARFARE IS THE CORRECT ROAD

In elaborating the theses we have presumed that it is possible for people eventually to accept the idea of armed struggle and the proposition that guerrilla warfare is a method of fighting. Why do we think that guerrilla warfare is the correct road in the conditions obtaining in America today? Why must the guerrilla movement be the principal means of struggle in America? As we see it, the basic reasons are as follows:

First, since it is acknowledged that the enemy will fight to maintain his political power, it is necessary to take into consideration the elimination of the repressive army. But, to eliminate this army, there must be a people's army to oppose it. This people's army does not come into existence by itself; it must be armed by the weapons presented by the enemy. This determines the ruthless and protracted character of the struggle in which, without adequate facilities for defence and mobility, the people's army and its leaders will be constantly subjected to attacks by a stronger force of the enemy.

On the other hand, the guerrilla nucleus stationed in areas favourable for struggle will ensure the security and continuity of the revolutionary command. The urban detachments commanded by the general staff of the people's army can perform actions of extreme importance. Even if these small units are incidentally destroyed, the nerve centre of the revolution (the revolutionary command) will not be wiped out, and the leadership of the revolution will continue to arouse the revolutionary spirit of the masses from the rural bases and organize new forces for the next battle.

Moreover, in this area, the future state apparatus will begin to take shape. It will be responsible for the effective exercise of class dictatorship in the entire transition period. The longer the struggle drags on, the greater and more complicated the problem of administrative affairs will become. To solve this problem, a group of cadres must be trained to deal with the difficult task of consolidating state power and developing economy at a later stage.

Secondly, account should be taken of the general condition of the Latin American peasantry and the increasingly explosive character of its struggle against the feudal structures under a social situation where the local exploiters work in collusion with foreign exploiters. . . .

ERNESTO CHE GUEVARA   *277*

Thirdly, the continental character of the struggle should be taken into consideration. . . .

The Yankees will intervene in order to consolidate their interests, since they regard the struggle in America as a decisive one. As a matter of fact, they have already taken part in fostering repressive forces and formed an organization for continental struggle. From now on they will do so with all their might and will try to suppress the people's forces with all the destructive weapons available. They will not allow any revolutionary regime to be consolidated and should a revolutionary regime be consolidated in a country, they will attack it, refuse to recognize it, try their best to split the revolutionary forces, send in all kinds of saboteurs, create border troubles, line up some other reactionary countries to oppose it, and try to strangle the newborn country economically, in short to destroy this newborn country.

In view of this situation in America, it is very difficult for a single country to achieve victory and consolidate it. The alliance of the repressive forces must be countered by the alliance of the people's forces. In all those countries where suppression has reached an unbearable point, the banner of uprising must be raised, and this banner, because of historical necessity, will bear a continental character. As Fidel said of the Andes Mountains inevitably becoming a Sierra Maestra, the whole extensive territory of this continent will become an arena of life-and-death struggle against imperialist power.

HOW TO OPEN UP A GUERRILLA CENTRE

Let us consider how a centre for guerrilla activities can be opened up.

Small units with few people in them chose some places favourable for guerrilla activities, from where they can advance for counter-attack and to where they can retreat for refuge, and they begin to take actions in these places. But one point must be made perfectly clear: at the initial stage, when the guerrillas are still rather weak, they should only concentrate on getting a firm footing, familiarizing themselves with the surroundings, establishing contact with the inhabitants, and consolidating places which can be turned into bases.

If the guerrilla units are to survive in the struggle under such conditions, they must possess three qualities: constant movement, constant vigilance and constant precaution. Misapplication of these elements of military tactics will make it difficult for the guerrillas to survive. It must be remembered that at such a moment the heroic deeds of the guerrillas lie in enlarging the predetermined objective and making a series of great sacrifices for the fulfilment of the objective.

These sacrifices do not mean everyday battle or a face-to-face struggle with the enemy; they are more bitter and more difficult for the guerrillas to endure physically and mentally.

They may sustain severe blows from the enemy forces and sometimes may be routed or killed when captured. They may be hunted down like wild game in the areas they have selected for operations and kept constantly in a state of alarm for fear that the enemy might be on their track. They must guard against credulity in everything, because the intimidated peasants, sometimes at a loss to find a pretext and out of a desire to clear up themselves, may hand them over to the repressive army. Either victory or death; there is no other alternative. At these moments death is a stark reality while victory is a myth which only a revolutionary can contemplate.

Such is the heroism of the guerrillas. It therefore follows that to move along is also a form of fighting, and at a particular moment, to avoid fighting is a form of fighting. Our way of putting it is, confronted with the general superiority of the enemy, to employ a form of tactics which will help to gain a relative superiority at a chosen point, either by concentrating a more numerous force than the enemy or by occupying favourable terrain, so that the balance of forces is changed. The winning of tactical victories can be ensured under such conditions; it is best not to go into action when the relative superiority is not so manifest. As long as a choice can be made as to "how to fight" and "when to fight," a battle should not be fought when victory is not certain.

BUILDING GUERRILLA BASES

The guerrillas will continue to grow and consolidate in a tremendous politico-military movement, and bases will be formed gradually, constituting the basic factor for the continuous growth of the guerrillas. They will become strongholds which the enemy cannot break into without paying a heavy price in casualties. They are the fortresses of revolution and the havens for the guerrillas who become bolder and bolder in launching attacks towards far-away regions.

A day will come when they overcome the tactical and political difficulties at the same time. The guerrillas should at no time forget that they are the vanguards of the people, nor should they forget the task resting on their shoulders. They should therefore create the political prerequisites for the establishment of a revolutionary regime wholly supported by the masses. The important demands of the peasants should be satisfied according to circumstances, so that the entire population may become united as a solid body.

If the military situation is difficult at the initial stage, politically it is no less delicate. If a single military error may lead to the destruction of the guerrillas, a political error may arrest the growth of the guerrillas for quite a long time.

The struggle is both military and political and therefore must be developed and understood as such.

As a guerrilla unit grows steadily, there will come a time when it will have an excessive number of men and an over-concentration of forces in the area which its capacity for action can cover. Then there will begin the beehive pattern effect in which one of the guerrilla leaders, an outstanding guerrilla fighter, leading his men, leaps to another area and repeats the chain development of guerrilla warfare, of course, under the central command.

To sum up, it must be pointed out that victory cannot be achieved without building up a people's army. The guerrillas may be numerically expanded to a certain magnitude and the people's forces may inflict damages on the enemy in some cities and enemy-occupied areas, but the military strength of the reactionaries may still remain intact. It should always be borne in mind that the ultimate outcome must be the elimination of the enemy. So all the newly opened areas, all areas deep in the enemy's rear and all forces operating in the major cities, must be subordinate to the command. It is not a strict system of level-by-level subordination as in the regular army, but a relation of subordination in strategy. A guerrilla unit is allowed some latitude of action, but it must carry out all the strategic orders of the general command, which is located in a most reliable and most powerful area in order to prepare conditions to use the forces in a concentrated form at a certain stage.

THREE STAGES OF GUERRILLA WARFARE

A guerrilla war or a liberation war generally covers three stages. It begins with the stage of strategic defence, when the fast-moving and quickly disappearing small units will now and then take a bite at the enemy, but do not retire in a small area for passive defence. Their defence means launching every small-scale attack that can be made. This is then followed by the stage of stalemate when there will be activities by both the enemy and the guerrillas. Later on it will come to the final stage of the collapse of the repressive army. The guerrillas will now capture the big cities, fight large-scale decisive battles and wipe out the enemy thoroughly and completely.

Having reached the stage of stalemate between the armies of both sides, guerrilla warfare will take on new characters in its further development. The concept of manoeuvre will begin to take shape; large units capable of attacking well-fortified strongholds will come into existence; mobile warfare which calls for a movement of considerable number of troops and deployment of offensive weapons will begin to be fought. But since the enemy still retains the power to resist and counter-attack, mobile warfare cannot yet wholly replace guerrilla warfare. It is only a form of operation in the development of guerrilla warfare and the largest concentration of guerrilla forces until several armies of the people's forces are eventually formed. Yet, even by that time, the guerrillas, in coordination with the operations of the main forces, will continue to use the method of "pure" guerrilla fighting to undermine the transport and communications facilities and disrupt the whole defensive machine of the enemy.

We have predicted that the war will be continental in character. That also means it will be protracted; there will be a great number of battle-fronts, and it will cost much blood and countless lives over a long period. Moreover, the phenomenon of polarization of forces which is appearing in America and the clear division between the exploiters and the exploited in the future revolutionary wars indicate that once the armed vanguard of the people rises to seize state power, the country or countries where state power has been seized will eliminate the oppressors, both imperialists and domestic exploiters at the same time. The first stage of the socialist revolution will be realized; the people will set out to heal the wounds and embark on socialist construction.

Is there a possibility which is less cruel?

The world has long since been carved up and the United States has seized the lion's share on our continent. Today the imperialists of the Old World are staging a comeback; the powerful might of the European Common Market is threatening even the United States. All this may lead some people to think that there may be a possibility to form an alliance with the more powerful national bourgeoisie, to watch with folded arms the struggle between the imperialists and to seek for a chance to make some headway. It must be understood that a passive policy in class struggle will never bring good results, for however revolutionary the bourgeoisie may appear to be at one time, the alliance with it can only be a temporary one. Skipping over these two points, people should take another road if the time factor is taken into consideration. The basic contradictions in America are sharpening so rapidly that they have come to interfere with the "normal" development of the contradictions between the imperialist camps scrambling for markets. . . .

The Alliance for Progress is trying to restrain what cannot be restrained. . . .

Not a single position, not a single weapon and not a single secret should be given up to the class enemy, or everything will be lost.

As a matter of fact, the struggle in America is already here. Will there not be whirlpools of struggle taking shape in Venezuela, Guatemala, Colombia, Peru, Ecuador. . . ? Is it true that the present fighting is only a demonstration of rash impulse which will be fruitless? The outcome of today's struggle is immaterial. The movement may be temporarily disrupted, but this will be of little effect on the final outcome. What is important is the daily maturing determination to struggle, the realization of the necessity for revolutionary change and the firm conviction of this possibility.

This is a prediction. We are firmly convinced that history will show that we are right. An analysis of the subjective and objective factors in America and the imperialist world has made it clear to us that the assertions made on the basis of the Second Havana Declaration are correct.

PART THREE

Strategies in Conflict

Introduction to Part Three

Crucibles of Theory

Theory must be converted to practice in direct encounters between the states of the three worlds. Many such confrontations have taken place since 1945, but three are presented here as case studies of strategies in conflict. The first, the Berlin crisis, peaked in 1961; the other two, the Cuban missile crisis and the Himalayan boundary dispute, erupted almost concurrently — late in 1962. As of 1965 none of the basic issues in these disputes has been resolved. Each confrontation had had its unique historical origins and setting. However, these three conflicts will be examined to determine what common features characterized them and what light, if any, these similarities shed on the nature of the present state of world politics.

Not all powers are satisfied with the present territorial and political distribution of power. Some states are willing to utilize force, indirectly or directly, to alter the status quo. The three cases given here stem primarily from Communist attempts to modify existing arrangements. This selection thus focuses attention on the relationship of major tension between the Communist and Western worlds. But other conflicts could have been included to illustrate Western aggression against the third world (e.g., the 1956 Suez crisis), aggression originating in the third world (such as Indonesia against Malaysia), armed hostilities between Communist countries (as along the Sinkiang frontier), or clashes between NATO allies (e.g., over Cyprus).

The three cases represented here were selected for (1) their heavy ideological component, of special relevance in a book on "world perspectives"; (2) their involvement of states from all three worlds in each other's affairs; (3) their ability to illustrate the problems resulting from political challenges to the legal status quo; and (4) their close time sequence and its relations to expected shifts in the military balance of power. Finally, the Berlin and Cuban crises are of particular significance because they put the superpowers on a collision course, while the Himalayan affair (like the 1956 Suez crisis) saw Washington and Moscow join in backing a nonaligned nation against an ally of a superpower.

The Internationalization of Politics

The ideological component is only one element in the three disputes, but its saliency produces global concern over each confrontation due to the all-out, total character of conflicts between allegedly alien and hostile systems.[1] The number of states directly involved in each of these disputes is relatively small, but all three confrontations quickly provoked criticism, mediation, and various forms of intervention from members of all three worlds. Thus, while the Berlin dispute engages primarily the former allies of the anti-Hitler coalition of 1945 and the present German governments, the nonaligned powers have exerted their influence to moderate and resolve the conflict. The readings here present the Belgrade Conference appeal to the disputants and the response of Moscow and Washington to importuning visits by neutralist leaders.[2]

The Cuban and Himalayan crises were also quite potent in eliciting universal concern. The Caribbean affair involved directly the superpowers and Latin America, but the matter was debated in the United Nations as well as the Organization of American States. It soon became

[1] Of the governments directly engaged in the three disputes only the Indian regime under Nehru was not actively hostile to its adversary government's ideology and structure.

[2] See readings No. 26–29.

grist for Chinese diatribes and Muscovite boasting in the Sino-Soviet dispute. Similarly, the Chinese-Indian frontier war quickly became the object of mediation by six Afro-Asian powers meeting in Colombo, Ceylon, and of U.S. and (to a lesser extent) Soviet military intervention in support of New Delhi.

Legal Uncertainties

Another characteristic of the three disputes is that they represent a political challenge to the legal status quo. In each instance the lawful existence of some institution — a government, a state, a frontier, or a doctrine — is doubted. A classic problem of international law results: Should treaties be observed in perpetuity (*pacta sunt servanda*), or should they be revised if the underlying conditions change (*rebus sic stantibus*)?[3] If the possibility of revision is admitted, what are the precise conditions which warrant it? Is it sufficient that one party to a treaty having become more powerful wants to revise it? Or must the conditions relate to the narrow circumstances which make execution of an obligation impossible, such as the inundation of an air base to which landing rights have been promised? By what procedure will it be determined what, if any, revisions are in order? And how will this determination be enforced?

In the Berlin dispute Moscow and Pankow question the validity of four-power obligations entered into at the end of World War II and the special arrangements by which the West has secured access to and defense of its sector in Berlin. More fundamentally, however, the Soviet Union calls on the West to accept as an accomplished fact the changes made in the political and territorial structure of East Central Europe since 1945. While the West is concerned to protect its rights in Berlin and make its alliance commitments credible, the aspect of Western behavior most troublesome to Moscow is the refusal to recognize the German Democratic Republic, the Oder-Neisse frontier with Poland, and the cession of East Prussia to Russia.[4]

Again in the Cuban case it is the United States which refuses to

---

[3] For discussion see William W. Bishop, Jr., *International Law: Cases and Materials* (2nd ed.; Boston: Little, Brown, 1962) pp. 133–134, 198–208.

[4] See item No. 25. For an East German statement, see Walter Ulbricht, "The Historical Task of the G.D.R. and the Future of Germany," *World Marxist Review,* V, No. 7 (July 1962) 3–8.

accept a present reality: a socialist regime and a hostile military base in the Western hemisphere. Washington favors a return to what might be called the status quo ante — a non-socialist Cuba (though not necessarily of the Batista coloring). Such sentiments are reciprocal. Neither Castro nor the Latin and North American governments which oppose him have resigned themselves to one another's prolonged existence. Each side, therefore, has some pretext for regarding its own offensive actions as defensive.

The Soviet military establishment in Cuba provides an implicit denial of the validity of the Monroe Doctrine. But many observers doubted the legality of the U.S. quarantine to force a withdrawal of Soviet missiles, the justification for which was variously attributed to the Rio Pact (Articles 6 and 8), the U.N. Charter (Article 51), and finally a supporting resolution of the Organization of American States.[5] Antedating the missile crisis, the concepts by which Moscow and Washington defined "offensive" and "defensive" weapons also appeared to clash.

As in the other cases, many considerations in addition to legal ones guided the policies of the participants in the Himalayan dispute. That conflict more than the other two suggests the profound need for an internationally accepted procedure for peaceful revision of treaties. Peking's legal position is strongest in casting doubt on the continued validity of a frontier (the 1914 McMahon Line) imposed on a disorganized China by imperial England in favor of British interests in India.[6] Should such an "unequal" treaty endure for all time? Will it endure when the weaker party becomes the stronger? India's action in forcibly retaking Goa from Portugal answered these questions in the negative. India, in any event, seeks to restore the status quo ante prior to China's advance, while Peking has sought negotiations on the basis of the new status quo.

The Military Threat System

Underlying each confrontation is a dynamic military balance which leads one disputant to believe it can command favorable changes in

[5] For a fuller explanation of the United States government's point of view see Abram Chayes, "Law and the Quarantine of Cuba," *Foreign Affairs*, XIL, No. 3 (April 1963) 550–557.
[6] For an interpretation favorable to India see J. S. Bains, *India's International Disputes* (Bombay: Asia Publishing House, 1962) pp. 136–164.

the political and legal status quo. Intense Soviet pressure for a German Peace Treaty recognizing the existence of the German Democratic Republic began in 1958, after the Soviet Union in 1957 became the first country to test successfully an ICBM and an earth satellite. This pressure reached a high point in 1961 when time was running out on Western belief in a "missile gap" favorable to Russia. Early in 1961 the first Kennedy budget and the procurement plans of Defense Secretary McNamara were designed to allow the West to negotiate quickly from a position of absolute nuclear and improved conventional strength. Each side demonstrated its resolve at the height of the 1961 crisis by increasing its military spending sharply and by recalling reserve forces to duty. Aware that the United States would soon achieve a significant lead in numbers of strategic delivery systems, Moscow used the occasion to resume nuclear testing to develop giant warheads.

The desperate nature of the Soviet effort in 1962 to emplace medium-range missiles in Cuba can be interpreted as another attempt to redress the strategic balance of power which had shifted sharply to U.S. favor.[7] Moscow, in any event, manifestly underrated Washington's willingness to take great risks to force a Soviet withdrawal.[8] The manner in which Khrushchev responded to the U.S. riposte confirms the supposition that Moscow perceived its military position to be considerably inferior to the American.

The Soviet failure to alter the military balance during the Cuban episode, coupled with the apparent desire each side displayed in maintaining peace, had the paradoxical result of initiating a *détente* and reconciling both parties to a ban on nuclear testing in three environments.

One positive achievement of the Soviet Cuban gambit was a U.S. promise not to attempt a forcible overthrow of the Castro government. On the other hand, the ability of the Cuban regime to carry on subversion in other Latin American countries is somewhat inhibited by the paucity of Soviet forces to defend Cuba against retaliation. Cuba —

---

[7] For further discussion of Soviet motives in Cuba see Zbigniew Brzezinski, "Cuba in Soviet Strategy," *New Republic*, November 3, 1962, pp. 7–8; Jean Daniel, "Unofficial Envoy: An Historic Report from Two Capitals," *New Republic*, December 14, 1963, pp. 18–19; Arnold L. Horelick, "The Cuban Missile Crisis: An Analysis of Soviet Calculations and Behavior," *World Politics*, XVI, No. 3 (April 1964) 363–390; Herbert L. Matthews, *Return to Cuba*, Institute of Hispanic American and Luso-Brazilian Studies, Bolivar House, Stanford University, 1964.
[8] J. Malcolm Mackintosh, "Soviet Motives in Cuba," *Survival*, V, No. 1 (January–February 1963) 16–19.

like Berlin — remains an exposed outpost of one superpower, highly vulnerable to pressure from the more proximate power, serving therefore as a kind of hostage to restrain the more distant party.

The immediate strategic objective of China's move in Ladakh was probably to consolidate her hold over Aksai Chin, through which Peking had already built a road connecting Sinkiang Province with Tibet. One reason for the Chinese military move was that the Indian Army was re-establishing outposts in eastern Ladakh in an effort to contain the Chinese infiltration of Aksai Chin. By unilaterally declaring a cease-fire, Peking succeeded in keeping India and the neutrals from organizing more effective resistance and preventing massive Western intervention on India's behalf. The Chinese advance to new positions helped to make India's northern border permanently vulnerable to renewed Chinese attack.

The broader motives for China's action are open to speculation. It was presumably intended to impress on Nepal, Burma, and other Asian countries the price of resisting Chinese territorial claims. Another objective may have been to show that neutralism affords little protection and that alignment with Peking is the only safe course. Alternatively, Peking may have hoped to goad Nehru into seeking Western aid and thus damaging his position as leader of the *tiers monde*.

Internal considerations may also have played a part — the move into India probably improved the flagging morale of the Chinese army and helped to rally popular, chauvinistic support for the regime. In general, the Chinese initiative showed Peking's independence from Soviet dictation.

The effectiveness of China's move is difficult to measure. As of 1965 Peking enjoyed unquestioned control over Aksai Chin and part of eastern Ladakh up to a cease-fire line separating Chinese and Indian forces. Politically it appeared that Cambodia and other states showed a greater inclination to follow Peking's wishes, but the Himalayan conflict had galvanized India's defense planning and sharpened for other countries the question whether they, too, should not prepare to resist restoration of the Middle Kingdom.[9]

[9] For further information on the Sino-Indian border question see Margaret W. Fisher, Leo E. Rose, and Robert A. Huttenbeck, *Himalayan Background: Sino-Indian Rivalry in Ladakh* (New York: Praeger, 1963) ; *The Report of the Officials of the Government of India and the People's Republic of China on the Boundary Question* (New Delhi: Government of India, Ministry of External Affairs, 1961) ; *The Sino-Indian Boundary Question* (Peking: Foreign Languages Press, 1962).

Short- and Long-term Restraints:
Realpolitik and Moralpolitik

The three confrontations suggest that fear of one's own physical destruction is a much more potent restraint than legalistic or moralistic concerns. The immediate factor inhibiting an increase in the level of violence has probably been the fear that such escalation might produce damage beyond any possible gain. A certain delicacy and appearance of restraint is also induced by the desire of all the parties to the disputes to appear reasonable to "world public opinion," as witnessed, for example, in the Khrushchev and Kennedy replies to the Belgrade Conference appeals. But the extent to which the disputants were willing to move toward the brink of war appears to have been determined primarily by a judgment on the national interest at stake, weighed against the probability of major war.

The "five principles of peaceful coexistence" signed by India and China in 1954 did not prevent Peking's invasion. And the efforts of the six nonaligned powers to mediate the conflict had little visible impact on the dispute.

The United Nations and the International Court of Justice have not been utilized to resolve either the Berlin or the Himalayan conflicts, partly because the two Germanys and mainland China are not seated in these organs. But the main reason for keeping Berlin out of U.N. debate has been the superpowers' preference to deal directly with each other on this vital issue.[10] The Cuban crisis suggests a shift in this attitude, however, as the superpowers seemed to welcome an agency which offered both sides a means to step away from the brink. Communications were facilitated by U Thant, and a U.S.-Soviet agreement on U.N. inspection procedures was frustrated in the first instance by Cuba — the country to be inspected.[11]

[10] However, the Soviet Government has sometimes suggested that the United Nations play a role in ensuring the status of Berlin as a "free city." Secretary General Hammarskjold, recognizing the potential disruptive consequences of U.N. participation in this great power confrontation, indicated some reluctance to involve the U.N. in the Berlin crisis, as have the Western governments including Bonn. See Alexander Dallin, *The Soviet Union at the United Nations* (New York: (Praeger, 1962) p. 180.

[11] Khrushchev's correspondence with Bertrand Russell during the Cuban missile crisis was probably aimed more at propaganda effect than communicaiton, although it offered at least a plausible indication of the Soviet Premier's interest in containing the conflict.

The relative ease of constructing an attractive propaganda position is illustrated by the diverse interpretations to which the three disputes have been subjected. Few persons even in the West command the facts to enable them to discern which interpretation is most valid. The attitude of most persons toward the disputes will be a function of their own predilections, usually quite nationalistic, and the simple themes reiterated by their own governments. These governments, in turn, are under a compulsion to take a strong stand in order to mobilize their constituents and to avoid charges of appeasement.

Western media have pictured Khrushchev's initiatives in the Berlin dispute as "ultimatums" designed to "end Western rights in Berlin" and prepare the way for a Communist takeover. The West's resistance to these initiatives is explained in the Communist press as a demonstration of Western scheming to keep alive the coals of World War II and to use Berlin as a forward base for renewed Fascist aggression against Eastern Europe. At a more refined level of debate it has been asked whether the Soviet campaign for a German Peace Treaty represents an offensive designed to push back the West or a reasonable proposal to settle by negotiation a major source of international tension. The West's response may also be judged according to the alternative evaluations of Soviet objectives.[12]

The movement of Soviet missiles into and out of Cuba has been justified in the Moscow press as a successful strategem to prevent U.S. aggression against Havana. Only when Washington gave its assurance that it would not use force to upset the Castro regime were the missiles withdrawn. Khrushchev's speech cited here reveals, however, that the main U.S. "attack" force was assembled in response to the discovery of Soviet missiles in Cuba, a fact which undermines somewhat any claims of a Soviet "victory."

The U.S. interpretation, on the other hand, begins by denying any U.S. plan to invade Cuba. That medium-range missiles might be used to deter as well as to attack was not acknowledged by official Washington, which stressed the duplicity in Soviet statements affirming the "defensive" character of all equipment sent to Cuba.

Peking, for its part, found a formula to denounce Khrushchev no matter which way he moved. The shipment of missiles was "adven-

---

[12] For an objective review of the Berlin problem see Elisabeth Barker, "The Berlin Crisis, 1958–1962," *International Affairs* (London), XXXIX, No. 1 (January 1963) 59–74.

turism"; their withdrawal, "capitulationism." The impact of such criticism on Soviet policy, of course, will vary according to Moscow's concern to keep China and/or revolutionaries elsewhere under Soviet influence.

The virtual identity of Indian and Chinese charges against one another in the Himalayan dispute is particularly striking. Each accuses the other of revising maps as early as 1955, of advancing into the other's legitimate territory, and of refusing to negotiate. Such opposed interpretations in the Sino-Indian conflict, as in the other encounters, are made possible by the existence of facts which, distorted by ethnocentric perception and cynical propaganda, lend themselves to half-truths favorable to one side or the other.

Despite the desire of the various governments to placate public opinion, the fact is that in the last analysis they control the means to shape decisively the views of their own constituents or, failing that, to ignore them. Considerations of public opinion, morality, and law have long-term power, but are subordinate to concern over naked power in crisis situations.

Thus, the three cases illustrate the strong antagonisms which persist between and among nation-states of the three worlds, the unsettling effect of an open-ended military balance which leaves unanswered the question of who gets what, the inability of present legal machinery to deal with challenges to the status quo, and the consequent reliance upon military force to defend and extend national interests — even while propaganda is cranked out and served to justify national strategies in moral and legal terms to appeal to public opinion at home and abroad. The changing nature of the superpowers' response to the three confrontations, however, also suggests an increasing desire on their parts to avoid head-on encounters, such as Berlin and Cuba, from which it is difficult to back down, and to damp the conflicts of other states in order to minimize the chances of great power involvement.

A Confrontation in Europe:
Berlin and Divided Germany

"Pacta Sunt Servanda"

24 LUCIUS D. CLAY
Berlin

Time and time again during the past fifteen years our people have
had to confront a new Berlin crisis. Thus they are well aware that we
have a continuing Berlin problem. However, it is not always recognized that the critical Berlin situation which has prevailed since the
end of World War II is in reality a challenge to the survival of Europe.
Many of us have forgotten why and when the Berlin problem came
about. For a proper understanding of it and of its relationship to our
foreign policy, we must look back occasionally to find how it did develop.

In the fall of 1943 when President Roosevelt and Prime Minister
Churchill met in Quebec, the Soviet armies had stopped the German
offensive and were advancing doggedly toward Central Europe. The

General Lucius D. Clay, Commander-in-Chief, U.S. Forces in Europe and Military Governor of the U.S. Zone in Germany 1947–49, was President Kennedy's
personal representative in Berlin during the crisis under discussion. These excerpts
are reprinted from an article in *Foreign Affairs*, XLI, No. 1 (October 1962) 47–58,
copyrighted by the Council on Foreign Relations Inc., New York.

British representatives at Quebec were already concerned as to where and when the Western Allied armies would meet the Soviet armies. They urged that an early conference be arranged with the Soviet Government to fix the lines of demarcation between these armies and to draw an agreement for the occupation of a defeated Germany. As a result, this question was placed on the agenda for the meeting of foreign ministers in Moscow in October 1943. There it was agreed that a European Advisory Commission would immediately be established in London to negotiate agreements for the future zones of occupation and for the postwar treatment of occupied Germany. This Commission was composed of the United States and Soviet ambassadors to Great Britain and a representative of the British Foreign Office, Sir William Strang.

Shortly after the Commission met in London in January 1944, the British representative submitted a proposed plan of demarcation with provision for a Berlin enclave to be carved out of the Eastern or Soviet zone, and this proposal was immediately accepted by the Soviet representative. Our government demurred somewhat as the War Department had suggested a counter-proposal which would have made Berlin the center of a pie to be carved in three slices. Since it was obvious that this proposal would have disrupted natural administrative and communication lines, it was not pushed vigorously. In point of fact, our government was more concerned about whether we could occupy the northwestern or southwestern zone than it was about the location of the line between the Western Allies and the Soviet forces. Thus, in April 1944, President Roosevelt approved the British proposal. It is important to know that the boundaries which exist today between East and West Germany as well as within the Berlin enclave are exactly the lines proposed in January 1944 and approved in April 1944, some weeks before the Western Allies had landed in northern France. Certainly, the existence of this agreement had some bearing on the political importance given to the possible capture of Berlin by the Western Allies. Since the future zonal boundaries had been laid down many months in advance, it did not appear to matter which armies were the first to enter Berlin.

In any case, at the time of the German surrender, the Western Allies had passed well to the east of the proposed boundary line and were in physical possession of much of Thuringia and Saxony. Under the occupation agreement, our forces were to retire behind the line of demarcation as soon as joint military government was established, and concurrently we would enter Berlin and occupy the assigned sectors there. In June of 1945, the Allied commanders met in Berlin to issue the declaration regarding the defeat of Germany and the rules of conduct of military occupation. The agreements, which had been negotiated by the three governments through their representatives on the European Advisory Commission, had already received formal approval at Yalta. Under these agreements an Allied Control Council composed of the three commanders-in-chief, with headquarters in Berlin, was to be responsible for the government of Germany. However, each commander-in-chief was to exercise final authority in his zone, thus making the Allied Control Council able to function only by unanimous consent. Berlin, however, was not included in any of the zones, but was to be governed by an Allied Kommandatura which reported directly to the Allied Control Council. At Yalta, France was added as an occupying power, although its government was not represented either at Yalta or at Potsdam. The Soviet Government offered no objection to the inclusion of France as an occupying power other than to insist that its zone in Germany be carved out of the American and British zones of occupation.

It is important also to remember that at Yalta the Western Allies agreed in principle to the transfer of lands in eastern Poland to the Soviet Republic with compensation to be provided to Poland from land in Eastern Germany. However, the eastern boundary of Germany was not fixed either at Yalta or at Potsdam and we insisted that this boundary could be fixed only with the signing of a peace treaty with a new and representative German government. We did accept at Potsdam the removal of the area in dispute from the jurisdiction of the Allied Control Council, and its being placed under Polish occupation and control until the final boundary was established. Very little else was accomplished at Potsdam other than to confirm the Yalta decisions, except that it was agreed that Germany was to be treated as a political and economic unit and that the German people were to be given the opportunity to establish a government of their own choice for all of Germany through democratic elections.

Much has been written about the failure of the Western Allies to obtain written guarantees of free access to Berlin, particularly as no such provision had been made in the agreement for the joint occupation of Germany. Philip Mosely, who was intimately connected with all of the negotiations of the European Advisory Commission, states that this was not included in the agreement as it was a matter to be negotiated directly by the military commanders.[1] Interestingly, despite my responsibilities as General Eisenhower's deputy in charge of our entry into Berlin, I had not been informed of this intention. However, the question arose immediately. At our first meetings Marshal Zhukov requested that our initial access to Berlin be effected over a specified highway route and a specific railway route, as all others were needed for the demobilization of the Soviet army. While this arrangement could have been obtained in writing, I refused to regard it as other than a temporary measure, since it seemed obvious to me that the joint occupation of Berlin clearly conveyed with it the right of access by any and all routes. More importantly, we were then concerned only with Allied access, as the right of access for Germans was not even discussed; in all the negotiations up to then it was taken for granted that Germany was to be treated as a political and economic unit. No one then foresaw the ultimate division of Germany and the blockade of Berlin which was aimed principally at throttling its German population. Since we had free access in the air, no blockade on the ground represented at any time a serious threat to our supply. For safety reasons we did establish specific flight corridors for the Allied aircraft flying to and from Berlin. This established, under written agreement among the four powers, three airlanes for use by the Western Allies, and these airlanes have been in daily use by the West ever since 1945.

The United States tried in every way to make the Allied Control Council a real government for all of Germany, only to find that the Soviet Government merely kept the Council alive while exploiting East Germany as a bolster to the Russian economy and simultaneously converting it into a police state. For a few months while we still had powerful military forces in Europe there seemed to be a chance for Allied government to function. Much to our surprise, shortly after our entry into Berlin, Soviet representatives had agreed to hold free elections in the city. It seems likely that they did this in the belief that their consolidation of the K.D.P. (Communists) and S.D.P. (Socialists) into the new S.E.D. (Socialist Unity) party would win the election. Fortunately there were strong and wise leaders in the S.D.P. who rejected this shotgun marriage and when the election was over the S.E.D. party had failed completely in its quest for power. From then on our diffi-

---

[1] Philip E. Mosely, "The Occupation of Germany: New Light on How the Zones Were Drawn," *Foreign Affairs*, July 1950.

culties in Berlin began, starting with the Soviet refusal to recognize the properly elected mayor, Ernst Reuter.

However, the final breaking point came with the currency reform that was put into effect in the American, British and French zones in June 1948. This reform, which had been prevented by Soviet veto for two years, was essential if Germany was to become self-supporting. Soviet representatives refused to accept any currency reform unless they were provided with a separate set of plates to print the new bank notes. Their prior flagrant abuse of plates for printing the occupation currency of course made it unthinkable that we provide them with this ready means of wrecking the new currency at any time. The decision of the Western Allies to proceed was violently denounced by the Soviet representatives who walked out of the Allied Control Council, thus putting an end to the last symbol of allied cöoperation.

In recognition of the special Berlin situation, the currency reform introduced in Western Germany was not made effective immediately in West Berlin. However, the Soviet military government quickly introduced a new currency into their zone and into East Berlin, and this led necessarily to the inclusion of West Berlin in the currency reform already placed in effect in West Germany. At this time the city government still had its headquarters in East Berlin. After the blockade by Soviet forces in June 1948, it came under increasing pressure from the Communists so that it could not hold its deliberations except in disorder and under threat of physical violence; in September 1948 it moved from East to West Berlin.

The blockade of Berlin by the Soviets was not caused by their desire to take over the city, which was not then the asset it is today. It came primarily from their desire to weaken our position in Europe. With the end of the war we had rapidly demobilized our great military strength as evidence of our faith in the United Nations. We had worked diligently with our Allies and the Soviet Government to establish peace treaties with the countries which had fallen under Hitler's domination, and we had accepted coalition governments to rule these countries until free elections could be held. These free elections never took place, as the powerful Soviet armies were kept intact and the threat which they represented led one by one to Communist domination of the countries of Eastern Europe. This threat was stopped only in mid-Germany by a thin line of American, French and British soldiers.

Fortunately, it had become evident to us in 1947 that even though this line defended Western Europe against the threat of Soviet force, it could not forever stop Communist political penetration into the countries of Western Europe where the economic chaos which followed war had created a despair favorable to such penetration. Our leaders had the political wisdom and our people had the political maturity to recognize the full extent and danger of this threat and they extended financial and economic aid to the countries of Western Europe that wanted to regain their economic independence and their political stability. We did not make this offer as a challenge to Communism; it was made to all of the countries of Europe which needed and wanted our aid. When it was refused by the Communist countries, we still made it clear that our assistance was not to be used to strengthen the military defenses of Western Europe.

Thus, the Soviet Government was still not sure whether we intended to stay in Europe or not. It was fully aware of our traditional policy of remaining free of foreign entanglements and it determined to test our intent by a blockade of Berlin, which was obviously the most vulnerable and difficult spot for us to defend. I am sure the Soviet Government expected the Western Allies to withdraw from Berlin. The consequence would have been to destroy the confidence of a defenseless Western Europe in the determination of the United States to support and defend it until it could recover. We recognized immediately that the loss of Berlin might well mean the loss of Europe, and with the support of our British and French Allies we determined to maintain our position. Although we alone had atomic power at the time, we did not want to be the first to use force. An airlift supplying a city of over two million people enabled us to break the blockade without the use of force. Since that was a success, it renewed the confidence of Western Europe in the United States and in the will of its own peoples to remain free and independent. The immediate Communist threat to Western Europe had been halted, and when it became apparent that the unsuccessful blockade was no longer worth the risk, the Soviet Union lifted it in May 1949. Berlin had become a symbol of American determination to remain in Europe and of the will of the peoples of Western Europe to remain free.

II

The chain of events which had started with our economic aid program in 1947 and which was accelerated by the blockade did not end with the lifting of the blockade. In Berlin, the city government which had been forced by Communist pressures to move to West Berlin was confronted with the creation of a separate Communist-dominated puppet government in East Berlin. The free elections which were to take place under the city constitution in December 1948 were prohibited in East Berlin and the unhappy division of the city became a fact.

Meanwhile, in Western Europe the Allies had agreed to establish the Federal Republic of Germany and to convey to it a large degree of sovereignty [in 1949]. They then moved to form the North Atlantic Treaty Organization [also in 1949], dedicated to collective security against aggression, and in a few years the Federal Republic of Germany, with its sovereignty fully restored, was added as a member [in 1955]. Moreover, we began rebuilding our own military strength and encouraged the countries of Western Europe to rebuild theirs. The economic recovery sparked by our foreign-aid program moved more quickly than anyone had expected and brought to the countries of Western Europe a political stability which made new Communist gains most unlikely. As these countries regained full economic strength and political stability, the movement toward unity accelerated. The Soviet Government, already disturbed at the success of the Common Market, recognized that, once this unity had become a fact, it would end forever any prospect of Communist domination of Western Europe. Thus, once again it embarked in November 1958 on a new challenge to Europe and its growing unity. Once again the spot chosen for this challenge was Berlin.

For several years the Soviet Government, with the support of the Warsaw Pact countries, had been threatening to sign a peace treaty with East Germany under which, so it claimed, the rights exercised by the Allied powers under their agreements with the Soviet Government would be cancelled completely and the Western powers would have to negotiate with the East German régime some new arrangement for access to West Berlin. And then, of course, the Ulbricht government might simply deny that right of access! During this period of heightened tension the flow of refugees from East Germany through Berlin continued to increase until it threatened to undermine the already shaky East Germany economy. To survive, Ulbricht had to close this avenue of escape. So on August 13, 1961, the East German government, certainly with Soviet backing, erected a wall through the heart of Berlin to stop further escapes. The fact that this wall separated thousands of families and cut off thousands of workers in East Berlin from their jobs in West Berlin meant nothing to a ruthless régime which could survive only as a police state and which could not successfully establish

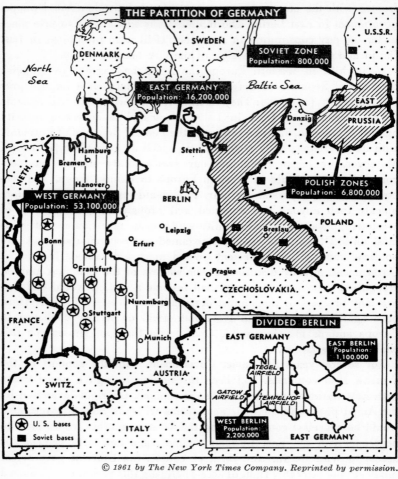

THE PARTITION OF GERMANY

SWEDEN

DENMARK

North
Sea

Baltic Sea

U.S.S.R.

SOVIET ZONE
Population: 800,000

EAST GERMANY
Population: 16,200,000

EAST
PRUSSIA

Danzig

NETH.

Hamburg
Bremen

Hanover

Stettin

WEST GERMANY
Population: 53,100,000

BERLIN

POLISH ZONES
Population: 6,800,000

Bonn

Leipzig

POLAND

Erfurt

Breslau

Frankfurt

Nuremberg

Prague

CZECHOSLOVAKIA

Stuttgart

FRANCE

Munich

DIVIDED BERLIN

AUSTRIA

EAST GERMANY

EAST BERLIN
Population:
1,100,000

SWITZ.

TEGEL
AIRFIELD

GATOW
AIRFIELD

TEMPELHOF
AIRFIELD

ITALY

WEST BERLIN
Population:
2,200,000

EAST GERMANY

⍟ U. S. bases
■ Soviet bases

GERMANY AND BERLIN
June 18, 1961

its full police control as long as an avenue of escape remained open.

Thus the Berlin Wall was built to serve two purposes: to stop the escape of refugees, and to create fear and confusion in Europe. The Communist leaders believed that a walled-in West Berlin could not endure and that its people would flee to safety in West Germany, leaving the Allies holding a hollow shell. Western Europe would lose not only its faith in the determination of the United States, but also its confidence in its own future, and the Soviet Government would be able to negotiate separate agreements with each individual Western European country. To add to the fears of West Berlin, continuing harassing actions were taken against Allied personnel; if these had been accepted without resistance, they would have demonstrated a lack of Allied determination to defend the city.

These harassments, it is important to note, were limited to actions against the Allies and were not directed against the movement of German goods and persons to and from the city. The first reason for this was that the movement of German goods and persons to and from West Berlin is not regulated by any of the existing agreements between the Allies and the Soviet Government; it is based on a trade agreement between the Federal Republic of Germany and the East German régime, whose economy is in very poor shape. The loss of this trade would be serious, even though a major effort is being made to reorient the East German economy to those of the Warsaw Pact countries. Secondly, the Soviet Government wanted to persuade the Federal Republic of Germany that the Allied powers would not defend Berlin and that West Germany and West Berlin would fare better by making a separate treaty with Russia than by continuing their close association with the West.

Fortunately, these were serious miscalculations. The United States and its Allies met the threats of the Soviet Government with sufficient show of force to convince it that harassing actions could be effective only if carried to lengths that might indeed cause war. The Federal Republic of Germany did not lose faith in the United States or its NATO Allies and refused to heed the Soviet overtures. The people of West Berlin, to whom the division of their city had been a great shock, realized that West Berlin must continue to grow and to prosper as a symbol of hope to their countrymen in East Germany and indeed to all enslaved peoples. The initial exodus of people and capital from the city stopped, and there was a renewal of the determination to keep West Berlin as the most important industrial center between Paris and Moscow and to add to its standing as the major cultural and educational center in Germany. Western Europe continued to prosper economically and the Common Market countries took the Soviet pressure as a warning to accelerate their progress toward full economic unity and the beginnings of political unity. . . .

. . . While the three Allied powers, the Federal Republic of Germany, and indeed all the countries in NATO, are pledged to the defense of

Berlin, there is still a lack of Allied unity as to the exact meaning of this pledge. We have been much more specific in our commitments than have our Allies. With them, of course, we hold firm to the commitment made to the Federal Republic of Germany when it was admitted into NATO that no other government would be recognized as having the right to speak for any of the German people until collectively they had selected a government of their own choice. We remain committed to the position taken at Potsdam that the final eastern boundary of Germany cannot be fixed except in a peace treaty to be negotiated with a united Germany. To the people of Berlin we have pledged ourselves to defend their freedom. Specifically, we are committed to maintain free access for Allied personnel and goods on the ground and for all who travel by air, and to protect the viability of West Berlin; and this viability obviously includes the safe movement of West German persons and goods in and out of West Berlin. We are committed to maintaining our garrison as long as the people of West Berlin want it there. We have also taken the position that there should be no lessening of the ties which now exist between West Berlin and West Germany. We have encouraged the investment of additional capital in West Berlin and the construction of new cultural and educational facilities. We hope and believe that full Allied agreement can be obtained, for we realize that a negotiated solution that is unacceptable to any ally cannot be accepted by the other allies. Otherwise, the Soviet Government might well accomplish its purpose of driving a wedge between the Allies which could threaten the continued existence of NATO and disrupt the progress toward political unity in Western Europe. Perhaps the most difficult question still to be resolved is what would constitute recognition of the illegal East German régime as a sovereign power. Here the views of the Federal Republic of Germany and the people of West Berlin must be taken into consideration in light of the commitments made when the Federal Republic became a part of NATO. . . .

It is difficult to know what will happen next in Berlin. Any interference with the movement of German persons and goods to and from Berlin that was serious enough to destroy or even threaten its economic life would lead at once to the cessation of all trade between East and West Germany and, if continued, would undoubtedly bring about other types of massive economic retaliation. Most of the actions directed against the Western Allies since August 13, 1961, have had as their purpose to bring about the West's recognition of East German authority in some form, and future Soviet actions can be expected to pursue the same purpose. It is not easy for us to understand the nature of these harassments, many of which seem too petty to warrant countermeasures; yet they have resulted in substantial deterioration of the Allied position in Berlin. Many people have wondered why it is important for us to refuse to show to East German police the credentials which we are prepared to show to Soviet soldiers. To accept this illogical demand would mean granting to Ulbricht's police the right to supervise, and hence to grant or deny, our right of access to West Berlin.

I believe that if further harassing tactics are undertaken by the Soviets to bring about panic in West Berlin they will have to include the use of force. This does not seem likely. However, we must be on our guard in Berlin to maintain the rights which we now possess and to prevent any encroachment by the puppet East German régime. There, as elsewhere, we must be prepared to interpose our troops step by step as threats materialize so that these threats can be carried out only by the use of force. Thus we shall place the responsibility for the use of force squarely on the shoulders of the Communist leaders. If this involves the risk of war it is a risk we must take. If we are less willing to risk war to save freedom than the Communists are to further their plan for world domination, we may be sure they will continue to gain.

There is little we can concede in Berlin although there is perhaps some room for trading concessions provided we get at least as much in exchange as we give. To make a compromise in which something of equal or superior value is gained in exchange for a concession is not in itself unworthy and may be wise. We must, however, establish clearly on the ground those principles which we will not compromise and for which we are prepared to fight, and we must be ready to use all of our strength and resources to protect these principles. Only in this way can an eventual solution be found which will enable the people of West Berlin to live in freedom and in economic independence.

We are in Berlin both by right of victory and by right of agreements under which we turned over to Soviet occupation a large part of what is now East Germany. It is unthinkable that we should let anyone take this right away from us. Moreover, if we remain true to our lifelong support of self-determination, we cannot allow the people of West Berlin to fall into the hands of a régime which they have rejected again and again in free elections. We must remain firm in Berlin, not just because of this obligation, not just because of our deep concern for its courageous people, but also because the Berlin crisis is really a European crisis and any threat to Western Europe is a direct threat to our own freedom and independence.

If we fail or falter in Berlin the present confidence under which Western Europe thrives and grows closer in political unity could well disappear in the minds and hearts of those people who seem today most apprehensive. No one in the West can afford to forget that the abandonment of Berlin might well lead to the permanent eclipse of democracy in Europe.

New Realities Require New Solutions

25 N. S. KHRUSHCHEV
On German Revanchism

. . . We cannot view with indifference how the aggressive quarters of the Western powers with Chancellor Adenauer's help are mobilising all material and spiritual forces of Western Germany for the preparation of a third world war. The Federal Republic of Germany is no longer the country which sixteen years ago bowed its head to the victors and pledged to follow the road of peace and democracy. Today the revenge-seekers of Western Germany have raised their heads; they have a mass army which is being trained and equipped for offensive operations. The Federal Republic of Germany has become a party to the North Atlantic military bloc directed against the Soviet Union and other socialist countries. Militarisation, an orgy of revengeful passions, the cult of hatred and enmity for communism and everything that is new and progressive, revival of pan-German traditions and sentiments — that is what determines today the face of the West German state.

By the will of the Western powers more inflammable material has been stockpiled in the centre of Europe than in any other region of the world. It is here that the flame of a world war again threatens to break out.

Nikita S. Khrushchev, until October 12, 1964 First Secretary of the Communist Party of the Soviet Union, Chairman of the Council of Ministers of the U.S.S.R., and member of the Supreme Soviet, gave this speech over radio and television on August 7, 1961. These excerpts are reprinted from *Soviet Policy on Germany: Speeches of N. S. Khrushchev and Documents of the Soviet Government June–September 1961*, Soviet Booklet No. 79 (London: Farleigh Press, Ltd., 1961) 38–48.

Since the Western powers have trampled underfoot the allied agreements on the demilitarisation and democratisation of Germany, only a peace treaty can forestall the dangerous development of German militarism and revenge-seeking. That is why we propose that the Soviet Union, the United States, Britain, France, Poland, Czechoslovakia, Yugoslavia, all the countries that took part in the war against Hitler Germany, on the one hand, and the German Democratic Republic and the Federal Republic of Germany as the lawful successors of the former German Reich on the other, conclude a peace treaty which would meet the legitimate interests of all parties. This would make it possible, observing all legal standards and international customs, completely to put an end to the state of war and to clear the way towards peace and peaceful co-existence in Europe.

The conclusion of a peace treaty with Germany would make it possible to normalise the situation in West Berlin and thus to remove grounds for a sharp clash between states. We must not permit West Berlin to become a kind of Sarajevo, the Serbian town, where rang out the shots heralding the outbreak of the First World War. Should West Berlin be made a free city, as the Soviet Union suggests, that would not affect either the interests or the prestige of any state. We propose that it should be stipulated in the peace treaty that the free city of West Berlin shall be granted freedom of communications with the outside world. We agree to the establishment of any and the most effective guarantees of the independent development and security of the free city of West Berlin.

Insisting on the conclusion of a peace treaty, the Soviet government declares: We stand for the freedom of West Berlin, but not on the basis of the maintenance of the military occupation status. It is common knowledge that occupation has never meant freedom and never will. For it is said, not without reason, that "it is not convenient to sit on bayonets."

All eastern neighbours of Germany agree on the need for concluding a German peace treaty and granting West Berlin the status of a free city. The government of the German Democratic Republic on whose territory West Berlin lies has also agreed to our proposals and has issued a statement to this effect. The Western powers replied by a refusal, but did not advance, however, their own proposals for a peace settlement with Germany. It would be well worthwhile for them to ponder over the dangerous development of Western Germany, and to look back, too. Is it not a fact that after the First World War the

Western powers also helped Germany in the hope that she would march towards the East? However, this did not prevent her from directing arms, in the first place, against those who helped the German militarists to get on their feet, and from unleashing her war for world domination.

Both the Yalta Declaration and the Potsdam Agreement clearly established that the occupation of Germany must help the German people to eradicate militarism and nazism. The Western powers violated all the principles regarding the occupation of Germany agreed upon at Yalta and Potsdam. The conspiracy by the Western powers late in 1946 on the merger of the two occupation zones was the beginning of the division of Germany and the restoration of the power of the militarists and revenge-seekers in Western Germany. The Western powers finally and unilaterally tore up the Potsdam Agreement by setting up a separate West German state, concluding the Paris Agreements and including Western Germany into NATO. It is not accidental that a special tripartite occupation status was established for West Berlin in this connection. By this tripartite occupation status the Western powers confirmed themselves that they had destroyed the foundation of their occupation régime in West Berlin under international law and that this régime rests solely on undisguised armed force.

The governments of the United States, Britain and France recently replied to the aide-memoire on the German question which was handed to President Kennedy at our meeting in Vienna. The Western powers once again seek to evade the conclusion of a peace treaty. They counterpose to it the idea of self-determination of the Germans and the reunification of Germany. It would be fine if genuine friends of freedom and the independence of peoples would advocate self-determination for the Germans. But it is strange, to say the least, to hear calls for self-determination from those who for centuries kept peoples in slavery and retaliated with bullet and whip to any attempt of the peoples to get rid of alien oppression and to achieve self-determination. . . .

The Soviet Union understands full well how dear the cause of Germany's national unity is to the German people. This unity can be achieved only by the Germans themselves. The Western powers want to persuade someone that they stand for reunification. But those who stood for German reunification would not reserve the right to intervene in what is exclusively the internal affair of the German people, as the governments of the United States, Britain and France did under the Paris agreements of 1954. Then the government of the Federal Republic of Germany willingly sacrificed the national interests of the Germans in exchange for participation in NATO.

It is significant that the government of the Federal Republic of Germany most persistently clamours for the revision of those articles of the Paris agreements which put some restrictions on armaments production in Western Germany. But it never raises the question of rescinding the articles which leave the Western powers the final say on matters of German reunification. And after all this the government of the Federal Republic of Germany and the Western powers pretend that they have no other concern except German unity, throwing in self-determination to boot.

What can't they in the West think up in order to distort our position on a peace treaty with Germany!

In his recent speech the President of the United States said that the United States faced a challenge of some kind from the Soviet Union, that there was a threat to the freedom of the people of West Berlin, that the Soviet Union was all but ready to use force. But he did not say a single word about the essence of the matter, about the fact that the Soviet Union proposes the conclusion of a peace treaty with Germany, and that it is striving to work out the terms of this treaty jointly with all states that took part in the war against Germany. After listening to the speech of their President, the American people might indeed get the idea that it is not the vestiges of the last war that we want to eliminate, but to start a third world war!

So what provisions of the Soviet draft of a peace treaty with Germany could give the American President a pretext to contend that the Soviet Union "threatens" to violate peace? Could it be those which envisage the renunciation of nuclear weapons by Germany, the putting of a legal seal on the existing German frontiers, the granting of full sovereignty to both German states and their admission to the United Nations?

If anyone did allow himself to resort to threats it was the United States President. He did not stop at presenting us with something in the way of an ultimatum in reply to the proposal to conclude a peace treaty with Germany. As if to reinforce his threats, the President announced an increase in the strength of the armed forces by 217,000 men and the American Senators started a fanfare about the need for mobilising certain classes of reservists.

Military hysteria is now being drummed up in the United States. At the same time, there are some who are conditioning the American people to the idea that there would be nothing particularly terrible even if war did break out. But it would be criminal thoughtlessness on the part of American leaders seriously to expect that after unleashing war against the socialist states it would be possible to keep it within certain bounds. . . .

Comrades, it must be said frankly that at present the Western powers are pushing the world to a dangerous brink, and the emergence of a threat of armed attack by imperialists on socialist states cannot be excluded.

I should like to assure you that the central committee of the C.P.S.U. and the Soviet government are doing and will continue to do everything in their power to prevent war from breaking out. But not everything depends on us. If a moment really comes when imperialism would dare to commit an act of madness and unleash a military gamble, a highly dangerous situation to the entire world would develop. We must be on our guard.

We are convinced that if the question of whether or not there would be a war depended on reasonable people in the western countries, they would not allow war to break out. But if people possessed by a suicidal mania take the upper hand, one cannot vouch for them. . . .

Let us see why the conclusion of a German peace treaty is so urgent for the consolidation of world peace! What would it mean if the conclusion of the German peace treaty was put off for several more years? That would mean conniving with aggressive forces, retreating under their pressure. Such a position would still further encourage NATO and the Bonn government to form more and more divisions in Western Germany, to equip them with atomic and thermonuclear weapons, to convert Western Germany into the main force for unleashing a new world war.

It is not because the Soviet Union is seeking some special privileges for itself that it is insisting on the conclusion of a German peace treaty without delay. We do not intend to seize West Berlin, we do not strive to alter the present frontiers of Germany, we do not encroach on Western Germany. The only thing we strive for is to strengthen peace through the conclusion of a German peace treaty.

If the Western powers reconsider their position, hearken to the voice of reason and express readiness to conclude a peace treaty together with us, we shall be only too glad. If they have any remarks to make or amendments to our draft peace treaty, or their own peace proposals on this question, we are ready not only to hear them but also to discuss most thoroughly all their considerations. We don't in the least want to impinge on the lawful interests of the Western powers, we are not seeking to change the state frontiers which took shape after the Second World War. This I proclaim once more today on behalf of the Soviet government.

If the Western powers persist in refusing to sign a German peace treaty, we shall have to settle this problem without them. The other day a conference of the First Secretaries of the Central Committees of Communist and Workers' Parties of the Warsaw Treaty countries took place in Moscow. They exchanged views on matters involved in preparing for the conclusion of a German peace treaty. The communiqué on this conference says that if the Western powers continue evading the conclusion of a German peace treaty, the states concerned will be compelled to conclude a peace treaty with the German Democratic Republic.

It goes without saying that in that case the German Democratic Republic would attain full sovereignty and therefore the question of the use of communications with West Berlin running across its territory would have to be decided by agreement with the G.D.R. government. As for the agreements between the U.S.S.R. and the Western powers on the question of access to West Berlin concluded during the occupation period, they would become null and void.

It would seem that all this is natural and quite fair and should not evoke objections or discontent on anyone's part. Is it not a fact that one cannot use communications on the territory of a state without dealing with the government of that state? Anything else would be absolutely abnormal, would run counter to the elementary principles of international law.

But here are American statesmen claiming that the Soviet Union, by concluding a peace treaty with the G.D.R., wants to humiliate in some way America, Britain and France, that it is impossible for representatives of America to ask Germans for permission to communicate with West Berlin, because they (the Americans), together with the peoples of the Soviet Union, fought against Hitler Germany. They even declare that the position of the U.S.S.R. on this question is against the principles of comradeship and is immoral!

But all this talk is absolutely inconsistent. Firstly, if we are to speak about ethics and legal grounds I should like to draw attention to an example set us by the United States and other allies of ours in the war against Japan, when they concluded a separate peace treaty with Japan and deprived us of all rights following from her surrender, including the right to take part in the agencies controlling Japan's fulfilment of the terms of surrender. So it would seem that there are two standards of ethics, two approaches — one for themselves and another for us.

Secondly, on what grounds do the Americans proclaim — a statesman of theirs told me this straight — that on the question of access to West Berlin they cannot deal with the G.D.R. government because, allegedly, this government was elected by an undemocratic procedure? But this is crude slander. However, there is no sense in arguing with the ruling circles of the United States on the principles of democracy. Our approaches to this matter are different. The United States, for instance, maintains friendly, allied relations with such "great democrats of the free world" as the fascists Franco and Salazar!

Incidentally, we, too, have to deal with governments with which we have no friendly relations. But we do deal with them. I can cite such an example in this respect. The Soviet Union had to enter into negotiations with the Federal Republic of Germany in order to ensure through train traffic on the Moscow-Paris line via the territory of Western Germany. And what came of it? We did come to terms and signed an appropriate agreement with the Federal government. At present the direct Moscow-Paris railway line is functioning effectively. In the given instance we acted as realists: although there had been a hard-fought war against Germany, it was over long ago and therefore it was necessary to normalize relations and reckon with the practical situation that existed.

The question of the right to dispose of the territory of some state or other is not a question for third countries to decide but for the people of the given state, and it must be settled by the government representing this people. . . . This is a real fact following from international law which cannot be disregarded.

I should like to repeat once more that by concluding a peace treaty with the G.D.R. we do not intend to infringe upon any lawful interests of the Western powers. Barring of access to West Berlin, a blockade of West Berlin, is entirely out of the question. All this is only a figment of the imagination of those who want to inflame the atmosphere in order to prepare war. But the peoples will see whose efforts are aimed at consolidating peace and whose at stirring up passions and preparing a third world war.

What is the point, anyhow? Why did the Western powers raise such an uproar in connection with our intention to turn over to the G.D.R. full sovereignty over communications leading to West Berlin after the conclusion of the peace treaty? Why are they even attempting to threaten us, and talking about a test of strength?

Taking a closer look at what is going on, one cannot fail to draw the conclusion that much more serious issues are at stake here. The imperialists do not want to recognise the fact that the German Democratic Republic, as a sovereign state, is entitled to exercise full control over its entire territory. The imperialists believe that the present situation provides them with a convenient loophole which enables them to obstruct the development of the G.D.R. as a socialist state.

They are using West Berlin as a base for subversion against the G.D.R. and other socialist countries, are sending over their agents, sharpening the military situation there. The imperialists think of nothing but ways and means of enlarging this loophole, of undermining the German Democratic Republic, but they are told: "Stop, gentlemen. We know full well what you want, what you are after. We shall sign a peace treaty and close your loophole into the G.D.R.!"

Someone might say, however: "But is it all that necessary to sign a peace treaty with Germany now? Why not wait another two or three years, or even more, for the conclusion of this treaty? Perhaps that would eliminate tension, remove the danger of war?" No, this line of action is impermissible. The truth must be faced: the Western powers are refusing to conclude a peace treaty with Germany on an agreed basis. At the same time they threaten with war and demand that we should not conclude a peace treaty with the G.D.R. They want nothing more nor less than to impose their will on the countries of the socialist camp.

To them the question of access to West Berlin and the question of the peace treaty as a whole is only a pretext. If we renounced the conclusion of a peace treaty, they would regard this as a strategic break-through and would widen the range of their demands at once. They would demand the elimination of the socialist system in the German Democratic Republic. Were they to attain that, too, they would of course set the task of annexing from Poland and Czechoslovakia the territories restored to them under the Potsdam agreement. And these are Polish and Czechoslovak lands. And were the Western powers to attain all this, they would advance their main claim, the abolition of the socialist system in all countries of the socialist camp. This is what they would like to do right now.

That is why the settlement of the question of a peace treaty cannot be postponed.

N. S. KHRUSHCHEV   *313*

The conclusion of a peace treaty with the G.D.R. will be of tremendous positive significance for the development of the entire international situation. Like the needle of a compass, the peace treaty will indicate to the entire German people the true direction of developments, ensuring for them peace, freedom, independence and sovereignty in the community of peace-loving peoples of Europe.

We address our people and tell them frankly about the present situation. You already know that the Soviet government had decided to increase expenditure for the defence of the country, to discontinue cuts in our armed forces which hitherto we had been carrying out unilaterally.

In a word, essential measures are being taken in order to make the defence might of the Soviet Union even stronger and more dependable. We shall watch the further developments and act in accordance with the existing situation. . . .

Why is the Soviet government considering such measures? These are measures in the nature of a reply. The United States is in fact carrying out mobilisation measures, is threatening to unleash a war. The allies of the United States in military aggressive blocs are supporting this dangerous course. The British government has announced that it will transfer additional troops to Western Germany; France is recalling troops from Algeria to Europe.

With such a situation taking shape, it would be impermissible for us to sit with our arms folded. The experience of history teaches: when an aggressor sees that no rebuff is given to him he grows more brazen, and in reverse, when he is given a rebuff, he calms down. It is this historical experience that should guide us in our actions. . . .

The Soviet Union does not want to go to war with anyone. We do not need anyone's territories, anyone's wealth. How could we covet anyone's wealth, considering that the Soviet Union possesses vast natural resources, a highly developed industry and wonderful cadres of scientists, engineers, technicians, workers and agriculturalists.

How many times, speaking both officially and unofficially have spokesmen of the Soviet government, of our public circles, told the United States of America, its government, its people: Let us trade, let us develop economic and cultural contacts. The United States is rich and strong, and we are rich and strong. When relations between us enter a calm channel, this benefits the peoples of all countries.

This is why we address the governments of the United States of America, Britain and France once more: Let us honestly meet round the conference table, let us not create war hysteria, let us clear the atmosphere, let us rely on reason and not on the power of thermonuclear weapons. . . .

We should like to address the peoples and governments of neutral countries and tell them now: You cannot stand aside. It is only through the efforts of all peoples that it will be possible to put the aggressor in a strait-jacket and rid mankind of the threat of a third world war. It is only through the efforts of all peoples and governments that the triumph of the great principles of peaceful coexistence can be assured, that agreement on general and complete disarmament under strict international control can be achieved. On the question whether or not there will be war neither governments nor peoples can remain neutral.

Such is the situation in which we are living today, such is the world of the middle of 1961, with its troubles and anxieties. Thinking whether there were such complex situations in past years, whether we succeeded in tiding them over in a reasonable way without war, historical experience indicates that such or similar situations have already occurred and reason has triumphed. The central committee of our Party and the Soviet government has done and will do everything in their power to see to it that the Soviet people, the peoples of all countries, tide over this tense moment, too, without war. We do not want war, but our people will not waver in the face of trials: to force they will reply with force, and will crush any aggressor.

We cannot allow ourselves to be complacent, we cannot expect everything to blow over by itself. Only energy, persistence, firm faith in the justice of our cause, devotion to the ideas of Marxism-Leninism and cohesion behind the Party and the Soviet government, only these qualities will lend us more and more strength, will help us to surmount obstacles. . . .

Let it be known to everyone that we shall continue to work persistently in the name of peace, that the entire Soviet people will raise their voice, will concentrate their efforts on preventing the outbreak of a new war, on preserving peace.

N. S. KHRUSHCHEV   *315*

The Nonaligned Nations and the Great Powers

26 L. ERVEN
About the Berlin Crisis

The main issue over which world relations have progressively deteriorated ever since the Soviet Government [in 1958] announced its
decision to sign a peace treaty with the German Democratic Republic
has been the question of Berlin. But the Berlin problem is certainly not
the most important or the most complex issue in the present dispute over
Germany, and the difficulties involved are hardly as great as to appear
insurmountable. Indeed, they are almost insignificant compared to what
their consequences could be if they were to be insisted upon. What is
more, both sides agree that a solution to the present Berlin crisis could
be found by way of negotiation. In spite of this, however, relations are
steadily deteriorating and demonstrations of strength are constantly
being staged on both sides, each believing that it will thereby convince
the other of the soundness of its arguments. Now, what is the essence
of the crisis and the danger which is so strongly emphasized in the
interested press?

The thesis of the Western Powers as regards Berlin has several
variants, but they can be reduced to two basic demands — one relating
to the essence of the matter, and the other concerning procedure. As
regards the former, the Western Allies insist on the maintenance and
defence of their present rights in West Berlin and on the preservation
of its present status. The Western rights include their military presence
in that part of the city, guarantees for the maintenance of the political
system established in it and free access to it, by land and air, over the
territory of the German Democratic Republic. With regard to procedure,
the Western Allies consider that, because communications to West Berlin
lead over the East German zone (not the state) which is under the
occupation of the Soviet Army, control over traffic across that territory
can only be carried out by organs of the Soviet Occupation Administration. The Western Allies have recognized the Government established
in their occupation zone and its sovereign authority over that territory.

L. Erven is a Yugoslav journalist and a regular contributor to the *Review of
International Affairs,* published in Belgrade; excerpts of this article are reprinted from this periodical, Vol. XII, No. 276 (October 5, 1961) 7–8.

But they have not recognized the Government set up on the same principle in the Soviet occupation zone and, consequently, do not recognize its right to control traffic over that territory. Why this attitude towards the question as to who has the right to supervise traffic with West Berlin has never led to complications before is primarily because the Soviet Government did not transfer the right of controlling traffic to the German Democratic Republic's Government earlier. It is this fact that has made it possible for the West to ignore the government of the German Democratic Republic for so long, the crossings and flights over German territory having been made under Soviet control. . . .

From the legal point of view and that of international law, the Western Allies may be right in the part of their thesis that relates to the essence of the matter. The status of West Berlin and the rights of the Western Allies on the basis of this status derive from earlier agreements, and they cannot be modified by the unilateral decision of any one of the parties to them. Consequently, it is possible to defend the thesis that an agreement signed between the Soviet Government and the German Democratic Republic's Government as *res inter alios acta* cannot affect the Western Allies' rights, established on another basis. But from what is known today, the Soviet thesis too is within the limits of these principles. While it does not deny the Allies' rights in Berlin legally, it does condemn them politically. The status of West Berlin and the Western Powers' rights relating to this status will remain unaffected, but after the signing of a peace treaty the Government of the German Democratic Republic will assume control over the traffic on its territory. The procedure and methods of control will then be a matter to be agreed upon between the Western Allies responsible for the traffic and the Government on whose territory the traffic takes place. Placed one against the other, or side by side, the Western and Eastern theses do not appear to be either irreconcilable or insoluble. This, however, is not the essence of the dispute. The two theses differ, greatly indeed, only as regards the future of the Berlin question and the final solution of the German problem, of which Berlin forms part. Yet, there is no serious ground for the present dispute arising from the Soviet decision to conclude a peace treaty with the German Democratic Republic, or its immediate effect on the Berlin question, since the Soviet Government recognizes the *status quo* in the rights of the Western Allies in West Berlin and the Government of German Democratic Republic does not refute it. The difficulty is over the procedure of control of the Allies' traffic with West Berlin, and accordingly concern the other part of the Western thesis.

In this the West is obviously in the wrong. There is not a single well-founded reason or legal basis to support the Western demand that the Soviet Government should control traffic in the German Democratic Republic indefinitely. In the first place, this aspect of control as well as all others has been regarded both by the East and the West as a right of the respective victorious power, and not as its obligation. Now, it will be admitted that the beneficiary of a right is free to renounce it to his own will. Had control been regarded as obligation and not a right of an occupation force the Western Allies would not have been able to renounce unilaterally their control in Western Germany as indeed they did. Consequently, the Soviet Government too, is fully entitled to give up this right and pass it over to the Government exercising sovereign authority over the territory concerned.

The transfer of the right of control will be effected on the basis of a separate peace treaty. While the war was still in progress, the Governments of the nations united in the anti-Hitlerite coalition pledged themselves in the Washington Declaration of the United Nations of January 1st, 1942, not to sign a separate truce or peace treaty with the enemy. These obligations, however, merely constituted a declaration of solidarity in days of war, and it was impossible to adhere to them in later, changed conditions. They were respected by neither the East nor the West. Today, one part of Germany has ceased to be the enemy of the Western side, while the other is no longer the enemy of the Eastern side. Having failed to agree on the terms of a peace treaty with Germany, the Western and the Eastern sides have each settled themselves in their own occupation area without having signed a formal peace treaty which would provide for a separate German state, with all the attributes of independence and sovereignty. It can now be argued that while the Soviet Government may be the first to sign a separate peace treaty with one of the two German States, the Western Allies' Government were the first to create a separate German State outside the scope of a peace treaty.

The West, which has no legal ground to object to the Soviet Government's decision to transfer the right of control to the Government of the German Democratic Republic, equally lacks the right to aspire to passage over the territory of the German Democratic Republic free of any control, on the grounds that the Soviet Government has renounced this control, and that the Western Allies do not recognize a legitimate

German Government on that territory. Such a position would be untenable on account of the fact that the interests and rights were territorially divided among the former allies, and because after the division of German territory and Berlin into occupation zones, neither the Western Allies nor the occupation administration in the Eastern zone retained or exercised any form of sovereign authority, so that such authorization could not be acquired simply by abolishing Soviet control either.

Whether the Western Allies reject or not the Soviet suggestion for a permanent solution of the Berlin problem, — a solution which there is still no ground to conclude that the Soviet Government intends to achieve unilaterally — the mere fact of the conclusion of a peace treaty with the German Democratic Republic does not presuppose any change in the status of West Berlin or the Rights of the Western Allies but only introduces certain alterations in their present attitude towards the German Democratic Republic Government. This calls for reasoning along the following lines.

By signing a peace treaty with the German Democratic Republic, the Soviet Government obviously cannot relieve the former of its obligation to respect the present status of West Berlin, which is not within the range of the Soviet occupation zone, since nobody can transfer to another any rights higher than he himself exercises. West Berlin is the consequence of war, and agreement among the victors in that war, and it remains beyond the unilateral authorization of any one side. The Soviet Government, however, is not called upon, obliged or authorized to regulate the future procedure of control of access to West Berlin on behalf of the Western Allies. Nor could such a clause affect or sanction future relations between the Government of the German Democratic Republic and the Western Allies, who would not be a party to such agreement. In order to settle the matter, the Western Allies would have to establish, in one way or another, legal contacts with the Government of the German Democratic Republic, and thereby, though perhaps merely *de facto* and implicitly, recognize the fact of its existence and the legitimacy of its functioning, which they have so far persistently denied or ignored. Western diplomacy will have to be very skilful indeed in order to succeed in finding a formula and an explanation which, at least apparently will not imply capitulation in the face of reality. Perhaps it is this element which is the most difficult in the entire Berlin crisis. Its essence is that it is too unpleasant to be suffered, and yet not serious enough to risk the danger of an open international conflict. . . .

The Berlin crisis will probably be eliminated, but the question of

Berlin will remain unsolved. The problem of Berlin, as a town divided in two parts, has become a political absurdity. The division of Berlin was explicable to a certain extent, if not justified, while the solution of the German problem through the creation of a unified German State appeared to be an immediate solution of the liquidation of war with Germany. With the creation of the two German States, however, this solution was postponed for an indefinite period and certainly was not expected to be settled at an early date. The prospects of a city divided into two politically and ideologically different parts, with different internal systems and different foreign-political orientation, are not at all encouraging. The present status of West Berlin and the position of the Western Allies, protracted over so long a period, are becoming more and more absurd. Perhaps it is this protracted state that will contribute first towards a more reasonable solution. For, in politics, it is absurdity more often than logic that helps to find a solution.

27 CONFERENCE OF NONALIGNED NATIONS
Declaration at Belgrade,[1] September 6, 1961

[Extracts] The conference of heads of state or Government of the following nonaligned countries: Afghanistan, Algeria, Burma, Cambodia, Ceylon, Congo, Cuba, Cyprus, Ethiopia, Ghana, Guinea, India, Indonesia, Iraq, Lebanon, Mali, Morocco, Nepal, Saudi Arabia, Somalia, Sudan, Tunisia, United Arab Republic, Yemen and Yugoslavia, and the following countries represented by observers: Bolivia, Brazil and Ecuador, was held in Belgrade from September 1 to 6, 1961, for the purpose of exchanging views on international problems with a view to contributing more effectively to world peace and security and peace for cooperation among peoples.

The heads of state or Government of the aforementioned countries have met at a moment when international events have taken a turn for the worse and when world peace is seriously threatened.

Deeply concerned for the future of peace, voicing the aspirations of the vast majority of people of the world, aware that, in our time, no people and no Government can or should abandon its responsibilities in regard to the safeguarding of world peace, the participating countries — having examined in detail, in an atmosphere of equality, sin-

---

[1] *The New York Times*, September 7, 1961.

cerity and mutual confidence, the current state of international relations and trends prevailing in the present-day world — make the following declaration:

* * *

27. The countries participating in the conference consider that the German problem is not merely a regional problem but liable to exercise a decisive influence on the course of future developments in international relations.

Concerned at the developments which have led to the present acute aggravation of the situation in regard to Germany and Berlin, the participating countries call upon all parties concerned not to resort to or threaten the use of force to solve the German question or the problem of Berlin, in accordance with the appeal made by the heads of state or governments on 5 September, 1961.

The heads of state or government of nonaligned countries resolve that this declaration should be forwarded to the United Nations and brought to the attention of all the member states of the world organization. The present declaration will also be forwarded to all the other states.

28 JOHN F. KENNEDY
Statement[1] at Conclusion of Visit of President Sukarno and President Keita, September 13, 1961

We have welcomed the visit of President Sukarno and President Keita on behalf of the nations which recently met in Belgrade, because we have viewed with growing concern the heightening tension in world affairs. Statesmen everywhere have an urgent responsibility to make every effort to preserve the peace and to solve their differences by peaceful means. This can be done if all approach these differences with full understanding of the rights, obligations and vital interests of others.

The situation in Berlin is filled with danger. I have made it clear that the position of the West and of the West Berliners will be defended. I have also made it clear that we are ready to discuss these matters with other governments, including the Government of the Soviet

[1] Statement released by the Office of the White House Press Secretary, September 13, 1961.

Union, and to search for the means to preserve an honorable peace. If that is the purpose on all sides, there is no need for resort to force.

The Foreign Ministers of the Western powers are meeting in Washington tomorrow. Next week the Secretary of State will head the United States Delegation to the General Assembly of the United Nations. We understand that Foreign Minister Gromyko will also be present. This will provide an opportunity for serious talks about Germany and other problems if the Soviet side proves willing. The channels of diplomacy are open for the exploration of constructive steps toward a reduction of tension. Other means are available when they can serve a useful purpose. Meanwhile, it is clearly of the utmost importance that there be no unilateral acts which will make peaceful progress impossible.

29 SOVIET FOREIGN MINISTRY
Statement,[1] September 14, 1961

President John Kennedy of the United States declared on September 13 that the United States was ready to enter into serious talks with the Soviet Union on the German and other problems if the Soviet side would show such a desire. He remarked that an opportunity for such talks would be provided in connection with the arrival in New York of the United States Secretary of State and the Foreign Minister of the U.S.S.R. for the sixteenth session of the United Nations General Assembly.

On the same day the British Foreign office welcomed this statement made by the United States President.

In view of the aforesaid desire of the Government of the United States and President Kennedy personally, and taking into consideration the positive attitude to this proposal of the Government of the United Kingdom, the Ministry of [Foreign] Affairs of the U.S.S.R. is authorized to state that Andrei Gromyko, the Minister of Foreign Affairs of the U.S.S.R. who will head the Soviet delegation to the sixteenth session of the United Nations General Assembly, is ready to enter into a relevant exchange of opinions with Dean Rusk, the Secretary of State of the United States.

The Soviet Government proceeds from the assumption, as its head

---

[1] Statement as issued at Moscow by Tass; *The New York Times*, September 15, 1961.

Nikita Khrushchev emphasized more than once, that the sides will display a serious attitude to the talks and will jointly search for a solution of the problem of the conclusion of a German peace treaty and a settlement on its basis of the situation in West Berlin.

Such is the Soviet Government's reply to the statement by the President of the United States and the British Foreign Office.

30 N. S. KHRUSHCHEV
Letter[1] to Prime Minister Nehru, September 16, 1961

Esteemed Mr. Prime Minister,

I have studied with close attention and interest the letter from the recently ended conference of the heads of state and government of 25 nonaligned nations, and I am deeply touched that you took the trouble to bring it to Moscow and deliver it to me in person. I express heartfelt gratitude to all the distinguished conference participants for this letter.

It is gratifying that the views of the Soviet Government on the present world situation coincide in many respects with the considerations set forth in the letter from the conference participants. I was also favorably impressed by the other conference documents full of concern for the destiny of the world.

How can one fail to rejoice that the governments of neutral states, whose population comprises a third of mankind, have lifted their voices in defense of peace and resolutely denounced the policy of war preparation. This will be of greater importance for world developments since the struggle to prevent war and consolidate peace was and remains the backbone of the entire foreign policy of the socialist states, which compose another third of mankind.

This is how broad the circle of states which regard concern for peace as their vital cause has become.

The conference's insistent call for the immediate conclusion of a treaty on general and complete disarmament will unquestionably attract the attention of all people. Yes, it is indeed the most pressing and urgent matter, as in it we have a reliable key to stable peace on earth. . . .

One cannot escape the thought that the policy of the NATO Powers is being increasingly influenced by circles which simply seek war, push

[1] Soviet Embassy at Washington, press release 201, September 22, 1961.

toward war. They apparently realize that time is working against the old imperialist system founded on domination and oppression, on flouting the basic rights of the peoples, and are considering if the time has not come to stake everything on an attempt to stop by war the great shifts that are taking place in the life of the peoples throughout the world, and especially on the continents which only yesterday groaned under the whip of colonial overseers. . . .

I should like to avail myself of this opportunity to declare that we are deeply convinced that the measures we have taken are in the interests not only of the Soviet people, of our allies, who like ourselves defend the cause of peace, the need for drawing a line through World War II and concluding a German peace treaty for this purpose, but also in the interests of all other peoples who crave a peaceful life. We express satisfaction with the fact that on the whole our defensive measures have been understood correctly by most broad public circles in many countries. . . .

In their letter the participants in the conference of noncommitted nations urge negotiation between the Great Powers to remove the danger of war. In particular they suggest direct talks between the Chairman of the U.S.S.R. Council of Ministers and the President of the United States of America.

What can one say to that? You know, of course, that the Soviet Union has always stood for a negotiated settlement of outstanding issues. Naturally now too we believe that talks between states, especially between the U.S.S.R. and the United States, as the mightiest and most influential countries, can and must play an important role in cleansing the international atmosphere. In the name of ensuring peace we are ready for talks any time, any place and at any level. . . .

A Confrontation in Latin America:
The 1962 Cuban Crisis

In Defense of Peace

3 | OSVALDO DORTICÓS TORRADO
    On Yankee Aggression

We have appeared before the United Nations specifically because surrounding the so-called Cuban problem or question, there is being created a series of circumstances and an entire atmosphere that, despite our will and . . . determination, transformed this question, or endeavors to transform it, into a case which implies . . . the threat of war. That is why I think it is appropriate for me . . . to put before you exactly what the Cuban situation is and what is the clear-cut position of the Revolutionary Government of Cuba. . . .

It is well to recall that the tense situation existing with relation to my country — that is, the tense situation existing between the United States and Cuba — began a long time before our revolutionary process acquired the socialist characteristics which it displays today.

The promulgation of our laws affecting the interests of the North American monopolies in our country and the promulgation of the

Osvaldo Torrado Dorticós, President of Cuba 1960–   , delivered this speech (from which excerpts are reprinted here) in the United Nations General Assembly on October 8, 1962.

agrarian reform law at a stage in our revolutionary development that was not yet in conformity with the principles of socialism — these sufficed to bring about the start of the aggressive actions against our country on the part of the Government of the United States. Then began the series of insolent diplomatic notes and the piratical incursions into the airspace over our territory. These were closely followed by the cutting of the sugar quota on the North American market and the discontinuance of the supply of oil to our country together with diplomatic activities aimed at the isolation of Cuba in the continent. In a word, there was a whole series of pointedly aggressive actions which gave rise to the present state of tension — I repeat — long before we proclaimed the socialist character of our revolution. . . .

The setting up and creation of exportable reserves to be ploughed into our agriculture, the development of our international trade, and the obviously necessary preliminary stages that will lead to a later industrial development, will entirely transform the characteristics and the structure of our underdeveloped industries. And hand in hand with this, there are measures of health improvement that are a privilege in this continent, and there are fundamental achievements in our educational policies. . . .

But we have had to carry this out beset at every step by multiple aggressions, and the very campaign against illiteracy in our country in itself had to go through some painful and dramatic moments, because the counterrevolutionary bands, organized and supplied by the Government of the United States, went so far as to murder teachers . . . who had gone out to our fields to wipe out the scourge of illiteracy from among our peasants.

All this progress, all this advance — which I think warrants the support and applause of those who may have differing ideological viewpoints from ourselves — all this success, and the enemies' failures, have also not taught the great lesson. The aggressions continued; the provocations continued; the training of counterrevolutionary groups on North American soil and on the soil of Caribbean countries continued; the provocations coming from the American naval base that is still rooted in our country continued; and the violation of the territorial waters and the airspace of my country continued. . . . American warships continue . . . lurking around our island, with their warlike aspect, and if not warlike as yet, at least with the aspect of preparing for war. . . .

This is taking place in the middle of, and surrounded by, a press, radio, and television campaign that fills the political stage of the United

States with a warlike hysteria. Together with this, there are the reiterated and insolent and insulting statements made by Senators and Representatives of the United States. . . .

We know that this atmosphere of hysteria, this campaign, this interminable series of slander and libel are part and parcel of pressures being exerted by the United States Government — and on it, too — so that once and for all there will be a decision taken for armed aggression, direct armed aggression, against my country. We know that these pressures exist. But we also believe that, when all is said and done, it is the United States Government itself that is responsible for the existence of these pressures, which are the inevitable corollary, the unavoidable result, of the policy of constant and permanent aggression and harassment that the United States Government has followed since the new Administration took over in this country. . . .

For example, not in the United Nations, but with obvious contempt for the United Nations, an invitation is sent out to the Foreign Ministers of Latin America to meet at the State Department. They are invited to conspire, to join in the domestic subversion of my country. Once again, the so-called inter-American system is wielded, that system which the United States Government itself has been good enough to disdain. Why was the system not invoked at the time of the aggression? Why was the system sidestepped at the time of the invasion of Playa Girón? Doubtless the same system will also be overlooked in the case of a new armed aggression against my country.

We have noticed that the Secretary of State of the United States is not very present at the United Nations. He has not shown any concern for disarmament, peace and tranquility. He has been outside our Organization, taken up with his work of subversion, of conspiracy against my country.

We also know full well that at the meeting of Latin American Foreign Ministers, respectable representatives of countries of Latin America despite their ideological differences with our revolution, defended the principles of nonintervention and the self-determination of peoples. From this rostrum I praise some of those Foreign Ministers. I challenge them to tell us what was discussed at that meeting, and what was discussed outside the meeting, too, so that one and all may know that it is not Cuba that is upsetting peace. . . .

Outside the Organization of American States, and without consulting any of the international bodies, showing contempt for one and all, the United States Government takes unilateral decisions and continues to engage in activities which flagrantly flout and violate the principles of the United Nations Charter. . . .

This is most bizarre. We can only turn to recent history. Was it perhaps Cuba that carried out aggressive or subversive activities against other countries of this hemisphere? No, it was quite the contrary. Cast your minds back for one moment and recall the invasion of Playa Girón, supported and organized, as President Kennedy himself admitted, by the Government of the United States. The mercenary troops were trained in a Central American country, and these troops set forth to invade another American nation. Was it Cuba that carried out subversive activities in this hemisphere, or was it rather these other Governments which, in one way or another, supported that invasion? . . . Cuba said in the past, and repeats it here, that we do not intend to carry out, nor shall we ever carry out, any activities extending the ideology of our own revolutionary process to any other countries or parts of this hemisphere.

But let us go back to this Joint Resolution of the United States of America in Congress assembled. In its third operative paragraph, it says:

"To work with the Organization of American States and with freedom-loving Cubans" — and may I enter a parenthesis here: Cuban counter-revolutionaries — "to support the aspirations of the Cuban people for self-determination."

Let us see what this means. Does it mean: to continue to support the subversive and aggressive activities against our country; to finance, to protect, to cover new piratical incursions on our shores; to finance and militarily to cover and protect new armed aggression against our country? . . .

In sub-paragraph b) of this Joint Resolution, the Congress of the United States of America states that it is determined "To prevent in Cuba the creation or use of an externally supported military capability endangering the security of the United States." In other words, the Congress of the United States *a priori* legitimizes the use of weapons, legitimizes armed aggression, against my country to prevent the setting up in Cuba of a military capacity that might endanger the security of the United States. Cuba endangering the security of a great power — Cuba, the victim of aggression, Cuba, the invaded country. This country, Cuba, fills the leaders of this great Power with panic, and their hearts tremble. I do not think I need to stress to you, gentlemen, the ludicrous nature of such a declaration. . . .

What can we say about this? We can say that Cuba has armed itself. We have a right to arm ourselves, to defend ourselves. . . . It is undeniable that we would have preferred to have channeled all those human and material resources, and all the energies that we have had to expend in the strengthening of our military defense, toward the development of our economy and the growth of our culture. We have armed ourselves against our will, against our better nature, because we were forced to. We were forced to strengthen our military defenses. Otherwise we should be jeopardizing and undermining the sovereignty of our country and its independence. We have armed because the Cuban people has the legitimate right, given to it by history itself, to defend its sovereign decisions. . . .

We were forced to arm — not to attack anyone, not to assault any nation, but only to defend ourselves. And to the Joint Resolution of the American Congress, we replied in due course with a declaration, agreed to by our own Council of Ministers:

Were the United States able to give Cuba effective guarantees and satisfactory proof concerning the integrity of Cuban territory, and were it to cease its subversive and counterrevolutionary activities against our people, then Cuba would not have to strengthen its defenses. Cuba would not even need an army, and all the resources that are used for this could be gratefully and happily invested in the economic and cultural development of the country.

. . . Furthermore, . . . we do not have to render an account to any power or to any foreign congress. While the dramatic circumstances require it, we shall continue to strengthen our military defense, to defend ourselves, not to attack anyone. If we are attacked, the enemy will meet the resistance of our weapons, but, at the same time, he will meet the resistance of our patriotism.

Obviously, the most serious point in this Resolution of the United States Congress is that it takes upon itself the so-called right unilaterally to decide when, in its opinion, these conditions set forth in the Joint Resolution have been fulfilled, at which time the United States will be able to carry out what previously was made legitimate, namely, aggression against my country. . . .

Surely this constitutes unheard-of contempt for international law, surely this is a barefaced flaunting of an international organization, surely this is a violation of the United Nations itself. By this artificial means, pretexts for aggression are prefabricated and a pretext for aggression is drawn from the supposed possibility that, by armed force, Cuba may try to take over the territory at present occupied by the United States military base at Guantanamo. We have stated more than once, and we repeat, our right to recover that territory. That region was torn from us by force, following an American incursion. International conferences, such as the Belgrade Conference, fully recognized and expressly stated the right of the Cuban Government to recover that territory. We know what that military and naval base is for today. It is to recruit and train counterrevolutionaries, to undertake acts of provocation against our frontier posts, to offend and insult our citizens, to infiltrate agents of conspiracy, espionage, and subversion into our territory. . . .

Where do we stand in the face of this aggressive conduct? From the beginning of the deterioration in Cuban-United States relations, Cuba has constantly been ready to negotiate, to negotiate through normal diplomatic channels or by any other adequate means, to negotiate the differences between the United States and Cuba. As our Council of Ministers stated in its declaration, Cuba was even prepared to indemnify American citizens and interests that might have been affected by the laws of the revolution, had it not been for the economic aggression, had the Government of the United States been ready to negotiate on a level commensurate with the sovereignty, dignity, and independence of our people. Our eagerness for a negotiated peaceful settlement was published many times. It was included in official notes sent to the United States Government. . . . The repeated refusals of the United States Government to negotiate proved conclusively that it had one single aim, namely, the overthrow of the Revolutionary Government of my country, the destruction of the Cuban Revolution and interference in the exercise of self-determination by our people. . . .

Cuba, and I say this clearly, has been ready and is ready to do everything we deem useful to lighten the tension that surrounds Cuban-American relations and that threatens world peace. Since Cuba is ready to do this, so we have a moral right to challenge the delegation of the United States Government to tell us whether that Government is equally ready to take the necessary and useful steps to overcome the present international tension which surrounds Cuba. Unfortunately, we are pessimistic, and we can anticipate the answer that will be given to us. . . . Unfortunately, and you can stand as witnesses, those steps will not be taken. . . .

It has been very often stated here that Cuba is not a bone of contention between the East and the West. Cuba is a problem of sovereignty and independence. . . . Cuba does not wish to add its name to the roster of those involved in the Cold War. Cuba only wishes to develop its economy and advance its culture and to plan and carry out a good future in peace.

Cuba is ready at any moment to prove its aims, and if it be true that there is no intention to attack our country, and if we can believe that to be a fact, then in this Assembly we urge the head of the United States delegation to be good enough to stand here and give us true guarantees that his Government does not intend to attack Cuba. But we urge him to give us these guarantees not only in words, but, over and above all, with deeds. Guarantees of words were offered to us before Playa Girón.

Let us not be told that the problem of Cuba is not a bilateral difference between Cuba and the United States, that Cuba is really a problem of the Hemisphere. We have said before and we have repeated, and we repeat once more, that we respect the principle of nonintervention. We have always proclaimed our respect for the sovereignty and independence of the rest of the countries of Latin America. Cuba is not a problem of this continent or of this Hemisphere. Underdevelopment is a Hemisphere problem; we are not a Hemisphere problem. . . . The United States is, because of its lack of respect for the sovereignty of other States. Cuba is no problem for the countries which respect it. Cuba can be a problem only for those Governments which fear it — not our capacity for subversion or for hypothetical aggressive intentions, but only the example of the Cuban Revolution. . . .

32 JOHN F. KENNEDY
The Soviet Threat to the Americas

Good evening, my fellow citizens. This Government, as promised, has maintained the closest surveillance of the Soviet military buildup on the island of Cuba. Within the past week unmistakable evidence has established the fact that a series of offensive missile sites is now in preparation on that imprisoned island. The purpose of these bases can be none other than to provide a nuclear strike capability against the Western Hemisphere.

Upon receiving the first preliminary hard information of this nature last Tuesday morning [October 16] at 9:00 A.M., I directed that our

The late President John F. Kennedy delivered this address from the White House by television and radio on October 22, 1962. The speech is reprinted from *The Department of State Bulletin*, XLVII, No. 1220 (November 12, 1962) 715–720.

surveillance be stepped up. And having now confirmed and completed our evaluation of the evidence and our decision on a course of action, this Government feels obliged to report this new crisis to you in fullest detail.

The characteristics of these new missile sites indicate two distinct types of installations. Several of them include medium-range ballistic missiles capable of carrying a nuclear warhead for a distance of more than 1,000 nautical miles. Each of these missiles, in short, is capable of striking Washington, D.C., the Panama Canal, Cape Canaveral, Mexico City, or any other city in the southeastern part of the United States, in Central America, or in the Caribbean area.

Additional sites not yet completed appear to be designed for inter-mediate-range ballistic missiles capable of traveling more than twice as far — and thus capable of striking most of the major cities in the Western Hemisphere, ranging as far north as Hudson Bay, Canada, and as far south as Lima, Peru. In addition, jet bombers, capable of carrying nuclear weapons, are now being uncrated and assembled in Cuba, while the necessary air bases are being prepared.

This urgent transformation of Cuba into an important strategic base — by the presence of these large, long-range, and clearly offensive weapons of sudden mass destruction — constitutes an explicit threat to the peace and security of all the Americas, in flagrant and deliberate defiance of the Rio Pact of 1947, the traditions of this nation and hemisphere, the Joint Resolution of the 87th Congress, the Charter of the United Nations, and my own public warnings to the Soviets on September 4 and 13.

This action also contradicts the repeated assurances of Soviet spokes-men, both publicly and privately delivered, that the arms buildup in Cuba would retain its original defensive character and that the Soviet Union had no need or desire to station strategic missiles on the territory of any other nation.

The size of this undertaking makes clear that it has been planned for some months. Yet only last month, after I had made clear the distinction between any introduction of ground-to-ground missiles and the existence of defensive antiaircraft missiles, the Soviet Government publicly stated on September 11 that, and I quote, "The armaments and military equipment sent to Cuba are designed exclusively for defensive purposes," and, and I quote the Soviet Government, "There is no need for the Soviet Government to shift its weapons for a retaliatory blow to any other country, for instance Cuba," and that, and I quote the Government, "The Soviet Union has so powerful rockets to carry these nuclear warheads that there is no need to search for sites for them beyond the boundaries of the Soviet Union." That statement was false.

Only last Thursday, as evidence of this rapid offensive buildup was already in my hand, Soviet Foreign Minister Gromyko told me in my office that he was instructed to make it clear once again, as he said his Government had already done, that Soviet assistance to Cuba, and I quote, "pursued solely the purpose of contributing to the defense capabilities of Cuba," that, and I quote him, "training by Soviet specialists of Cuban nationals in handling defensive armaments was by no means offensive," and that "if it were otherwise," Mr. Gromyko went on, "the Soviet Government would never become involved in rendering such assistance." That statement also was false.

Neither the United States of America nor the world community of nations can tolerate deliberate deception and offensive threats on the part of any nation, large or small. We no longer live in a world where only the actual firing of weapons represents a sufficient challenge to a nation's security to constitute maximum peril. Nuclear weapons are so destructive and ballistic missiles are so swift that any substantially increased possibility of their use or any sudden change in their deployment may well be regarded as a definite threat to peace.

For many years both the Soviet Union and the United States, recognizing this fact, have deployed strategic nuclear weapons with great care, never upsetting the precarious *status quo* which insured that these weapons would not be used in the absence of some vital challenge. Our own strategic missiles have never been transferred to the territory of any other nation under a cloak of secrecy and deception; and our history, unlike that of the Soviets since the end of World War II, demonstrates that we have no desire to dominate or conquer any other nation or impose our system upon its people. Nevertheless, American citizens have become adjusted to living daily on the bull's eye of Soviet missiles located inside the U.S.S.R. or in submarines.

In that sense, missiles in Cuba add to an already clear and present danger — although it should be noted the nations of Latin America have never previously been subjected to a potential nuclear threat.

But this secret, swift, and extraordinary buildup of Communist missiles — in an area well known to have a special and historical relationship to the United States and the nations of the Western Hemisphere, in violation of Soviet assurances, and in defiance of American and hemispheric policy — this sudden, clandestine decision to station strategic

CUBA

weapons for the first time outside of Soviet soil — is a deliberately provocative and unjustified change in the *status quo* which cannot be accepted by this country if our courage and our commitments are ever to be trusted again by either friend or foe.

The 1930's taught us a clear lesson: Aggressive conduct, if allowed to grow unchecked and unchallenged, ultimately leads to war. This nation is opposed to war. We are also true to our word. Our unswerving objective, therefore, must be to prevent the use of these missiles against this or any other country and to secure their withdrawal or elimination from the Western Hemisphere.

Our policy has been one of patience and restraint, as befits a peaceful and powerful nation, which leads a world-wide alliance. We have been determined not to be diverted from our central concerns by mere irritants and fanatics. But now further action is required — and it is under way; and these actions may only be the beginning. We will not prematurely or unnecessarily risk the costs of world-wide nuclear war in which even the fruits of victory would be ashes in our mouth — but neither will we shrink from that risk at any time it must be faced.

Acting, therefore, in the defense of our own security and of the entire Western Hemisphere, and under the authority entrusted to me by the Constitution as endorsed by the resolution of the Congress, I have directed that the following *initial* steps be taken immediately:

September 9, 1962

First: To halt this offensive buildup, a strict quarantine on all offensive military equipment under shipment to Cuba is being initiated. All ships of any kind bound for Cuba from whatever nation or port will, if found to contain cargoes of offensive weapons, be turned back. This quarantine will be extended, if needed, to other types of cargo and carriers. We are not at this time, however, denying the necessities of life as the Soviets attempted to do in their Berlin blockade of 1948.

Second: I have directed the continued and increased close surveillance of Cuba and its military buildup. The Foreign Ministers of the OAS in their communique of October 3 rejected secrecy on such matters in this hemisphere. Should these offensive military preparations continue, thus increasing the threat to the hemisphere, further action will be justified. I have directed the Armed Forces to prepare for any eventualities; and I trust that, in the interest of both the Cuban people and the Soviet technicians at the sites, the hazards to all concerned of continuing this threat will be recognized.

Third: It shall be the policy of this nation to regard any nuclear missile launched from Cuba against any nation in the Western Hemisphere as an attack by the Soviet Union on the United States, requiring a full retaliatory response upon the Soviet Union.

Fourth: As a necessary military precaution I have reinforced our base at Guantanamo, evacuated today the dependents of our personnel there, and ordered additional military units to be on a standby alert basis.

Fifth: We are calling tonight for an immediate meeting of the Organ of Consultation, under the Organization of American States, to consider this threat to hemispheric security and to invoke articles 6 and 8 of the Rio Treaty in support of all necessary action. The United Nations Charter allows for regional security arrangements — and the nations of this hemisphere decided long ago against the military presence of outside powers. Our other allies around the world have also been alerted.

Sixth: Under the Charter of the United Nations, we are asking tonight that an emergency meeting of the Security Council be convoked without delay to take action against this latest Soviet threat to world peace. Our resolution will call for the prompt dismantling and withdrawal of all offensive weapons in Cuba, under the supervision of U.N. observers, before the quarantine can be lifted.

Seventh and finally: I call upon Chairman Khrushchev to halt and eliminate this clandestine, reckless, and provocative threat to world peace and to stable relations between our two nations. I call upon him further to abandon this course of world domination and to join in an historic effort to end the perilous arms race and transform the history of man. He has an opportunity now to move the world back from the abyss of destruction — by returning to his Government's own words that it had no need to station missiles outside its own territory, and withdrawing these weapons from Cuba — by refraining from any action which will widen or deepen the present crisis — and then by participating in a search for peaceful and permanent solutions.

This nation is prepared to present its case against the Soviet threat to peace, and our own proposals for a peaceful world, at any time and in any forum — in the OAS, in the United Nations, or in any other meeting that could be useful — without limiting our freedom of action.

We have in the past made strenuous efforts to limit the spread of nuclear weapons. We have proposed the elimination of all arms and military bases in a fair and effective disarmament treaty. We are prepared to discuss new proposals for the removal of tensions on both sides — including the possibilities of a genuinely independent Cuba, free to determine its own destiny. We have no wish to war with the Soviet Union, for we are a peaceful people who desire to live in peace with all other peoples.

But it is difficult to settle or even discuss these problems in an atmosphere of intimidation. That is why this latest Soviet threat — or any other threat which is made either independently or in response to our actions this week — must and will be met with determination. Any hostile move anywhere in the world against the safety and freedom of peoples to whom we are committed — including in particular the brave people of West Berlin — will be met by whatever action is needed.

Finally, I want to say a few words to the captive people of Cuba, to whom this speech is being directly carried by special radio facilities. I speak to you as a friend, as one who knows of your deep attachment to your fatherland, as one who shares your aspirations for liberty and justice for all. And I have watched and the American people have watched with deep sorrow how your nationalist revolution was betrayed and how your fatherland fell under foreign domination. Now your leaders are no longer Cuban leaders inspired by Cuban ideals. They are puppets and agents of an international conspiracy which has turned Cuba against your friends and neighbors in the Americas — and turned it into the first Latin American country to become a target for nuclear war, the first Latin American country to have these weapons on its soil.

These new weapons are not in your interest. They contribute nothing to your peace and well-being. They can only undermine it. But this country has no wish to cause you to suffer or to impose any system upon you. We know that your lives and land are being used as pawns by those who deny you freedom.

Many times in the past the Cuban people have risen to throw out tyrants who destroyed their liberty. And I have no doubt that most Cubans today took forward to the time when they will be truly free — free from foreign domination, free to choose their own leaders, free to select their own system, free to own their own land, free to speak and write and worship without fear or degradation. And then shall Cuba be welcomed back to the society of free nations and to the associations of this hemisphere.

My fellow citizens, let no one doubt that this is a difficult and dangerous effort on which we have set out. No one can foresee precisely what course it will take or what costs or casualties will be incurred. Many months of sacrifice and self-discipline lie ahead — months in which both our patience and our will will be tested, months in which many threats and denunciations will keep us aware of our dangers. But the greatest danger of all would be to do nothing.

The path we have chosen for the present is full of hazards, as all paths are; but it is the one most consistent with our character and courage as a nation and our commitments around the world. The cost of freedom is always high — but Americans have always paid it. And one path we shall never choose, and that is the path of surrender or submission.

Our goal is not the victory of might but the vindication of right — not peace at the expense of freedom, but both peace *and* freedom, here in this hemisphere and, we hope, around the world. God willing, that goal will be achieved.

33 N. S. KHRUSHCHEV
Speech to the Supreme Soviet, December 12, 1962

Cuba is terrible to the imperialists because of her ideas. The imperialists do not want to reconcile themselves to the idea that little Cuba dared to live and develop independently as her people want to and not in the way which would please the American monopolies. But the question of how people are to live, what road they are to take, is an internal matter for each people!

Flouting generally accepted standards of international relations, the United States reactionary forces have been doing everything from the first day of the victory of the Cuban revolution to overthrow Cuba's revolutionary Government and to restore their domination there. They broke off diplomatic relations with Cuba, were and are conducting subversive activity, established an economic blockade of Cuba. Threatening to apply sanctions, the United States began pressing its allies not only to stop trading with Cuba but even not to make available ships for carrying food to Cuba from the socialist countries which came to the assistance of their brothers. This is an inhuman policy — a desire to starve a whole nation.

But even this seemed little to them. Assuming the functions of a policeman, they decided to take the road of the military suppression of the Cuban revolution. In other words, they wanted to usurp the right to the export of counterrevolution.

United States policy in relation to Cuba is the most unbridled, reactionary policy. To declare that Cuba allegedly threatens America or any

Former Soviet Premier N. S. Khrushchev delivered a speech before the Supreme Soviet on December 12, 1962. Excerpts are reprinted by permission from *The Worker Supplement*, December 23, 1962.

other country and to usurp on this plea a special right to act against Cuba is just monstrous.

Seeking to justify its aggressive actions, American reaction is repeating that the crisis in the Caribbean was created by Cuba herself, adding that blame rests also with the Soviet Union which shipped there rockets and IL-28 bombers.

But is this so? It is true that we carried weapons there at the request of the Cuban Government. But what motives guided us in doing that? Exclusively humanitarian motives — Cuba needed weapons as a means of containing the aggressors, and not as a means of attack. For Cuba was under a real threat of invasion. Piratical attacks were repeatedly made on her coasts, Havana was shelled, and airborne groups were dropped from planes to carry out sabotage.

A large-scale military invasion of Cuba by counterrevolutionary mercenaries was launched in Cuba in April of last year. This invasion was prepared and carried out with full support on the part of the United States.

Further events have shown that the failure of the invasion did not discourage the United States imperialists in their desire to strangle Cuba. They began preparing another attack. In the autumn of this year a very alarming situation was created. Everything indicated that the United States was preparing to attack the Cuban Republic with its own armed forces.

Revolutionary Cuba was compelled to take all measures to strengthen her defense. The Soviet Union helped her to build up a strong army standing guard over the achievements of the Cuban people. In view of the mounting threat from the United States, the Government of Cuba in the summer of this year requested the Soviet Government to render further assistance.

Agreement was reached on a number of new measures, including the stationing of several score Soviet IRBM's in Cuba. These weapons were to be in the hands of Soviet military.

What were the aims behind this decision? Naturally, neither we nor our Cuban friends had in mind that this small number of IRBM's, sent to Cuba, would be used for an attack on the United States or any other country.

Our aim was only to defend Cuba. We all saw how the American imperialists were sharpening knives, threatening Cuba with a massed attack. We could not remain impartial observers in face of this bandit-like policy, which is contrary to all standards of relations between states and the United Nations charter. We decided to extend a helping hand to Cuba. We saw a possibility of protecting the freedom-loving people of Cuba by installing rockets there so that the American imperialists, if they really decided to invade, would realize that the war which they threatened to start stood at their own borders, so that they would realize more realistically the dangers of thermonuclear war.

Such was the step we took because of the serious aggravation of the situation. We were confident that this step would bring the aggressors to their senses and that they — realizing that Cuba was not defenseless and that American imperialism was [not] all powerful — would be compelled to change their plans. Then the need for retaining rockets in Cuba would naturally disappear.

Indeed, had there been no threat of an invasion and had we had assurances that the United States would not invade Cuba, and would restrain its allies from this, had the United States guided itself by this course, there would have been no need for the stationing of our rockets in Cuba.

Some people pretend that the rockets were supplied by us for an attack on the United States. This, of course, is not wise reasoning. Why should we station rockets in Cuba for this purpose when we were and are able to strike from our own territory, possessing as we do the necessary number of intercontinental missiles of the required range and power?

We do not, in general, need military bases on foreign territories. It is known that we have dismantled all our bases abroad. All people who have any understanding of military matters know that in the age of intercontinental and global rockets, Cuba — this small, far-away island, which is only 50 kilometers wide in some places — is of no strategic importance for the defense of the Soviet Union. We stationed rockets in Cuba only for the defense of the Cuban Republic and not for an attack on the United States. Such a small country as Cuba cannot, naturally, build up such forces as could launch an offensive against such a big country as the United States.

Only those who are not "all there" in the head can claim that the Soviet Union chose Cuba as a springboard for an invasion of the American continent — the U.S. or countries of Latin America. If we wanted to start war against the U.S., we would not have agreed to dismantle the rockets installed in Cuba, which were ready for launching, for battle. We would have used them. But we did not because we did not pursue such aims.

Thus, all talk that Cuba was being converted into a base for an attack on the United States of America was a vicious lie. The purpose of this lie was to cover up the plans of aggression against Cuba. We are loyal to Lenin's principles of peaceful coexistence and hold that all disputes among states should be settled by peaceful means, by way of negotiations.

The developments in the Caribbean confirmed that there was a threat of such aggression. By the third week of October, a large-scale buildup of U.S. naval and air forces, paratroopers and marines began in the South of the U.S., on the approaches to Cuba. The U.S. Government sent reinforcements to its naval base at Guantanamo lying on Cuban territory. Big military maneuvers were announced in the Caribbean. In the course of these "maneuvers," a landing was to be made on Vieques Island. On October 22, Kennedy's Administration announced a quarantine of Cuba. The word "quarantine" by the way, was merely a figleaf in this case. Actually it was a blockade, piracy on the high seas.

The events developed rapidly. The American command alerted all its armed forces, including the troops in Europe, and also the Sixth Fleet in the Mediterranean and the Seventh Fleet based in the area of Taiwan.

Several airborne, infantry, and armored divisions, numbering some 100,000 men, were set aside for an attack on Cuba alone. Moreover, 183 warships with 85,000 naval personnel were moved to the shores of Cuba. The landing on Cuba was to be covered by several thousand military planes. Close to 20 per cent of all planes of the U.S. Strategic Air Command were kept in the air around the clock with atomic and hydrogen bombs on board. Reservists were called up.

On October 23, immediately after the United States proclaimed the blockade of Cuba, the Soviet Government, besides taking defensive measures, issued a Statement resolutely warning that the United States Government assumes a gave responsibility for the destinies of the peace and is recklessly playing with fire. We frankly told the United States President that we would not tolerate piratical actions by United States ships on the high seas and that we would take appropriate measures with this object in view.

At the same time, the Soviet Government urged all peoples to bar the road to the aggressors. Simultaneously it took certain steps in the United Nations. The peaceful initiative of the Soviet Government in settling the Cuban crisis met with full support by the Socialist countries and the peoples of most other United Nations member states.

However, the Government of the United States of America continued to aggravate the situation. United States militarist forces were pushing developments towards an attack on Cuba. On the morning of October 27, we received information from the Cuban comrades and from other sources which bluntly said that the invasion would be effected within the next two or three days. We assessed the messages received as a signal of utmost alarm. And this was a well founded alarm.

Immediate actions were needed to prevent an invasion of Cuba and to maintain peace. A message prompting a mutually acceptable solution was sent to the United States President. At that moment, it was not yet too late to put out the fuse of war which had already been lighted. Forwarding this message we took into consideration that the messages of the President himself expressed anxiety and the desire to find a way out of the obtaining situation. We declared that if the United States undertook not to invade Cuba and also would restrain other states allied with it from aggression against Cuba, the Soviet Union would be willing to remove from Cuba the weapons which the United States call "offensive."

The United States President replied by declaring that if the Soviet Government agreed to remove these weapons from Cuba the American Government would lift the quarantine, i.e., the blockade, and would give an assurance on renunciation of the invasion of Cuba both by the United States itself and other countries of the Western Hemisphere. The President declared quite definitely, and this is known to the whole world, that the United States will not attack Cuba and will restrain also its allies from such actions.

But we shipped our weapons to Cuba precisely for the prevention of aggression against her! That is why the Soviet Government reaffirmed its agreement to the removal of the ballistic rockets from Cuba.

From the above follow some evident results of the beginning of normalization of the situation over Cuba.

First, it has been possible to avert an invasion which threatened the Republic of Cuba from day to day, and, therefore, to avert an armed conflict, to overcome a crisis which was fraught with the danger of universal thermonuclear war.

Second, the United States publicly, before the entire world, pledged not to attack the Republic of Cuba, and to restrain its allies from doing so.

Third, the most rabid imperialists who staked on starting a world thermonuclear war over Cuba have not been able to do so. The Soviet Union, the forces of peace and socialism, proved that they are in a position to impose peace on the exponents of war.

Which side triumphed, who won? In this respect one may say that it was sanity, the cause of peace and security of peoples, that won. Both sides displayed a sober approach and took into account that unless such steps are taken as could help overcome the dangerous development of events, a World War III might break out.

As a result of mutual concessions and compromise, an understanding was reached which made it possible to remove dangerous tension, to normalize the situation.

It is, of course, true that the nature of imperialism has not changed. But imperialism today is no longer what it used to be when it held undivided sway over the world. If it is now a "paper" tiger, those who say this know that this "paper tiger" has atomic teeth. It can use them and it must not be treated lightly. It is possible in the relations with imperialist countries to make reciprocal compromises, while, on the other hand, having all means in order to smash the aggressors should they unleash war.

Some people confined themselves to cursing when difficult conditions were created for Cuba. Noisy statements do not reduce the strength of the imperialist forces and Cuba will hardly get any relief from this. The Soviet Union acted differently. It not only exposed the U.S. imperialist intrigues against Cuba. It sent its weapons to Cuba, sent people who were ready to lay down their lives in the struggle for defense of Cuba. And when Cuba was threatened, our men were ordered to defend Cuba against invasion, to fight shoulder to shoulder with the Cubans, to stand to death with the Cuban people. These are genuinely fraternal sentiments, fraternal attitudes, fraternal solidarity.

Of course, this was a critical time and the Government of the United States understood the possible development of events.

They understood that if their Armed forces set alight the conflagration of war in Cuba and both Cubans and Soviet men in Cuba would be burnt in this conflagration, no force could restrain the Soviet Union from striking a crushing retaliatory blow. That is why the United States Government displayed reason at the crucial moment of the crisis.

Offering a mutually acceptable solution, we took into consideration the whole complex of circumstances and war was averted. . . .

Macao is situated at the mouth of the Chuchiang River, on the coast of China. It is a small territory and not easily spotted on the map. The Portuguese leased it way back in the middle of the sixteenth century and in 1887 wrested it completely from China and made it their colony. There is also the British colony of Hongkong there. It lies in the delta of the Hsichiang River, literally below the heart of such an important town as Kwangchow (Canton). The smell coming from these places is by no means sweeter than that released by colonialism in Goa.

But no one will denounce the People's Republic of China for leaving intact these fragments of colonialism.

It would be wrong to prod China to actions of some kind which she considers untimely. If the Government of the People's Republic of China tolerates Macao and Hongkong it clearly has good reasons for doing so. Therefore it would be ridiculous to levy against it the accusation that this is a concession to British and Portuguese colonialism, that this is appeasement.

But maybe this is a retreat from Marxism-Leninism? Nothing of the kind. This means that the Government of the People's Republic of China takes into account the realities, the actual possibilities.

And this is by no means because the Chinese are less sensitive to colonialism than the Indians, that they are more tolerant towards Salazar than India.

Both sides made concessions. We withdrew ballistic rockets and agreed to withdraw IL-28 planes. This gives satisfaction to Americans. But both Cuba and the Soviet Union received satisfaction too: The American invasion of Cuba has been averted, the naval blockade lifted, the situation in the Caribbean area is returning to normalcy. People's Cuba exists, gains strength and develops under the leadership of its Revolutionary Government, its dauntless leader Fidel Castro.

We solemnly declare that the Soviet Union was and remains with Revolutionary Cuba. We shall continue to help the Cuban people to build a happy future. The solution of the crisis enables it to return to peaceful labor, but the forces of peace must remain vigilant.

The Soviet Government hopes that the United States will honor its pledges concerning Cuba. For violation of these pledges would be dangerous not only to the area in question — as it would inevitably produce a new conflict, create a new threat to peace — what is more, it would destroy all faith in such pledges, and this would preclude the use in the future of the method of peaceful adjustment which played a positive role in the solution of the crisis around Cuba.

We, for our part, will firmly abide by the agreement reached as a result of the exchange of messages with the President of the United States. We would like to make the clear warning that our commitments will stand so long as the other side, too, abides by theirs.

Peking versus "Adventurism" and "Capitulationism"

34 THE EDITORS OF "PEOPLE'S DAILY"
Editorial, December 31, 1962

Some people have repeatedly charged China with creating difficulties in the Caribbean situation and with wanting to plunge the world into a thermonuclear war. This slander against China is most malicious. . . .

How can one possibly interpret the resolute support which the Chinese people gave to the Cuban people in their struggle against international inspection and in defense of their sovereignty as meaning that China was opposed to peaceful coexistence or wanted to plunge others into a thermonuclear war? Does this mean that China, also, should have applied pressure on Cuba to force it to accept international inspection, and that only by so doing would China have conformed to this so-called "peaceful coexistence"? . . .

The Chinese Communist Party and the Chinese people have always maintained that the course of history is decided by the great strength of the masses of the people and not by any weapons. On more than one occasion we have made it clear that we neither called for the establishment of missile bases in Cuba nor obstructed the withdrawal of the so-called "offensive weapons" from Cuba. We have never considered that it was a Marxist-Leninist attitude to brandish nuclear weapons as a way of settling international disputes. Nor have we ever considered that the avoidance of a thermonuclear war in the Caribbean crisis was a "Munich." What we did strongly oppose, still strongly oppose, and will strongly oppose in the future is the sacrifice of another country's sovereignty as a means of reaching a compromise with imperialism. A compromise of this sort can only be regarded as 100 percent appeasement, a "Munich" pure and simple. . . .

The Chinese Communist Party and the Chinese Government have always stood for peaceful coexistence between countries with different social systems. China was an initiator of the well-known five principles of peaceful coexistence. On the basis of those principles, China has established friendly relations with many countries, concluded treaties of

These excerpts are taken from an editorial in the *People's Daily* (Peking), as reprinted in the *Peking Review*, VI, No. 1 (January 4, 1963) 9–21.

friendship or treaties of friendship and mutual nonaggression with Yemen, Burma, Nepal, Afghanistan, Guinea, Cambodia, Indonesia, and Ghana, and achieved a satisfactory settlement of boundary questions with Burma, Nepal, and other countries. No one can deny these facts.

Yet there are persons in the international Communist movement who vilify and attack China as being opposed to peaceful coexistence. The reason they do this is to cover up their own erroneous and anti-Marxist-Leninist views on this question.

On the question of peaceful coexistence, our differences with those who attack us are the following: We believe that Socialist countries should strive to establish normal international relations with countries having different social systems on the basis of mutual respect for territorial integrity and sovereignty, mutual nonaggression, mutual noninterference in domestic affairs, equality and mutual benefit, and peaceful coexistence.

So far as the Socialist countries are concerned, this presents no difficulties whatsoever. The obstacles come from imperialism and from the reactionaries of various countries. It is inconceivable that peaceful coexistence can be achieved without struggle. It is still less conceivable that the establishment of peaceful coexistence can eliminate class struggles in the world arena and can abolish the antagonism between the two systems, socialism and capitalism, and the antagonism between oppressed nations and oppressor nations.

The Moscow Statement of 1960 points out: "Peaceful coexistence of states does not imply renunciation of the class struggle as the revisionists claim. The coexistence of states with different social systems is a form of class struggle between socialism and capitalism." But Comrade Togliatti and those who attack China hold that through "peaceful coexistence" it is possible to "renew the structure of the whole world" and to establish "a new international order," to build throughout the world "an economic and social regime capable of satisfying all the aspirations of men and peoples to freedom, well-being, independence, all round development of a full respectful human personality, and peaceful cooperation of all states" and "a world without war."

This means that it is possible through "peaceful coexistence" to change a "world structure" in which there exists antagonism between systems of socialism and capitalism and between oppressed and oppressor nations; and that it is possible to eliminate all wars and to realize "a world without war" while imperialism and reactionaries still exist.

In taking this stand, Comrade Togliatti and other comrades have completely revised Lenin's principles for peaceful coexistence and discarded the Marxist-Leninist doctrine of class struggle; in reality they are substituting class collaboration for class struggle on a world scale, advocating a fusion of the Socialist and Capitalist systems. . . .

On peaceful coexistence we have another difference with those who are attacking us. We hold that the question of peaceful coexistence between countries with different social systems and the question of revolution by oppressed nations or by oppressed classes are two different kinds of questions, and not questions of the same kind.

The principle of peaceful coexistence can apply only to relations between countries with different social systems, not to relations between oppressed and oppressor nations, nor to relations between oppressed and oppressing classes. For an oppressed nation or people the question is one of waging a revolutionary struggle to overthrow the rule of imperialism and the reactionaries; it is not, and cannot be, a question of peaceful coexistence with imperialism and the reactionaries. . . .

We hold that the emergence of nuclear weapons has not changed and cannot change the fundamental Marxist-Leninist theory with regard to war and peace. In reality, the numerous wars that have broken out since the appearance of nuclear weapons have all been the continuation of politics, and we still have just and unjust wars. . . .

On the question of nuclear weapons and nuclear war, the second difference between us and those who attack the Chinese Communist Party is — whether one should view the future of mankind with pessimism or with revolutionary optimism.

Togliatti and certain others talk volubly about "the suicide of mankind" and the "total destruction" of mankind. They believe that "it is in vain even to discuss what could be the orientation of these fragments of survivals regarding social order."

We are firmly opposed to such pessimistic and despairing tunes. We believe that it is possible to attain a complete ban on nuclear weapons in the following circumstances: The Socialist camp has a great nuclear superiority: The people's struggles in various countries against nuclear weapons and nuclear war become broader and deeper; having further forfeited their nuclear superiority, the imperialists are compelled to realize that their policy of nuclear blackmail is no longer effective and that their launching of a nuclear war would only accelerate their own extinction. There are precedents for the outlawing of highly destructive weapons. One such precedent is the Geneva protocol concluded by various nations in 1925, for the prohibition of the use in war of asphyxiating, poisonous, or other gases, and of bacteriological methods of warfare.

If, after we have done everything possible to prevent a nuclear war, imperialism should nevertheless unleash nuclear war, without regard to any of the consequences, it would result in the extinction of imperialism and definitely not in the extinction of mankind. The Moscow Statement points out that "should the imperialist maniacs start war, the peoples will sweep capitalism out of existence and bury it." All Marxist-Leninists firmly believe that the course of history necessarily leads to the destruction of nuclear weapons by mankind, and will definitely not lead to the destruction of mankind by nuclear weapons. . . .

We hold that in order to mobilize the masses of the people against nuclear war and nuclear weapons it is necessary to inform them of the enormous destructiveness of these weapons. It would be patently wrong to underestimate this destructiveness. However, U.S. imperialism is doing its utmost to disseminate dread of nuclear weapons in pursuit of its policy of nuclear blackmail. In these circumstances, while Communists should point out the destructiveness of nuclear weapons, they should counter the U.S. imperialist propaganda of nuclear terror by stressing the possibility of outlawing them and preventing nuclear war, by transmuting the people's desire for peace into righteous indignation at the imperialist policy of nuclear threats and by leading the people to struggle against the U.S. imperialist policies of aggression and war. In no circumstances must Communists act as voluntary propagandists for the U.S. imperialist policy of nuclear blackmail. . . .

A Confrontation in Asia:

The Indian-Chinese Frontier

India's View

35 K. S. SHELVANKAR
China's Himalayan Frontiers: India's Attitude

The "boundary dispute" between India and China stems from the Chinese demand for over 50,000 square miles of territory adjoining the frontier, territory which is, and has always been, a part of India. . . . it is clear that if the Chinese demand were conceded, the Himalayas and its ancillary ranges would cease to be the frontier between the two great civilizations, as they have been for ages past, and Chinese power would reach down to the edge of the Indian plains.

This state of affairs is in sad contrast to the good relations which prevailed at first between the newly-independent India and the People's Republic of China. Looking back, the manner in which China abused India's confidence and eventually brought this claim into the open is itself significant — and disturbing.

For some years after independence India continued to believe, as on

K. S. Shelvankar is European correspondent for *The Hindu*. These excerpts, from *International Affairs* (London), XXXVIII, No. 4 (October 1962) 472–477, are reprinted by permission.

the record she had every right to do, that her northern boundary was firmly fixed and universally accepted, not least by China. But from 1954 onwards, there were a series of border violations. India promptly brought them to the attention of the Chinese Government, in polite and friendly terms. Her Notes went unanswered, or she was told that the area was in Chinese territory. Then, in 1958, came the incident at Longju, in the Eastern Sector, when the Chinese opened fire on the Indians and captured the outpost. This was followed in October by the attack on an Indian patrol near the Kongka Pass, in Ladakh, with some loss of life on the Indian side.

Even before 1954, India had begun to express concern at Chinese maps, which wrongly showed large tracts of Indian territory as belonging to China. Mr. Chou En-Lai was soothing, at first; he assured Mr. Nehru that these were reprints of old maps which would be revised in due course. In November 1958, in response to repeated Indian complaints, a somewhat enigmatic Chinese Note curtly informed India that "a new way of drawing the boundary would be decided upon" after "consultations." A few months later, in January 1959, China for the first time took exception to the Indian maps, "particularly in the Western sector." There was still no suggestion that the Chinese maps were correct. Finally, in September and December of that year, Mr. Chou En-Lai showed his hand: in two Notes to Delhi he repudiated the existing frontier along its whole length, and demanded that it be shifted back a considerable distance to the south and west.

Thus, towards the end of 1959, the two series of events came to a head more or less simultaneously — frontier incursions resulting in bloodshed on the one hand, and on the other the progressive deployment of China's unprecedented claims. It is easy to think of other ways, consistent with good will and good faith, in which the Chinese could have raised the problem, if there *was* a problem. They chose to hide their intentions and spring their claim only after breaching the frontier at various points from west to east — i.e. after committing aggression.

If there is anything more in the Chinese attitude and actions than a brutal challenge to a trial of strength, the issue turns on the exact location of the frontier, particularly as it was before the present troubles began. China agrees that there *is* a frontier, an ancient one, based on custom and tradition; and her conception of the frontier is not too far apart from that of India, in the Middle sector, i.e. between Kashmir and Nepal. But in the Western Sector, and in the East, the Chinese line cuts deep into India, taking in large chunks of Indian territory. To whom do these disputed areas belong? Who has the more valid title, India or China? Is it possible to weigh the charges and counter-charges, and form an unbiased judgment?

There is an enormous accumulation of evidence on this subject. But even a brief review of some of the more important facts and arguments involved should leave one in no doubt as to the merits of the case.[1] To start with, the Chinese have never been too clear or consistent in defining the frontier they are claiming. Not only are there no official maps published in China before the rise of the People's Republic which bear out their present claims, but even the maps issued since then do not uniformly show the same alignment.

In 1959, Mr. Chou En-Lai informed Mr. Nehru that their 1956 map should be taken as authoritative; but by 1960 the claims it reflected had already been exceeded, and this year Chinese troops are reported to be active further forward still. The Chinese have offered no explanation for changing and enlarging their claims in this fashion. Moreover, Chinese officials have been unable, in relation to a number of places, to describe even the physical features of the frontier claimed, or to give other details about it. In answer to Indian inquiries they have asserted both that the traditional boundary was "broad and approximate," and that it was "precise, clear and well-defined" — whichever served their polemical purpose at the moment.

This lack of precision, and indeed the ignorance shown, casts doubt from the outset on the genuineness of the claim — all the more because the Chinese insist that they have been in possession of these areas and administered them for centuries. They hold, in fact, that administration is the acid test for determining to which side an area belongs. Yet it is on this very point that their evidence is least convincing. They have not produced a single Chinese law or administrative regulation, let alone any Chinese local maps, referring specifically to any of the areas in dispute, nor any official document showing that the regional authorities in Sinkiang or Tibet even knew much about them. . . .

There are, besides, some damaging inconsistencies which cut at the root of the Chinese case. In the Western Sector, for example, the Chinese contend that Ladakh was a Tibetan province until it was taken by Gulab Singh in the 1840s. They have, however, also put forward a certain

[1] Apart from the Government of India's *White Papers*, the main source in English is a volume entitled *Report of the Officials of the Government of India and the People's Republic of China on the Boundary Question*, issued by the Ministry of External Affairs, New Delhi, February 1961.

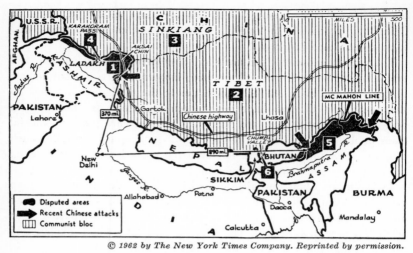

DISPUTED AREAS BETWEEN INDIA AND CHINA
November 11, 1962

alignment in this region as the traditional and historic boundary between India (Ladakh) and Tibet. The contradiction is obvious: if this
was indeed the old international frontier, Ladakh could not have been
a part of Tibet up till about 120 years ago. If, on the other hand, it is
represented as a feudal dividing line within Tibet, it was not an international frontier; if it has since become one, it cannot be called ancient
and traditional.

There is a similar lack of coherence in the Chinese stand on the
Eastern Sector. In contesting the significance of the so-called McMahon
Line, they claim that it marked the frontier *not* between Tibet and India
but between Tibet and China. Yet they have themselves expended much
ingenuity in trying to prove that this area, to the south of the McMahon
Line, had traditionally belonged to Tibet and was ruled from Lhasa.

In general, the Chinese allege that the Indian frontiers were fixed
arbitrarily by the British, as far north as they could reach in the days
of their maximum power, and that India is seeking to hold on to the
ill-gotten gains of the British imperialism. The implication is that these
areas were stolen from China by guile or force. Whatever one may
think of British policies, this particular charge does not bear examination. No doubt, India as a unified modern State took shape under
British rule; it is also undeniable that Central Asia in the last century

was the scene of rivalries and intrigues involving the three big Empires, Britain, Russia, and China. It is one thing to recognise these facts; quite another to assert that the *raison d'être* of India's present frontier is that it happens to mark the line at which British expansion, at the cost of China, suddenly came to a halt.

On the contrary, the extension of British power in these regions was part of the process of completing and consolidating the conquest of India. The Karakoram and Kuen Lun mountains formed the traditional boundary of Sinkiang — even Chinese documents testify to this — and the territory to the south of these ranges, including Aksai Chin, belonged to Kashmir and Ladakh, sovereign principalities, linked to India, but with a long history of their own. Ladakh was briefly and loosely associated with Tibet, but broke away nearly a thousand years ago, and, after a period of independence, it was absorbed into the Mughal Empire. Following the downfall of the Mughals, it was united with Kashmir in the new State which was founded about the middle of the nineteenth century. As a province of Kashmir, it subsequently came into India and has been under Indian (Kashmir) administration since then.

The history of the Eastern Sector is likewise far from being a blank, nor had it much in common with that of China. The region is inhabited mostly by people ethnically akin to the hill tribes in the interior of India, and owing no allegiance to Buddhism, or the Lamaist faith. For centuries it was under the sway of the Hindu dynasties of Eastern India. In the thirteenth century it passed to the Ahom rajas (who came from the Burmese hills, but were soon Hinduised), and later on from them to the British, who annexed the entire province (Assam) in 1842.

India's northern frontier is thus much older than the British raj, and was determined by geographical factors and a historical process which did no violence to Chinese rights. Besides, it was not an abstract or theoretical line, but one which marked the limits up to which India exercised effective jurisdiction — and still does, except where the Chinese have intruded. For obvious reasons, the administrative system could not be of the same type as in the plains. Ladakh is a desolate region, sparsely populated, if at all; and in the North-east, it was at one time thought best to leave the tribal organizations more or less intact, so far as their internal affairs were concerned.

Subject to these conditions, the Government of India discharged all the usual administrative functions, including the basic ones of tax collection and the maintenance of law and order. There are stacks of official records relating to the now disputed regions which provide ample proof of this. They contain a regular sequence of reports, stretching over decades, on such varied matters as revenue assessments and police activities, public works projects and the control of trade routes, as well as periodical census returns and detailed reports of survey and mapping operations. There is nothing comparable to this wealth of documented evidence to support the Chinese pretension to have administered these areas until recent times; indeed, there cannot be, for two different administrations could not have been functioning for long over the same territory.[2]

India's stand is further vindicated by several inter-governmental agreements, of different dates, and relating to different parts of the frontier. One of them, the tripartite Simla Agreement of 1914 between India, Tibet, and China has acquired special prominence in this controversy. Its effect was to formalize the traditional alignment in the Eastern Sector under the name of the McMahon Line. The Chinese now refuse to recognize the legality of this Line, not only because the Chinese Government of the time did not ratify the agreement, but on the grounds that Tibet was not competent to conclude treaties.

It would take us too far afield to pursue the ramifications of this question, but it should be said that here again we have one of those curious contradictions which make the Chinese case puzzling, if not incomprehensible. Much of the material that China herself relies upon to support her claims in the Middle and Western Sectors comes from the Tibetan archives, and carries the implication that that Government was entitled to negotiate with foreign powers. What is more, China has herself been ready, in other contexts, to recognize the validity of treaties signed by Tibet. Her 1956 Treaty with Nepal, for example, expressly abrogated the 1856 Treaty between Nepal and Tibet; and in 1947 she took the initiative in asking India whether, on attaining independence she assumed the treaty rights and obligations existing till then between India and Tibet. Such moves would surely have been superfluous if Tibet had been considered to have had no treaty-making powers.

It is true that this long frontier is not everywhere demarcated on the ground — the nature of the terrain precludes it. But it has solid support in history and tradition as well as in a series of inter-State transactions,

[2] During the joint meetings of Indian and Chinese officials in 1960, India proposed that the evidence submitted by each country on these and other points in dispute should be presented in a form which would enable a reader to view the two sets of submissions side by side and draw his own conclusions. The Chinese objected to the suggestion and it had to be abandoned.

and, above all, in India's unbroken record of continuous administrative control. Moreover, it conforms for the most part with the generally accepted principle that where a mountain range forms the boundary the watershed constitutes the natural frontier.

Allowing for some sporadic minor troubles and disagreements, this has been on the whole a remarkably peaceful frontier. There was never any secret about its location: it was defined from point to point, and publicly and authoritatively affirmed in different forms and on different occasions by the Government of India. It was also specifically referred to, at various dates, before and after independence, in communications between India and China, or India and Tibet. No government in Peking, or Lhasa, ever challenged it wholesale, or made even a perfunctory protest, or asked for clarification, or raised any serious complaint or objection. And it is only eight years since China signed a treaty with India, containing promises of mutual non-aggression and respect for territorial integrity. She was fully aware at the time of the extent of India's territory; but she did not reveal, and India was not to know, until five years later that she had her own plans for redrawing the map.

China's pretext for tearing up this treaty — and denying all the history it embodied, and the hopes it epitomized — is that there is no formal boundary agreement between the two Governments. This is true enough, but not in itself unusual, or an occasion for a dispute. Even today there are a large number of international boundaries which have not been defined in a boundary agreement; nor does a long-established frontier necessarily require treaty sanction to make it legally valid. Secondly, the Chinese argue that it has become necessary to delimit the India-China frontier through "joint surveys" and "consultations." This seems an innocuous proposal; but a procedure which may be excellent for negotiating minor adjustments of a recognized frontier is hardly relevant when what is at stake is the cession, under duress, of territory about the size of England.

Failing to secure India's compliance, China is endeavouring to seize what she can by force. At the same time, and contrary to her earlier attitude, she has begun to take a hand in the Kashmir dispute by siding with Pakistan, and is apparently preparing for a move into Sikkim and Bhutan by questioning India's responsibility for their defence and territorial integrity. This whole policy of violence and intimidation, with its ill-defined objectives, is buttressed by a ramshackle structure of highly questionable arguments, replete with contradictions, disdainful of facts and indifferent to the pledged word.

K. S. SHELVANKAR   *355*

It is hard to believe that it is only territorial ambition which is driving China on this course. Other explanations are, however, equally unsatisfactory. Retaliation for the hospitality extended by India to the Dalai Lama and other Tibetan refugees? Fear that some day India may allow these mountains to serve as a springboard for an attack on China? Some esoteric calculation deriving from the ideological divisions in the Communist world? Whatever the answer, and whatever the vicissitudes of the totally unnecessary conflict that has been thrust upon India, one thing is already patent and is bound to have a long-term effect: it has spread disillusionment and revulsion amongst a people who would have willingly lived in peace and friendship with their neighbour.

China's View

36 THE EDITORS OF "PEOPLE'S DAILY"
More on Nehru's Philosophy in the Light of the Sino-Indian
Boundary Question

For several years past, Nehru has obstinately rejected the Chinese Government's proposals for settling the Sino-Indian boundary question peacefully through negotiations, and has moved troops to make incursion after incursion into China's territory. On October 12, 1962, haughtily disregarding the consequences, he publicly ordered Indian troops to "free" the Chinese frontiers of the Chinese troops stationed there. Soon afterwards, aggressive Indian troops launched large-scale armed attacks in the eastern and western sectors of the Sino-Indian border, thus bringing about unprecedentedly serious military clashes between China and India.

China has always hoped to avert a conflict. Though we have every time exercised forbearance and self-restraint, what we least wished to see happen has come to pass. China has at no time occupied or intruded into any part of India; but the Indian side, which has occupied vast tracts of Chinese territory, has been using force deliberately to change the status quo of the boundary and extend its aggression. China has

This item was first printed in the *People's Daily* (Peking) on October 27, 1962, and is excerpted from *The Sino-Indian Boundary Question* (Peking: Foreign Languages Press, 1962) pp. 93–134.

proposed again and again to the Indian Government that negotiations be held at once without pre-conditions, but Nehru wants the Chinese troops to withdraw from large tracts of their own territory as a precondition for negotiations, thereby rejecting negotiations without any reason whatsoever.

Even after Indian troops had intruded time and again into Chinese territory in the western and eastern sectors of the Sino-Indian border, China's frontier guards strictly observed the People's Government's order to avoid conflict. They never fired the first shot even when under their very eyes they saw their territory being occupied by Indian troops, their links with the rear being cut off by Indian troops and strongpoints for aggression being set up by Indian troops only a few hundred metres, a few dozens of metres or only a few metres away. It was in these circumstances that many of our soldiers were killed or wounded by Indian troops. The Nehru government took our forbearance and self-restraint as an indication that we are weak and can be bullied. Indian troops pressed forward steadily and penetrated deep into Chinese territory, set up more and more strongpoints for aggression and advance positions. After completing their dispositions for attack, the Indian troops finally launched a large-scale general offensive on October 20, 1962. ...

I

Just like their interference in China's Tibet, the provoking of Sino-Indian border incidents by India's ruling circles headed by Nehru, leading to their large-scale armed invasion of China, is no accident. Both are determined by the class nature of India's big bourgeoisie and big landlords, whose interests are closely connected with those of the imperialists.

To explain this point, let us recall some history.

Readers are invited first to read the following passage written by Nehru in his book *The Discovery of India* in 1944.

Though not directly a Pacific state, India will inevitably exercise an important influence there. India will also develop as the centre of economic and political activity in the Indian Ocean area, in southeast Asia and right up to the Middle East. Her position gives an economic and strategic importance in a part of the world which is going to develop rapidly in the future. If there is a regional grouping of the countries bordering on the Indian Ocean on either side of India, — Iran, Iraq, Afghanistan, India, Ceylon, Burma, Malaya, Siam, Java, etc.,— present-day minority problems will disappear, or at any rate will have to be considered in an entirely different context.

. . . the small national state is doomed. It may survive as a cultural autonomous area but not as an independent political unit. (Meridian Books, Ltd., London, 3rd ed., 1951, pp. 510–511.)

This enables one to understand two things clearly:

First, the goal pursued by this ambitious Nehru is the establishment of a great empire unprecedented in India's history. The sphere of influence of this great empire would include a series of countries from the Middle East to Southeast Asia and far surpass that of the colonial system set up in Asia in the past by the British empire.

Secondly, this ambitious Nehru believes that when the "regional grouping" with India as "the centre of economic and political activity" is set up, or, in other words, when the great empire conceived by Nehru comes into existence, "minority problems will disappear" in this region. According to Nehru, "the small national state is doomed," "it may survive as a cultural autonomous area but not as an independent political unit." In a word, it can only be a vassal in Nehru's great empire.

These remarks of Nehru were written 18 years ago. Nehru was dreaming of a great Indian empire long before India's proclamation of independence. This is a real "discovery" of the expansionism of the big bourgeoisie and big landlords of India!

These reactionary, expansionist ideas of India's big bourgeoisie and big landlords form an important part of Nehru's philosophy.

India was for a long time under the colonial rule of British imperialism. The Indian big bourgeoisie is a parasitic class fostered by British imperialism. Its close relations with the British monopoly capitalist class are clearly seen in Nehru. . . . Fostered by the British imperialists, the economic forces of the Indian big bourgeoisie began to develop already under British rule. They developed further, especially after World War I and during World War II. As a large country, India was regarded by British imperialism as the economic and political centre of its colonial system in the East, and was called "the brightest jewel in Britain's imperial crown." This view of India held by the British imperialists was an insult to the great Indian people. However, the Indian big bourgeoisie which depended on British imperialism took over from the British imperialists this concept of India as "the centre of Asia," and this has led to Nehru's idea of a great Indian empire.

After India's proclamation of independence, the Indian ruling circles headed by Nehru inherited and have tried their best to preserve the bequests of the British colonialist rulers; they have become increasingly brazen in carrying out their chauvinistic and expansionist policy. India is the only country in Asia that has a protectorate. The Indian ruling circles have used every means to interfere in the internal and external affairs of countries around India, to control their economy and trade and demand their absolute obedience. This is no secret. . . .

It is precisely from this expansionist viewpoint that the Indian ruling circles regard China's Tibet region as an Indian sphere of influence. In 1950, the fourth year after India's proclamation of independence, the Nehru government interfered with the Chinese people's liberation of their own territory of Tibet; later they instigated and backed up the treason and rebellion of the reactionary clique of the upper social strata in the Tibet region. It was from this series of concrete facts that we began to understand Nehru's expansionist "philosophy."

Nehru's policy on the Sino-Indian boundary question and the whole process by which he engineered the Sino-Indian border clashes have shed new light on the expansionist philosophy of the Indian big bourgeoisie and big landlords.

It is a well-known fact that the Sino-Indian boundary has never been formally delimited, but that there is a traditional customary line which was formed long ago in the course of history. While it ruled over India, British imperialism continuously nibbled away at China's Tibet region, and so boundary disputes were of constant occurrence.

After India's declaration of independence, the Indian ruling circles regarded as India's both those Chinese territories which the British imperialists had occupied and those which they had wanted to occupy but had not yet succeeded in occupying. Taking advantage of the fact that in the period soon after its founding New China had no time to attend to the Sino-Indian boundary and that China's security was seriously threatened by the U.S. imperialist war of aggression in Korea, the Indian ruling circles brazenly did what the British imperialists had not dared to do. They forcibly pushed India's northeastern boundary up to the vicinity of the so-called McMahon Line which China has never recognized, and occupied more than 90,000 square kilometres of China's territory. Following on this, they further crossed the so-called McMahon Line at several points.

Again and again, the Indian authorities arbitrarily and unilaterally altered their map of the Sino-Indian boundary to incorporate large areas of Chinese territory into India. On March 22, 1959, that is, the fourth day after the reactionary clique of the upper social strata of the Tibet region started its rebellion and attacked the People's Liberation Army units in Lhasa, Nehru hastily wrote to Premier Chou En-lai, making territorial claims on China based on the map arbitrarily altered by the Indian Government. He demanded that there should be incorporated into India not only the more than 90,000 square kilometres of Chinese territory in the eastern sector and the about 2,000 square kilometres of Chinese territory in the middle sector, but also the over 33,000 square kilometres of Chinese territory in the western sector which had always been under Chinese jurisdiction. The total area so claimed is about the size of China's Fukien Province, or four times as large as Belgium or three times as large as Holland.

Over the past three years and more, Nehru has insisted that China should accept these preposterous demands, and has persisted in the use of force continually to invade and occupy Chinese territory. Nehru's expansionist "philosophy" boils down to this: "The places I have occupied are mine, and so are those I intend to occupy. Since I was able to occupy an inch of your territory yesterday, I certainly can occupy a yard of your territory today." This is downright unreasonable, not to say utterly outrageous!

The Chinese Government has consistently held that, since China and India suffered the common experience of being subjected to imperialist aggression, with India having gained her independence and New China founded, they ought to live together amicably and settle their differences through peaceful negotiation. After the Indian side provoked border clashes in 1959, the Chinese Government on its own initiative proposed that talks be held between the Prime Ministers of the two countries. In April 1960, Premier Chou En-lai visited New Delhi with the desire to settle the Sino-Indian boundary question, held talks with Indian Prime Minister Nehru and made earnest efforts to reach a preliminary agreement that would help settle the boundary question. However, there was no response from the Indian side to the sincere efforts of the Chinese side. The subsequent meeting of Chinese and Indian officials also failed to produce the results as it should.

The Chinese Government has always held that even if the two sides cannot for the time being achieve a meeting of minds on the boundary question, this should not lead to border clashes. As early as in 1959, it repeatedly proposed that the armed forces of each side withdraw 20 kilometres all along the border and stop border patrols so as to disengage the armed forces of the two sides and avoid clashes.

After the Indian side rejected these proposals, China unilaterally stopped patrols on its side of the border in the hope of helping to ease the border tension. The adoption of this measure by China led for a certain period to some relaxation in the situation along the Sino-Indian border. If the Indian side had agreed to the Chinese proposal about the withdrawal of 20 kilometres by each side, it would certainly have been possible to avert the military clashes between the armed forces of the two sides. Even when the Indian side did not agree to withdraw, these clashes would have been prevented if the Indian side had respected the situation of the unilateral Chinese cessation of patrols, instead of taking the opportunity to invade China.

Contrary to our expectations, the Nehru government, taking advantage of the unilateral cessation of patrols by the Chinese frontier guards, pressed forward steadily all along the Sino-Indian border, penetrated deep into China's territory, built scores of aggressive strongpoints and continuously provoked armed clashes, first in the western and middle, then in the eastern, sectors. It is easy for everybody to see that China has tried by every means to disengage the armed forces of the two sides along the Sino-Indian border, while the Nehru government, bent on maintaining military contact, has again and again adamantly rejected China's reasonable proposals.

Disengagement of the armed forces of the two sides would not prejudice the stand of either side on the boundary question; it is a practical and most effective method of avoiding border clashes. . . . For what reason has the Nehru government adamantly rejected the Chinese proposals and insisted on maintaining military contact? Does it not prove that the Nehru government is deliberately prolonging tension along the Sino-Indian border? Does it not prove that the Nehru government intends to provoke armed clashes at any time in order to attain its ulterior aims?

While pushing ahead with his policy of expansion into China, Nehru has continually used the boundary question to fan the anti-China campaign. A rough count shows that in the past three years Nehru has made more than 300 speeches on the Sino-Indian boundary question on various occasions. He used the most malicious language in attacking and vilifying China. . . .

In addition to slandering China noisily on the boundary question, Nehru has mounted a series of attacks on China on much broader terms than the boundary question; he has also tried in the most despicable and sinister way to sow dissension between China and other countries.

Witness the following statements made by Nehru:

. . . a strong China is normally an expansionist China. Throughout history that has been the case. . . . [China's] population problem itself, the vast population and the pace of growth greater than almost any in the wide world . . . is likely to create a very novel and very dangerous situation not so much for India, but for India also. (November 27, 1959)

Even if we are a hundred per cent friendly with them, the fact remains that here is a mighty power sitting on our borders. That in itself changes the whole context, the whole picture. . . . So, we face each other there and we face each other in anger at the present moment and we are going to face each other, not today or tomorrow but for hundreds and hundreds of years. (December 9, 1959)

Basically, the truth is that China has been expansionist whenever it is strong. But the present push also comes from rapid developments inside China, in military and industrial fields. (December 12, 1959)

A tremendous explosive situation is being created by the rapid growth, industrially, and in the population of China. (May 2, 1960)

China is at present affected by bad harvests, which is a terrible thing considering the growing population of China. . . . The continuous failure of harvest has created an explosive situation. (May 2, 1962)

What was Nehru driving at in these utterances? The meaning is:

(1) China should not become a strong country, but should remain a poor and weak one with an impoverished people beset with internal and external troubles, as it was under the rule of imperialism, feudalism and bureaucrat-capitalism before liberation.

(2) China should not develop its industry rapidly, but should continue to be a backward, agricultural China.

(3) China should not have the necessary military strength to consolidate its national defence, though it is faced with aggression and the threat of war by U.S. imperialism.

(4) China should not have so large a population, still less increase its population.

(5) When China develops its industry rapidly, this will create "an explosive situation"; when China is affected by bad harvests, this too will create "an explosive situation."

(6) China should not be India's neighbour but should change its geographical location.

In short, it seems to Nehru that, unless China ceases to exist or moves to some other place, China and India are bound to "face each other in anger . . . not today or tomorrow but for hundreds and hundreds of years"!

We would like to ask: Whose spokesman is Nehru? Is he speaking for the Indian people? By no means. The Indian people, including the Indian workers, peasants, politically conscious intellectuals, oppressed national bourgeois elements and open-minded public men and women, that is, the overwhelming majority of Indians, wish to have as their neighbour a powerful, prosperous, industrialized and populous China, where the people are the masters of the country, just as the Chinese people wish to have as their neighbour a powerful, prosperous, industrialized and populous India, where the people are the masters of the country. . . .

It is true that historically China had been powerful and had invaded other countries, but that occurred under the rule of the feudal landlord class. China today is a people's China, a socialist China; its social system is fundamentally different and its domestic and foreign policies are fundamentally different. A powerful and prosperous socialist China can only benefit peace and the fight against aggression, can only be of benefit to its neighbours and to friendship among nations. It will be a disadvantage only to the imperialists, who are aggressive by nature, and their lackeys. People throughout the world who love peace and uphold justice hold this view, and they believe that the more powerful and prosperous socialist China is, the better. Since Nehru so hates to see a powerful and prosperous socialist China, where does he stand? Has he not put himself in the very position of a lackey of the imperialists?

China has all along pursued a foreign policy of peace and stood for peaceful co-existence of the basis of the Five Principles with all countries having different social systems. China has signed treaties of friendship and mutual non-aggression or treaties of peace and friendship with the Yemen, Burma, Nepal, Afghanistan, Guinea, Cambodia, Indonesia and Ghana. Similarly, China has always wanted to live in friendship with India. But Nehru, on the contrary, holds that India cannot live in friendship with China. This runs diametrically counter to the wishes and interests of the Indian people. . . .

Nehru has his ulterior motives for refusing to make it up on the Sino-Indian boundary question over a long period of time and continuously creating tension. To understand this, we must examine the class nature of the Indian big bourgeoisie and big landlords, represented by Nehru, whose interests are closely connected with those of the imperialists; we must examine the needs of the Indian reactionary ruling circles, represented by Nehru, in domestic and international politics; and we must broadly examine the background, both inside India and in regard to its international relations.

II

Everybody knows that before India attained independence, Indian society was colonial and feudal. The task facing the Indian people then was to carry out a national and democratic revolution against imperialism and feudalism. The great Indian people waged a prolonged and heroic struggle for the complete overthrow of the colonial rule of British imperialism in India and for the genuine independence and liberation of their homeland. After World War II, the national-liberation movements carried on by the people of the Asian and African countries rose to unprecedented heights and the anti-British struggle of the Indian people forged ahead. The Chinese people have always had a deep sympathy and high respect for the national-liberation struggle of the Indian people.

The Indian bourgeoisie has a blood relationship with the British bourgeoisie and the Indian landlord class. But in its own class interests, it participated in the Indian people's anti-British movement in varying degrees at different stages. However, as determined by its economic position, it had from the very beginning a strong tendency towards compromise in the anti-British movement. In the national-independence struggle, the Indian bourgeoisie, on the one hand, carried on the non-co-operation movement against British colonial rule and, on the other hand, used the slogan of "non-violence" to paralyse the people's struggle and restrain their revolutionary movement. . . .

In the course of the Indian people's movement for national independence, the British colonialists reached a compromise with the big bourgeoisie and big landlords of India and turned over their rule to the latter on conditions which basically kept the economic interests of the British colonialists intact. Thus, the fruits gained by the Indian people in their anti-British struggle were seized by India's big bourgeoisie and big landlords.

After India proclaimed independence, Nehru, who once represented to a certain degree the interests of the Indian national bourgeoisie, gradually, as the class struggle developed at home and abroad, became a loyal representative of the interests of the big bourgeoisie and big landlords of India. The Nehru government has substituted reactionary nationalism for the anti-imperialist and anti-feudal revolution, and tied up ever more closely with the imperialist and feudal forces. Of course, certain contradictions exist between the big bourgeoisie and big land-lords of India and foreign monopoly capital; their interests are not in full conformity. Therefore, when the contradictions between imperialism and the Indian nation sharpened, the Nehru government, under the pressure of the masses of the people, showed a certain degree of differ-ence from imperialism. But the class nature and economic status of the Indian big bourgeoisie and big landlords determine that the Nehru government depends on and serves imperialism more and more.

India did not gain economic independence after its proclamation of independence. Imperialism still retained its economic influence in India. Foreign capital still controlled many vital branches of the country's economy. . . .

In recent years, foreign investments in India have increased rap-idly. . . .

At the same time, the number of enterprises which are jointly owned by Indian monopoly capital and foreign capital but are actually under the control of the latter has also grown rapidly. . . .

What is particularly noteworthy is the fact that the Nehru government has become increasingly dependent on foreign aid. Foreign aid ac-counted for 9.6 per cent of the total expenditure under India's first "Five-Year Plan," and for 20.6 per cent under its second "Five-Year Plan"; it will account for 30 per cent under its third "Five-Year Plan." . . .

The overwhelming proportion of the large amount of foreign aid received by the Nehru government consists of loans repayable with interest and the annual interest rates of these loans run as high as 6 per cent. As a result, India's foreign debt burden grows heavier and heavier, and it becomes more and more difficult for India to extricate itself from its economic dependence on foreign monopoly capital. . . .

These facts prove that economically India has not freed itself from dependence on imperialism. What is different from the past is that U.S. imperialism is gradually taking over British imperialism's monopoly position in India.

The Nehru government has established a number of state-run enter-prises in India which are nothing but state-capitalist enterprises domi-nated by the big bourgeoisie and big landlords and actually dependent on foreign monopoly capital. Such enterprises serve the interests of both the Indian big bourgeoisie and big landlords and of foreign monopoly capital. They are in essence Indian bureaucrat-monopoly capital. This bureaucrat-monopoly capital is developing. It develops at the expense of the Indian working people and even of the capitalist owners of small and medium-sized enterprises.

. . . The living standards of the masses of the Indian working people have been deteriorating in recent years. Prices have been mounting continuously and taxes increasing. The number of unemployed has become even greater, and the life of the peasantry has become increasingly hard.

India's basic domestic problem is the peasant problem.

When they ruled India, the British imperialists, to serve their predatory ends, supported the feudal landlord class. The broad masses of the peasants were subjected to all kinds of exploitation in the form of rent, taxes and usury, and agricultural production was at a very low level.

After India's proclamation of independence, what policies did the Nehru government adopt in regard to the feudal land system?

In the initial period of India's independence, the Nehru government, in order to meet the needs of the big bourgeoisie and big landlords to concentrate power in their own hands, abolished the political privileges of some of the local feudal princes and the *zamindari* (tax-farming) privileges of some landlords, but the Indian feudal land system as a whole was preserved. . . . As a result of large-scale evictions by feudal landlords in recent years, the concentration of landholdings has become even greater, and the ranks of the poor peasants and farm labourers have grown. . . .

In view of the economic conditions mentioned above, the prestige of Nehru's Congress Party is steadily declining and dissatisfaction and opposition among the broad masses of the people are growing day by day. Big-scale strikes and struggles for land have flared up one after another. . . .

Nehru constantly slanders Marxism as being "out of date," and trumpets his philosophy of "tolerance," "non-violence" and "peaceful means." But the realities in India are a great mockery of Nehru's philosophy. Nehru is indeed tolerant of imperialism and the feudal forces, but he is not "tolerant" of the people and the progressive forces, nor "non-violent" towards them. Since coming to power, Nehru has used violence to suppress the masses of the people and the progressive forces; he has become an old hand at opposing communism and the people. . . .

The Nehru government has used extremely brutal measures of repression against many minority nationalities in India. Available information indicates that over many years Indian troops have killed tens of thousands of the Naga people in the northeastern part of India, and detained tens of thousands more in concentration camps. . . .

In view of the actual economic and political conditions in India, is not the building of a "socialist pattern of society" in India, as advertised by Nehru, an out-and-out hoax? Commenting on Nehru's "socialism," Harriman, spokesman for the U.S. monopoly groups, said on May 4, 1959:

> I think it is a good thing that they [Nehru and his like] use this word ["socialism"]. It is a highly popular word among the Asian peoples, where capitalism has become closely identified — almost synonymous — with colonialism. The Indians [Nehru and his like] have taken it away from the Communists.

Harriman's remarks serve to show what Nehru's "socialist pattern of society" is really worth.

With any country, a given foreign policy is necessarily the continuation of a given domestic policy. Like its domestic policy, the foreign policy of the Nehru government reflects its reactionary class nature.

At one time some actions of the Nehru government were helpful to world peace. It refused to join imperialist military blocs, turned down the imperialists' request to establish military bases in India and declared its adherence to the policy of "non-alignment." It stood for peaceful co-existence with socialist countries and joined with China in initiating the Five Principles of Peaceful Co-existence. The Nehru government played a positive role in sponsoring the first Asian-African Conference.

However, even in that period, Nehru seldom voiced opposition to the major acts of aggression by imperialism, especially U.S. imperialism, but constantly came out against the just struggles of the people of various countries, and against the socialist countries. On many important, key international questions, Nehru always stood on the side of imperialism, adopting in the main a policy of "criticizing in a small way and helping in a big way" towards imperialism. For instance, during the war of U.S. aggression in Korea, the Indian Government put forward a proposal in the United Nations in November 1952 supporting the forcible retention of prisoners of war by the United States. In the counter-revolutionary event in Hungary in 1956, Nehru maliciously slandered the Soviet Union and attacked the Hungarian Workers' and Peasants' Revolutionary Government. . . .

With the changes in India's domestic situation and in the international situation in recent years, Nehru's foreign policy has leaned more markedly towards imperialism. In addition to intensifying its suppression and exploitation of the people, the Nehru government has relied more and more on imperialism as a major means of coping with the economic and political difficulties and crisis in India. On the other hand, in order to counter the influence of socialism, particularly that of China's socialist revolution and socialist construction, to obstruct the national-liberation movements, and to fight for control of the intermediate zone, U.S. imperialism now attaches greater importance to the part played by Nehru. . . . As a result, the United States in recent years has made an obvious shift in policy towards the Nehru government, from opposition to its policy of "non-alignment" to vigorous aid to it; from refusal to supply machinery and technical knowledge to the Indian big bourgeoisie to co-operation with the Indian big bourgeoisie in joint exploitation of the Indian people. In a word, U.S. imperialism pursues a policy of paying a high price to buy over the Indian big bourgeoisie represented by Nehru. . . .

It is precisely in these circumstances that over the past few years Nehru has practically thrown away the banner of opposition to imperialism and colonialism in international affairs, suited himself to the needs of U.S. imperialism, become a busy spokesman for U.S. imperialism, and even openly made Indian troops serve as an international policeman for U.S. imperialism in its suppression of national-liberation movements. . . .

It is at a time when their entire home and foreign policy has become increasingly reactionary that the Indian ruling circles headed by Nehru have instigated the Sino-Indian boundary dispute, provoked China and finally launched large-scale armed attacks on China. They have done so because they persist in their expansionist policy and, by sabotaging Sino-Indian friendship and stirring up reactionary nationalist sentiment, attempt to divert the attention of the Indian people, intensify their exploitation and oppression of the people, and strike at the progressive forces. They have done so, too, because they seek to make use of the anti-China campaign to curry favour with U.S. imperialism and get more U.S. dollars. In a word, in the effort to satisfy their own needs and meet the demands of U.S. imperialism, the Indian ruling circles headed by Nehru have become pawns in the international anti-China campaign. This is the root cause and background of the Sino-Indian boundary dispute.

III

Marxism-Leninism points out that bourgeois nationalism under different conditions plays different historical roles. Marxism-Leninism has always drawn a distinction between the nationalism of the oppressed nations and the nationalism of the oppressor nations, between progressive nationalism and reactionary nationalism, and has taken different attitudes to nationalism in accordance with this distinction.

In modern times, the national bourgeoisie of the colonial and semi-colonial countries, because of their contradictions with imperialism and the feudal forces, can take part in the revolutionary anti-imperialist and anti-feudal struggle during certain historical periods and to a certain extent and therefore play a progressive role in history. . . .

On the other hand, however, the bourgeoisie of the colonial and semi-colonial countries, because of their class status, are inclined to compromise with imperialism and feudalism and are liable to waver in the anti-imperialist and anti-feudal revolution. One section, the big bourgeoisie, whose interests are closely connected with those of imperialism and domestic feudalism, are the reactionaries among the bourgeoisie. Under certain circumstances, they may join in the national-independence movement, but, when the broad masses of the people have really stood up, when class struggle becomes acute, and when bribed by the imperialists, then they will betray the revolution, suppressing the people, the Communist Party and the progressive forces at home and selling out to imperialism and opposing the socialist countries abroad. . . .

The basis of China's policy towards the nationalist countries is this: Firstly, the primary common task of China and all nationalist countries is to oppose their common enemy, imperialism and colonialism, especially U.S. imperialism. They must support one another in the struggle against imperialism and colonialism. China has consistently given active support to the struggles waged by the various nationalist states against imperialism and colonialism. Secondly, it is necessary and entirely possible to establish and develop, between China and these countries, relations of friendship and co-operation on the basis of the Five Principles of Peaceful Co-existence. It is necessary and fully possible to bring about, through friendly consultations, a reasonable settlement of all outstanding disputes among them in accordance with the Five Principles and the Bandung spirit.

Similarly, China stands firm in its desire to live for ever in friendship

THE EDITORS OF "PEOPLE'S DAILY" *369*

with India. The relations of friendship between the Chinese and Indian peoples have a long history. There is no conflict of vital interests whatsoever between the peoples of our two countries. In 1954 the Chinese and Indian Governments jointly initiated the Five Principles of Peaceful Co-existence, and Sino-Indian relations built on this basis were once good. The Chinese people, like the Indian people, cherish the memory of the years when the two countries were on friendly terms.

But even in the period when Sino-Indian relations were good, the Indian ruling circles headed by Nehru repeatedly interfered in China's Tibet and harboured expansionist designs against it, thereby revealing their policy of reactionary nationalism. Then in 1959, when the rebellion of the reactionary clique of the upper social strata of the Tibet region instigated by Nehru was defeated and Nehru's expansionist dream about Tibet was shattered, and when he took a more reactionary line in all his home and foreign policies, Nehru immediately turned against his friend, switching from professions of friendship for China to frantic hostility to China. . . .

The principles of China's foreign policy and of its policy towards India have been consistent. Despite incessant provocation by the Nehru government, China has still maintained an attitude of maximum restraint. It was only when the Nehru government had recently launched large-scale attacks that China was compelled to hit back in self-defence to safeguard its sovereignty and territorial integrity and to repulse the attacks of the Indian reactionaries. It is fully necessary and perfectly just for China to do so, and it is the least a sovereign state should do. It is precisely for this reason that China has won the sympathy and support of the people of the world who cherish peace and uphold justice. . . .

Marxism-Leninism always points to the fact that bourgeois nationalism and proletarian internationalism are two different world outlooks which represent two different classes and are fundamentally antagonistic to each other. While supporting progressive bourgeois nationalism, Communists must draw a clear-cut line between themselves and bourgeois nationalism and must combat reactionary bourgeois nationalism. . . .

As a result of the reactionary policy of the Nehru government, the Indian Communist Party and progressive forces are subjected to persecution. Each time the Nehru government stirs up an anti-China campaign, he simultaneously mounts an attack on the Indian Communist Party and progressive forces. But large numbers of Indian Communists and progressives, large numbers of politically conscious workers, peasants, intellectuals and fair-minded people have not been deceived by the reactionary propaganda of the Indian ruling circles, nor have they knuckled under to their attacks. . . .

In this article while we touch upon certain aspects of the Indian situation in order to elucidate the truth, we are not in any way gloating over the difficulties facing the Indian people. On the contrary, we note with profound concern that since the Nehru government has ignored the sufferings of the Indian people and has aggravated the tension on the Sino-Indian border and extended the armed clashes, the Indian people will have to shoulder heavy military burdens in addition to the exorbitant taxes which are weighing down on them. Indian soldiers are being used as pawns by the selfish ruling circles; they are making meaningless sacrifices in the border clashes, while India's big capitalists and big landlords are taking the opportunity to feather their own nests. The Chinese people have the greatest sympathy for the broad masses of India's working people who are facing such sufferings. The Chinese people sincerely hope that the Indian people will free themselves from this lot, that India will soon become prosperous and strong, and that the Indian people will be able to lead a happy life. We hope to see a progressive, democratic and strong India on the continent of Asia.

We are firmly convinced that all complicated questions between China and India left over from history can be settled, provided friendly negotiations are conducted in accordance with the Five Principles of Peaceful Co-existence. Like the Sino-Burmese and Sino-Nepalese boundary questions, the Sino-Indian boundary question can be settled in a friendly way through peaceful negotiations. The Chinese people have never wavered in this conviction. We are willing to do everything possible and, together with the Indian people and all countries and people concerned with Asian peace and Afro-Asian solidarity, continue to work for the cessation of the border clashes, for the reopening of peaceful negotiations and for the settlement of the Sino-Indian boundary question. The Nehru government should make corresponding efforts on its part if it still has some respect for India's national interests and for the aspirations of the Indian people, and if it does not want to bruise its head against a stone wall in further expanding the border clashes to the advantage of the imperialists.

To safeguard and strengthen the friendship between the Chinese and Indian peoples not only accords with the common interests of the 1,100 million people of the two countries but also conforms to the common wish of the peace-loving people in Asia and throughout the world. No force can undermine or shake this great friendship.

Moscow's View

37 "PRAVDA"
Serious Hotbed of Tension in Asia

Unfortunately, there is still much inflammable material in the world that threatens at any moment to kindle and become a serious menace to the cause of peace. One of the sources of tension, a source that has already become chronic but has not lost its acuteness, is the Chinese-Indian border dispute in the Himalayas.

Recently the Chinese press has carried a whole series of pronouncements — "Statement by a Representative of the Ministry of Foreign Affairs of the C.P.R.," articles and editorials in leading Chinese newspapers — about the Chinese-Indian border dispute. The common feature of all these pronouncements is the effort to justify completely all the C.P.R.'s actions in the border quarrel and to blacken the policies of other states. These pronouncements abound in slanderous inventions on the subject of the Soviet government's stand on the Chinese-Indian dispute.

The Chinese leaders have gone to absurd lengths, upbraiding the Soviet Union for "collaborating with American imperialism," for "uniting with India to combat China." They find the Soviet government at fault for regarding India as belonging to "an important sector of the peace zone." In this they completely ignore the position of the 1957 Declaration, which emphasizes that the peace-loving states of Asia and Africa are an important factor in the struggle to prevent war and that, together with the socialist countries, they form "a large peace zone." The C.P.R. government's actions in the Chinese-Indian dispute run counter to the general concerted course of the Marxist-Leninist parties

The condensed translation of this article, which originally appeared in *Pravda* on September 19, 1963, is excerpted from the *Current Digest of the Soviet Press*, XV, No. 38, 18–19, which is published weekly at Columbia University by the Joint Committee on Slavic Studies, appointed by the American Council of Learned Societies and the Social Science Research Council. Copyright © 1963; by permission.

on peaceful coixstence and supporting the national-liberation movement.

At the recent session of the Executive Committee of the Afro-Asian Solidarity Organization, the Chinese representatives, distorting the nature of Soviet aid to India, went so far as the monstrous assertion that the Soviet Union was "inciting India to clash with China." This absurd statement, it goes without saying, is supported by no facts whatsoever. And this is understandable, since such facts do not exist. It is well known to the C.P.R. government that the aid given to India by the U.S.S.R. is of precisely the same nature as the aid to many other young developing states.

The U.S.S.R.'s stand with regard to the Chinese-Indian dispute, no matter how the Chinese leaders try to distort it, has unchangingly amounted to assisting the fastest possible settlement of this dispute. It would be natural to expect that this Soviet stand would find understanding and support among the C.P.R. leaders. However, strange as it may be, everything possible is being done in Peking to distort this stand. As for the Chinese leaders' recent pronouncements on the question of the U.S.S.R.'s stand on the Chinese-Indian border dispute, it is difficult to tell which is uppermost here — hostility to the first country of socialism, the effort to discredit the policy of peaceful coexistence consistently pursued by the Soviet government, or the attempt to disguise behind verbal camouflage their own departure from the concerted line of the Communist and Workers' Parties of the whole world on questions of the socialist countries' policy toward young independent states. . . .

The clashes in the Himalayas have caused great concern among the peace-loving public. The Soviet people and the peoples of the socialist countries greeted the news of them with particular anxiety. . . . The Soviet Union has proceeded and still proceeds from the premise that this conflict can be advantageous only to the imperialist and reactionary forces, which have an interest in preserving hotbeds of international tension.

However, the Chinese leaders are dissatisfied with the U.S.S.R.'s peace-loving stand. Did they perhaps wish to settle the border quarrel with India by military means and hope to obtain support from the Soviet Union in this? If that is what the Peking leaders wanted, then it goes without saying that they have grounds for being "indignant" at the U.S.S.R.'s stand. However, no matter what is said in Peking, the Soviet government, true to the Leninist policy of peace, has always done and always will do everything so as not to stir up but to eliminate hotbeds of international tension, resolutely to promote the preservation and consolidation of peace. We have thought and continue to think that there are not and have never been any reasons for the border dispute between India and China to arise, and even less for carrying this dispute as far as armed conflict. . . .

Since the cease-fire on the Indian-Chinese border, on the Chinese side's initiative, in October of last year, all people of good will have hoped that the dispute would be quickly settled and that a tragic page in the relations between India and China would be closed forever. These hopes were all the better founded since the C.P.R. government had found the way to settling unresolved territorial questions with other neighboring countries. Border agreements were reached with Nepal and Burma, even though, as Premier Chou En-lai of the C.P.R. State Council noted, "the question of the border between China and Burma was much more complicated than the question of the Chinese-Indian border." . . .

As is known, as early as last December, on the initiative of Sirimavo Bandaranaike, Prime Minister of Ceylon, leading figures of six non-aligned countries (Ceylon, the U.A.R., Ghana, Burma, Indonesia and Cambodia) in conference at Colombo worked out a proposal for the peaceful settlement of the conflict. . . .

The Colombo conference's proposal represented nothing but the friendly desire of states that were sincerely trying to help find a mutually acceptable solution to the border dispute.

Unfortunately, the voice of reason expressing the will of the peoples of Asia and Africa was not heard in Peking. . . .

The press of many Afro-Asian countries is calling attention to the fact that at first the C.P.R. government declared its acceptance "in principle" of the Colombo meeting's proposal. Then it declared that it could not accept it fully because "not all was clear" and asked amplification. When such amplification was given, the C.P.R. government declared that it was given only by the representatives of a few of the countries that had participated in the Colombo meeting, and therefore, as [People's Daily] put it, "was not a legal document of the meeting." . . .

It is no accident that many are now beginning to say that the C.P.R. government, while praising the initiative of the non-aligned countries and declaring that it "values" and "gives due credit" for their good offices, is in fact ignoring their efforts and making no move to apply the proposals worked out at Colombo. . . .

Noteworthy is the fact that the Chinese leaders have recently strenuously propagandized assertions that the Nehru government is an imperialist, expansionist government, allegedly striving to set up a huge empire that would surpass even the British Empire in magnitude. In the light of such assertions, it is difficult to believe in the sincerity of the Chinese leaders who swear that they are seeking peaceful settlement of the border dispute with India.

An impression is created that in the capital of the C.P.R. they do not want to understand who benefits by the present conflict. This conflict has done and continues to do enormous harm to the peoples. As is known, the imperialists promptly seized on the Chinese-Indian dispute, attempting to fan the flames of war in the Himalayas. They linked it to far-reaching plans, vying in offering India arms and joint military measures. The imperialists were particularly gladdened by the circumstance that one of the parties to the conflict is a socialist state. They would like to make use of this fact to discredit the idea of the peaceful coexistence of states with different social systems, to discredit the friendship and cooperation of the socialist countries with the young independent states of Asia and Africa. Behind all this stands the desire to utilize the conflict for preserving a dangerous hotbed of tension.

To what, in actual fact, has the Chinese-Indian conflict led, and what are its consequences?   . . .

Reactionary forces in India are using the conflict to raise a chauvinistic fever, to attack the progressive forces in the country, so as to force India from the path of neutralism and draw her into the military-political blocs of the West. . . . Some time ago an extraordinary statute curtailing the people's democratic rights was introduced in the country. Many hundreds of Communists and trade unionists have been arrested and imprisoned, and Indian reactionaries are demanding that the economic development program be cut back and the country's limited resources be used for military purposes, to set up an enormous war machine. . . .

The tension being maintained on the Chinese-Indian border is fraught with serious consequences. When soldiers of neighboring states stand face to face with rifles at the ready, particularly if they have already had a bitter battle in the past, there naturally exists the danger that bloodshed might begin with an accidental rifle shot. . . .

Peaceful settlement of the Chinese-Indian dispute would advance the interests of the Indian and the Chinese peoples, would end this serious hotbed of tension, would render good service to the cause of peace in Asia and the entire world.

There are no rational reasons justifying the maintenance of tension in this part of the world. . . . As for the Soviet Union, it treats the countries that border on it with respect. It understands that good-neighborliness is possible only when there is respect for the borders that have formed between states. . . .

The most difficult negotiations are better than war, and disputed issues must be decided not by military but by peaceful means, by negotiations at the round table. The Soviet people resolutely advocate that a way be found to a peaceful solution of the Indian-Chinese border dispute, that the hotbed of serious tension in this part of the world be eliminated as soon as possible.

PART FOUR

The Ordering of Conflict

Introduction to Part Four

Military Strategy: The Control of Violence

Just as war offers a possible (if not desirable) instrument for continuation of policy, so may the control of war and the regulation of armaments. The need for such controls result in part from the intersection of the major tensions and the driving forces at work in the modern world, for they produce an explosive situation without precedent for its potential danger to the survival of the species, as well as individual nations. On the one hand are the tensions between Communism and the West, between the impoverished and the developed nations, and between man and his technology. These fault lines are sharpened by the destabilizing effects of nationalism, rising economic expectations, ideological fanaticism, the population explosion, and rapid technical and military innovation. The dangers inherent in this combination of tensions and forces are implicit in the preceding chapters on political and military strategy and explicit in the studies of strategies in conflict.

The desirability of certain arms controls[1] is eloquently stated in the

[1] The distinction between "disarmament" and "arms control" varies with time, place, and author. "Disarmament" usually implies a reduction or abolition of armaments, although it has been used, especially between the World Wars, to denote

selections in Part IV, especially those from nonaligned or developing countries. The President of Ghana expresses the natural desire of an African to have his continent free of the great political and military struggle.[2] Israeli writer Simha Flapan asserts the desirability of keeping a nuclear arms race from further complicating Arab-Israeli relations.[3] Aftab Ahmad Khan,[4] a Pakistani member of a select U.N. committee to investigate the economic and social consequences of disarmament, reports the unanimous conclusion of the group that disarmament would bring great benefits to all economies, provided the conversion of military production were planned in advance.[5] Professor Melman's critique of what he regards as superfluous military stockpiling is also predicated on the assumption that reduced defense expenditures would profit the U.S. and the world economy.[6] Finally, the official U.S., Soviet, and even the Chinese positions on disarmament affirm, if only for propaganda purposes, the theoretical advantages accruing to large reductions of defense spending and procurement.[7]

A world without arms, no matter how desirable, may not be immediately attainable. As with other problems of world politics, one may have to forgo the utopian for the feasible, the immediate ideal for the gradual improvement, the maximum for the minimum goal. In this context the relevant question becomes: How can the danger of war be reduced and the greatest savings be made from defense expenditures?

It is widely recognized that a vicious circle drives the arms race to ever higher levels of quantity and quality: Tensions produce armaments, but armaments increase tensions. To stop the spiral it may be necessary to reduce or stabilize both tensions and armaments.

---

mere limitation of arms. "Arms control" is a more inclusive concept having to do with any regulation or limitation on the construction, maintenance, or use of arms. It could therefore provide for a severe reduction, but possibly for an increase in arms. The term "disarmament" is favored in Moscow and the phrase "arms control" in Washington. Steps such as the nuclear test ban are euphemistically labelled "partial disarmament measures" by Soviet spokesmen.

[2] See item No. 42.
[3] See item No. 43.
[4] See item No. 44.
[5] *Economic and Social Consequences of Disarmament*, Report of the United Nations Secretary-General Transmitting the Study of His Consultation Group, New York, 1962. United Nations Document E/3593/Rev. 1, February 1962.
[6] See item No. 39.
[7] The Chinese opposition to the 1963 test ban is justified on the ground that it does not result in real disarmament but only in a limitation designed to freeze the size of the nuclear club. See also items No. 38, 40 and 41.

Some of the preceding readings indicate why the spiral exists and why it is hard to curtail. Confrontations over Berlin, Cuba, the Himalayas and other troublespots are a constant possibility. China and Cuba, among other countries, follow revisionist territorial policies and foreign subversion. Political and ideological tensions aside, the chance of a technological breakthrough and the present uncertainties regarding the effectiveness of different weapons systems stimulate further military research and development. The manifest reluctance of France and China to rely for their defense on either superpower is another factor exacerbating the competition on arms.

The readings in Part II on "adversary relations," however, point to ways that international tension might be contained. The very title of Kennedy's address, "Toward a Strategy of Peace," implies that peace like other policy objectives may gain from being carried out according to a long-term plan.[8] The speech is designed to allay Soviet fears of U.S. aggression and to stress — for an American and Russian audience — the mutual advantages of peaceful cooperation.[9] This speech contrasts vividly with earlier official statements hinting that Washington would consider initiating a pre-emptive attack;[10] with the Strausz-Hupé and Kintner "Forward Strategy" positing an all-out struggle until one side or the other is vanquished;[11] and with the 1964 Republican Presidential candidate's attack on what he called the "no-win" foreign policy of the incumbent administration — a sharp reminder of the possible impact of domestic affairs upon external.

Similar in some ways to the Kennedy address, the Suslov and Arzumanyan statements on peaceful coexistence stress that Communist aims cannot and should not be advanced by violence. While the Soviet declarations should not be taken at face value, their plausibility gains some from high-level repetition and more from the vehemence of Chinese rebuttals insisting that Moscow has forsaken revolutionary ways.

The Glagolev-Larionov article in this section argues that human survival, if a choice must be made, is more important than maintenance of the ideologies which strategists such as Herman Kahn and Mao Tse-

---

[8] See item No. 3.

[9] Khrushchev welcomed the Kennedy address (*Pravda*, June 15, 1963), while Peking labeled it "Kennedy's Big Conspiracy" (*Peking Review*, VI, No. 26 [June 28, 1963] 12–14).

[10] See the views attributed to the President in Stuart Alsop, "Kennedy's Grand Strategy," *Saturday Evening Post*, CCXXXV (March 31, 1962) 11–17.

[11] See item No. 4.

tung would defend at a high cost.[12] Moscow, however, continues to oppose "ideological disarmament" and the allegation that Communist and Western societies are converging.[13] The fact remains that political dogmatism tends to wane as education and prosperity increase, thus strengthening support for pragmatic compromise instead of fanatical holy wars in international politics.

One of the more positive developments attested to in these readings is the growing rapport between Moscow and Washington. It is manifested in a general way in their tacit agreement to avoid direct confrontations and in their parallel action to support India against Peking. More specifically the U.S.-Soviet dialogue on arms control and disarmament shows signs of increasing mutual understanding. For decades Moscow maintained that to think of arms control in relation to defense policy was virtually immoral. But this selection by Glagolev and Larionov — an economist and a military strategist — specifically justifies Soviet military posture by arguing its contribution to international security. Glagolev, it should be noted, has travelled widely in the United States, meeting with many arms control and disarmament analysts. His article with Larionov, like other Soviet writing since about 1959, shows considerable familiarity with Western scholarship. It even rebuts a U.S. critique of the 1962 treatise edited by Marshal Sokolovskii, *Military Strategy* (second edition in 1963).

Probably the most significant point in the Glagolev-Larionov article, however, is its defense of the nuclear umbrella principle, the notion that the superpowers should retain a limited number of strategic delivery systems until the end of a three-stage disarmament process. This principle appears to have first been broached to Soviet scholars by U.S. scientists in 1960. It was later endorsed by Gromyko at the 1962 and 1963 General Assemblies. This endorsement marks a high point in an increasingly realistic Soviet assessment of arms control problems. It reflects a belief that collaboration is possible with the United States in the defense of peace and an awareness of the utility for Moscow in retaining vastly superior weapons in the face of challenges from Peking and elsewhere to Soviet interests.

Whether the United States should reduce its strategic forces to a level with the Soviet Union is, of course, quite controversial. Any judgment on this question will reflect an opinion on Soviet intentions — security

[12] See reading No. 40.
[13] See footnote on pp. 30–31.

alone or dynamic expansion — and on the reliability of present deterrent capabilities. Professor Melman argues that there is an absolute level of destructive power beyond which it is politically, economically, and technically unnecesary and imprudent to procure additional strategic weapons.[14] If this thesis were correct, it might be in the U.S. interest to reduce to parity with the Soviet Union. Offical Washington, however, is not convinced that either the present or a vastly reduced deterrent system is entirely adequate for future contingencies.[15]

That the superpowers have been interested in at least controlling the arms race is suggested by the 1963–1964 agreements on the direct communications link, the limited test ban, the declaration against bombs in orbit, and the reduction of fissionable materials production.

The pressure of the third world upon the Communist and Western alliances to resolve their conflicts and to negotiate has probably been a positive factor in advancing the cause of arms control and disarmament. A nuclear test ban, for example, was called for by Nehru in 1954 and by the Bandung Conference in April 1955, and quickly appeared among Soviet proposals made on May 10, 1955. The U.N. committee on the Economic and Social Consequences of Disarmament was composed of representatives from nonaligned, as well as aligned, powers. One rationalization offered for the creation in 1961–62 of a somewhat unwilling Eighteen-Nation Disarmament Committee was that the presence of the nonaligned states would contribute to the great power deliberations. The danger of grandstand plays to impress the neutrals has been reduced by the privacy of the meetings and the growing sophistication of the nonaligned delegations. The almost universal support of the 1963 test ban adds to the momentum for further progress in the negotiations.

International Strategy: The United Nations and the Rule of Law

The two views of world politics — the outward perspective of national strategy and the overview of the international system — have alternated throughout the preceding chapters. Both recur in this final section which illustrates the efforts of individual nations to shape international or-

[14] See reading No. 39.
[15] See E. H. Hartsook, " 'Overkill': Theories and Implications," and Herbert O. Horn and John Ponturo, "Stable Deterrence Proposals: Some Questions," *Orbis*, VII, No. 4 (Winter 1964) 709–718, 821–832.

ganization to their needs and the gradual response of the United Nations to the challenges before it.[16]

The readings in this chapter deal primarily with the changing nature of the United Nations. The U.N. Charter placed prime responsibility for peace and security upon the permanent members of the Security Council, the Big Five, on the assumption that responsibility and power should belong together. The fundamental change in the "parliament of mankind" has been to shift this responsibility from the Big Five to the other members represented in the General Assembly where each state possesses an equal vote, regardless of its material prowess or financial contribution to the organization. This shift has developed over time, but three key developments have spurred it: (1) the efforts of the West led by the United States in 1950 to authorize the General Assembly to deal with disputes on which the Security Council was deadlocked, efforts which led to the Uniting for Peace Resolution; (2) the influx of the new African and Asian nations into the United Nations since 1955; and (3) the struggle between the Communist and Western worlds which created and creates a vacuum and opportunities which the smaller powers are pleased to exploit.

The growth in U.N. membership is of particular importance in an analysis of the third world. The United Nations began in 1945 with 51 members; the number rose in 1961 alone from 99 to 104; in 1962 it climbed to 110; in 1963 it reached 113, adding two more members in 1964. Within the next few years as many as 25 or 30 additional states might request membership as further dependent territories are emancipated and divided countries such as Germany, Korea, and Vietnam are accepted for admission.[17]

A breakdown of the principal groupings among the 104 members in 1961–1962[18] shows the possibilities for diplomatic coalitions:

The Asians, including the Asiatic Arabs but excluding, on political grounds, Israel, China, and Outer Mongolia — 20;

[16] The focus here is on the central organs of the United Nations. A rounded picture would have to take account of the functional cooperation (like that of the U.N. Specialized Agencies), regional integration (e.g., in the Organization of African Unity or the Comecon), and the non-governmental international organizations alluded to above. (See p. 7.)

[17] Richard P. Stebbins, *The United States in World Affairs, 1963* (New York: Harper and Row, 1964) p. 325.

[18] H. G. Nicholas, *The United Nations as a Political Institution* (2nd ed.; New York: Oxford University Press, 1963) p. 118.

The Africans, including Arab states in Africa, but excluding South Africa — 28;

The Arabs — 10;

The Latin-Americans, if Cuba is included — 20;

The Communists, excluding Yugoslavia — 10;

The West European and North American countries — 19;

The Commonwealth Countries, excluding South Africa but including several states which also feature in other groupings — 12.

The political implications of this distribution of voting power are clear. In the present Assembly of 115, where a two-thirds majority requires 77 positive votes, the Afro-Asians can operate a virtual veto. If the Arab states join them, this group constitutes over half the U.N. membership. If the Latin Americans vote with this coalition, it carries more than two-thirds of the votes in the General Assembly. As the over-all membership rises from 115 to 120 and more, the major alteration of the above pattern will be the increment of African votes.

All of these groupings do not operate with the same discipline and unanimity. Further, the interests of the African, Asian, Arab, and Latin nations do not necessarily coincide. Hence, it is by no means assured that they will exploit their potential numerical advantages. They are restrained, among other reasons, because their capacity for action is ultimately dependent upon the participation of at least some great powers.

The permanent members of the Security Council smart under the impact of this political upsurge which leaves them relatively weaker. The West pushed through the Uniting for Peace Resolution at a time when it dominated the General Assembly, but already the Assembly majority has voted against French, British, and U.S., as well as Soviet, policies.

The Soviet article which follows in this section indicates that Moscow is no less concerned about "The U.N. in a Changed World" than the West.[19] Moscow's advocacy of the trioka principle in U.N. affairs has provided a tacit admission that the third world would not necessarily vote with the Communist. The United Nations offers the nonaligned nations a pivotal role which they could not otherwise play in world affairs, but they have opposed Moscow's attempts to cripple the organization. The opposition of the *tiers monde* forced Moscow to abandon its

[19] See item No. 47.

insistence that the U.N. Secretariat operate under three Secretaries or, failing that, that the lone Secretary-General make certain prior commitments to the states sponsoring him. Even before U Thant's election in 1961, the Assembly voted 87 to 11 to appeal to the Soviet Union to call off its impending 50-megaton bomb tests. A week later it voted 72 to 11 to appeal to all nuclear powers to refrain from further testing. The neutralist resolution, opposed by Moscow and Washington alike, had a clear majority of U.N. members behind it. Still earlier, in 1960–1961 the U.N. handling of the Congo operation, in Alexander Dallin's words, showed that the Afro-Asians were by no means in "Khrushchev's pocket."[20] As the Pakistani analysis indicates, some Afro-Asians are quite proud of their responsible use of U.N. power and their contributions to U.N. police actions.[21]

Moscow has steadfastly resisted all attempts to revise the U.N. Charter in any way that would diminish national sovereignty or the privileged position of the five permanent members of the Security Council. Late in 1963 the Soviet Government was confronted with two General Assembly resolutions for Charter amendments to expand the Security Council from eleven to fifteen seats and the Economic and Social Council (ECOSOC) from eighteen to twenty-seven seats. The United States and United Kingdom agreed to a moderate expansion of both Councils, but abstained on the two resolutions because the proposed increases seemed excessive and the procedure somewhat hasty. France and the Soviet Union, whose concurrence was needed to effect the proposed amendments, cast negative votes. Moscow's excuse was that its loyalty to Communist China prevented its consenting to any enlargement of the two Councils so long as Peking is denied U.N. representation. This rug was immediately pulled from beneath the Soviet delegation by a Peking statement on December 12, 1963, denying any connection between the issue of Chinese representation and the proposed enlargement. In linking the two problems Moscow was said to be attempting to blame China for Soviet unwillingness to accommodate the Afro-Asian countries. The Soviet Government then announced, after the Assembly had gone home, that its position might be reconsidered if Peking had in fact released Moscow from its obligations.[22]

Moscow had sought in recent years not only to expand and defend its

[20] Alexander Dallin, *The Soviet Union at the United Nations* (New York: Praeger, 1962) pp. 176–177.
[21] See article No. 46.
[22] Stebbins, *op. cit.,* pp. 327–328.

influence in U.N. voting procedures, but to obtain more positions for Communist personnel in the U.N. Secretariat. A Soviet spokesman complained to the General Assembly on December 11, 1963, that of 1,390 professional posts in the Secretariat, 68 per cent were held by the Western countries and their allies, 20 per cent by nonaligned countries, and only 12 per cent by the "Socialist countries." He added that "almost all" Western officials were on permanent contracts. Moscow proposed the elimination of permanent positions and their replacement by appointments on short-term contracts.[23] The same complaint was registered in 1964 in connection with Soviet financial obligations to the United Nations. Soviet citizens, it was argued, hold only 74 posts in U.N. bodies, although the Soviet Union's financial contributions would enable it to claim 193 posts.[24]

The Russian sensitivity over representation in the U.N. Secretariat is an indication of the greater importance which Moscow now attaches to the world organizations. One reason the Soviet quota is not filled is that Moscow showed little interest in sending high quality staff personnel to the Secretariat in earlier years.

Soviet sensitivity is sharpened still more by the belief that there are no truly neutral men or truly international civil servants. *Izvestiia* on September 9, 1964, however, took pains to refute the allegation of Western officials that Soviet citizens "cannot act as independent international officials."

A major shift in Soviet policies may have been adumbrated in 1964 when Moscow hinted it might be ready to accept the principle of a U.N. police force composed of units from non-Big Five powers, but subject to the Security Council. Such a system would fall short of Western advocacy of a veto-free force, but would represent a step forward from general Soviet hostility toward all U.N. peacekeeping machinery.[25]

France, as noted above, joined Moscow in 1963 to cast negative votes against expansion of the Security Council and ECOSCOC. Paris is perhaps less resigned to the changing nature of the United Nations than the Soviet Union, because France has no comparable material power to fall back on. President de Gaulle's remarks suggest a wish to return to the legalistic status quo ante of 1945.[26] This would assure a paper

[23] *The New York Times*, December 12, 1963.
[24] *Izvestiia*, September 9, 1964. The same article stated that the U.S. occupied 267 such posts.
[25] See *The New York Times*, July 8, 1964; August 7, 1964.
[26] See item No. 45.

grandeur in the United Nations parallel to the symbolic nuclear sanctuary France pursues in military affairs. The termination of French colonial rule, a subject of much U.N. debate, and the gradual improvement of France's cultural and business relations in the third world may come to obviate some of the grounds for French anxiety over structural change at the United Nations.

The Chinese People's Republic continues to feed its resentment against Western imperialism on Peking's exclusion from the United Nations. Declaratory policy has been contradictory, but it seems likely that Peking would like the prerogatives of permanent membership in the Security Council. At the same time, it welcomes the strengthening of the Afro-Asian bloc on the assumption that this weakens the United States, the Soviet Union, and other imperialist powers. The projected expansion of the two councils in 1963 gave Peking an opportunity both to rebuff Moscow and to court the third world.[27] Until there is some prospect of the C.P.R.'s representation in the United Nations, there is of course no point to Peking's excessively lamenting its absence. Since the C.P.R.'s seating seems inevitable, Peking may well calculate that the longer the delay, the greater Chinese bargaining power on the various political conditions at stake will grow.

As noted earlier, it does not automatically follow that the wealthier the power, the more intensive its attempts to preserve the status quo. Enlightened self-interest dictates that the present advantages of a great have nation may best be maintained by helping to channel pressures for change, rather than suppressing them. The wealthy, in a sense, can afford magnanimity, because of their margin of relative security.

The statement in this section by Secretary of State Rusk may illustrate the point.[28] The United States can view the rising influence of the smaller nations in all U.N. bodies with greater equanimity than Moscow or Paris. Washington can acknowledge the danger of voting-power dissassociated from material power and responsibility, but it can also appreciate the potentially crippling effects of the veto power in the Security Council. The United States need not attempt to turn back the clock to the legal defense assured the Big Five in 1945 by the U.N. Charter and the smaller membership of the organization. Unlike Russia, the United States can count on three or four allies in the Security

[27] See item No. 48.
[28] See item No. 49.

Council to save it from relying on the Big Five unanimity rule. Under the pressure of greater dependency upon domestic support than Moscow or Paris, however, Washington is less free to deal flexibly with issues such as the seating of Peking.

In the spirit of the great international civil servant, the Dag Hammarskjold Memorial Lecture of Secretary Rusk stresses the dominant reality of interdependence, resulting from modern technology and shared economic and political problems. His address states eloquently one of the major themes of this book: that the nation-states are intimately linked in a transnational net of forces and values which requires international cooperation to deal with common needs of peace and development.

Rusk attempts to balance the desirable with the possible. He calls on all states to make the sacrifice of formal sovereignty required to advance the cause of international security and prosperity. He calls specifically for international cooperation to place the financing of U.N. operations on a sound foundation . . . to assist the developing nations to grow economically within a framework of political stability . . . to provide effective U.N. peacekeeping machinery . . . and to refrain from using the United Nations as a forum for self-serving propaganda.

The intersection of tensions and forces operative in the atomic age results in unprecedented opportunities as well as dangers. The long-term hope is that the United Nations, if oriented in the direction set out in Rusk's Dag Hammarskjold Lecture, may develop the potential not only to control armaments but also to render them superfluous, by mitigating the tensions and ethnocentrism which drive the arms race. While world federation and general disarmament appear only as distant possibilities, the United Nations and its Specialized Agencies already offer the instrumentalities by which the basic actors can cooperate to cope with their immediate functional and political needs and, in that very process, build the consensual foundations of a more stable and fraternal order in which many worlds may become one. The superpowers, this book has argued, have not only a common responsibility but also the greatest interest and opportunity to lead in the creation of a world in which diversity may flourish amid cooperation and friendly competition. Whether this responsibility, interest, and opportunity will be perceived and acted on, only history will divulge.

Military Strategy:

The Control of Violence

WESTERN STRATEGY

Stabilized Deterrence and Arms Control

38 GEORGE E. PUGH
Restraints, Strategy, and Arms Control

According to the legislation which established the U.S. Arms Control and Disarmament Agency, "An ultimate goal of the United States is a world which is free from the scourge of war and the dangers and burdens of armaments; in which the use of force has been subordinated to a rule of law; and in which international adjustments to a changing world are achieved peacefully." In the present international climate it seems unlikely that this goal of a disarmed world under international law will be achieved in the near future. It is therefore appropriate to inquire what steps can be taken, in the absence of enforceable world law, to improve international security and contribute to an environment

George E. Pugh is Deputy Assistant Director of the U.S. Arms Control and Disarmament Agency. These excerpts are reprinted from *Orbis*, a quarterly journal of world affairs, published by the Foreign Policy Research Institute of the University of Pennsylvania, and are taken from an article with the same title which appeared in Vol. VII, No. 2 (Summer 1963) 209–225.

where world law would be possible. While the ultimate goal may involve revolutionary changes in the international environment, those steps which can be taken in the absence of world law are necessarily evolutionary. They must be soundly based on military and political realities and well integrated with other aspects of national strategy.

In an environment without enforceable international law, arms control arrangements are, in essence, mutually accepted restraints on the size, the type, deployment or employment of military forces. Considering the historical role of restraint in conflict situations, the principles which govern arms control proposals should not differ widely from those involved in other forms of self-restraint observed by sovereign nations.

THE HISTORICAL ROLE OF RESTRAINT

The impression is widespread that the consideration of such restraints in actual or possible military conflict situations is in some way new, and perhaps unrealistic. The fact is that many examples of mutually accepted restraints have become so commonplace that they have almost ceased to be recognized for what they are. Examples of restraints commonly accepted by nations at opposite poles of a political power confrontation include: freedom of the seas; respect for the integrity of neutral nations; restraint in the use of chemical and biological warfare agents; restraint in the use of military methods to harass potential enemies in time of peace; recognition of "open-cities"; and the immunity of diplomats. Thus, an analysis of restraints is not an academic pursuit. As the above examples indicate, they have played a real and important role in international relations. Some restraints have been honored even in wartime, others only in peacetime.

The appropriate conventions of restraint for any period of history should be matched to the political and military environment of the time. Since strategic deterrence (which in itself is only a method of enforcing restraint) has now become a primary security objective, it is appropriate to re-examine the traditional concepts of restraint, and to inquire how modifications of these concepts might contribute to improved security in the present military environment.

Examination of the existing examples of restraint reveals a common motivation for observance: In every case these restraints have been observed, not because of any direct advantage to be gained, but because of the indirect advantage secured when restraints are mutually respected by other powers. Restraints have operated most effectively a) where any advantage to be gained from unilateral violation of the restraint would not be decisive, and b) where mutual violation of the restraint could have serious consequences for both sides.

While the conventions of restraint can be important elements in strategy, it is foolhardy to allow one's security to become overly dependent on the restraint of an opponent. All the above restraints have one element in common: they have all been violated at one time or another.

Violation is always possible, and in fact, likely, if it can give one side a decisive advantage over the other. It is irrelevant whether the restraint has been incorporated into a formal treaty (e.g., the Washington naval limitation agreement of 1922) or based on no more than an informal understanding (as was the case with the [1958–61] nuclear test moratorium). Treaties and informal agreements between sovereign nations can and will be broken when it appears that an important net advantage can be gained. This net advantage must, of course, compensate for any loss of prestige or bargaining power. The Soviet Union has demonstrated by its past behavior that it places a relatively low value on these considerations. For example, although the U.S.S.R. had concluded treaties of friendship and nonaggression with Poland, Latvia, Lithuania and Estonia, it invaded and communized all these nations.

One may reasonably ask why the United States should enter into a formal agreement with the U.S.S.R. at all, since the latter appears to place such a low value on honoring its treaty commitments and preserving a reputation for honest bargaining. However, where it is desirable to establish conventions of restraint that are too involved for an informal agreement, a formal treaty can provide a clearer definition of the rules and thus improve the chances that the agreement will survive. . . .

ROLE OF RESTRAINTS IN A DETERRENT STRATEGY

The tremendous firepower in easily deliverable packages, which thermonuclear weapons have made possible, has made an effective defense against thermonuclear attack exceedingly difficult because even a few penetrating warheads can do enormous damage. Consequently, the U.S. and other major powers have moved toward dependence on a deterrent rather than a classical defensive strategy.

The major advantage of a deterrent strategy is that it can provide a degree of national security without the necessity for a successful physical defense. The disadvantage is that it makes the national defense dependent on the restraint of potential enemies. Thus, it would not be chosen as a desired strategy except for the fact that the successful physical defense does not, at present, appear possible. The high cost of providing a defense against nuclear firepower, and the relatively low cost of increasing the available firepower, makes it unlikely that a satisfactory defense will be achieved in the foreseeable future.[1] Thus, both the United States and the Soviet Union can be expected to continue for some time to depend for their own protection on the restraint of the other. The primary role of the deterrent forces is, in fact, to provide the motivation for this restraint.

The restraint which is imposed by strategic deterrent forces does not stop with its effect on the employment of these forces. Indeed, it extends throughout the entire spectrum of the conflicts between the East and the West, for without some restraint in methods and objectives any limited East-West dispute could escalate to a full-scale nuclear exchange. It is, therefore, highly appropriate that serious thought be given to the conventions of restraint, since the success or failure of the strategy of deterrence is dependent on the satisfactory operation of a variety of such mutual restraints.

Restraints may include political and economic as well as military factors. The military restraints might include restrictions on the use of military forces, or on the production and deployment of forces as well. Both East and West are faced with a central dilemma: excessive restraint in the East-West confrontation may lead to setbacks in the Cold War. However, with too little restraint, the Cold War could lead to thermonuclear war. A difficult task which confronts the strategist today is how to encourage the establishment of a set of conventions of mutual restraint which will reduce the risk of such a war and still be consistent with the realities of the East-West conflict, in which neither side can be expected to relinquish its own power position.

Restraint conventions can be modified in a variety of ways: by formal treaties, by threats and promises, by observance of new restraints, or by violation of old ones. Each of these factors can influence the expectations of a nation concerning the consequences of various actions it may wish to take, and thereby can influence the development of various modified conventions of restraint.

It does not follow that formal treaties or informal understandings, which would place restraints on the size or deployment of military

[1] While effective defense against full-scale attack by the U.S.S.R. does not appear probable, effective defenses against small-scale attacks, or attacks by minor powers, may be quite feasible.

forces, would necessarily add to, rather than detract from, stability and national security. Thorough examination of all proposals to ensure that they do indeed add to, rather than jeopardize, stability and security is of highest importance. . . .

OBJECTIVES OF ARMS CONTROL PROPOSALS

The conventions of restraint can be influenced by arms control negotiations themselves whether or not any treaty is signed. Moreover, the dialogue of such negotiations inevitably becomes an important factor in the Cold War. The present pressure of public opinion (particularly in Free Europe) for efforts to reduce the threat of nuclear devastation makes it advisable for the U.S. to engage in active arms control negotiations, regardless of any expectation of success. However, the U.S. must assure its allies that any proposals made are in their best interest. Similarly, the dialogue of the negotiations can have an impact on the extent to which the U.S. will be able to obtain or sustain support among the uncommitted nations of the world; consequently, the proposals made by the U.S. must be evaluated, in part, in terms of their potential impact on these nations. The decision to propose any sort of arms control must be influenced by the impact the proposal will have, whether it is accepted or not.

The objectives of any arms control proposal, therefore, should be: a) if accepted, to provide an improvement in U.S. and Free World security; b) if rejected, to provide a demonstration of the sincere intentions of the U.S. and to do this without producing any disadvantageous change in the conventions of restraint.

It follows that U.S. proposals for arms control should be evaluated in terms of their potential contribution to the security of the entire world, as well as in terms of their value for the security of the United States. Certainly the Soviets will refuse to accept any proposal which they feel does not serve their own security interests and will break any agreement when they deem it to be no longer in their best interests. Thus, no agreement can be implemented, remain in operation, and contribute to U.S. security *unless* the Soviet Union is convinced that the agreement also contributes to Soviet security. The U.S. is not likely to be credited with a serious effort, and both our allies and other Free World nations will doubt our sincerity, *unless* the U.S. proposals appear to be consistent with the legitimate security interests of the U.S.S.R. as well as those of the Western nations.

Because of the essentially irreconcilable conflict between the U.S.

and U.S.S.R., it is inevitable that both sides will attempt to inject into potential agreements certain elements which are designed not to contribute primarily to mutual security, but rather to further unilateral long-range objectives at the expense of the opponent. Paradoxically, however, it is not necessarily to the advantage of either side to drive a "hard bargain," since an agreement which holds little advantage for the other signatories is most likely to be broken. Thus, to increase the chance of success in the negotiations it is important to try to include *only* those items which contribute to mutual security, and to eliminate from both U.S. and Soviet proposals those items which appear to contribute primarily to unilateral objectives. It may be preferable in the future to seek agreements, where possible, on an informal basis; the false sense of security which can result from formal agreements may tend to make such treaties less viable and thus more deceptive than informal agreements where the option to violate is obvious to all concerned.

CHARACTER OF POTENTIALLY USEFUL AGREEMENTS

One of the most common of all disarmament proposals involves across-the-board reductions in military forces of both sides to some agreed fraction of existing forces. While this type of agreement can provide a simple and apparently equitable way to initiate a disarmament agreement, as an arms control agreement it can contribute little to military stability. It leaves untouched all the basic instabilities of the *status quo ante*.

Such agreements on across-the-board proportional reductions in forces can contribute to world security only insofar as they provide a basis for first steps toward enforceable world law, reduction in secrecy, or a reduction in the probable level of damage if war occurs. U.S. military thinkers have logically been skeptical about this general type of proposal. Certainly, other types of agreements which are deliberately designed to reduce instabilities, as well as minimize damage in the event war ensues, are much more likely to contribute to security. Examples of such agreements might be:

a. Selective reduction or elimination of certain types of systems from both sides:

(1) Systems which are particularly useful to a potential aggressor in an offensive rather than a defensive role;

(2) Systems which are particularly vulnerable, and therefore invite attack;

(3) Systems which threaten excessive collateral damage beyond the needs of legitimate military tasks:

b. Unsymmetrical agreements to redress force inequalities in different locations or in different types of armament, such as:

(1) A reduction in force at one level of escalation in return for a reduction in force by the other side at a different level of escalation (for example, a reduction of U.S. nuclear forces in Western Europe in return for a reduction of Soviet conventional ground forces in Eastern Europe).

(2) A reduction in deployment in one area which appears to be a threat, in return for a compensating reduction by the other side in some other area.

c. Agreements to improve the availability of information in order to decrease the risk of miscalculation or accident, or — looking further into the future — agreements to introduce or strengthen the machinery of enforceable international law.

Because agreements must remain acceptable to both sides, they cannot be designed to obtain an obvious major military or political advantage, but should, in general, tend to stabilize an existing military balance and minimize the risk of miscalculation or accident. If either side believes it has a chance to obtain military or political dominance in a given region, then agreements are likely to be much more difficult to obtain. Even when the intended method of obtaining this dominance is political or economic, the importance of military realities cannot be denied. . . . Thus, where a region is in political ferment and the expectations and future goals of both sides are different, agreements which would affect respective military postures in these areas are likely to be difficult to obtain. On the other hand, where there is a stalemate politically and militarily, or where a stalemate is clearly imminent, the chances for an agreement should be relatively good.

CONCEPT OF DEFENSE IN AN AGE OF DETERRENCE

The dominant feature of the present deterrent environment is the fact that both major powers can maintain a capability to inflict crippling damage on the other, irrespective of any foreseeable defensive measures which either side can take. To understand the role of military forces in this environment, one must bear in mind that all actions by both sides take place under this threat of ultimate retaliation. The threat of ultimate retaliation, however, is only the cap on the bottle. By itself, it could not convincingly restrain a number of possible aggressive acts below the threshold of all-out war. The restraint of lesser forms of aggression must be achieved by applying defense strategies at lower levels of violence, and by threats of lesser retaliation (not necessarily military) commensurate with the values involved.

These threats of less-than-total retaliation may be employed in the immediate area in question, and may be integrated with a basic defensive operation. Alternatively, they may be purely punitive and be applied in any other related or unrelated area. It is only necessary that they be clearly recognized as retaliatory responses. They might embrace, for example, local military actions, economic sanctions, blockade, or even threats of limited nuclear attack. They could be, in the aggregate, a "mix" of any one of a number of these potential combinations. Ideally, they should be so selected that they require a relatively low level of commitment on our part and a relatively high level of commitment for the opposition.

We can assume that we will be harassed in those areas, such as Berlin, where a low commitment by the Soviet bloc requires a high level of commitment from us. In any such situation we will face a difficult dilemma. We can choose to respond locally and limit the area of crisis despite the adverse commitment levels, or, alternatively, we can expand the area of crisis to include new elements for which the commitment levels are more in our favor. The decision will always be difficult; our actual course of action will have to be decided in each case by a detailed evaluation of relative strengths and weaknesses and of relative commitment requirements along the entire spectrum of escalation, up to and including thermonuclear exchange.

There is a wide diversity of possibilities in this area of limited military and nonmilitary conflict which tends to complicate the problem. For instance, it is even conceivable that the U.S. could attempt to deter Soviet action against Berlin by threatening some retaliatory action against a place as far away as Cuba. Thus, given the ubiquity of the East-West power struggle, one cannot reach definitive conclusions through the examination of security problems in only one area at a time.

However, from the point of view of arms control negotiations, there are certain rules of thumb which help to simplify the consideration of possible proposals. Since one Western objective usually will be to limit the area of conflict, it will generally be better to have deterrent assets on the spot, rather than to be compelled to depend on countering the enemy's moves by provoking or fanning crises in other parts of the world. Similarly, it will generally be better for the West to be able to defend at a low level of escalation, rather than to have to depend on raising the level of escalation. Thus, while a successful defense of disputed areas does not absolutely require Western superiority or even equality in all areas, it is nevertheless true that a military environment which is relatively balanced at all levels and in all areas will generally be preferable to one in which we are dependent on the credibility of threats in other areas or at other levels of escalation.

None of this is intended to mean that communist aggression is deterred only by our military posture. The Soviets, to a large extent, are deterred from aggression in some areas by their own strategy. If they were to attack Iran, for example, they might jeopardize the success of their strategy in other areas of primary interest such as Western Europe. If their primary objective is to divide the NATO alliance, an overt attack on Iran or some other small state might serve to strengthen NATO, a development which the U.S.S.R. would seek to avoid, even if it meant revising lesser policy goals.

In any event, the dialogue of threat and counterthreat in areas of limited military and nonmilitary conflict is a significant part of the East-West struggle in the deterrent environment. Western threats of limited retaliation, necessitated as this dialogue develops, do not require the same high level of Western commitment as threats of massive strategic response, since the former are less likely to cause the enemy to invoke full-scale retaliation. Our behavior in such comparatively "minor" crises can demonstrate our willingness to pay a price to restrain aggression, and can imply a risk of escalation to higher levels of retaliation if aggression is carried out. Thus under the ultimate threat of strategic retaliation, the international power arena no longer resembles a competitive game which is likely to end with a victor and a vanquished. It is, instead, more analogous to labor-management negotiations where negotiations take place either during a strike, or under threat of a strike, which would injure both parties and, if the impasse is not broken, might result in a permanent work stoppage. In this type of conflict situation, gains and losses by the competitors are likely to be influenced by: a) their degree of commitment to various objectives; b) their willingness to make sacrifices; c) their ability to communicate to the opponent the degree of their commitment to the various objectives involved; and d) their ability in individual situations to make the required commitment level higher for the opponent than for themselves.

The physical ability to defeat the opponent at the highest level of violence which, in a sense, is possessed by both sides, is no longer the primary controlling factor. The modified role of military forces in this environment which relates primarily to items c) and d) above can be summarized briefly as follows: a) to raise the price associated with lesser aggressive acts to such a level that lesser aggression will also appear undesirable, and to do this at as low a level of military commitment as possible; and b) to maintain the ultimate retaliatory capability as a final deterrent to a major attack and to do whatever is possible to limit damage to ourselves if deterrence fails. . . .

Thus, while the gains and losses of East and West are likely to be governed in large degree by the extent of their commitment to their objectives and their willingness to make sacrifices, the military capability of both sides still plays an important role because it serves to increase or to decrease the relative sacrifices required by both sides in any specific conflict situation. A well-designed military force for this new type of environment is clearly one which in each area of confrontation can demand a large commitment or sacrifice on the part of the opponent and can keep the level of commitment required of one's self as low as possible. . . .

Obviously, the ideal U.S. military posture would be one which could provide for a successful defensive operation in every region of the world and at each level of violence, up to that level at which the total national resources of the disputed territory are necessarily destroyed. Because of the essential dominance of destructive capability over defense, the defense cannot physically stop an attack designed to destroy the country. Consequently, the only possible protection against attacks of this magnitude is to deter them. An effective defensive strategy must assure that the aggressor cannot benefit from such an attack. If the primary object of the attack were to capture the existing economic assets of the nation, the fact that these assets could not be captured intact would remove the primary motive for the attack. However, if the purpose of the attack were to achieve a psychological or military objective, deterrence of the attack might require a plan for the destruction of assets within the aggressor's sphere of influence which he considered more valuable than the prize of successful aggression. Such a response should more than offset any benefit sought as a consequence of the attack.

Clearly, such an ideal defense in every region and at all levels of violence is not economically feasible. In some areas, it is necessary to defend by threatening to escalate any engagement which begins at a low level of escalation, where the defender's weaknesses are obvious, to some higher level where either defense is possible or the prize is destroyed.

In those cases where the destruction of the values to be defended is inevitable if the conflict escalates, the defender's threat of escalation may not be credible unless it can occur either accidentally or by automatic processes inherent in the defender's war plans and pattern of deployment. This requirement to enhance the credibility of a threat to "raise the ante" by providing in advance for automatic escalation devices has influenced much of our deployment in Free Europe. Despite this fact, a posture dependent on automatic escalation is undesirable, if a workable defense can be found at lower levels of violence. Such a posture is also undesirable because it automatically commits the defense to a course of action which might not be justified by the nature of the enemy attack. In short, it eliminates escalation as a deliberate decision taken by the defender to improve the likelihood of his successfully countering the aggressor. This is a particularly serious a priori commitment since the defense might have had other options had there been a longer "pause" to identify the magnitude of the enemy effort. Moreover, the greater the flexibility of response implied by the defender's pre-attack deployments and weapons "mix" in the area, the more uncertain the potential aggressor will be about how to assess correctly in advance the ultimate outcome of any attack plan he may contemplate. Decreasing the enemy planner's ability to predict a successful outcome can, in itself, contribute to deterrence.

In all cases of this type, it is to the advantage of the defense to try to hold violence at the lowest possible level consistent with successful termination of the war. Similarly, it is to the advantage of the attacker to keep the level of violence at as low a level as is consistent with the attainment of his objectives. A primary function of any limited conflict is to demonstrate a level of commitment and thereby to modify or limit the objectives of the opposition. In designing military forces for this type of mission and in considering arms control proposals which might modify the effectiveness of military forces on both sides, it is important to take these general principles into account. It is equally essential to understand the implications of these considerations in terms of our unilateral preparation for various types of engagements that we must be prepared either to fight or to threaten to fight.

Clearly, we will be better off if we have selectively allocated our military expenditures in favor of those types of forces which can play a crucial role at the various potential levels of escalation. However, in order to accomplish this it is necessary to have a well-defined concept of the distinguishable levels of escalation, and to understand the role of various types of military forces at each such level.

DISTINGUISHABLE LEVELS OF RESTRAINT OR ESCALATION

In any discussion of levels of escalation, it is easy to stray into an unresolvable controversy about the probability of any set of restraints being respected by both sides in an actual military confrontation. Lacking a well-defined geopolitical and military context, such speculation is necessarily fruitless. In any given situation, restraints will be observed *only* if both sides believe the restraints to be advantageous within that particular context. Even when the context is real and well-defined, one can only conjecture about the viability of specific restraints. Either side can violate the restraints at any time, and neither the course of the battle, nor the motives and degree of commitment of the opposition, ever can be predicted with confidence.

In the heat of conflict, restraints will not be effective unless they are fairly simple and can be readily discerned by both participants. Therefore, the restraints must be defined by some clearly distinguishable parameters, known and accepted by both sides, so that their observance by one side can be easily recognized by the other. For example, a restraint which confined the use of nuclear weapons to tactical rather than strategic applications would almost surely fail (even if both sides were strongly motivated to honor it) because of the nebulous line between the tactical and strategic applications of such weapons. Such a restraint would necessarily be unworkable unless the international dialogue preceding the conflict had resulted in a clear and unambiguous distinction between the tactical and strategic applications of nuclear weapons. In order for a restraint to be viable during a prolonged conflict, which necessarily would include periods of reversal for both sides, it must be founded on an unambiguous and mutually recognizable distinction.

This is not to imply that qualitative and somewhat ambiguous distinctions have no role to play. Occasions can certainly arise where it may be desirable — in order to provide a demonstration of commitment and willingness to escalate to a higher level — to move into the next distinguishable level of escalation. Under such circumstances, one can anticipate that the enemy also may move in the same direction. The initiation of such a move is, in effect, a challenge. The opponent, depending on his degree of commitment, can reply in any of the following ways: a) by an immediate effort to negotiate; b) by a limited reply at the new level or at some higher level in an effort to achieve a more favorable political settlement; or c) by extending the conflict *in toto* to the suggested new level or even to some higher level of escalation. Unless the opposition interprets the move as a bluff, he cannot expect to continue his conduct of the engagement at the lower level of escalation with any prospect of winning.

Such limited maneuvers into higher levels of escalation, with deliberate intent to limit the level of violence within the new level of escalation, may be useful for their political and psychological effect. These moves are designed primarily as demonstrations of intent rather than as decisive military operations. Such limited military operations should not ordinarily tax the capability of either side to fight at the next level of escalation. Therefore, the fact that such incidents may occur should not be a primary consideration either in structuring military forces or in weighing the relative strengths and weaknesses of both sides for purposes of negotiation.

An evaluation of the strengths and weaknesses of opposing military forces must be based on an assessment of their *maximum* capability within each *distinguishable* level of escalation. In order to proceed with such an evaluation, we must first determine what potentially clear distinctions exist which could serve to define these identifiable levels of escalation. However, the mere fact that two levels of escalation are theoretically distinguishable will not make these levels distinguishable in the real world unless the dialogue between the participants has served to make both sides aware of the potential dividing lines which separate them. Since the existence of such distinctions can, in itself, contribute to military security by providing potential stopping points in the escalation process, one of the functions of arms control negotiations might be to contribute to the clarification of useful distinctions.

Based on the fact that the most effective distinctions should be simple, clearly defined and unambiguous, we can now list some of the most important factors which could serve to delineate potential levels of escalation. Some possible distinguishing factors are:

    a. The use or nonuse of nuclear weapons:
        (1) Airburst only
        (2) Both air and groundburst.
    b. The use or nonuse of chemical or biological weapons.
    c. Geographic sanctuaries or limitations on the extent of the combat area, or on the use of atomic, biological and chemical (ABC) weapons within the

area. Possible geographic distinctions could involve present (or in some cases even historical) national boundaries, or topographical features such as rivers and coastlines. The use of ABC weapons might be restricted to sea warfare, or to air defense, or to "defensive" application only, i.e., within friendly territory.

    d. Direct versus indirect U.S. and U.S.S.R. participation:

      (1) Moral support only
      (2) Supply of armaments
      (3) Supply of combat personnel and armaments.

The above factors, in a variety of combinations, can provide potential distinctions which could be used to limit the level of violence. While there is no assurance that in specific cases the distinctions could or would be recognized, there does not appear to be any sound basis for ruling out any of them as potentially useful criteria for introducing restraints. . . .

In some instances, for sound reasons of strategy, the U.S. government may find it advisable to assert our intention to ignore some of the broader restraints suggested. For example, it has long been U.S. policy to insist that the West would resort to nuclear weapons to counter any significant communist attack on a portion of NATO Europe. Furthermore, we have declared that any major attack in that area could trigger U.S. nuclear retaliation against the Soviet homeland. This position is, in effect, a statement of intent to respect neither the distinction between nuclear and conventional weapons nor the political boundaries of Europe as restraint criteria in the event of an attack on NATO. The existence of such a declaration of policy does not contradict the idea discussed above which states, in effect, that if both East and West believed it in their best interest to avoid the use of nuclear weapons or to accept geographic limitations on their employment in the European theater, it might be possible to abide by these restraints.

CONCLUSION

Arms control and strategy are intimately related. Thus, arms control can be successful only if it is soundly based on military strategy and capabilities — whether it be by formal agreement or by tacit understanding. Indeed, a measure of arms control automatically inheres in a defense policy which offers a wide range of choices below the level of general nuclear war. The formulation of a feasible arms control policy must begin with a careful assessment of the range of military options available. This does not mean, of course, that military capabilities and strategy must remain inflexible. In some instances, it may be possible to facilitate arms control by modifying the existing strategic concept or posture. But any Western effort to formulate an arms control scheme which seeks in procrustean fashion to make military force posture and strategy fit a preconceived arms control plan will inevitably fail either to gain the necessary domestic and foreign acceptance or to provide international security.

Enough Is Enough

39 SEYMOUR MELMAN
Too Much U.S. War Power? A Scientist's View

Soon after President Kennedy presented a 1964 military budget request totaling $56.7 billions, Secretary of Defense McNamara told the Congress, "We calculate that our forces today could still destroy the Soviet Union without any help from the deployed tactical air units, or carrier task forces, or Thor or Jupiter intermediate range ballistic missiles."

The military fact behind this judgment is an American military overkill capability that exceeds almost anyone's comprehension. The idea of "overkill" is a thermonuclear invention. Never before could one think of military power sufficient to kill a population more than once. Washington officialdom has yet to understand the meaning of this new power for the military and other aspects of security policy.

A group of colleagues and myself recently completed a set of studies on "A Strategy for American Security." What we found is a combination of surplus destruction on the military side, with technological and economic depletion in basic civilian industry; in short, a net weakening of America's security position.

The United States currently has about 3,400 strategic aircraft and missiles. These vehicles can deliver warheads with explosive power equivalent to 22 billion tons of TNT, that equals more than seven tons of TNT for each person on our planet. The stockpile of nuclear warheads is more than twice that amount.

Seymour Melman is Professor of Industrial Engineering at Columbia University. This article is reprinted from the *New York Herald Tribune*, July 7, 1963, Section 2, p. 1.

What is the military significance of this much nuclear power? Here are the results of calculations that are at once nightmarish and realistic. We will designate the relationship — 100,000 persons killed by 20,000 tons of TNT — as a "Hiroshima equivalent."

In the Sino-Soviet bloc, the population of 370 cities equals 1,400 "Hiroshima equivalents." Allowing for 30 percent loss of delivery weapons, U.S. overkill capability for the entire Sino-Soviet area is 500 times. The Soviet Union alone contains 140 cities and industrial centers of 100,000 population or over: altogether, approximately 500 "Hiroshima equivalents." Allowing 50 percent failure to deliver warheads, the U.S. alone could deliver about 25 million tons per "Hiroshima equivalent," amounting to a U.S. overkill capability of 1,250 times.

In these calculations, we have omitted any contribution that might be made by U.S. fighter planes, intermediate and short-range missiles, torpedoes, mines, cannon, and smaller "tactical" rocket launchers.

We can also estimate U.S. strategic power under a set of extreme conditions of possible missile and plane losses from all causes, with the following resulting nuclear delivery:

Effective U.S. Strategic Power, Assuming Massive Losses

Remaining Vehicles	Vehicles	Total Warhead Power Vehicles in Mill. Tons TNT Equivalent
10% of 600 B47 bombers	60	600
10% of 600 B52 bombers	60	1,200
10% of 100 B58 bombers	10	200
10% of 1150 Navy Aircraft	115	115
5% of 200 Atlas-Titan missiles	10	10
25% of 240 Polaris missiles	60	60
25% of 500 Minuteman missiles	125	125
Total	440 vehicles	2,310 million tons TNT

This effective power has an overkill factor of 231 on the population-industrial centers of the U.S.S.R. after drastic allowances for losses from defensive systems, breakdowns, etc. Such losses might occur if a successful surprise attack was launched against the U.S. and if the Soviet had anti-missile capability of hitherto unheard of effectiveness. Still, 231 times overkill should suffice.

The destructive capability of Soviet forces is estimated on the same basis as our first set of calculations: there are 404 NATO area cities of 100,000 people or more; the Soviets could deliver about 9 megatons per 100,000 city people, allowing for a 30 percent attrition of delivery systems. This is an overkill capability of 450 times. For 192 American cities of 100,000 or larger, U.S.S.R. medium-range vehicles are excluded as out of range, and an attrition of 50 percent is assumed. Yet the Soviets could deliver about 2.9 megatons per 100,000 city people — an overkill factor of 145 times.

Furthermore, Western military manpower exceeds that of the Communist bloc. The armed forces of the U.S. treaty powers come to a grand total of 8 million men. Total Communist-bloc forces are 7.7 million men.

All this means that a new military condition has been created. Neither side can defend its population against the nuclear attack of the other. Even a 99 percent effective defensive system against overkill in excess of 100 will not prevent total kill. What remains then of nuclear military strategy is deterrence, a thermonuclear threat system — and we obviously have sufficient military power now to deter.

ADDING TO SURPLUS DESTRUCTION

Why then does the proposed 1964 military budget include about $12 billion for additional strategic weapons, and the development of such weapons? There are three main explanations for the Pentagon proposal.

During a recent visit with the Assistant Secretary of Defense and his staff, I discovered, first, that they have not learned to face the new fact — that offensive and defensive strategic power is now at a stalemate because of the overwhelming power of offensive nuclear capability.

Some of the senior Defense Department people are still devoted to "counterforce" strategy — the theory that advises an attempt to knock out the military system of an opponent, thereby making a nuclear war primarily into a duel of military systems. This is advocated, despite the fact that the Secretary of Defense, in his budget message to the Congress, indicated that such a strategy is unworkable, since the Soviets have also been hardening missile sites on land and locating missiles in submarines.

The search for counterforce capability is very expensive: it requires an advantage of the order of ten to one in missiles, and unattainable precision in locating submarines, etc. There is no known way to prevent society-destroying counterblows in the event of first strike, either by the Soviets or by the United States.

The second explanation for more overkill spending is historical and institutional. The search for nuclear military superiority produced enormous overkill capability, which changed the conditions of offensive and defensive strategy. But this transformation went unnoticed by the people who made it happen, for they were immersed in the detailed technical aspects of this process. Also, the Pentagon, like other large organizations, practices "suboptimization," a theory which assumes that the improvement of the system will be the sum of the improvements of the parts. This is no longer possible, for the new condition of overkill has closed the way to militarily decisive improvements. A population can be killed only once.

Finally, the military equate security with military security. They don't perceive that military power, coupled with economic and political weakness, is poor security policy.

COST OF SURPLUS DESTRUCTION

One of the most disturbing aspects of the current defense procurement of surplus destruction is the cost.

Our military spending is 10 per cent of the Gross National Product. But the crucial figure is the use of three-quarters of the engineering and scientific talent of the country for these purposes; these men are attracted by the higher salaries of military industry. This pressure is undermining our civilian industrial economy, and restrains the growth of America's domestic industrial efficiency. The capability to manufacture quality producers' goods at low cost and price is diminished and thus depresses the United States toward a second-rate position as a supplier of industrial goods for the developing nations of the world. Such a condition is bound to have profound weakening effects on the political position of the United States relative to Europe and the Soviet Union. For the supply of basic industrial goods to the developing countries is one of the basic ways by which political relationships are established.

Security means not only military power, but a combination of military, economic, and political strength.

INDUSTRIAL DEPLETION

The United States now has the oldest stock of metalworking machine tools of any major industrial country. In 1963, 64 percent of our machine tools are 10 years old or older. In West Germany, the figure is 55 percent. Productivity in every class of metalworking production is limited, and our whole industrial system is affected.

Technological stagnation and economic decay are to be seen in a host of industries that are the base for a modern industrial system. Our steel industry has been neglectful of research and development; the shipbuilding industry of the United States has long ceased to be competitive. It has been neglectful of research and development and has not pursued technological opportunities, such as standardization of design and modern industrial engineering. The same conditions prevail in many classes of electrical machinery, printing machinery, textile machinery and manufacture of scientific instruments, elevators, large electric motors, materials-handling equipment, typewriters and sewing machines.

In 1948, we manufactured virtually all of the typewriters that were sold here. At present, 60 percent or less of America's requirements are manufactured here. The remainder is imported due to lack of technological development in the typewriter industry in this country.

In the sewing machine industry, there now is only one major firm manufacturing household sewing machines, with only one factory in the United States and 27 plants abroad, many supplying our domestic market.

The second side of the depletion of civilian industry is the relative shortage of capital for productive investment. This shortage has been due to the depleting effect of the tax process.

TO HALT DEPLETION IN CIVILIAN ECONOMY

I am certain that very few Americans are willing to watch this nation slip into a second rate security position due to waste of vital national resources on the production of surplus destruction. Accordingly, I have made a preliminary analysis of the proposed military budget in order to estimate the cost of operating and maintaining present strategic and conventional forces, and to gauge the resources that could be released to renew the depleted sectors of civilian activity. The . . . table [on page 410] indicates where cuts ought to be made from the proposed $56.7 billion military budget.

The recommendation is based upon the test of providing a "maintenance of present forces budget." In this analysis, the Administration's personnel proposals are held intact, as is the entire operational and maintenance budget. The procurement item, however, should be reduced by between $7.5 and $14 billion. The military stalemate caused by already overwhelming nuclear power suggests sharp curtailment of the military research and development and construction items.

Procurement	Proposed Budget	Possible Budget Reductions
		(In $ Billions)
Procurement of equipment & missiles, Army	$ 3.2	$ 1.0 — $ 2.0
Procurement of aircraft & missiles, Navy	3.0	2.0 — 3.0
Shipbuilding & conversion, Navy	2.3	1.0 — 2.0
Other procurement, Navy	1.2	.5 — 1.0
Aircraft procurement, Air Force	3.5	2.0 — 3.0
Missile procurement, Air Force	2.1	1.0 — 2.0
Other procurement, Air Force	1.0	.0 — 1.0
Total	$16.3	$ 7.5 — $14.00
Research, Development, Tests & Evaluation		
R & D, Tests and Evaluation, Army	$ 1.4	$ 1.0 — $ 1.2
R & D, Tests and Evaluation, Navy	1.5	.8 — 1.3
R & D, Tests and Evaluation, Air Force	3.6	3.6 — 3.6
R & D, etc., Defense Agencies	.4	.4 — .4
Emergency Fund, Defense	.15	.15 — .15
Total	$ 7.05	$ 5.95 — $ 6.65
Atomic Energy Commission	$ 2.0	$ 2.0 — $ 2.0
Military Assistance	1.5	.5 — 1.0
Miscellaneous	2.0	1.0 — 2.0
GRAND TOTAL (In Billions)	$29.75	$16.45 — $25.55

The Administration's recommendation on atomic energy deserves to be cut by about two-thirds, since further production of warheads makes no sense. Civil defense should be cut out as technically ineffectual and politically dangerous. The same logic applies to the bloated industrial stockpiling activity — already an economic and physical embarrassment.

Such cuts and the transfer of these billions to the civilian economy would free the resources needed to solve five pressing national problems.

(1) The civilian economy of the U.S. needs a massive infusion of capital and technical talent to stop industrial stagnation, to modernize our industries, and to generate productive employment. These are essential for solving the economic problems of our youth, the job needs of Negroes, and to compensate for automation displacement.

In 1960, for example, while we spent about 10 percent of our goods and services for military purposes, the countries in the Common Market spent 4 percent. During the same year, we spent 5 percent for machinery and equipment for our industries, while the countries of the Common

Market spent 10 percent for theirs. The result has been plain for all to see: full employment and rapid economic development in the countries of the Common Market, and economic stagnation in many regions of the United States.

(2) The flight of gold from the Federal Treasury has reached the point where it jeopardizes the international value of the dollar. (Twelve years ago the U.S. government held $24 billion in gold bullion. Today the gold stock has been reduced to about $15 billion. This compares to $12 billion that is legally required as the basis for our currency. At the same time, about $19 billion in claims against U.S. gold is held by the central bankers of foreign countries and by various private individuals.) The cause of the adverse balance of payments is composed of many elements, but one element dominates and converts a favorable balance of trade into an unfavorable balance of payments: heavy dollar spending abroad for military purposes.

(3) We have developed a new condition in American life, a bureaucracy that rules a military-industrial complex in the United States. Highly concentrated in particular states and regions (25 percent of industrial work in California, but 2 percent in Detroit), the military manufacturing industry takes orders directly from the Department of Defense and delivers its goods to that customer only. We have yet to see serious steps by these military industrialists toward blueprinting the conversion of their firms from military to civilian economy.

(4) Thirty to forty million Americans live in deep poverty, with family income of less than $1,000 per year; they are poorly housed, poorly fed, poorly clothed. A capital fund and the technical talent to raise the productivity of these people is being used elsewhere. One result is that one out of six Americans is virtually removed from the market for consumer goods.

(5) While concentrating on military development at home and abroad, we have left more than half the population of the earth in bleak poverty, and thus vulnerable to Soviet penetration. Our foreign assistance program has been overwhelmingly military. So long as economic development is left to be carried out by a process of extracting taxes from an impoverished peasantry, a police state becomes a reasonable, necessary form of government. This will continue to be the case until we organize our enormous productive resources to make possible the option of economic development together with a measure of personal and political freedom.

SEYMOUR MELMAN   *411*

The large savings that are possible in our military expenditures, even while maintaining enormous military power, allow us to raise fresh questions about our whole world strategy. The policy of the United States has been based on the assumption that military power is the indispensable instrument for resolving national conflicts.

What are the possible alternatives to this view? Could the productive capability of the United States be used as an instrument of power?

If we use our productive might to generate economic development at home and abroad, then we could create a new situation: an industrial thrust from the United States of such power and political consequences that in order to meet it the Soviets, for their part, would have to take disarmament seriously. Could such a strategy, a peace race, break the negotiating deadlock which now plagues all our disarmament efforts?

A prudent national budget can maintain the present military capacity while liberating vast resources. These resources are the proper size for ameliorating grave national problems, and for mounting an alternative system of power politics based upon our industrial, productive might.

COMMUNIST STRATEGY

Disarmament and Peaceful Coexistence

40 I. GLAGOLEV AND V. LARIONOV
Soviet Defense Might and Peaceful Coexistence

Thermo-nuclear and rocket weapons make world war in our day cataclysmic. In such a war, hundreds of millions of people would inevitably die, and whole countries, great and small, would be turned into radioactive wasteland.

Such a war is espoused only by the ultra reactionary "wild men" of the West, who do not care what happens to the human race, or by the myopic dogmatists from among the leaders of the Chinese Communist

I. Glagolev is an economist specializing in economic problems of disarmament, while V. Larionov is a Soviet military analyst. These excerpts are from an article in *International Affairs* (Moscow), XI (November 1963) 27–33.

Party, who trample on the highly humanitarian ideas of Marxism-Leninism. They operate with obsolete concepts and fail to take account of the new world situation. They refuse to recognise that as a result of the formation of the Socialist world system the balance of world forces has radically changed in favour of peace and Socialism, that another world war is no longer inevitable, and that peaceful co-existence is the only correct foreign policy for the Socialist states to follow. . . .

An ideological offensive to denigrate the policy of peaceful co-existence is now being mounted by its opponents in the West and in the East, each group going about it in its own peculiar way. Thus, they have discovered "contradictions" in the very substance of Soviet foreign policy: Western critics say that the strengthening of the defence might of the U.S.S.R. and the whole Socialist camp makes nonsense of peaceful co-existence; by contrast, the Chinese leaders say that peaceful co-existence disarms the Socialist countries.

It turns out that in the long run these critics have the same purpose: they want to destroy confidence in the Soviet Union's policy of peace. That states with different social systems should co-exist in peace is not a new idea: it was the Soviet Union's guiding light even when the country was militarily much weaker than the combined forces of world imperialism; it continues to be guided by the idea today, when the military might of the country and the whole world Socialist system is greater than that of the forces of international reaction. This proves that the Soviet Union does not proclaim its policy of peaceful co-existence out of any sense of weakness. . . .

In view of the open and frankly slanderous campaign now being conducted by the "wild men" in the West and the Chinese dogmatists in the East, an analysis of the connection between the consistent Leninist policy of peaceful co-existence and the efforts of the Soviet people and Government to strengthen their country's defence capability is necessary and appropriate.

I

Looking for contradictions between the Soviet policy of peaceful co-existence and the propositions of Soviet military strategy on the strengthening of the U.S.S.R.'s defence capability is one of the latest fads among Western reactionaries.[1]

---

[1] A symposium edited by Marshal of the Soviet Union V. D. Sokolovsky, published at the end of 1962, is often quoted as evidence of the "glaring" contradiction between the general line of Soviet foreign policy and Soviet military strategy.

Some American and British writers and Washington spokesmen cast doubt on the peaceful co-existence policy, which, they say, does not accord with the idea of building up Soviet defences and preparedness on the part of the Soviet Armed Forces to use every means at their disposal to inflict decisive and total defeat on any aggressor. . . .

The real aim of these absurd anti-Soviet charges is to help the wild votaries of the arms drive to vindicate the military preparations in the U.S.A. and other NATO countries.

Everyone knows that the preparedness of the Soviet Armed Forces and the Soviet Union's possibilities of beating back any aggressor are now not in any way unequal to the capability of the imperialist countries to strike first. All Western leaders who take a more or less sober view of the situation now realise this, as otherwise they would not have declared an equal interest in averting a military catastrophe. That is why they have to voice — always with an effort and often inconsistently — their acceptance of co-existence. . . .

Only those for whom logic is a closed book will see any contradiction between the policy of peaceful co-existence and the desire for general and complete disarmament, on the one hand, and the strengthening of Soviet defences, on the other. Soviet military strategy is completely dependent on the policy of the state, and deals with the various aspects of national defence in conformity with its general line. So long as there is any danger of an outside attack, so long as general and complete disarmament remains to be negotiated, the policy of the Socialist state must reckon with the need of taking appropriate measures to safeguard national security.

If disarmament and international security were achieved, this function of the Soviet state would disappear, and the armed forces would become superfluous. . . .

The Soviet Union does not need war to attain its goal — to build Communism. It will do this much faster and with much greater success in conditions of peace. Consequently, the Communist Party, the Soviet Government, and the country's military leaders are concerned with strengthening their Armed Forces for purely external reasons: owing to the force of circumstances they *must* constantly devote attention to matters of defence.

Those in the West who see this as a "contradiction" would apparently like to see the Soviet Union and the other Socialist countries disarmed in the face of impending attack, as this would allow the imperialist Powers to dictate their will with impunity. However, the Soviet Union conducts its policy of peaceful co-existence out of a certitude of its strength and preparedness to safeguard peace and the security of nations.

"We do not hold to that well-known maxim: offence is the best defence," says Soviet Defence Minister Marshal Rodion Malinovsky. "It is a maxim that does not suit the Socialist states in principle, for they are peaceable by nature. Ours is different: the best form of defence is to warn the opponent of our strength and readiness to crush him at the very first attempt to commit an act of aggression."[2]

In short, there is no contradiction, but a direct connection between the policy of peaceful co-existence and our preparedness to rout an aggressor. The officers and men of the Soviet Armed Forces, like all Soviet people, have an interest in averting war and the wholesale annihilation of the peoples.

It undoubtedly takes more than an army to ensure the security of the U.S.S.R. and of other countries, for security is also based on economic, scientific, technical and political might.

Under general and complete disarmament, security will be ensured by the liquidation of the armaments of all countries, international control over disarmament, the remaining security forces and also by international organisations. The economic, political, scientific and technical might of the countries of the Socialist community will by then undoubtedly have been greatly enhanced and will play an even greater part in this.

The Armed Forces of the Soviet Union have the capability of instant devastating retaliation to any imperialist aggressor. However, their *principal aim* is not to annihilate the nations but to *avert a nuclear attack on the U.S.S.R. and the other Socialist and peace-loving countries, to avert world wars*. In this context they are a powerful factor for peace and an obstacle to the military gambles which some in the West are hatching.

So long as imperialism exists there remains the danger of its using force in international affairs. That is why the U.S.S.R. strives to conduct its policy of peaceful co-existence and disarmament in such a way as not to jeopardise the security of the Socialist countries or to allow the imperialist circles to obtain unilateral military advantages, engage in espionage on the territory of the Socialist countries, or violate international treaties. It is a deliberate lie for the Chinese leaders to say

---

[2] R. Ia. Malinovskii, *Bditel'no stoiat' na strazhe mira* (Moscow: Voennizdat, 1962) p. 25.

that the U.S.S.R. has proposed the *unilateral* disarmament of the progressive forces. Upon the other hand, the U.S.S.R. does not demand capitulation on the part of the other countries or any unilateral advantages for itself.

The Armed Forces of the U.S.S.R. — the mightiest Socialist country and the world's first space Power — differ in principle from the armed forces of states in the past, and from those of all socio-economic formations now on the way out. The Soviet Armed Forces are not designed for attacking other countries or seizing foreign territory. Their main purpose is to defend the freedom and independence of our country and the other Socialist and peaceable countries, the gains of Socialism and democracy, universal peace and international security. This not only makes them a force of national security but also assigns to them the international mission of serving as a reliable guarantee of peace and the security of other Socialist nations, including the Chinese People's Republic, and of all peace-loving nations.

All the peoples now realise that at the most critical moments the Soviet Union has never wavered in throwing the full weight of its international authority and military might to tip the scales and stay the aggressor's hand about to fall on any country, big or small. Such was the case during the Caribbean crisis, in the period of tension in the Taiwan Strait, during the Anglo-French-Israeli aggression, and during the 1958 events in the Middle East, when the Soviet Union used its nuclear rocket might to shield Socialist Cuba, to avert aggression against the Chinese People's Republic, and safeguard the independence and freedom of Egypt, Syria and Iraq.

"Nor will the Soviet people," says the Soviet Government's statement of August 21 [1963], "ever waver in the future, in any time of ordeal; they have everything they need to deal a crushing blow at anyone who makes an attempt on the security of the Soviet Union or its friends and allies. But despite Peking's exhortations, the Soviet Union will not be drawn into acts of foolhardiness and irresponsible gambling with hundreds of millions of human lives."

It must be emphasised that the Chinese leaders' arsenal of foolhardy "theories" now contains another highly dangerous idea. Without canvassing the opinion of the Poles, Czechs, Mongols, Rumanians, Hungarians or the peoples of other Socialist countries, the Chinese leaders, having lost all sense of responsibility for the destiny of peace and Socialism, proclaim from the rooftops the doctrine of "strategic autarky," which is based on the patently harmful idea that "in the struggle against imperialist aggression, in defence of its own security, every Socialist country relies above all on its own defence capacity." For most relatively small states this idea was a patent absurdity even in the prenuclear age. But to say this in the nuclear age is to ignore the actual balance of forces and reveal utter incomprehension of the processes taking place in the world. Every one knows that the manufacture of nuclear and rocket weapons is an extremely costly business which tends to tax the economy even of highly developed countries. Clearly not all Socialist countries have such possibilities.

That is why the Socialist countries, including the Chinese People's Republic, all the assertions of the Chinese leaders to the contrary, base their defence planning on the Soviet Union's nuclear might, which is a deterrent to the aggressive circles of the Western Powers.

It is not surprising, therefore, that the peoples of the Socialist countries have firmly rejected the doctrine of "strategic autarky" put forward by the leadership of the Chinese Communist Party. . . .

The Soviet Union is ready to come to the defence of all the Socialist countries, and has sufficient means to do this. But this is a matter of ensuring the security of these countries against possible encroachments by aggressors and not of preparing an attack against other countries.

The Soviet people still have a vivid recollection of the U.S. President's recent statement that in certain circumstances the U.S.A. could use nuclear weapons first.* Efforts are being made in the U.S.A. to justify this bellicose statement. Some say it envisions the "possibility of an attack" by conventional Soviet forces on Western Europe, which allegedly does not have enough conventional forces to defend itself; hence U.S. nuclear "retaliation." However, this argument does not hold any water. A few years ago, it could be said (for purely demagogic purposes, of course) that the French army was engaged in Algeria, and that the West German Bundeswehr was embryonic. Today, West Germany is a place of arms where battle-ready German, American and British troops are deployed, while the bulk of the French forces has been transferred to Europe.

Neither official Soviet spokesmen nor Soviet military theorists have ever put forward the doctrine that nuclear war was acceptable as a means of obtaining advantages for the Soviet Union at the price of hundreds of millions of deaths.

---

* Apparently a reference to an interview with President Kennedy published in the *Saturday Evening Post.* See p. 381. — Ed.

The Chairman of the Council of Ministers of the U.S.S.R., N. S. Khrushchev, has made this clear-cut statement: "We have our rockets armed with the most powerful thermo-nuclear weapons in constant readiness for action. But the Soviet Union will never be the first to use these weapons and start a world war. We place all our might on the scales of peace, working for the strengthening of peaceful co-existence between the Socialist countries and the capitalist countries."

By contrast, there are "theorists" in the U.S.A. who are trying to prove that in modern conditions nuclear war is acceptable. Just this year, Herman Kahn, Director of the Hudson Institute — which investigates the role of military technology, particularly nuclear weapons, in U.S. foreign policy — had the gall to tell in *War/Peace Report* that nuclear war was preferable to certain systems of peaceful international relations in which the countries of Asia, Africa and Latin America would play a prominent part. Kahn's theory is shared by some U.S. Senators and other Western statesmen.

If there must be a quest for contradictions between official government declarations and the military policy advocated, it should be conducted in the United States. Is there not a glaring contradiction between the monstrous doctrine espousing nuclear war and President Kennedy's statement of June 10, 1963, that such a war is absurd?*

The Soviet Government must see to it that the Soviet Union's security is reliably guaranteed and spotlight the practical measures being taken by the U.S.A. and the other NATO Powers to step up their armament for no other reason than that imperialism is militaristic and predatory, and that the Western Powers are engaged in military preparations, while their politicians and top brass keep turning out aggressive doctrines. In the circumstances, the strengthening of Soviet defences is of great importance in safeguarding the gains of the working people in the Soviet Union and the other Socialist countries and in defending peace and the security of all nations. That is why Soviet military analysts have to show the material, moral and political possibilities of checking aggression and the ways of parrying it, including the rout of the forces encroaching on the Soviet people's peaceful labours.

Those who insist that this is in "contradiction" with the policy of peaceful co-existence ought to bear in mind that all Soviet writers on military affairs speak of defence preparations only because war can break out if the forces of imperialism and aggression risk taking this

---

* A reference to the *Toward a Strategy of Peace* address, pp. 78–85. — Ed.

suicidal step despite all the measures taken by the U.S.S.R. to avert it. It follows, therefore, that those who have no intention of attacking the Soviet Union or of unleashing war against the peace-loving countries need have no fear of Soviet military might and the preparedness of the Soviet Armed Forces to crush any aggressor.

Soviet military strategy is the strategy of ensuring reliable security for the Soviet Union and the Socialist world. It is in complete accord with the policy of peaceful co-existence being conducted by the Soviet state. Upon the other hand, the security of the U.S.S.R. and its allies is not weakened, as the Chinese leaders assert, but is strengthened by the policy of peaceful co-existence.

II

What then is the basis and point of departure of the Soviet concept of defence? It rests, above all, on the economic might of the U.S.S.R. and the other Socialist countries; the policy of peace and the support of this policy by other nations; the identity of interests of the Socialist countries and the combat alliance of their armed forces, as sealed by their mutual commitments under the Warsaw defence pact; and the moral and political unity of the peoples of the U.S.S.R. and its allies.

The Soviet concept of defence is based on the might of the Soviet Armed Forces, which have at their disposal all modern means of warfare, including highly powerful nuclear weapons, super-range ballistic rockets of excellent quality and hairline precision, and other means capable of instantly dealing a devastating unavertible counterblow with fatal consequences for the aggressor. It is this proposition of Soviet military strategy that has caused displeasure in the imperialist camp.

The bourgeois advocates of the arms drive and military pressure on the U.S.S.R. slander the Soviet policy of peace by saying that the Soviet strategic concept is rigid and does not set any limits to the use of nuclear weapons in the event of war. They say the Russians take a critical attitude to the Anglo-American doctrine of "limited war."

These charges fly in the face of elementary logic.

The Soviet Government has said again and again — and has proved by its works — that it wants a total ban, and not a mere limitation, on the use of nuclear weapons. When the Soviet proposal for a total ban on the use of nuclear weapons (and their eventual destruction) is weighed against the idea of their limited use, everyone will see which, from the standpoint of humanity's destiny, is found wanting.

To accept the Western doctrine of limiting the use of nuclear weapons to geographical areas, specified targets, or size of warheads would be to recognise as lawful the annihilation of millions of people through the use of dozens or hundreds of "small" nuclear missiles or rockets, and to draw comfort from the thought that a great service has been rendered to mankind because it is not going to lose hundreds of millions of lives in a nuclear strike with the use of mammoth bombs. After all, it will be cold comfort for the war casualty to have been blasted by a 20-kiloton bomb instead of a 50-megatonner. Moreover, the "limited war" doctrine is false, because nuclear war differs in principle from all previous wars in that it *cannot be limited*.

The Soviet Union, in resisting the stirring up of a world nuclear conflagration, is fully aware that with the pattern of international ties being what they are in present-day conditions and with nuclear stockpiles providing enough overkill capacity to destroy whole nations many times over, any nuclear conflict is liable swiftly to escalate into a world nuclear war. The Soviet Union, working as it does to avert nuclear war, will not encourage any kind of secret agreement legalising the prelude to such a war.

The limitations on the use of nuclear weapons suggested by Western military theorists, when analysed, turn out to be far-fetched and impracticable, and this is now and again admitted by the authors of the "limited war" doctrine themselves. The well-known American military analyst, Henry Kissinger, says, for instance: "Many argue that a limited nuclear war will automatically escalate because the losing side will always invest more resources to restore the situation."[3]

U.S. critics accuse Soviet military strategists of projecting a counter-strike at the entire complex of enemy military objectives, not excluding the cities. They ask whether it is not better to wage a war with strikes only at military objectives. This U.S. doctrine of the "controlled strike," whatever its purpose, misleads people into thinking that a nuclear war could be waged with small civilian losses. Experience in the use of nuclear weapons must not be ignored. The first U.S. bombs dropped on Hiroshima and Nagasaki made it clear that they were primarily weapons of mass destruction. What ground is there to believe U.S. theorists when they say that their strategists would avoid striking at populated localities?

It is self-evident that any belligerent, if only to reduce his own losses, will first strive to knock out the enemy's military targets, especially

[3] *Foreign Affairs*, July 1962, p. 531.

his nuclear strike means. This does not at all mean that in the massive use of nuclear weapons cities and their inhabitants would be able to escape without huge losses. How can a multi-megaton bomb strike be limited to selected military targets when their area usually runs to no more than two figures, and the area directly hit by the bomb blast, to four or five figures? Besides, many important military objectives are located in the cities or in their vicinity, and in heavily populated areas. All this quite apart from the spread of radioactive fallout, fire storms, and the disruption of supply systems and medical services. . . .

The open letter of the Central Committee of the C.P.S.U. of July 14, 1963, is sharply critical of the Chinese leaders who suggest that a "beautiful future" could be built on the thermo-nuclear war ruins of the old world. The letter emphasises that the working class, the toiling peasantry and the working intelligentsia constitute the bulk of the population in the capitalist countries. Like many other Party and Government documents of the U.S.S.R., the letter makes it abundantly clear that the Soviet Union will never use nuclear weapons first.

"If the Chinese leaders' view were to prevail," says the Soviet Government's statement of September 21, 1963, "if Communists, instead of working for peace, were to engage in aggravating international tensions and accepted that world war was fatally inevitable, mankind would be plunged into a thermo-nuclear holocaust. In vain do the Chinese leaders deceive themselves and others by saying that this would bring nearer the triumph of the world revolution. . . . No, regardless of the cover-up of revolutionary phrases, the peoples would never forgive those who, in one way or another, pushed mankind towards thermo-nuclear war. It is quite plain that the Chinese leaders' course is directed against the vital interests of the masses of people in all countries. What it means in practice is betrayal of world Socialism, the working class and national-liberation movement, and betrayal of the cause of world revolution."

U.S. critics of Soviet defence concepts should make a more sober appraisal of Soviet policy and strategy. Soviet strategy, while stating the U.S.S.R.'s readiness to apply the full force of its military potential against an aggressor, has always emphasised that the Soviet Armed Forces would resort to such a measure only under compulsion. At the same time the Soviet state is intensifying its effort to stop the arms drive; ban nuclear weapons; achieve elimination of foreign military bases and withdrawal of troops from foreign territories; attain general and complete disarmament; and exclude war from the life of society.

Foreign military analysts who say that Soviet nuclear rocket weapons are highly vulnerable and are designed mainly for a first and not for a counterstrike, are talking through their hats.

It is obvious that even in the most favourable conditions, an aggressor would be unable to destroy all the counterstrike means with his first salvo, for these means — rockets, bombers, submarines, etc., — are dispersed, hidden underground and under water, and camouflaged. A considerable part of them is constantly on the move. Another, even greater part, such as bombers on airfields, are in a state of almost instant readiness to take off. It is physically impossible not only to knock out all the counterstrike means simultaneously, but even to pinpoint their location as the first salvo missiles reach their targets.

The element of surprise, rather important in past wars, now has a different character. Even such weapons as instant-action rockets, launched at any time of day or night and in any weather, can be detected in the first section of their flight path by ever vigilant radars and other instruments. In this age of radioelectronics and targeted ready-to-fire rockets, a counterstrike will follow the first strike in a matter of minutes. The first rockets and bombers of the side on the defensive would take off *even before the aggressor's first rockets, to say nothing of his bombers, reached their targets.*

If the attacker is to achieve a measure of even relative surprise — an advantage of a few minutes — he would have to use in his very first salvo a small but most efficient part of his means of attack. Thus, existing bombers, whose speed is only a fraction of that of rockets, would hardly produce any element of surprise, in the modern sense. Upon the other hand, after the aggressor's strike the attacked could discount the element of surprise and would use all his counterstrike means set in motion before the first explosions on his territory or remaining intact after the start of the enemy's nuclear bombardment.

But in order to deal an instant nuclear counterstrike the means of that strike must always be in a state of heightened readiness for action, and the Soviet Government's efforts are directed precisely at maintaining such a state of preparedness; it is precisely this capability of the Soviet Armed Forces that is now an important factor of Soviet defence might.

The modern Armed Forces of the U.S.S.R., even in the event of a surprise attack by an aggressor, are capable of delivering an instant counterblow, which would be equivalent in power to thousands of millions of tons of T.N.T.

It is quite safe to say that an aggressor cannot now derive any economic or political advantages from nuclear war, for it merely puts the seal on his own destruction. These propositions are a matter of principle. They indicate that *the basic change in the world balance of forces and the new properties of the weapons at the disposal of the Soviet Union* are a powerful deterrent to the unleashing of another war by the most aggressive circles of imperialism.

The Soviet Government, proceeding from the need to work up to the main goal — general and complete disarmament — has made a number of proposals to that end. It should be emphasised that acceptance by the Western Powers of these proposals which are based on complete reciprocity and do not involve any risk for either side, would clarify the military and political aims of the two sides.

Peaceful co-existence which is the general line of the foreign policy of the Soviet Union and the other Socialist countries does not imply a temporary absence of war, or a breathing space between clashes. Not at all. Peaceful co-existence is the only positive, constructive policy which promotes economic, social and cultural progress all over the world. Peace and disarmament will give scope to the development of the forces of Socialism, democracy and national liberation. At the same time they will tend to isolate and weaken the force of imperialism and reaction.

The "dissenting" opinion expressed on this issue by the Chinese Communist Party leaders, who are trying to foist their reckless "blow-for-blow" policy on the Socialist community, is alien to Marxism-Leninism. The illusion of "independence," of which there is so much talk in Peking these days, turns out to be nothing but a very prosaic betrayal of the cause of peace and Socialism which puts in jeopardy the future of millions of ordinary men. The "theories" now being propounded by leading Chinese Communists in their efforts to "refute" the Leninist principles of peaceful co-existence merely serve to whet the appetites of the ultra reactionary circles, and are, in essence, provocative.

The Soviet Union has always conducted and continues steadfastly to conduct the class, proletarian foreign policy of safeguarding the great gains of Socialism and preserving world peace. Its steadily strengthening armed might has always served — and continues to serve — the vital interests of ordinary people.

Through Revolution to Disarmament

41 | CHINESE GOVERNMENT STATEMENT Against the Test Ban

. . . The whole world knows that the tripartite treaty is designed to manacle all the socialist countries other than the Soviet Union and all the peace-loving countries, and that it has no restraining effect whatsoever on U.S. imperialism. It does not hinder the United States from using nuclear weapons in time of war, manufacturing and stockpiling nuclear weapons and proliferating nuclear weapons among its allies. After the conclusion of the tripartite treaty, U.S. imperialism has continuously declared that it is not bound in any way, and the Soviet leaders have not uttered a sound of protest. The Soviet statement pretends ignorance of all this and maintains that the Soviet leaders' position on the question of preventing the proliferation of nuclear weapons is perfectly reasonable.

The Soviet statement says it would not mean much if one or two more socialist countries came into possession of nuclear weapons, but it would be terrible if one or two more capitalist countries did so; that the Soviet Union cannot on the one hand give nuclear weapons to China and on the other oppose the United States giving nuclear weapons to West Germany; and that if the Soviet Union did so, the United States would surely arm West Germany with nuclear weapons. The Soviet statement boastfully proclaims this to be the Soviet leaders' "principled stand" on the question of preventing nuclear proliferation.

The Soviet statement asserts that in refusing to sign this treaty, China is assuming the role of those in the right-wing of the ranks of the U.S. "madmen," the West German revanchists and the French extremists. If that is the case, do not Chiang Kai-shek, Adenauer and Franco, who have signed, become left-wing forces of peace?

Finding themselves unable to put up any defence for the tripartite treaty, the Soviet leaders resort to slandering China. One of the slanders is that China is opposed to the tripartite treaty because the Soviet Union has denied it the atom bomb. This is a deliberate distortion of China's position.

These excerpts of the Chinese Government Statement of September 1, 1963 are taken from the text appearing in *Survival*, V, No. 6 (November–December 1963) 263–268, published by the Institute of Strategic Studies Ltd.

In our last statement we explained in detail how, as far back as 1959, the Soviet leaders made a gift to the United States of their refusal to provide China with the technical data required for the manufacture of nuclear weapons, but, for the sake of larger interests, we never mentioned this before, not even between fraternal parties. If it were not because the Soviet leaders have colluded with the U.S. imperialists in an effort to force China to undertake not to manufacture nuclear weapons, we would not have wanted to talk about this.

Our exposure has enraged the Soviet leaders, who declare that it amounts to divulgence of confidential documents and information relating to the defences of the countries in the socialist camp, and that they will draw their own conclusions.

Please do not pretend innocence. You know very well that long before we published our last statement you told the Americans the secrets between China and the Soviet Union concerning nuclear weapons.

As for drawing conclusions, have you not already done that long ago? Not only have you perfidiously and unilaterally scrapped the agreement on providing China with nuclear technical data, but you have blatantly given more and more military aid to the Indian reactionaries, who are hostile to China and have made incessant armed provocations against it. What is this if not your "own conclusions"?

The real point is that the Soviet leaders hold that China should not, and must not, manufacture nuclear weapons, and that only the few nuclear powers, and particularly U.S. imperialism, the enemy of the peoples of the whole world, are entitled to the continued production of nuclear weapons.

The Soviet statement asserts that China can rely on the nuclear weapons of the Soviet Union and need not manufacture them itself; that if it tries to manufacture them it will result in a great strain on China's economy.

Should or should not China itself master the means of resisting U.S. nuclear blackmail?

True, if the Soviet leaders really practised proletarian internationalism it might not be necessary for China to manufacture its own nuclear weapons.

But it is equally true that if the Soviet leaders really practised proletarian internationalism, they would have no reason whatever for obstructing China from manufacturing nuclear weapons.

The Soviet statement says that if China were to produce two or three atom bombs, the imperialists would aim many more atom bombs at China. This is in effect instigating the imperialists to threaten China with atom bombs.

Of course the fact that the U.S. imperialists may wish to aim more atom and hydrogen bombs at China merits attention and vigilance. But there is nothing terrifying about it. At this very moment the United States has many such bombs already poised against China. It will not make much difference if the United States listens to the Soviet leaders and adds a few more. The Chinese people will not tremble before U.S. nuclear threats. But one must ask: where do the Soviet leaders place themselves in making such instigation?

The main feature of the Soviet government's latest statement is its slander that we want socialism to win by means of thermo-nuclear war and that we would sacrifice 300 million Chinese and half of mankind in order to create a greater civilization on the corpses and the ruins. Railing at China, the Soviet statement asserts that China is carrying out "an inhuman policy" and following a "bestial conception."

This is really hair-raising stuff. How shocking! The Chinese communists are nothing but a bunch of bloodthirsty monsters, worse than Hitler, worse than any tyrants past or present, and, needless to say, hundreds of times worse than the U.S. imperialists.

TWO COUNTS

But how is this possible? What do the Soviet leaders base themselves on in making such fantastic charges against China? Their charges, however varied, boil down to two counts: First, that some responsible Chinese leaders have talked about the possibility that in a war people may die by hundreds of millions; second, that the Chinese journal *Red Flag* has made the assertion that the victorious people would create a beautiful future for themselves on the ruins of imperialism.

The references are to certain remarks made by Comrade Mao Tse-tung in his speech at the Moscow meeting of the Communist and Workers' Parties on 18 November, 1957 and to a passage in the article "Long Live Leninism!" (written by the editorial department of the *Red Flag*).

Let us now see what the Chinese Communist Party actually said. Comrade Mao Tse-tung said:

It is my opinion that the international situation has now reached a new turning point. There are two winds in the world today, the east wind and the west wind. There is a Chinese saying, "either the east wind prevails over the west wind or the west wind prevails over the east wind." It is characteristic of the situation today, I believe that the east wind is prevailing over the west wind. That is to say, the forces of socialism are overwhelmingly superior to the forces of imperialism.

Proceeding from that estimation, Comrade Mao Tse-tung pointed to the steadily growing possibility of preventing imperialism from launching a new world war.

Comrade Mao Tse-tung then added:

At present another situation has to be taken into account, namely, that the war-maniacs may drop atomic and hydrogen bombs everywhere. They drop them and we act after their fashion; thus there will be chaos and people will be lost. The question has to be considered for the worst. The political bureau of our party has held several sessions to discuss this question. If fighting breaks out now, China has got only hand-grenades and not atomic bombs — which the Soviet Union has, though. Let us imagine, how many people will die if war should break out? Out of the world's population of 2,700 million, one-third — or, if more, half — may be lost. It is they and not we who want to fight; when a fight starts, atomic and hydrogen bombs may be dropped. I debated this question with a foreign statesman. He believed that if an atomic war was fought, the whole of mankind would be annihilated. I said that if the worst came to the worst and half of mankind died, the other half would remain while imperialism would be razed to the ground and the whole world would become socialist; in a number of years there would be again 2,700 million people and definitely more. We Chinese have not yet completed our construction and we desire peace. However, if imperialism insists on fighting a war, we will have no alternative but to make up our minds and fight to the finish before going ahead with our construction. If every day you are afraid of war and war eventually comes, what will you do then? First I have said that the east wind prevails over the west wind and that war will not break out, and now I have added these explanations about the situation in case war should break out. In this way both possibilities have been taken into account.

The passage in "Long Live Leninism!" reads:

We consistently oppose the launching of criminal war by imperialism, because imperialist wars would impose enormous sacrifices upon the peoples of various countries (including the peoples of the United States and other imperialist countries). But should the imperialists impose such sacrifices on them, we believe that, just as the experience of the Russian Revolution and the Chinese Revolution shows, those sacrifices would be rewarded. The victorious peoples would very swiftly create on the ruins of imperialism a civilization thousands of times higher than the capitalist system and a truly beautiful future for themselves.

The meaning of these words is very clear:

(1) China wants peace, and not war;

(2) It is the imperialists, and not we, who want to fight a war;

(3) A world war can be prevented;

(4) Even in the eventuality that imperialism should impose a war on the peoples of the world and inflict tragic losses on them, it is the imperialist system, and not mankind, that would perish, and the future of mankind would still be bright.

In effect, we make the point in these four sentences. These four sentences are interrelated. But the Soviet leaders have seized hold of half the sentence in which we mention the possibility that the peoples of the world might suffer tragic sacrifice, quoted it out of context, and turned the other three and a half sentences inside out. Hence the conclusion: China wants to launch a nuclear world war and bring about the death of half of mankind so as to attain a bright future for mankind. It is indeed pitiable that the leaders of a great power, and a great socialist power at that, should resort to such low fabrications.

In the 14 July open letter of the Central Committee of the C.P.S.U., the Soviet leaders said, "The nuclear rocket weapons that were created in the middle of our century changed old notions about wars." In reality, this means that, after the emergence of nuclear weapons, war is no longer the continuation of politics, there is no longer any difference between unjust and just wars, imperialism is no longer the source of war, and the peoples of various countries should no longer wage just wars against imperialist armed aggression and armed suppression by the reactionary regime for such just wars cannot possibly be won but will only bring about the annihilation of mankind.

The conclusion must be: the only thing for all the oppressed peoples and nations and for all countries and peoples subjected to aggression and oppression to do, if they do not want to court self-destruction, is to capitulate to imperialism which possesses nuclear weapons. Anyone who dares to resist imperialist oppression, aggression and threats and to wage revolutionary war for independence and liberation, and anyone who dares to support such revolutionary war, is guilty of the error of adventurism and will be held responsible for the disaster of the so-called annihilation of mankind. In the opinion of the Soviet leaders, in this nuclear century to remain alive is everything, and there is no aim in life. This is the philosophy of willing slaves which demands of the peoples of the world that they should submit to the tender mercies of imperialism. It is a reactionary theory in the service of imperialism. It is a truly bestial conception.

At the end of World War Two, after it had dropped two atomic bombs on Hiroshima and Nagasaki in Japan, U.S. imperialism assumed that armed with this "ultimate weapon" it could ride roughshod over the world and do whatever it pleased. At the time there was a kind of fear-mentality among the Chinese people as well as among the peoples of other countries. U.S. imperialism, possessed of atomic weapons, appeared to them so powerful that they thought it could put down peoples' revolutions at will.

Precisely at that crucial moment Comrade Mao Tse-tung said in his talk with the American correspondent Anna Louise Strong in 1946:

> The atom bomb is a paper tiger which the U.S. reactionaries use to scare people. It looks terrible, but in fact it isn't. Of course, the atom bomb is a weapon of mass slaughter, but the outcome of a war is decided by the people, not by one or two new types of weapon.
>
> All reactionaries are paper tigers. In appearance, the reactionaries are terrifying, but in reality they are not so powerful. From a long-term point of view, it is not the reactionaries but the people who are really powerful.

This Marxist-Leninist thesis of Comrade Mao Tse-tung's was a timely exposure of the U.S. imperialists' plot of atomic blackmail and armed the Chinese people and the revolutionary peoples of all countries against it. The victory after victory which the peoples of many countries have won in their revolutionary wars against the aggression and enslavement by the imperialists and their lackeys in the past seventeen years have repeatedly proved the correctness of this thesis. . . .

Nuclear weapons in the hands of socialist countries should always be defensive weapons against the nuclear threats of the imperialists. In contrast to the imperialists, socialist countries have no need to, and must not, use nuclear weapons for blackmail or gambling. The question of using nuclear weapons is one that concerns the interests of millions upon millions of people; and the socialist countries must be extremely prudent on this question and never act recklessly. In this connection, both adventurism and capitulationism are extremely dangerous.

During the Caribbean crisis, the Soviet leaders committed both the error of adventurism and the error of capitulationism. Instead of criticizing themselves, they have prided themselves on the slap in their face, boasted of their "genuine proletarian internationalism" and proclaimed what they have called a "major victory of the policy of reason, of the forces of peace and socialism." They have wantonly attacked the Chinese Communist Party for the righteous position it took on this issue, alleging that China hoped for a head-on clash between the United States and the Soviet Union and tried to provoke a nuclear war. This is utterly loathesome. . . .

. . . the open letter of 14 July of the Central Committee of the C.P.S.U. said that "in case of aggression by American imperialists we shall come to the assistance of the Cuban people from Soviet territory, just as we would have helped them from Cuban territory. True, in this case the rockets would take slightly longer in the flight, but their accuracy would not be impaired by this." That being so, why did you have to ship rockets to Cuba? Was your purpose really to defend the Cuban Revolution? Would it not be more correct to say that what you did in the name of defending the Cuban Revolution was in reality political gambling?

The position and line of the Chinese Communist Party and the Chinese Government on the question of war and peace have always been clear and cannot be distorted.

We resolutely oppose world war and we resolutely defend world peace. Not long after World War Two, Comrade Mao Tse-tung stated definitely that a third world war can be prevented. For over a decade, the Chinese people have been firmly persisting in the struggle to oppose the imperialist policies of aggression and war, to prevent a new world war and to preserve world peace. We have consistently held that provided the peoples of the whole world become united, follow a correct line and persevere in struggle, a new world war can be prevented, a nuclear war can be prevented, and world peace can be preserved.

It is our view that imperialism is the source of modern wars and that U.S. imperialism is the main force of aggression and war. Unless a resolute struggle is waged against the U.S. imperialist policies of aggression and war, defence of world peace is completely out of the question. If one prettifies U.S. imperialism and obscures from the peoples of the world the targets of this struggle, this will only endanger world peace.

It is our view that in order to strive for world peace, it is necessary to unite in joint efforts all the peace-loving forces of the world, namely, the socialist camp, the national liberation movement, the revolutionary movement of the peoples of all countries, and all the peace-loving countries and peoples. If one despises the force of the masses of the people and blindly trusts nuclear weapons as omnipotent, this will only endanger world peace.

It is our view that in order to strive for world peace, it is necessary to strengthen the unity of the socialist camp and enhance the strength of the national defences of all the countries in the socialist camp. If one splits the socialist camp and weakens its defence forces, it will only endanger world peace.

It is our view that in order to strive for world peace, it is necessary to give full support to the national liberation movement and the revolutionary struggles of the peoples of all countries. The more these struggles develop, the more the imperialist forces will be weakened and the more possible it will be to prevent the imperialists from launching world war. If one refuses to support, and even sabotages, the national liberation movement and the revolutionary struggle of the peoples of all countries, this will only endanger world peace.

PEACEFUL CO-EXISTENCE

We consistently maintain that countries with different social systems should co-exist peacefully. It was China which initiated the five principles of peaceful co-existence. It has made unremitting efforts for peaceful co-existence with countries having different social systems on the basis of the five principles. For the socialist countries, peaceful co-existence must in all circumstances be based on principles and must not depart from them. Negotiation is one form of struggle against imperialism.

We are in favour of general disarmament and hold that the imperialists can be forced to accept certain agreements on disarmament through the unremitting struggle of the peoples of all countries. We are of the opinion that the complete and thorough prohibition of nuclear weapons can be achieved while imperialism still exists, just as poison gas was prohibited. This is because the use of such a weapon of mass destruction is completely contrary to the will of the peoples and, moreover, would subject the users to destruction. However, universal and complete *disarmament can be realized only after imperialism, capitalism and all systems of exploitation have been eliminated.* To make propaganda about the possibility of realizing "a world without weapons, without armed forces and without wars" through universal and complete disarmament while imperialism still exists, is to deceive the peoples of the world and is detrimental to the struggle for world peace. [Emphasis added.]

STRATEGY IN THE THIRD WORLD

Colonialism versus Peace

42 KWAME NKRUMAH
Africa, Disengagement and Peace

In thinking over the problems which you will be considering, what strikes me most forcibly is this. What the world today lacks is a code of international morality which measures up to its technological progress. . . .

THE HERITAGE OF WORLD WAR II

In my view, the tensions which have produced the "World with the Bomb" can be divided into roughly four classes.

First, there are the tensions resulting from the problems left over from the Second World War.

Secondly, there are the tensions arising out of the striving of the peoples of the less developed parts of the world to better their future and to throw off the burdens of imperialism, colonialism and racial discrimination.

Thirdly, there are the tensions resulting from a conflict of ideologies.

And fourthly, there are the tensions caused by the possession by some powers of weapons of mass destruction. . . .

Let me now deal with the first of my points — the tensions resulting from the problems left over from the Second World War. The very fact that peace is to-day threatened by tensions created by the Second World War underlines the point that world war cannot solve our difficulties. The victors in a world war, by their very victory, create problems which contain the seeds of a new world war. . . .

THE COLONIAL COUNTRIES AND CHANGE

Let me come now to my second point — the tensions arising out of the striving of the peoples of the less developed parts of the world to

Kwame Nkrumah, President of Ghana 1960–   , gave this speech as his opening address to the Accra Assembly on "The World without the Bomb," on June 21, 1962. These excerpts are reprinted from Document No. AA/5/1 (Accra, Ghana: Government Printing Department, 1962).

settle their future and to throw off the burden of colonialism, neo-colonialism and racial discrimination. . . .

The world is going to change. No power on earth can stop it, short of destroying all humanity. The choice before us is, therefore, peaceful change or change brought about by force. No international organization, however powerful, can stop the clock of history. I am a strong believer in peaceful change. In the Positive Action campaign which I initiated in Ghana during colonial times, and which led to a realization by the British authorities that the time had come to end colonialism here, I always insisted upon non-violent action.

I am, however, sufficiently a realist to understand that change cannot always, at every period in history, be brought by non-violent action. It is no coincidence that every single one of the five nations to whom permanent seats on the Security Council are allotted have had their revolutions or rebellions, which they look back to with justifiable pride and upon which, indeed, their present constitutions are based. The fact is that in certain periods of history the masses of the people in some particular country have no other means of escaping from a regime which is intolerable to them except by armed revolt. We must accept this fact and we must also accept the fact that the forces which produce a revolution, a revolt against colonialism or a movement for national unification, can occur at any point of time in history. . . .

One of the great difficulties of our age is that peace has become equated with compulsory political stagnation. The theory of balance of power results in this or that state being arbitrarily assigned to the zone of influence of one or other of the great power blocs. In consequence, any attempt by the people to alter the regime, whether it be by democratic or revolutionary means, is regarded not, as it should be, as a purely internal matter, but as an attempt to alter the balance of power between the power blocs. . . .

It is unrealistic, however, to hope that the people most intimately concerned will see the issue in this light. Oppressed peoples in a less developed country, made desperate by tyranny and corruption, are not going to be deterred from getting rid of an objectionable government on the ground that it might upset the balance of power between the Great Powers. People struggling to free themselves from colonial oppression are going to get help wherever they can find it. People artificially divided in the interest of the balance of power are going to continue to strive for reunification, and those suffering from racial discrimination are going to end it irrespective of the interests of those powers.

It is utterly unreasonable for the Great Powers to say to the less developed countries: "It is true we revolutionized our social systems. It is true that some of us executed our kings and emperors in the name of liberty, but this was a luxury to which we were entitled and to which you are not. You must bear all your present misfortunes because otherwise you will upset the balance of power on which we depend for our safety."

We must be realistic and understand that such a policy is in fact impossible. We must accept change, even violent change, in the less developed countries of the twentieth century. The highly developed countries of the world of today must realize that before they could become fully developed they had, in fact, to go through an exactly similar process. General and complete disarmament must presuppose complete and total liquidation of colonialism.

AFRICA AND THE IDEOLOGIES

Let me now turn to my third point: the tensions arising from a conflict of ideologies. . . .

The unity of Africa, which is to me and to many others the most important single international issue, may follow from either the system of capitalism, as practiced in the United States today, or the system of socialism, as practiced in the Soviet Union. To say this does not of course mean that those who think in these terms condemn either of these two systems, or suggest in any way that they are not suitable for the countries in which they are practised. Since, however, owing to Africa's colonial background, there is no class of indigenous African capitalists, it is impossible to build up a capitalist system in the same way as, for example, Japan has done. A capitalist system in Africa upon the United States' model, if it could be constructed at all, which is doubtful, would be essentially a system of the domination of Africa by foreign capital.

On the other hand, we have, throughout Africa, indigenous institutions as, for example, our traditional forms of co-operative undertakings in agriculture and commerce, which provide us with a basis upon which we can build. But in order to do so we must construct social and political systems of our own type and it would be quite unrealistic to think that this could be done by adopting wholesale the economic and political system of the Soviet Union.

We wish to learn from the capitalist and the socialist systems. In so far as is practicable we want to adapt to our own circumstances what is best in both of them, but we are not prepared to be forced to say we belong irrevocably to either camp. Unfortunately, this is often what the Eastern and Western blocs attempt to force us to do. They accept the view that he who is not for them wholeheartedly is at heart their opponent. This is not true. All that we wish to do is to live in friendship with all the countries of the world, irrespective of their political ideologies. All we ask in return for our friendship is that we be left alone to work out our own destiny. . . .

DISENGAGEMENT IN AFRICA

Co-existence and disengagement run together. The Great Powers cannot co-exist and at the same time compete for spheres of influence in the less developed parts of the world. . . .

Obviously there are many difficulties to be faced. Disengagement is impossible so long as former imperial powers retain in practice control over their former colonies. In the case of a number of African states, the former colonial power continues to control the Civil Service and the administration generally. It has a stranglehold over the central banking system. Further, states have been created which are so small as not to be economically viable, and these countries in fact are compelled to depend upon their former colonial rulers for subsidies in order to meet the ordinary expenses of administration. Under such circumstances, of course, there can be no disengagement, as the former colonial power in fact retains every attribute of government except for the purely nominal attitude of sovereignty. . . .

It is essential to realize that the continuance of [the colonial] system is in itself a threat to world peace. Colonial revolts are not only occasioned by the desire of a people to control their own political government. In fact, they are more often produced by economic oppression. . . .

If the European powers use their present economic strength to impose a similar system upon their ex-colonies, sooner or later the relationship will become intolerable, and there will be a people's revolt against the neo-colonialist regime. . . .

In regard to Africa, I should like the continent to become not only a non-nuclear zone, but also a zone where no foreign military bases are allowed. I should like this to be paralleled with an ideological truce and an agreement not to try to convert Africa into an economic ap-

pendage of any other continent. Africa should not become a battle-
ground for the cold war. The cold war and the cold war mentality should
be kept out of Africa. It is in the interests of world peace that this
should be so. . . .

MANKIND AND THE BOMB

It is unnecessary for me to deal at any length with my fourth point,
for it is abundantly clear that mutual fear, which is at the root of so
much of the mistrust in the world today, cannot be eliminated so long
as the Great Powers are in a position at one stroke to annihilate each
other. . . . Further, disarmament is essential if the productive forces of
the world are to be released for use in developing the less developed
areas of the globe. The mere fact of so using these resources would do
much to destroy these dangerous tensions to which I referred under my
third head, and which arise out of the disparity in wealth and opportunity for economic advancement between the more developed and the
less developed countries. . . .

Against Small Power Arms Races

43 SIMHA FLAPAN
    For an Atom-Bomb Free Middle East

. . . The dangers of war are increasing even more as atomic weapons
spread to additional countries, and even some of the smaller ones.
It is presently estimated that in addition to the four nuclear powers,
eleven other countries are capable, economically and technologically,
of engaging in the production of nuclear weapons. Eight more countries
have the economic resources for such a program though they are more
limited in science and technology. Still other countries may obtain
nuclear weapons as a result of military alliances. The inclinations of
even small countries to obtain nuclear weapons are encouraged by the
belief that they can thereby increase their military power far beyond
the limits of their own industrial and military potential.

Simha Flapan is the Director of the Arab Department of Mapam and a member of
New Outlook's Editorial Board. These excerpts are reprinted from *New Outlook,*
V, No. 4 (May 1962) 13–20.

Once the nuclear weapons have found their way to a large number of countries the prospects for nuclear control and disarmament will diminish towards zero. Smaller countries engaged in local or regional conflicts and possessing atomic weapons will endanger the uneasy balance achieved out of mutual fear by the Great Powers.

It is because of this danger that the proposals to prevent any further spread of nuclear weapons and to *establish non-nuclear and atom-bomb-free zones in centers of political conflict and military tension acquire such significance for world peace.*

The "deatomization" of such areas as Central Europe, the Middle East and South-East Asia, which have been breeding-grounds for international tension, is a necessary and unavoidable step in order to preserve any chance of agreement on nuclear disarmament. If the two Great Powers have not given up the hope of reaching an agreement and remain ready to renew their efforts to this end, they will have to take this step. In their efforts to break the deadlock in the disarmament talks the neutral countries have concentrated their efforts on preventing the spread of nuclear weapons into new countries. It was on their initiative that the U.N. General Assembly adopted the Irish and Swedish resolutions to undertake immediate steps to this direction.

The call issued by the Israeli professors has appeared while Israel is considering its reply to U.N. General Secretary U Thant's circular questionnaire to all non-nuclear countries concerning their readiness to refrain from producing, acquiring and storing nuclear weapons. Can there be any doubt as to what the Israeli reply should be? A people which lost one-third of its members in the Nazi extermination camps, the people of Israel must answer with an unqualified and unequivocal "yes," as an expression of their determination to prevent any aggravation of the international crisis by dragging the Middle East into the whirlpool of a nuclear armaments race.

The extrication of Israel and the Arab states from this race is vital not only for the cause of world peace but also for the prospects of an eventual peaceful settlement in the area.

It is true that at present the Arab states and Israel are the scene of an arms-race for superiority in conventional weapons as a result of their unsolved dispute, the Arabs' refusal to accept Israel's existence and Great Power competition for influence in the area. Even in its present dimensions the competition is a dangerous one; it has involved the countries concerned in undesirable political and military alliances and has led them to an ever-growing drain on their meager economic resources. The already heavy expenditures on modern "conventional" military equipment may soon reach such dimensions as to frustrate any large-scale development. It will be either the Aswan Dam or Ilyushins for Egypt and the irrigation of the Negev or Mysteres for Israel. Only highly industrialized countries have the resources to build up their national economies and their military potential at the same time. An undeveloped country like Egypt, which lacks capital for its program of industrialization and a higher standard of living, or Israel, which faces immense investments in order to develop its absorptive capacity for large-scale immigration, cannot perform this miracle. The attempt to escape this contradiction between the needs of economic development and of defense by resorting to nuclear weapons is like an attempt to avoid drowning by committing suicide. The transfer from even the most destructive conventional arms to nuclear weapons is not an additional, natural and unavoidable step in the development of national defense; it is a jump into the abyss.

The possession of an atom bomb by either Israel or an Arab country would give them only a very short-lived advantage. In the long run it would expose them to dangers greater than the extra security it afforded. Instead of acting as a deterrent it would stimulate the other side to engage in an all-out effort to produce or to obtain even larger and more destructive bombs. Under the present international circumstances, with the great advances in atomic technology and the continuation of the Cold War, atomic devices are becoming less expensive and more available. It would take either side only two or three years, at the most, to catch up. The restored equilibrium would not, however, guarantee even an unstable peace. Influenced not by what they had but by what they feared the other side possessed or was attempting to obtain, both sides will be dragged by mutual fear and suspicion into a disastrous and insane race for "better" atomic weapons.

The "balance of terror" theory is valid least of all in the Middle East. The complexities of long-range missiles to a certain extent inhibit the Great Powers. The short distances in the Middle East, however, make "delivery" a simple matter. The technology of short-range missiles or jet-planes is already available to both Israel and Egypt. There can be no such thing as safeguarding the invulnerability of the retaliatory forces in the Middle East. In Egypt the major part of the population and the industrial and administrative centers are concentrated in the small area of the Nile Delta. In Israel they are in a narrow coastal strip adjoining Haifa and Tel Aviv. Cold-blooded scientists of the U.S.A. or the U.S.S.R. may be able to estimate the chances of survival and recovery after tens of millions are blown to bits, burnt or suffocated under the debris of cities and towns. In the Middle East one or two bombs would be sufficient to wipe out the centers of national life and most of their populations. But even if an atomic race in the Middle East, because of international intervention or other inhibitions, did not lead to mutual destruction, the damage would still be great because of the tremendous investments wasted and the lost prospects of a peaceful settlement.

The U.S.A. and the U.S.S.R. are separated from each other by thousands of miles of land and ocean. Protected as they are by intricate radar and reconnaissance systems, each of the two countries may hope for at least the space of twenty minutes in which to give the alert and to put into motion the poised systems of retaliation. These twenty minutes and the almost inevitable retaliation they make possible form the margin of risk which has kept the peace.

The distances between Israel and any of the Arab countries are so small as to reduce the margin of preparation time to almost nothing. Human imagination can hardly conceive what life would be like if populations on both sides of the border lived under the constant danger of sudden and instantaneous death from the skies. Any hopes of a peaceful settlement would thus be ruined for a long time to come.

As long as any potential Israeli-Arab war is limited to conventional weapons the emergence of trends towards moderation and realism will still be possible, even under the present conditions of hostility and tension. It cannot, for instance, be doubted that the hopes of destroying Israel held by Arab governments and public have begun to lose their force as they begin to recognize the fact that the Arab armies are incapable of accomplishing it. Under the surface of violent threats there is sometimes an undertone testifying to an awareness of their ineffectiveness. This would almost surely vanish entirely under the conditions of an atomic arms-race. Even worse, the very engagement in an atomic arms-race would revive the Arabs' hopes of destroying Israel, not only as a "desirable solution" but also as a practical possibility, which could be achieved technologically by nuclear weapons without resort to conventional war and armies.

In addition, any initiative on the part of a Middle Eastern country to acquire nuclear weapons would transform local or regional problems into an international affair. No country in the Middle East is capable of engaging in an atomic program on the strength of its own economic, technological and scientific resources. It would necessarily have to work in cooperation and alliance with one of the nuclear powers. This would, in turn, involve it in the danger of becoming one of the committed countries on the Cold War and military strategy maps of the Great Powers. For any Middle Eastern country, that would create dangers far greater than any threatening it from its neighbors.

We feel compelled to dwell on two questions which may be raised here. Even if we agree on the desirability of the Middle East being kept free of nuclear armaments, what are the chances of this being done by both sides? Would a unilateral step on the part of Israel, for example, be a sufficient guarantee against an atomic venture on the part of the Arabs? The Middle East is, fortunately, still in a position where the anti-nuclear bomb forces must prevent unilateral nuclear *armament* instead of having, as in England, to campaign for unilateral *disarmament*.

TIME TO RE-ADJUST POLICY

One might ask: What if the Arab states were already engaged in building nuclear weapons or trying to obtain them from friendly powers, regardless of what Israel did? Israel's most effective measure probably would be to arouse public opinion and U.N. to the danger. Under the present circumstances both sides in the cold war are interested in keeping the "nuclear club" as exclusive as possible. Israeli initiative in preventing Middle East production of atomic weapons would have more than a reasonable chance of success.

It is probable, however, that the Arab countries have until now not been able to go far in atomic energy developments with their heavy investments and enormous drain on economic and technological resources. Their immediate economic and social problems and the level of their scientific and technological abilities make such a venture premature. It is not to Israel's interest to stimulate them to give atomic energy development an important place in their national planning for the near future. The possibility of obtaining atomic weapons from the Soviet Union seems even less likely under existing circumstances. The Soviet Union has not supplied atomic weapons to her closest allies, like China and the Popular Democracies. It has submitted proposals for the termination of nuclear tests and the arms race and even for the destruction of the existing stockpiles of atomic weapons though it has not conceded so easily to controls. Only extraordinary circum-

440   SIMHA FLAPAN

stances, in which Israeli foreign policy could also play a part, may lead the Soviet Union to any sharp deviation from this policy.

Some people may still ask what Israel is to do if and when the Soviet Union or China give atom bombs to the U.A.R. The only answer is to do everything possible so that the Soviet Union and China shall have no reason, excuse or interest in doing so. This would not require from Israel a full turn from her Western orientation towards the East but only a policy of non-identification with either of the great powers and support for the neutralization of the Middle East. Israel pursued such a policy from her inception up to the war in Korea, when it was abandoned in favor of an alignment with the U.S.A. Since then, the whole political structure and relationship of forces has changed radically. The Afro-Asian bloc has become a decisive factor against the background of an atomic stalemate between the U.S.A. and the U.S.S.R. And now both powers are competing for the sympathies of the neutralist bloc and are coming to recognize that the neutralization and "deatomization" of vital areas are the only way out of degeneration into war. It would now be a realistic and necessary adjustment to the international situation and a guarantee against the danger of an atomic arms race in the Middle East for Israel to make the neutralization of the Middle East the focal point of Israeli foreign policy.

It should be recalled that on February 12, 1956, the U.S.S.R. tendered a note to the U.S.A., Great Britain and France, suggesting a "hands-off" agreement for the Middle East. The six points of the Soviet proposal were:

1. The preservation of peace in the Near and Middle East by settling questions at issue exclusively by peaceful means.
2. Non-interference in the internal affairs of the countries of the Near and Middle East. Respect for the sovereignty and independence of these countries.
3. Refusal to undertake any attempts to draw these countries into military alignments with the participation of the great powers.
4. The liquidation of foreign bases and the withdrawal of foreign troops from the territory of countries of the Near and Middle East.
5. Joint refusal to supply arms to countries of the Near and Middle East.
6. Assistance in the economic development of countries of the Near and Middle East, without putting forward any political, military or other conditions incompatible with the dignity and sovereignty of these countries.

Events in the Middle East have since proved beyond doubt the soundness of such an approach. Now, viewed against the background of the nuclear dangers, it may have a greater chance of realization than ever if given sufficient support by the peoples of the area.

We might also raise the question whether the peoples of the Middle East should forego the advantages of atomic energy and give up the possibilities of research and experimental development because of the military dangers involved. Definitely not. However, any program of atomic research and use for peaceful purposes must be so conceived as to leave no doubts concerning its peaceful character. In this connection it is also worthwhile recalling some of the remarks made during the "International Conference on Science in the Advancement of New States" which took place at the Weizmann Institute in Rehovot in August 1960.

Mr. J. A. Jukes, a member of the United Kingdom's Atomic Energy Authority, told the Conference that:

Nuclear power is not at present being produced anywhere in the world at competitive costs. Most of the nuclear stations now under construction are unlikely to be fully competitive . . . New states may well find that their very scarce scientific resources would yield a much bigger return in other directions. Some new states have insufficient indigenous reserves of energy to support a major programme of industrialization and expansion and are therefore looking to nuclear energy as a means of meeting their potential requirements. In the long run they are undoubtedly right. But the important question is one of timing. At what stage in their development will they be able to make use of nuclear energy with advantage?

. . . The immediate prospects for nuclear power in new States are limited therefore to a few special cases. Perhaps those of you who are from new States find this discouraging. On the contrary, I believe you should find it greatly encouraging. You have no need to rush into this new technology and so consume your most valuable resources — your scarce scientific manpower and your scarce capital. Unlike some of the old industrial countries, you can afford to wait.

This view was also supported in Rehovot by Dr. Jules M. Gueron:

However satisfactory the planned power station may be, the power stations of the future may very well be significantly different from those which we know now. . . . It is a major problem of national planning whether one should devote enormous monies and manpower in this.

To conclude, therefore, from every point of view Israel will have to reply in the affirmative to the U.N.'s efforts to prevent the spread of nuclear weapons. It should be prepared to support such an agreement with regard to the Middle East even before the Great Powers come to an understanding on nuclear disarmament on a world scale. More than that, we might suggest that Israel come forward with some positive proposals of her own. Such proposals might include the following points:

1. A plan to prohibit the production, acquisition and use of any atomic weapons. This could be initiated by a commitment on the part of Israel and the Arab countries in the form of an unofficial but guaranteed understanding or an agreement by them and added to the existing armistice treaties, that they would not produce or purchase or acquire in any way atomic weapons or other weapons of mass destruction and that they would not use or train their armed forces to use, or establish any bases for the use of such weapons, neither by themselves nor in conjunction with other powers.

2. An agreement by the atomic powers to impose an embargo upon atomic weapons or other weapons of destruction in the Middle East.

3. An agreement to place all atomic reactors in Israel and the Arab states under international control by an agreed body.

Sooner or later nuclear energy will come to the Middle East. If it is brought into the area irresponsibly as part of the cold war between Israel and the Arab states it can be a cause of tremendous harm. But if it comes at the right time and under auspicious political circumstances, it will be a great lever lifting this area into development and prosperity. It must be the task of political wisdom to create those auspicious circumstances.

On the Economic Benefits of Disarmament

44 **AFTAB AHMAD KHAN**
Economic and Social Consequences of Disarmament

As you know, there is a lurking suspicion that very powerful vested interests, specially in the wealthy countries of the West, are interested in maintaining armaments at a high level so as to ensure that their profits are sustained. There is also a fear on the part of Governments

Aftab Ahmad Khan is chief economist on the planning commission of the government of Pakistan, and a member of the group appointed by the Secretary-General of the United Nations to study the economic and social consequences of disarmament. These excerpts, from an article in *Pakistan Horizon*, XV, No. 3 (1962) 177–184, are reprinted by permission of the Pakistan Institute of International Affairs, Karachi.

that, if the huge expenditure on armaments suddenly ceased, the world would probably be faced with an economic crisis such as that of 1929–1933. This fear of the Governments, combined with the pressure of the groups representing the vested interests, was one of the important causes in thwarting an agreement on disarmament. We tried to prove that, so far as economic consequences of disarmament were concerned, these would not pose any sort of problem, provided there was advance preparation to meet the challenge.

I think it is understood that disarmament is primarily a political problem. Once there is a favourable political milieu, we can sit down and work out its economic and social consequences. . . . I need not stress the political desirability of disarmament. Everybody knows that if there is another armed conflict, it might mean the end of civilization, and yet if armament expenditure goes on mounting and if the present tensions become aggravated, a time might come when war might be unavoidable. Therefore for the preservation of the human race and its civilization, there has to be disarmament. But the history of the effort for disarmament reveals that until today the problem in the political field has been in a morass. At the first Peace Conference, held in 1899 at The Hague, a resolution was adopted which required that disarmament should be undertaken for the material and moral advancement of mankind. It was a pious sort of resolution but even as early as 1899 when weapons were not so deadly as they are today people were conscious of the deleterious effects of armaments on the moral and material fabric of the world. At the second Peace Conference of 1907 the resolution of 1899 was reiterated. Still the First World War came, followed by the Treaty of Versailles, which was without morality, without justice and without imagination. The Treaty provided that there should be disarmament of Germany as a prelude to general universal disarmament. Annexed to the Treaty was the convention of the League of Nations, whose Article 9 made it a duty of the League to bring about universal disarmament. Several abortive attempts were made during the inter-War period, culminating in the dismal failure of the world Disarmament Conference of 1932. Then followed the Second World War. The destructive consequences of this War were much more catastrophic than those of the First War. In 1945 when the Charter of the United Nations was being hammered out, again disarmament was not forgotten. Article 26 of the Charter, as also its Article 11 and paragraph 1, specifically laid down as a duty of the

Security Council that it should undertake measures for the reduction and regulation of armaments. The General Assembly in its session of 1946 appointed the Atomic Energy Commission, specially designed to curb the use of atomic power for destructive purposes. In December 1946, there was set up another committee for bringing about reduction and regulation of conventional armaments. These two committees went to work but there were again differences on what was going to be the control mechanism and how it was to be brought about. The two committees merged in 1952 in a Disarmament Commission. An Experts Committee and a Sub-Committee of the Disarmament Commission are still wrestling in Geneva with the problems. All the same, there is an awareness in all quarters that whatever might be the present suspicions and difficulties in bringing about a complete and general disarmament, this is a problem that humanity cannot live with for long. That is why in its 1960 session, the General Assembly, on the motion of Pakistan, adopted the resolution by which the expert Group was set up to study the economic and social consequences of disarmament. A notable feature of the Group was that it was composed of men representing different economic, political and social systems. . . .

Actually when one looks at the total resources which are absorbed by armament expenditure and when one looks at the clamouring need of undeveloped countries, arising out of their abject poverty, the whole situation, measured in money terms, overwhelms you. According to conservative estimates the annual expenditure on armament is 120 billion dollars. Considering the national income of Pakistan, its total gross national product in terms of 1960–61 prices is about 6.3 billion dollars. The total requirement of our Second Plan period is 2.3 billion dollars which actually means .46 percent of the world expenditure on armaments. So this enormous expenditure of $120 billion is of staggering dimensions. It represents about 8 percent to 9 percent of the total world national income. It is equal in money value to the total volume of exports in the world. *i.e.*, the exports of all the countries in the world, in one year, are of the total value of this figure. It nearly equals, to give another figure, the total income of all the under-developed countries, that is those countries in which the level of *per capita* income is below $100 per year. It is equal again to nearly 1½ times the total gross capital formation that annually takes place in the world. If as a result of an international agreement armament expenditure were to stop, you could step up by 50 percent the rate of productive capital formation in the world. I do not say that all these figures are very precise. There are a number of conceptual difficulties but this is the order of the magnitude of the total resources involved in armaments. Again there are about 20 million people who are directly in the armed forces of the world. If we also take into account those persons who are indirectly associated with the armed forces as through working in ammunition factories or supplying them with other services or goods, the total comes to 50 million people. They are engaged in pursuits that are unproductive and indeed destructive.

Nearly 85 percent of the total expenditure is confined to seven countries, the U.S.A., the U.S.S.R., the People's Republic of China, France, Canada, the Federal Republic of Germany and the U.K. In advanced countries, like the United States, in percentage of national income, it comes to about 10 percent. In under-developed countries, the figure varies between 5 percent to 10 percent. But considering their level of national income and their *per capita* incomes which are dismally low, arms expenditure means a tremendous drain on the resources of the under-developed countries. The best talent, scientists and researchers and 50 percent of the expenditure on research and technical development are devoted to defence purposes. If somehow all this talent, which is the highest powered talent of the world, could be diverted to peacetime development projects, what a tremendous impact that would make on the world!

When discussing the economic and social consequences of disarmament, one has to make certain assumptions about the nature and timing of disarmament. First, if there is a ban on nuclear weapons and then reduction by stages of conventional weapons, the economic and social consequences will be of one character. But if there is to be sudden and complete disarmament, these consequences would partake of a different character. Our Committee considered what assumptions should be made. We thought that since the U.N. General Assembly had agreed on the objective of complete and general disarmament, we should accept that. We felt that if it could be proved that complete and general disarmament could have no adverse economic consequences, then phased disarmament or partial disarmament should pose no problems. So, we worked on the assumption that there should be complete universal disarmament, except for forces which would be required by each country to contribute to an international police force or a force for its own internal security purposes. The question arose as to what would be the immediate problems, specially in countries like the United States, where there is no central plan to regulate the entire national economy and where the maintenance of an effective demand is crucial to the health and growth of the economy. When studying the impact on the United States, the United Kingdom, West Germany and other similar countries, we found it should not pose any really serious problems. After all in all these countries conversion from war-time economies to peace-time economies had taken place and the cut-back in defence expenditure had been much greater than what it would now be if disarmament were to come about. In 1944–45, nearly half of the total productive resources of the world were earmarked for war purposes. In 1945–46, there was a switch-over and a sudden decline in defence expenditure even in the United States. Defence expenditure in the last year of the war was nearly 40 percent of the gross national product of United States and suddenly dropped to something like 5 percent after the war and about 9 million people were completely demobilised. Of course, in the Western European countries, because war devastation was much greater, the damage to productive capacity, to manpower and other things was much greater, the adjustment took much longer. There was the Marshall Plan Aid of 13 billion dollars and by about 1948–49 most of the Western European economies were on the way to recovery. In the U.S.S.R. destruction both of human and material wealth had been tremendous but by about 1948 even there the level of annual production was about one-fifth higher than what it had been during the last three war years. The whole recovery was remarkable. But in 1946, in the United States there was what is termed hyperliquidity. During the war years, people had about 160 million dollars shut up in banks. They were impatient to spend the money as soon as the war was over. This pent-up demand helped to sustain economic activity. This created a peculiar economic situation at the end of World War II, which is not going to be present now. Now the world's productive system balances effective demand and there are no pent-up needs. The war-time damages and obsolescences all have been made good. Quite true, these were special features.

Then we had the experience of the switch-over from the Korean war expenditure. That expenditure was on a limited scale, *i.e.*, one-tenth of that in 1945–46. The switch-over caused no consequences to the economy. I wish to say that it is quite possible even within the framework of a private enterprise economy to keep up effective demand at a level which could absorb for productive purposes all the funds which would be released by disarmament. It is just a question of the statesmen having sufficient wisdom and strength to follow certain policies. After all, as we have shown in our report, in the chapter on the Peaceful Use of Released Resources, there is so much to be done, even in the advanced countries, in the field of capital social expenditure on education, on health, on slum clearance and on what you call developing the pockets of poverty, such as there are even in a country like the United States, and on extending social service benefits. You can take measures like reducing taxes, reducing the hours of work, making the pay of men and women equal. These are needs of a vital and urgent character. In the report, we pointed out how much social imbalance there was even in American society. We have graphic figures to prove it. Governments should be prepared to follow monetary and fiscal policies, which would lead to better expenditure and thus off-set inflationary tendencies and the retarding effect of the cut-back in defence expenditure. The trouble unfortunately arises from the fact that we still have old-fashioned ideas. Each one of us is a slave to the ideas which we imbibe in our early reading. We have concepts like the balanced budget, not a very high figure of public debt, not more than a certain level of taxation and so on. We are not prepared to shed those concepts, even though they have ceased to have reality in the world of today. Sometimes even Congresses and Parliaments become silly and follow irrational economic policies. But so far as economics is concerned, it is not inevitable that if effective demand should fall off, the level of employment should fall off too. In under-developed countries, like Pakistan, India and the African countries, expenditure on armaments and the percentage of national income to it is much less. In the case of Pakistan, it is about 3 percent of our gross national product. If you want to avoid social imbalances and other economic upheavals, consequent upon the release of people, engaged in armament activities, in the under-developed countries, you have to speed up the process of economic development to a level, which would absorb all these people in constructive activities. To speed up that process, the whole of the developed world, the Western and the Communist powers, would have to step up their rate of capital and technical assistance to all those countries.

The Committee discussed the possible uses of the released resources. It collected an impressive survey of what needs to be done in the U.S., in the U.S.S.R. and in Europe, in the field of education, health, slum clearance and social security as well as what needs to be done in the under-developed countries. We found that the resources released by disarmament would be most insufficient for meeting the tremendous needs of all these various countries and even of the more advanced countries, where the level of per capita income was the highest. We were even apprehensive that the unfulfilled needs of the developed countries would be of such an order that they might absorb for their own needs all the funds that are released by disarmament and there might not be enough for the under-developed ones. Consequently, if a disarmament agreement comes about, a fixed proportion of the released funds should be earmarked for assistance to the under-developed countries.

In the under-developed world, there have been since the 1950's, various estimates of capital requirements. The rate of growth of per capita income in these regions has been less than 2 percent. Actually, it approximated 1 percent, increase in the national income having been eaten up by the growth of population. On the other hand, there is tremendous disparity in the level of per capita income between countries like Pakistan and the U.S.A. It is about $60 here and about $2400 there, i.e., 40 times. Then their rate of growth of national income per capita is about 3 percent and ours is about 1 percent. This disparity will go on worsening and, from a world point of view, that will lead to a very explosive situation. In the fifties the growth of the economies of the under-developed countries has been very very slow. Various individual economists and expert economic bodies have made their estimates of the capital requirements of the under-developed countries. These estimates vary. In 1957–58, according to some estimates, the transfer of resources from the developed to the under-developed countries was of the order of 3.5 billion dollars to 4 billion dollars of all types of flow. It has been estimated that if you wish to attain the target of 5 percent annual increase in national income, which would give these countries something like 2 to 3 percent increase in per capita income, there has to be a transference during the decade of the 1960's of something of the order of 20 to 30 billion dollars more than what the present level of transference is. Unless this is done, you will find that the under-developed countries will go on stagnating and the gap between the advanced and the retarded countries will go on widening. Twenty to 30 billion dollars over 10 years means 2 to 3 billion dollars a year more over the existing level. This is not impossible, considering that the developed countries now spend 100 billion dollars on armament. If disarmament be carried out, it would have a tremendous impact in ensuring and stabilising so many of the newly independent countries, whose people's expectations have been roused but whose rate of economic development is tardy, with consequent frustration and insecurity.

. . . assistance given by the developed countries to the under-developed countries, be it capital assistance or technical assistance, will not by itself solve the problems of the latter. The primary effort for development has to be made by the under-developed countries themselves. They have to undertake important institutional and other reforms. They have to step up their own domestic effort. They have to streamline their administrative structures. Foreign aid can supplement but cannot be a substitute for the domestic effort of the under-developed countries. Only if there is such effort can there be hope in the developing countries of their breaking the vicious circle of poverty or getting out of what is sometimes called by economists the low-level equilibrium.

We stated in our report another problem which is naturally causing a great deal of anxiety to some of the under-developed countries. Some of these countries depend on the export of primary commodities, which are used by armament industries or in armament products. There may be a sudden fall in the prices of these commodities, seriously disturbing the economies of the exporting countries. We find that commodities like tin, lead, zinc and copper are consumed by the armament industry to the extent of about 50 percent of their total production. These commodities are very sensitive to any fall in demand, leading to a sharp fall in prices. If the prices of primary commodities fall, its impact on the income of the countries may be disastrous. A 6 percent fall in the price of primary commodities would be equal to half the total amount of aid, which the entire developed world is giving to the developing world.

This is an important problem. We took the view that as a result of the cessation of expenditure on armament, there was bound to be other substantial expenditure and, as a result of that, the total reduction in the consumption of commodities like copper, zinc and petroleum should not be very large. It should be about 2 percent. But at the same time we recommended that in order to meet the problem, such measures should be devised as buffer stocks, commodity agreements and other special arrangements, so that prices of primary commodities do not fall. The Western world should not be in the position that what it gives with one hand, it takes away with the other, that it should buy primary products cheap and sell its own products at high prices. For this again there is no easy solution.

When we say that these problems can be tackled, it does not mean that there will be no areas of the economy, or politically special areas, where the problems will not be pronounced. Everybody knows that there will be problems for the U.S. economy. For instance, the aircraft and missile industry in the U.S.A. depends on the armament industry to the extent of 90 percent of its production, radio and electronics to the extent of 40 percent. Here the Government will have to do something for the reconversion of the plants for peace-time uses. There has to be proper planning of the impact of disarmament on special areas and on special industries, otherwise there is a possibility of depression. This process of conversion is going to pose problems, such as changes in the location of industries, changes in population centres and incomes and so forth. These have been taken account of in the report. . . .

International Strategy:

The United Nations and the Rule of Law

The Spirit and Letter of 1945

45 CHARLES DE GAULLE
Press Conference, April 11, 1961

The United Nations Organization and its institutions were created in 1945 on the basis of a Charter, and with purposes which France at that time approved. I was, myself, at that time at the head of my country and in that capacity I was one of the founders of the United Nations at the request of President Roosevelt and then of President Truman, who were its promoters.

There was an executive council, the Security Council, which was a sort of Government composed of the five big powers, that is to say, the United States, the Soviet Union, Great Britain, China and France. And then there was a kind of non-legislative deliberative parliament, the General Assembly. The General Assembly, at that time, was supposed to debate only on subjects which were submitted to it by the Security Council. I will add that the General Assembly then included

Charles de Gaulle, President of France 1958–   , was leader of the wartime Resistance movement. These excerpts are from his press conference on April 11, 1961 at Elysée Palace; the translation is courtesy of the Press and Information Division, Embassy of France.

only about forty States which had been in existence for a long time, which were endowed with cohesion and unity and which were used to international relations and to the traditions, obligations and responsibilities which these relations entail.

In the Security Council each of the members — each of the big powers — had the veto power. And then finally in the General Assembly, in accordance with what France had wanted and had obtained in San Francisco, it was necessary — and it still is— to have a two thirds majority in order to pass a resolution.

It seems that all these procedures would enable the States to establish contact with each other, to examine world questions jointly and to promote peace while restricting demagogic activities.

As for the Charter, it was designed to prevent the Organization from interfering in the affairs of each State and it could intervene only on the explicit request of a Government.

Finally, among the intentions which had inspired its creation, there was the desire, perhaps the illusion of the Western nations — in any case of the Americans — to bring the Soviets to cooperate with the West. We know what has happened.

Today it must be said that the United Nations really does not in any way resemble what it was or ought to have been at the start. First of all, the Security Council no longer comprises — it is far from comprising — only the big powers, but also several powers elected in turn, and then there is an undetermined number of delegations attending all debates of the Security Council, depending on the subjects under discussion. As for the General Assembly, at the present time it has assumed all powers. It can deliberate on everything, without and even against the advice of the Security Council which is thus dispossessed of its essential prerogative. In addition, this General Assembly now includes the representatives of more than 100 States — soon they will number 120 — most of which, at least many of which, are improvised States and believe it their duty to stress grievances or demands with regard to the older nations, rather than elements of reason and progress.

As for the Charter, it now inconveniences every one and there is no one who can enforce its application. As regards the hoped-for cooperation between East and West within the United Nations, we can see its results.

So that now the meetings of the United Nations are no more than riotous and scandalous sessions where there is no way to organize an objective debate and which are filled with invectives and insults thrown out, especially by the Communists and those who are allied with them against the Western nations.

And then as the United Nations becomes a scene of disturbance, confusion and division, it acquires the ambition to intervene in all kinds of matters. This is especially true of its officers. It is anxious to assert itself — even by force of arms — as it did in the Congo.

The result is that it carries to the local scene its global incoherence, the personal conceptions of its various agents and the individual partiality of each of the States which send their contingents with their own orders — send them, then withdraw them.

Under these conditions, France does not see how she can adopt any attitude toward the United, or disunited, Nations other than that of the greatest reserve. In any case, she does not wish to contribute her men or her money to any present or future undertaking of this organization — or disorganization. Of course we hope that the day will come when common sense will again prevail and when the reasonable nations, noting the results of experience, will wish to resume this great world undertaking on a new basis.

In my opinion, this will be achieved if Europe succeeds in organizing itself and consequently in asserting its power, its reason and its experience in the world. Then Europe will be able to take the necessary steps.

The Rise of the Third World in the United Nations

46 MOHAMMAD NAWAZ
Afro-Asians and the United Nations

The late Dag Hammarskjold once said that the United Nations Organization was for the small nations. Looking at the social, economic and political work of the Organization, one finds that most of it has been for the small nations and particularly for the Afro-Asian nations. Health, shortage of food and development are some of the major problems

Mohammad Nawaz is Lecturer in International Law at the University of Peshawar, Pakistan. These excerpts, from an article in *Pakistan Horizon*, XV, No. 1 (1962) 42–48, are reprinted by permission of the Pakistan Institute of International Affairs, Karachi.

facing the emerging countries of Asia and Africa. The United Nations is playing a very important role in solving these problems through its various Specialized Agencies. The present generation of lepers in Nigeria is to be the last to suffer from this crippling disease, thanks to the efforts of the U.N. There are many more such instances which support the view that the U.N. exists today largely for the benefit of Afro-Asian countries. All these nations at the U.N. are small either in area, or in population or in resources. Consequently they depend on some external agency for their development.

To-day the balance of power at the U.N. is not in the hands of great powers but in the hands of small nations, specially Afro-Asians. . . .

The Afro-Asian bloc . . . does not necessarily behave homogeneously on every issue but tends to behave as a single unit (with slight deviations) on issues of common interest. The stand of Afro-Asians on Algeria, Suez, Congo and other colonial issues is an example of such behaviour. It is on account of the growing importance of these countries of Asia and Africa that we have to look towards them for the preservation of the World Organization. . . .

To-day the Afro-Asian bloc and the U.N. seem to strengthen each other.

At the 15th session of the General Assembly in 1960, seventeen new members were admitted to the U.N., sixteen of whom were African states. It was the most important session of the General Assembly, not only for the reason that it was attended by so many heads of states, but also as a case study of Afro-Asian political behaviour. Soviet Premier Mr. Khrushchev had gone to New York with the intention of dislodging the then Secretary General of the Organization Dag Hammarskjold for having frustrated Russian expectations in the Congo. Mr. Khrushchev was till then under the impression that he would get support from the Afro-Asians. His presence at the U.N. put a great strain upon the Organization. His performance there created serious doubts about the future of the U.N. It was a great relief for the well wishers of the U.N. when the final outcome of his efforts was against the wishes of the Soviet Premier. . . .

The Afro-Asian bloc instead of helping Mr. Khrushchev in dislodging the late Secretary-General supported his continuance in office. They also supported his action in the Congo. To approve his action in the Congo, the session of the General Assembly was held on September 20, 1960. The Afro-Asian resolution approving the policies of the Secretary-General in the Congo was not even opposed. France, South Africa and the Soviet Union along with nine members of its bloc abstained. Seventy members supported the resolution. Opposed to this was a Soviet resolution, censuring the late Secretary-General. Its sponsors did not even dare to ask for a vote on it.[1]

Thus the 15th session of the General Assembly provided Afro-Asians with a chance to make their importance felt. It also proved that the neutralist members of the bloc were not necessarily pro-Russian. The neutralism of the majority of these states which the Soviet Premier was banking upon turned out to be one of the major causes of his defeat. Another very strong proof of the independent thinking of the Afro-Asians at the U.N. is the voting on Red China's admission to the Organization. At the sixteenth session of the Assembly last year, out of 51 Afro-Asians, 30 voted with the U.S. for not admitting Red China in the U.N. The admission of Mauritania is a still further proof of the growing importance of Afro-Asians at the U.N. . . .

The Congo dispute very significantly demonstrates the importance of the Afro-Asians at the U.N. On 2 February, 1961, the Security Council adopted a resolution which among other things gave authority to the U.N. command in Congo to use force for preventing civil war in this strife-torn African country. It was the most unusual resolution to be passed by the Security Council. It got the required majority, U.S.S.R. and France having abstained from voting. How could such an important resolution escape the veto specially when three great powers — the U.S.S.R., France and U.K. — were not interested in the success of the U.N. operations in Congo.[2] It could happen because the sponsors of the resolutions were three Afro-Asian nations — Ceylon, Liberia and the U.A.R. Therefore any country interested in vetoing it was aware of the consequence (displeasure of Afro-Asians). The big powers at the Security Council also knew that if the resolutions failed in the Council then under the provisions of the resolution for "Uniting for Peace,"[3] it would be placed before the General Assembly where

[1] *Keesing's Contemporary Archives*, 1960–61, p. 17938.
[2] Conor O'Brian, "My Case," *The Observer*, London, 10 December, 1961.
[3] Resolution 377A (V) of the General Assembly, 3 November 1950 GAOR, V, Supp. 20(A/1775), pp. 10–12. Part of paragraph A of the Resolution reads: "The General Assembly resolves that if the Security Council, because of lack of unanimity of the permanent members, fails to exercise its primary responsibility for the maintenance of international peace and security in any case where there appears to be a threat to the peace, breach of peace or act of aggression, the General Assembly shall consider the matter immediately with a view to making appropriate recommendations to Members for collective measures, including in the case of a

the Afro-Asians could definitely muster two-thirds majority in its support. Thus any vetoing of it in the Council would have been ineffective. It would have only annoyed the Afro-Asians who were all interested in the integration of Congo. It was the knowledge of the unity among Afro-Asians and the probable consequence of this unity in case the matter was brought up before the General Assembly that prevented any of the big powers from taking any step contrary to the wishes of Afro-Asians in the Council.

Still further proof of the strength of the Afro-Asians at the U.N. is in the dropping of the Troika proposal by the U.S.S.R. and the election of a Burmese diplomat U Thant, by a unanimous vote of the General Assembly, as Secretary-General of the Organization. After the death of Dag Hammarskjold Moscow had concentrated all her efforts in convincing Afro-Asians about the advantages of having a triumvirate of Secretaries-General instead of having just one person holding the office. The Afro-Asians were found in no mood to split the office upon which depended the success of the world organization. When the Soviet Union found no support among these countries it postponed the consideration of the question and accepted U Thant as the temporary successor to the late Secretary-General till March 1963. This was a wise diplomatic move on the part of the Soviet Union. The Soviet leaders did not want to incur the blame for breaking up the Organization. . . .

This shifting of influence in the Organization has caused a lot of annoyance to many. . . . The U.N. is becoming, due to the admission of new Afro-Asian nations, what it was not expected to be.

There is one very big disadvantage to the Afro-Asian bloc, namely, the lack of leadership. When talking of leadership, I am thinking of it in the sense in which U.S.A. leads her own western allies and the U.S.S.R. is the leader of pro-communist countries. Among Afro-Asians none can boast of being a leader in the above sense. Neither India, nor U.A.R. nor Ghana can claim this status. Nor is there any individual delegate who can claim this status. At the 15th session of the General Assembly Mr. Nehru did play a role of this nature but it was only a temporary phase.

How are these Afro-Asian countries important in an organization which is dominated by the Council in which five members are vested

---

breach of a peace or act of aggression the use of armed force when necessary, to maintain or restore international peace and security."

with veto power? To answer this question we must look at Articles 10 and 14 of the Charter. These two provisions of the Charter give concurrent jurisdiction to the Council and the Assembly to deal with international disputes. The only restriction on the powers of the Assembly in this regard is Article 12 of the Charter. Then there is the resolution on "Uniting for Peace." It is only in the light of this resolution that we can establish a correct relationship between the above mentioned three Articles of the Charter. An important question can be decided only by a two-thirds majority of the members present and voting in the Assembly.[4] It is this two-thirds majority requirement which gives importance to the Afro-Asian bloc and which is impossible without the support of some members of this bloc. In order to obtain it, Afro-Asians have to be kept happy. So long as the present voting formula in the United Nations exists the importance of this bloc will not diminish. India invaded Goa in violation of the Charter. Such an unlawful step could be taken by India only after calculating that no resolution against her would obtain two-thirds votes in the Assembly as the majority of Afro-Asians are anti-colonialists and Indian action was successfully represented as anti-colonial. In the Security Council the Soviet Union vetoed the resolution against India. U.A.R., Ceylon and Liberia, all three from the same bloc, also voted against the resolution and thus supported India in her action. Had the matter been moved in the Assembly after failure at the Council the outcome would have been the same, because the Afro-Asians in the General Assembly would have blocked the adoption of any resolution condemning India for her invasion of Goa, in the same way as the U.S.S.R. had done in the Council. But while it is gratifying for the Afro-Asian nations that they should have such great influence in the world body, too frequent an exercise of that influence, particularly in support of Afro-Asian nations which have used force, may result in paralysing the U.N. . . .

Thus the responsibility today for saving the United Nations lies very much on the Afro-Asians.

Another important outcome of the increased membership of the Afro-Asians at the U.N. is that they have turned the Organizations into a place where the great powers cannot practise their diplomacy very effectively. It is generally believed that the world Organization has been a theatre for the power politics of the big five. In certain cases this cannot be denied. But with the growing membership of small nations,

[4] Article 18(2).

specially the Afro-Asians and since the adoption of the resolution on "Uniting for Peace" the U.N. is today not as the framers of the Charter visualized it. In the Council of the League very important decisions required the unanimity of the members. In vesting the power of veto in only five of its members, the U.N. has definitely avoided the excessive democracy of the League. The Charter concept has been to provide leadership in the Organization to the big five. If we analyse the effect of this veto power on the Security Council we conclude that today these big five powers can block action in the Council but cannot take action due to the differences between them. The existence of this gulf between the big five powers has enhanced the importance of the General Assembly and thus indirectly of the Afro-Asian bloc.

Looking at the situation in the U.N. one realizes that the world has reached the stage where international affairs are no more the monopoly of any big or small powers. The Organization, if it is to be saved, needs the support of every member. Small powers and specially the Afro-Asians, have to realize that their help is also needed for saving the Organization. To-day they are collectively as important as any big power in the Council. It is the number which counts in making the decisions in the Assembly. Thus with such a dominating position in the Organization, this bloc and specially its African members have to realize that

. . . the future of the world Organization is tied to that of Africa. The African members represent the largest single bloc of nations, and their power is therefore considerable. Like no other group, they need the Organization because their number makes their strength, and because they would have no foreign policy outside it. Who would listen to Ghana or Guinea if the United Nations did not exist? No other single group could be more interested in preserving an organisation which is their sole shield against the great powers and the principal vehicle for the expression of their newly found personality.[5]

Thus not only Africans but all Afro-Asians must be sensible, wise and moderate in order to preserve an Organization which has provided them with the only means available to them of asserting themselves.

[5] "The U.N. and Africa," *The New Republic*, 2 October, 1961, p. 4.

The Troika in World Affairs

47 M. VOLODIN
United Nations in a Changed World

A most important task — to rid humanity for ever of the calamities of war — was set before the United Nations when it was organised during the Second World War. Its members solemnly undertook the obligation to practise tolerance and to live together in peace with one another as good neighbours. This provision of the Charter contains the principle on which U.N. members must base their relationships. It is the principle of peaceful co-existence of all states regardless of differences in their political, economic and social systems.

The U.N. Charter specifically states that the United Nations must be a centre for harmonising the actions of nations in the attainment of the U.N. purposes. It need not be explained that harmonising actions does not mean mechanical adoption of decisions by a majority, nor does it mean dictation by any one group of states; what it means is working out decisions which take account of the interests of all U.N. members.

The principal provisions of the U.N. Charter are in complete accord with the tasks for whose solution the organisation was set up. Life does not call for the amendment of these provisions, but for their strict observance.

This is something that cannot be said of the structure of the United Nations.

The U.N. Charter was drawn up at a Conference in San Francisco 17 years ago, when the world situation was very different from the present one. The Charter was signed by 51 countries, in their overwhelming majority capitalist countries of the American continent and Western Europe. Asia was represented by 10 states and Africa only by four.

In these 17 years, the world has undergone a radical change: the Socialist camp has become a mighty force uniting one-third of the population of the globe; the period of the final liquidation of colonialism has set in. The U.N. membership has changed accordingly. . . .

M. Volodin is a frequent contributor to *International Affairs* (Moscow). These excerpts are reprinted from that periodical, IX (September 1962) 6–9.

Much more important are the qualitative changes: three approximately equal groups of states have taken shape in the world — the Socialist, the neutralist, and the imperialist Western Powers.

Since its inception the United Nations has made a definite contribution to international peace-keeping and security. In 1956, it helped to rebuff the armed aggression of Britain, France and Israel in their attempt to encroach on Egypt's rights and freedom. In 1957, it helped to avert aggression against Syria. In 1958, it helped call to order the Anglo-American interventionists in the Middle East and assisted in withdrawing U.S. and British troops from the territory of the Lebanon and Jordan.

However, the United Nations has regrettably also taken action aggravating the international situation and endangering both the future of the United Nations and the preservation of peace. Witness the events in Korea and the Congo.

The basic reason for the many negative aspects of U.N. activities, above all of its Secretariat, is that its executive apparatus is one-sided. Most of the key operational posts are held by U.S. citizens and their allies in the aggressive blocs, so that the Secretariat often angles the solution of important questions in a way that benefits these countries. The real face of the U.N. Secretariat was most clearly revealed during the initial stages of the Congolese events in 1960.

What was the composition of the Secretariat which played such a negative role in the Congolese events? Of its 1,170 posts, which in accordance with Article 101 of the U.N. Charter must be filled on as wide a geographical basis as possible, almost 800 posts, i.e., two-thirds, were held by citizens of the U.S.A. and its allies in the military blocs. Citizens of the U.S.S.R. and the other Socialist member countries had 84 posts, i.e., only about 7 percent; the citizens of neutralist Afro-Asian countries — about 120 posts. British and American citizens filled 92 senior posts in the Secretariat, while the citizens of all the other member countries held 56 — only about half as many.

There was even less fairness in recruiting specialists for U.N. technical assistance. In 1959 alone, 2,291 experts were sent to various countries; of these 1,420, i.e., the overwhelming majority, were citizens of countries taking part in the aggressive NATO bloc. Only 52 specialists came from the U.S.S.R. and the other Socialist countries.

The U.S.A. and its allies, having built up positions within the U.N. apparatus which allow them to use the organisation as an instrument of their policy, are virtually trying to place this apparatus above the United Nations by ensuring for it the broadest freedom of action. The late Hammarskjold even tried to set up special "U.N. offices" in the nature of embassies in various small countries in order to pressure their Governments into following the foreign policy line of the imperialist Powers.

The future of the United Nations will be jeopardised unless measures are taken to stop this trend. Such measures have been proposed by N. S. Khrushchev, head of the Soviet Government, in his speech at the 15th General Assembly on September 23, 1960. It was proposed, in particular, that the post of Secretary-General, who runs the Secretariat alone and personally interprets and executes the decisions of the Security Council and the General Assembly, should be abolished and replaced by a collegiate body consisting of three secretary-generals representing the three main groups of states. This body would take agreed decisions.

Such a collegiate executive organ would be a definite guarantee that the activities of the U.N. Secretariat would not be detrimental to any of the existing groups of states. Such an executive organ would be truly democratic and would safeguard the interests of all member states regardless of social and political systems.

It was also proposed that the Security Council, the organ chiefly responsible for the maintenance of international peace, should be re-modelled in such a way as to give each of the three groups of states equal rights, equal possibilities and equal representation.

Three of the five permanent seats on the Security Council are held by the Western Powers, whereas the Socialist countries are represented by the Soviet Union alone. The seat of the Chinese People's Republic is occupied by the Chiang Kai-shek man, who does not represent the people of China. The neutralist states have no permanent seats on the Security Council, although such great Powers as India or Indonesia have every reason to be its permanent members. This, and the restitution of the legitimate rights of the Chinese People's Republic, would make the Council more representative, more faithfully reflecting the balance of world forces and, accordingly, more authoritative and effective.

The policy of discriminating against the Socialist countries in the election of non-permanent members of the Security Council is intoler-able. The Western Powers, above all the United States, in violation of the U.S.-initiated gentlemen's agreement reached in London in 1946 concerning the geographical distribution of the non-permanent seats on the Security Council, have been using every means of pressure to keep the Socialist countries out of the non-permanent seats on the Council.

This applies equally to elections to the Economic and Social Council, the International Court of Justice and auxiliary U.N. organs. Under the London agreement the Afro-Asian countries can expect to have only three or four seats of the 18 on the Economic and Social Council, but even this arrangement is time and again violated by the Western Powers.

The policy of discrimination pursued by the Western Powers in respect of the Socialist countries in the election of General Assembly Presidents is absolutely inadmissible and is injurious to the United Nations. At none of the . . . sessions held to date have the Western Powers allowed the election of a representative of the Socialist countries to the post of President. It is necessary to ensure that representatives of the three main groups of states should be elected in turn to the post of President of the General Assembly and Chairmen of its main committees, in particular the First Committee. This procedure should be written into official documents.

The recruitment of staff for the Secretariat, the main executive organ, requires special examination. According to the Charter it must be an international apparatus. It is a matter of record that the question of placing a collegiate organ instead of one Secretary-General at the head of the Secretariat had been discussed at the 1945 Conference in San Francisco, when the Charter of an International Security Organisation (United Nations) was being worked out. The delegations of the U.S.S.R., the United States, Britain and China tabled a joint proposal that the U.N. Secretariat should be headed by an organ consisting of a Secretary-General and four deputies, all of whom would be appointed by the General Assembly on the recommendation of the Security Council. This would have made the deputies of the Secretary-General independent of him and would serve as a guarantee that the Secretary-General would in his actions take account of the interests of all the groups of states within the United Nations.

This reasonable proposal was given wide support at the conference. Suffice it to say that it was twice put to the vote and both times received a majority. It was not incorporated in the Charter only because the vote in favour had been slightly less than two-thirds of the delegations taking part. Even at the time the majority of those who attended the Conference realised that the *concentration of broad powers in the hands of one Secretary-General could do great damage to the cause for which the United Nations was being set up.* Life has shown that these fears were fully justified.

For almost the entire period of the existence of the United Nations the responsible post of Secretary-General has been filled by direct agents of the imperialist Powers, Trygve Lie and Hammarskjold. They put their own interpretation in U.N. decisions and always implemented them in the interests of their masters. . . .

The opponents of collegial leadership in the Secretariat allege that the U.N. Secretary-General and the personnel of the Secretariat in discharging their duties act without bias and objectively, getting no directives from their Governments, and that collegial leadership will make the Secretariat inefficient. Such arguments are evidently designated for very naive people.

The U.S. authorities have very powerful instruments for prompting American employees of the Secretariat to act in their interests. There have been cases when the U.S. Department of State made the Secretary-General dismiss from the Secretariat several Americans who did not suit it. Moreover, U.S. citizens working in the U.N. Secretariat, remain Americans. Had the Governments of the United States and other Western Powers really believed that the employees of the Secretariat could be absolutely impartial, they would have had no reason to try and keep out citizens of Socialist countries from the Secretariat.

This was well understood by the U.N. Preparatory Commission, whose report was approved at the First Session of the General Assembly early in 1946. The report stressed, though with reservations, that it was impossible to expect the employees of the U.N. Secretariat fully to subordinate the special interests of their countries to international interests. . . .

Here is another fact that needs mentioning. Every month the U.N. Secretariat publishes staff lists of permanent delegations of U.N. member countries at U.N. headquarters in New York. Without any authorisation from the chief U.N. organs, the Secretariat has included in these lists the so-called "permanent observers of non-member countries" at the U.N. headquarters. These "observers" include representatives of the Federal Republic of Germany, South Korea and South Viet-Nam. They have been given full opportunity by the United States to set up their delegations in New York. These "observers" are provided by the Secretariat with passes to the United Nations, they are admitted to the sittings of U.N. organs, and are supplied with official U.N. documents. But the Secretariat has refused to do anything to make the U.S. authorities allow the representatives of Socialist non-member countries (for instance, the German Democratic Republic) to have their own observers at the United Nations.

At the 16th General Assembly, U Thant (Burma), the acting Secretary-General, announced the intention to set up a group of senior advisers from among the deputies of the Secretary-General and promised to consult with them on all important matters. At present this group of advisers consists of eight deputies of the Secretary-General (U.S.S.R., Czechoslovakia, U.S.A., France, India, U.A.R., Brazil and Nigeria) but for all practical purposes it is out of use. . . .

Such important posts as directors of departments and offices handling finance and personnel, economic and social affairs, the chiefs of the Technical Assistance Administration and the Technical Assistance Board are filled by citizens of Atlantic bloc countries. They raise all manner of obstacles to the enrollment of citizens of the Socialist (and of the neutralist) countries. Even when citizens of the Socialist countries are taken on they are kept away from actual operational work.

In operational matters the chiefs of departments and offices continue the line that was pursued under Hammarskjold, i.e., a line benefiting the Governments of the Western Powers. For example, technical assistance is not rendered first to countries which need it most but to those whose policy suits Washington and London.

A change in the structure of the Secretariat is also necessary if there is to be any solution of the cardinal problem of our day — the problem of general and complete disarmament — because at a certain stage there will arise the concrete question of setting up forces to maintain international peace. The question is: who is going to command and control these armed forces? To agree, in the present circumstances, that these forces should be placed under the command of the U.N. Secretariat, as the U.S.A. insists, would be to place oneself at the mercy of NATO and to allow that aggressive bloc to dictate its will to the Socialist countries and the world.

The only reasonable solution of the question of international peacekeeping in a world without arms (leaving aside for the moment the question of establishment and armament of the peace-keeping forces) would be a decision placing such forces under the control of an organ in which the three principal groups of states enjoy equal rights and equal possibilities.

Those who insist on preserving the present U.N. structure which is advantageous to the Western Powers, should understand that the time of their undivided rule of the United Nations is long past. They can no longer impose their will on other countries. The United Nations is not a national parliament in which members submit to majority decisions but an international council discussing important problems and looking for mutually acceptable decisions. Under the present relation of forces in the world, any decision adopted by a mechanical majority ignoring the opinion of the Socialist countries can only be harmful.

Only if the structure of the U.N. bodies is remodelled in the spirit of the Soviet proposals will the United Nations become a truly international instrument and make a useful contribution to the maintenance and strengthening of international peace and security.

China Supports Broader Afro-Asian Representation in the United Nations

48 THE EDITORS OF "PEOPLE'S DAILY"
Editorial, December 18, 1963

After several days' debate on the expansion of certain principal organs of the United Nations, the Special Political Committee of the United Nations General Assembly adopted, on December 16 [1963], three resolutions jointly tabled by 37 Asian and African countries. Two of the resolutions call for the revision of the United Nations Charter to increase the number of seats in the Security Council from 11 to 15 and in the Economic and Social Council from 18 to 27, so as to secure a broadening of representation from the Asian and African countries in these two organs. . . .

DISCRIMINATION AGAINST AFRO-ASIAN STATES

We have long and repeatedly pointed out that the way the seats in the principal U.N. organs are distributed is extremely unreasonable and unfair to the Asian and African countries. In recent years a fundamental change has taken place in the face of Asia and Africa; scores of countries there have attained independence by throwing off colonial fetters. The Asian and African countries are exerting an ever increasing

These excerpts, from the *People's Daily* editorial of December 18, 1963, are reprinted from the *Peking Review*, VI, No. 52 (December 27, 1963) 14–16.

influence in international affairs. It is unthinkable that existing major international issues can be solved without the joint participation of the Asian and African countries. It is therefore imperative that the voices of these countries be fully heard in the international arena. An end to discrimination against them in the United Nations is long overdue.

When the U.N. organization was founded in 1945, only 13 of its 51 foundation members were Asian and African countries, but now, of the 113 U.N. members, 58 are Asian and African countries, more than half of the U.N. membership.

In 1955, the Bandung Conference demanded in its resolution an increase in the number of seats of the Asian and African nations in the Security Council. The present distribution of seats in the principal U.N. organs, however, still remains as before. It fails to reflect the true position of these countries in the United Nations, much less their tremendous role in current international affairs. They have all along been denied the right to corresponding representation in the U.N. organs.

This situation has been caused solely by the control and manipulation of the United Nations by the imperialist countries headed by the United States. The U.S. propaganda machine has made no secret of the fact that the ruling circles in Washington very much fear that a strengthened position of the Asian and African countries in the United Nations would be unfavourable to U.S. control over this international organization. . . .

SOVIET ULTERIOR MOTIVES

We must express our greatest regret at the improper tactics employed by the Soviet delegate over this issue. Using as a pretext his allegation that China opposed an expansion of U.N. organs, the Soviet delegate refused to support the resolutions for broader Afro-Asian representation in the Security Council and in the Economic and Social Council. Even after the spokesman of the Chinese Foreign Ministry in a statement on December 12 gave a comprehensive and clear-cut explanation of the position of the Chinese Government, he still stuck to his misrepresentation of the Chinese position in an attempt to apologize for the action of the Soviet Union. This showed that the Soviet delegate was manoeuvring for ulterior motives. . . .

CHINA'S POSITION CANNOT BE DISTORTED

As we have pointed out before, there may be two ways of increasing the number of seats of Asian-African countries in the principal organs of the United Nations so as to satisfy their demand. One is to revise the relevant articles of the U.N. Charter. The other is to leave the Charter as it is for the time being, that is, while not altering the total number of seats stipulated in it, to make reasonable readjustments in the distribution of seats after consultation among the various parties concerned, so that at least half of them go to Asian-African countries.

We feel that it would be more convenient if the question could be settled by the latter method as it is simpler and easier to carry out under present circumstances. The first method involves more complex questions. That is why we believe endeavours should be made to obtain the adoption of the second method. However, if the second method does not work, the first method is the only alternative.

We have suggested two methods, both out of consideration for the interests of the Asian-African countries. They are put forward merely as suggestions for the settlement of this question, so that a comparatively practicable method can be found speedily to meet the legitimate demands of the Asian and African countries in the shortest time possible. The question of China only favouring one method and opposing the other does not arise at all. Our basic stand is to support every effort of the Asian-African countries to increase their seats in the principal organs of the United Nations. If it is impossible to redistribute the seats in the Security Council and the Economic and Social Council through consultation to satisfy the justified demand of the Asian-African countries and the method of revising the relevant articles of the Charter has to be adopted, then, in line with our consistent stand, we naturally favour the corresponding revision of the relevant articles of the Charter so as really to satisfy the justified demand of the Asian and African countries.

China's attitude towards the United Nations is well known. The People's Republic of China is a foundation member of the United Nations and also a Permanent Member of the Security Council. But because U.S. imperialism insists on a policy of hostility towards China and controls the voting machine in the United Nations, China has so far been illegally deprived of its legitimate rights and China's seat has all along been usurped by the Chiang Kai-shek clique. Until the restoration of China's legitimate rights, the Chinese Government holds that all activities of the elements of the Chiang Kai-shek clique in the U.N. are illegal. China will undertake no commitment on any activity or decision of the U.N. including the revision or non-revision of the U.N. Charter.

THE EDITORS OF "PEOPLE'S DAILY"   *469*

While it continues to be excluded from the United Nations, China naturally can undertake no commitment on the question of revision of the Charter by the United Nations. The Chinese Government has, however, always judged the activities of the United Nations on their intrinsic merits. We resolutely oppose all evil doings of the United Nations, but will have no objection to the good things, if any, done by the United Nations.

We resolutely demand that the United Nations drive the elements of the Chiang Kai-shek clique out of all its organs and fully restore China's legitimate rights. However, the question of restoring China's legitimate rights in the United Nations and the question of increasing the number of the seats of the Asian and African countries in the principal U.N. organs are two different matters and should by no means be lumped together. The question of broadening the representation of the Asian and African countries in the principal U.N. organs should be settled fairly and reasonably by those countries now in the United Nations in the spirit of no discrimination against the Asian and African countries. . . .

Retrospect and Prospect

49 DEAN RUSK
The First Twenty-Five Years of the United Nations —
From San Francisco to the 1970's

I regard this event as a welcome opportunity — and a command performance. Any invitation bearing the name of Dag Hammarskjold is compelling for me.

In my job I often think of Hammarskjold's reply to a newsman who asked about his interest in mountain climbing: "What I know about this sport," he said, "is that the qualities it requires are just those which I feel we all need today — perseverance and patience, a firm grip on realities, careful but imaginative planning, a clear awareness of the

Dean Rusk, U.S. Secretary of State 1961–   , under Presidents Kennedy and Johnson, and formerly President of the Rockefeller Foundation, presented this Dag Hammarskjold Memorial Lecture at Columbia University on January 10, 1964. The text was reprinted in *The Department of State Bulletin*, L, No. 1283 (January 27, 1964) 112–119.

dangers — but also of the fact that fate is what we make it and . . .
the safest climber is he who never questions his ability to overcome all
difficulties."

Dag Hammarskjold was an intensely practical idealist; and I think
this is why his name will live. He never wore his devotion to world
peace as a personal adornment. Instead, he worked for peace through
action. It was selfless and tireless action — and for this we honor the
man. But it also was rational, considered, calculated action — and for
this we respect his method.   . . .

THE U.N. A NECESSITY FOR OUR TIMES

I believe also that the executive capacity of the United Nations to
act in support of the purposes of the charter will be greater in the
1970's than it is today.   . . .

Let me begin by observing that it means little to study the performance of an institution against abstract standards without reference to
the realities — and even the illusions — of the total environment in
which it must operate. In that context the first thing that strikes one
about the United Nations is that international organization is a plain
necessity of our times. This is so for both technical and political reasons.

The technical reasons stem, of course, from the headlong rush of
scientific discovery and technological advance. That process has overrun
the hypothetical question as to whether there is to be an international
community that requires organization. It has left us with the practical
question of *what kind* of international community we have the wit to
organize around the scientific and technical imperatives of our time. In
the words of Ogden Nash:

> When geniuses all in every nation
> Hasten us towards obliteration,
> Perhaps it will take the dolts and geese
> To drag us backward into peace.

World community is a fact
— because instantaneous international communication is a fact;
— because fast international transport is a fact;
— because matters ranging from the control of communicable disease
to weather reporting and forecasting demand international organization;
— because the transfer of technology essential to the spread of industrialization and the modernization of agriculture can be assisted by
international organizations;

— because modern economics engage nations in a web of commercial, financial, and technical arrangements at the international level.

The advance of science, and the technology that follows, create an insistent demand to build international technical and regulatory institutions which lend substance to world community. Few people seem to realize just how far this movement has gone. The United States is now a member of 53 international organizations. We contribute to 22 international operating programs, mostly sponsored by these same organizations. And last year [1963] we attended 547 international intergovernmental conferences, mostly on technical subjects. We do these things because they are always helpful and often downright essential to the conduct of our national and international affairs.

It is obvious that in the 1970's we shall require more effective international organization — making for a more substantial world community — than we have today. We already know that in the next decade we shall become accustomed to international communication, including television, via satellites in outer space. We shall travel in aircraft that fly at speeds above a thousand and perhaps above two thousand miles per hour. Industrialization will pursue its relentless course. Cities and their suburbs will keep on growing. The world economy will become increasingly interdependent. And science will rush ahead, leaving to us the task of fashioning institutions — increasingly on the international level — to administer its benefits and circumscribe its dangers.

So, while nations may cling to national values and ideas and ambitions and prerogatives, science has created a functional international society, whether we like it or not. And that society, like any other, must be organized. . . .

ADJUSTMENT TO REALITY OF POLITICAL WORLD

The need for political organs at the international level is just as plain as the need for technical agencies.

You will recall that the decision to try to form a new international organization to preserve peace grew out of the agonies of the Second World War. The United States took the lead in this enterprise. President Franklin D. Roosevelt and Secretary of State Cordell Hull sought to avoid repeating what many believed to have been mistakes in political tactics which kept the United States from joining the League of Nations. They consulted at every stage the leaders of both political parties in both Houses of Congress. They insisted that the formation of this organization should be accomplished, if possible, *before* the end of the war.

Most of our allies readily endorsed this objective and cooperated in achieving it. You will recall that the charter conference at San Francisco convened before the end of the war against Hitler and that the United States Senate consented to ratification of the charter in July 1945, before the end of the war in the Pacific. The vote in the Senate was 89 to 2, reflecting a national consensus bordering on unanimity. The significance of that solemn action was especially appreciated by those of us who were in uniform.

The commitment of the United States to the United Nations was wholehearted. We threw our best efforts and some of our best men into getting it organized and moving. We set about binding the wounds of war. We demobilized our armed forces and drastically reduced our military budget. We proposed — not only proposed but worked hard to obtain agreement — that atomic energy should be put under control of an agency of the United Nations, that it should be devoted solely to peaceful purposes, that nuclear weapons should be abolished and forever forbidden.

What happened? Stalin refused to cooperate. Even before the guns were silent, he set in motion a program of imperialistic expansion, in violation of his pledges to the Western Allies and in contravention of the principles of the United Nations.

You will recall that the United Nations was designed on the assumption that the great powers in the alliance destined to be victors in the Second World War would remain united to maintain the future peace of the world. The United Nations would be the instrument through which these powers, in cooperation with others, of course, would give effect to their mutual determination to keep the peace against any threats that might arise from some future Mussolini or Hitler. World peace was to be enforced by international forces carrying the flag of the United Nations but called into action and directed by agreement among the major powers. Action without big-power agreement was not ruled out by the charter, but such agreement was assumed to be the prior condition of an effective peace organization. Indeed, it was stated repeatedly by early supporters of the United Nations that the organization could not possibly work unless the wartime Allies joined in collective action within the United Nations to exert their combined power to make it work.

That view of the postwar world rapidly turned out to be an illusory hope. One might well have expected — as many good people did — that when the conceptual basis for the United Nations fell to the ground, the organization would fall down beside it.

But all great institutions are flexible. The United Nations adjusted gradually to the political and power realities of the quite different world that came into being. In the absence of major-power agreement in the Security Council, it drew on the charter's authority to balance that weakness with a greater reliance upon the General Assembly.

By adapting to political reality the United Nations lived and grew in effectiveness, in prestige, and in relevance. It could not act in some of the ways the founding fathers intended it to act, but it went on to do many things that the founding fathers never envisaged as being necessary. The most dramatic reversal of its intended role is seen in the fact that, while the United Nations could not bring the great powers together, it could on occasion keep them apart by getting between them — by becoming the "man in the middle" — as it did in differing ways in the Middle East and in the Congo.

In short, the political organs of the United Nations survived and did effective work under the shadow of a nuclear arms race of awesome proportions, despite the so-called cold war between the major powers whose unity was once presumed to be its foundation.

This was not bound to happen. It is evident that in the political environment of the second half of the 20th century both technical and political reasons dictate the need for large-scale and diversified international organizations. But it does not necessarily follow that the United Nations was destined to work in practice — or even to survive. Indeed, its very survival may be more of an achievement than it seems at first blush. That it has steadily grown in its capacity to act is even more remarkable.

It has survived and grown in effectiveness because a great majority of the nations of the world have been determined to make it work. They have repulsed those who sought to wreck or paralyze it. They have remained determined not only to keep it alive but to improve and strengthen it. To this we owe in part the peace of the world.

PRESERVER AND REPAIRER OF WORLD PEACE

Indeed, it is difficult to avoid the conclusion that the existence of the General Assembly and the Security Council these past 18 years was a plain necessity for the preservation and repair of world peace. The failures would still have been failures, but without the U.N. some of the successes might not have been possible.

In the world of today any breach of the peace could lead to the destruction of civilization. In the thermonuclear age any instrumentality with a potential for deterring war can hardly be described as less than indispensable to mankind. In 18 brief years the United Nations has helped to deter or to terminate warfare in Iran and Greece, in Kashmir and Korea, in the Congo and the Caribbean, and twice in the Middle East and twice in the Western Pacific. It is not fanciful to speculate that any or all of us may owe our lives to the fact that these dangers were contained, with the active and persistent help of the processes of the United Nations.

With half a dozen international disputes chronically or repeatedly at the flash point, with forces of change bordering on violence loose in the world, our very instinct to survival informs us that we must keep building the peacekeeping machinery of the United Nations — and keep it lubricated with funds and logistical support.

And if we are to entertain rational hopes for general disarmament, we know that the U.N. must develop a reliable system for reconciling international conflict without resort to force. For peace in the world community — like peace in smaller communities — means not an end of conflict but an accepted system of dealing with conflict and with change through nonviolent means.

"SWITCHBOARD FOR BILATERAL DIPLOMACY"

Traditional bilateral diplomacy — of the quiet kind — has a heavier task today than at any time in history. But with the annual agenda of urgent international business growing apace, with the birth of more than half a hundred new nations in less than two decades, an institution that can serve as an annual diplomatic conference becomes almost a necessity. As a general manager of our own nation's diplomatic establishment, I cannot imagine how we could conduct or coordinate our foreign affairs if we were limited to dealing directly through bilateral channels with the 114 nations with which we have diplomatic relations tonight. . . .

. . . outside the formal agenda the General Assembly also has become the world's greatest switchboard for bilateral diplomacy. For many of the young and small nations, lacking a fully developed diplomatic service, the United Nations is the main, sometimes the only, general mechanism available for the conduct of their diplomacy.

Without formal decision the opening of each new Assembly has turned into something like an informal conference of the foreign ministers of the world community. . . .

I believe that too many items are placed on the agenda of the General Assembly. Too many issues are debated and not enough are negotiated. I feel strongly that members should take more seriously article 33 of the charter which pledges them to seek solutions to their disputes "first of all . . . by negotiation, enquiry, mediation, conciliation, arbitration, judicial settlement, resort to regional agencies or arrangements, or other peaceful means of their own choice" before bringing disputes to the U.N. at all.

But the point here is that it is hard to imagine the conduct of diplomacy throughout the year without a meeting of the General Assembly to deal in one forum and, in a more or less systematic manner, with subjects which demand widespread diplomatic attention among the members of the world community.

The need for an annual diplomatic conference, the need for a peacekeeping deterrent to wars large and small, and the need for an international monitor of peaceful change are plain enough. They seem to me to warrant the conclusion that the political organs as well as the technical organs of the United Nations have been very useful to the world at large for the past decade and a half. Common sense informs us that they can be even more useful in the years ahead.

RECOGNIZING THE PEACEKEEPING CAPACITY OF U.N.

I suspect that the near future will witness another period of adjustment for the United Nations. Some adjustments are, indeed, required — because the political environment is changing and so is the structure of the U.N. itself.

For one thing the cobweb syndrome, the illusion that one nation or bloc of nations could, by coercion, weave the world into a single pattern directed from a single center of power, is fading into limbo. That other illusion, the bipolar theory, of a world divided permanently between two overwhelming centers of power with most other nations clustered about them, is fading too. The reality of a world of great diversity with many centers of power and influence is coming into better focus.

Meanwhile, a first brake has been placed on the nuclear arms race, and the major powers are searching for other agreements in areas of common interest. One is entitled to hope that the major power conflicts which so often have characterized U.N. proceedings in the past will yield more and more to great-power cooperation. . . .

As long as a member possessing great power was intent on promoting conflict and upheaval — the better to coerce the world into its own image — that member might well regard the United Nations as a threat to its own ambitions. But suppose it is agreed that all members, despite their deep differences, share a common interest in survival and therefore a common interest in preventing resort to force anywhere in the world. Then the peacekeeping capacity of the United Nations can be seen realistically for what it is: an indispensable service potentially in the national interest of all members — in the common interest of even rival states.

If this reality is grasped by the responsible leaders of all the large powers, then the peacekeeping capacity of the United Nations will find some degree of support from all sides, not as a rival system of order but as contributor to, and sometimes guarantor of, the common interest in survival.

It would be a great service to peace if there could develop common recognition of a common interest in the peacekeeping capacity of the United Nations. That recognition is far from common now. My belief that it will dawn is based on the fact that it would serve the national interests of all nations, large and small, and because sooner or later nations can be expected to act in line with their national interests.

Peace will not be achieved by repeating worn-out propaganda themes or resetting rusty old traps. But if our Soviet friends are prepared to act on what Chairman Khrushchev says in part of his [1964] New Year's message — that war over territorial questions is unacceptable, that nations should not be the targets of direct or indirect aggression, that we should use the United Nations and every other means of peaceful settlement — then let us together build up the peacekeeping machinery of the United Nations to prevent even small wars in our flammable world.

For small wars could too easily, too quickly, lead to nuclear war, and nuclear war can too easily, too quickly, prove fatal to friend and foe alike.

PROBLEMS AFFECTED BY GROWTH

Meanwhile the internal structure of the United Nations has been changing radically over the past several years. The United Nations began life with 51 members. When its headquarters building was designed, United Nations officials believed they were foresighted in planning for an eventual membership of 75. This year major alterations will be undertaken to make room for the present 113 members and more. It is a fair guess that membership of the U.N. will level off during the next decade at 125 to 130 members.

This more than doubling of the U.N.'s membership is proud testament to the tidal sweep through the old colonial areas of the doctrine of self-determination of peoples. It is a triumph of largely peaceful change. It is a tribute to those advanced countries which have helped bring dependent areas to self-government and independence and made possible their free choice of their own destiny. It is a striking and welcome result of the greatest wave of national liberation in all time. It also has important implications for all U.N. members — the new members and the older members too — and for the U.N. itself.

The most prosaic — but nonetheless important — implication is for methods of work in the General Assembly. With more than twice as many voices to be heard, views to be reconciled, and votes to be cast and counted, on a swelling agenda of business there is obvious danger that the General Assembly will be swamped.

I already have suggested that the agenda may be unnecessarily bloated, that in many cases private discourse and real progress are preferable to public debate and symbolic resolution and that the U.N. might well be used more as a court of last resort and less as a forum of original jurisdiction.

But I think still more needs to be done. If the expanded Assembly is to work with reasonable proficiency, it must find ways of delegating some of its work to units less cumbersome than committees of 113 members. The General Assembly is the only parliamentary body in the world that tries to do most of its business in committees-of-the-whole. The Assembly has, in fact, moved to establish several subcommittees, including one to consider financing peacekeeping operations, and perhaps more thought should now be given to the future role of such committees in the work of the organization.

The radical expansion of the membership raises problems for the newer and smaller nations. They rightly feel that they are under-represented on some organs — notably the Security Council and the Economic and Social Council — whose membership was based on the U.N.'s original size and composition.

The growth of membership also raises problems for the middle-range

478   DEAN RUSK

powers, who were early members and have reason to feel that they are next in line for a larger voice.

And it raises problems — or potential problems — for the larger powers too.

The rapid and radical expansion of the General Assembly may require some adaptation of procedures if the U.N. is to remain relevant to the real world and therefore effective in that world.

Theoretically, a two-thirds majority of the General Assembly could now be formed by nations with only 10 percent of the world's population, or who contribute, altogether, 5 percent of the assessed budget. In practice, of course, this does not happen, and I do not share the dread expressed by some that the General Assembly will be taken over by its "swirling majorities."

But even the theoretical possibility that a two-thirds majority, made up primarily of smaller states, could recommend a course of action for which other nations would bear the primary responsibility and burden is one that requires thoughtful attention.

There are two extreme views of how national influence should be expressed in the work of the United Nations. At one extreme is the contention that no action at all should be taken by the United Nations without the unanimous approval of the permanent members of the Security Council. This is a prescription for chronic paralysis. The United Nations was never intended to be kept in such a box. The rights and duties of the General Assembly are inherent in the charter. The United Nations has been able to develop its capacity to act precisely because those rights were not blocked by the requirement of big-power unanimity.

At the other extreme are those few who feel that nothing should matter except the number of votes that can be mustered — that what a majority wants done must be done regardless of what states make up the majority. This notion flies in the face of common sense. The plain fact of the matter is that the United Nations simply cannot take significant action without the support of the members who supply it with resources and have the capacity to act.

Some have suggested that all General Assembly votes should be weighed to reflect population, or wealth, or level of contributions, or some combination of these or other factors. I do not believe that so far-reaching an answer would be realistic or practical. The equal vote in the General Assembly for each member — however unequal in size, wealth, experience, technology, or other criterion — is rooted in the idea of "sovereign equality." And that idea is not one which any nation, large or small, is eager to abandon. . . .

I would hope that the discussions which lie ahead will not only strengthen the financial underpinnings of the U.N. but, among other things, develop an acceptable way for the General Assembly to take account of capacity to act, of responsibility for the consequences, and of actual contributions to the work of the U.N. Such a way must be found if the United Nations machinery is to be relevant to the tasks that lie ahead — in peacekeeping, in nation-building, and in the expansion of human rights.

All adjustment is difficult. Adaption of the U.N. to recent changes in the environment may take time. It will require a shift away from some hardened ideas and some rigid patterns of action and reaction — perhaps on all sides. It will require — to come back to Hammarskjold's words — "perseverance and patience, a firm grip on realities, careful but imaginative planning, a clear awareness of the dangers. . . ."

To ask all this may seem to be asking a great deal. But I am inclined toward confidence because the U.N. already has demonstrated a capacity to adapt under the flexible provisions of the Charter to the realities of international politics.

I am further persuaded that all, or most, of the smaller members are realistic enough to know:

— that their own national interests lie with, not against, an effective United Nations;

— that the U.N. can be effective only if it has the backing of those who have the means to make it effective;

— that the U.N. is made less, not more, effective by ritualistic passage of symbolic resolutions with no practical influence on the real world;

— that only responsible use of voting power is effective use of voting power;

— that true progress on behalf of the world community lies along the path on which the weak and the strong find ways to walk together.

THE GREATEST GOAL — EXTENDING HUMAN RIGHTS

These are some of the reasons, derived from analysis of the current state of world affairs, why I expect the United Nations to evolve and to grow in executive capacity to act in support of its goals.

And apart from the issue of human survival, the greatest of these goals is, of course, the steady extension of human rights.

Dedication to the principle of the universality of fundamental human rights collides in practice with dedication to the principle of national sovereignty. For most violations of human rights are committed within the confines of national societies, often by the very governments that have ratified the charter's prescription for "fundamental freedoms for all." Yet securing equal rights for all individual members of the human race is the ultimate goal of world community — and the ultimate challenge to the United Nations as the elementary but principal expression of that community. Somehow the United Nations must learn how to increase respect for the rights of the human person throughout the world.

It is here that we sense the permanent value and the final force of the basic principles of a charter which dares to speak for "We the peoples of the United Nations." Sometimes I feel that we talk too much about the universality and brotherhood of man and too little about the valuable and interesting differences that distinguish all brothers. But the lessons of recorded history, and the teachings of the world's great teachers, make clear the basic wants of mankind.

Men and women everywhere want a decent standard of material welfare for themselves and their children. They want to live in conditions of personal security. They want social justice. They want to experience a sense of achievement, for themselves and for the groups with which they identify themselves.

But men and women everywhere want more. They want personal freedom and human dignity.

Individuals and societies place differing values on these aspirations. But surely these are universal desires, shared by all races in all lands, interpreted by all religions, and given concrete form — or lipservice — by leaders and spokesmen for every kind of political, economic, and social system.